VISUAL ADJECTIVES

PUBLISHING COMPANIE

PROUDLY PRESENTS:

SUBSCRIBE TODAY!

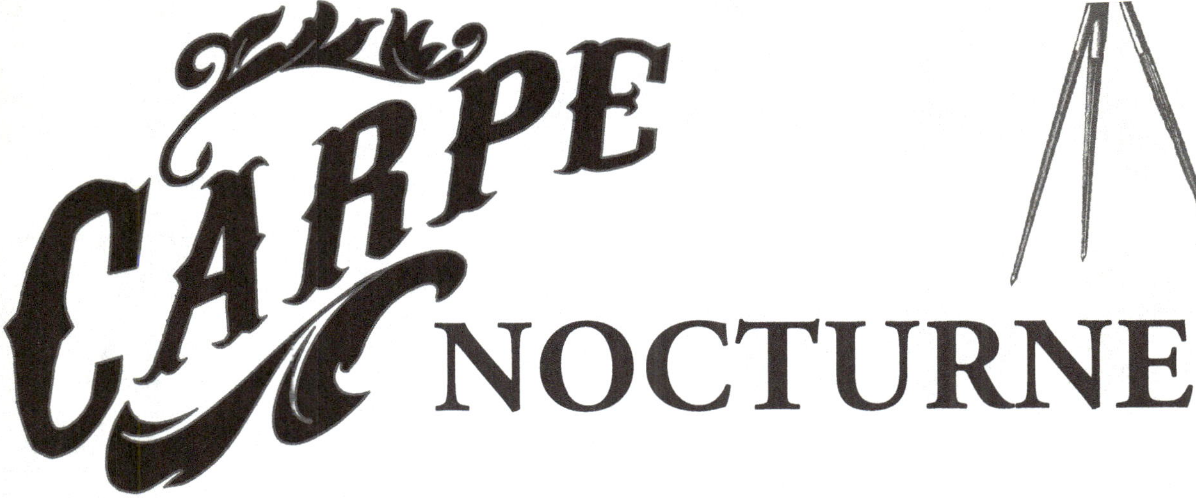

CARPE NOCTURNE

A MAGAZINE PUBLISHED AND PRINTED IN THE SUMMER OF THE YEAR TWO THOUSAND FIFTEEN.

VOLUME

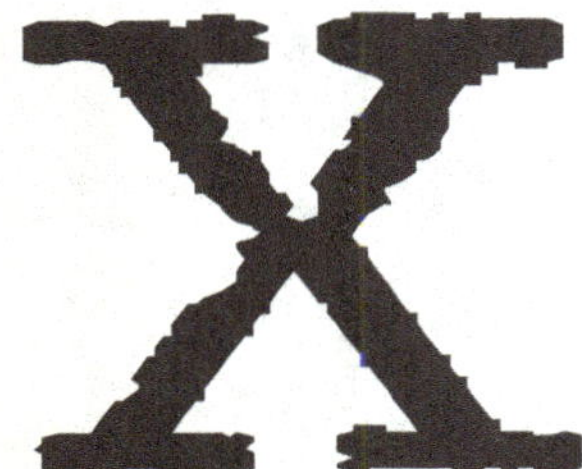

X

CONSTRUCTED BY:

PUBLISHER
Visual Adjectives

EDITOR IN CHIEF
Paula Andrews Powles

MANAGING EDITOR
Michael Jack

LAYOUT & DESIGN
Annabella Rios

Amunet Isfet
Asylum Attendant
Chirality
Dannette Tillery
Dawn Wood
Ethicus
Hyde Falkenstein
Jesse Orr
Jezibell Anat
KA Morris
Katheleen Sharkey
Katie McKensie
LinnieSarah Helpern

Lisa Walker England
Mark Hickman
Mary Crawley
Michele Combs
Miss Bella Blitz
Montague Jacques Fromage
Mr. Dark
Omen
Sergio Manghina
trixxi divine
XXX ZOMBIEBOY XXX
Yasaman Vrd'dhi
Zahara

KINDLY ADDRESS ANY CORRESPONDENCES TO:

Carpe Nocturne Magazine
ATTN: Subscribe
14280 Military Trail, #7501
Delray Beach, FL 33482

Carpe Nocturne Magazine
Volume X • Summer 2015
is a publication of Visual Adjectives, LLC and published four times a year.
All reviews and coverage expressed in this publication are the opinions of the writer and/or those being interviewed and may not be shared by Visual Adjectives.
Copyright © 2015 by Visual Adjectives, LLC. All rights reserved. July 2015.
14280 Military Trail, #7501, Delray Beach, FL 33482, USA.
No work may be copied or reproduced without the express permission of the editor or publisher.
Correspondence should be addressed to:
Visual Adjectives
ATTN: Publisher, Carpe Nocturne Magazine
14280 Military Trail, #7501, Delray Beach, FL 33482, USA.
E-mail: editor@carpenocturnemagazine.com
www.carpenocturnemagazine.com
561-809-3834.

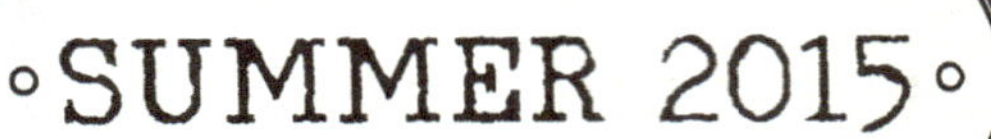

Carpe Nocturne

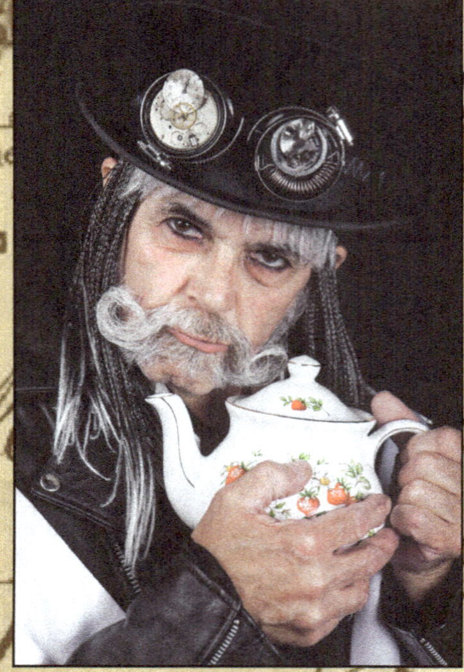

ON OUR COVER
Montague Jacques Fromage
Read more on page 7 and 85.

FEATURES

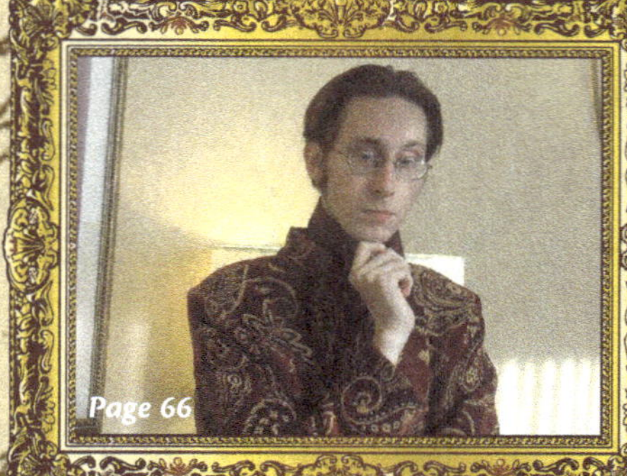

Page 50

Page 66

INTERVIEWS

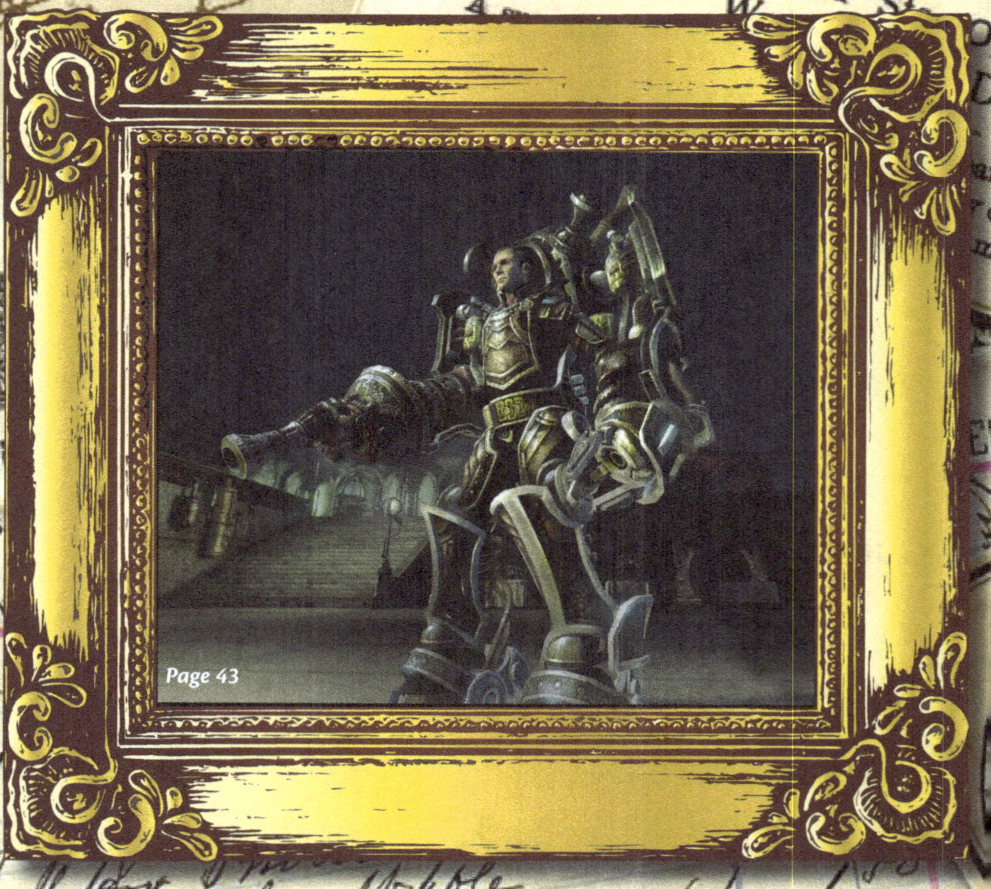

Page 43

OTHER THAN THE NORM

REGULARS

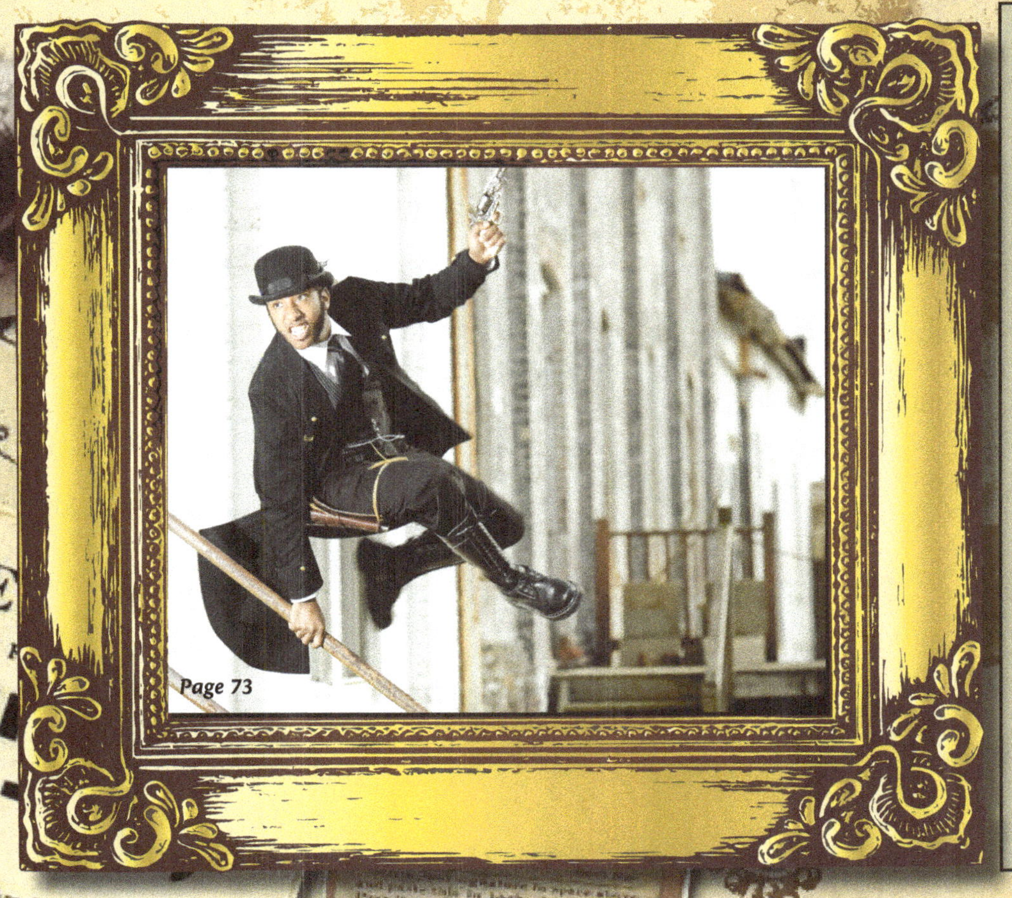

Page 73

REVIEWS

Page 40

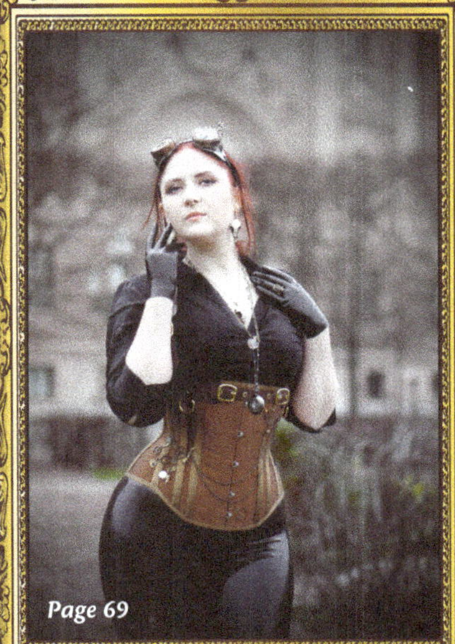

Page 69

THE AGE OF STEAM

FROM THE EDITOR

"What Steampunk is . . ." is the beginning of many debates on the subject. Is it:

- A mixture of Victorian style with a Science Fiction aesthetic?
- Retro-futuristic designs with steam technology at its core?
- A fantasy world, where steam is the magic that evolves humanity?

Or maybe it's a conglomeration of all?

Here at Carpe Nocturne, as we endeavored to bring you, our fans, this year's Steampunk Edition, we delved deep into the background and modern representation of what Steampunk truly is. In order to understand it, you must first know what you are attempting to understand.

This is what Steampunk means to us as stated by Cassie Bergman:

Steampunk is a progressive literary genre that evokes, imitates, and re-imagines the nineteenth century and favors the Industrial Revolution ideals of science and technology. In a historical framework, it mixes nineteenth-century conventions and retrofuturistic machinery with science fiction and fantasy elements.
~ Cassie Bergman

It is a fantastic culture and genre that deserves as much attention and respect as Fantasy, Sci-Fi, and Goth. Throughout this issue; we aim to bring you every aspect of the Steampunk culture! We look forward to your opinions and questions, so please feel free to contact us with any concerns you have or suggestions you'll have for the next issue!

Hissssst. Hissst.
You turn your head.
Oh! There it is.
The articulated arm that he's building to help him lift things.
There's still a whistle in the other room; it's the teapot.
That's right, it's teatime.

Steampunk draws all types together.
The adventurer, who wants a little extra.
The nobility, who enjoys adding to what they normally wear.

The truth about Steampunk and all the spinoffs,
Diesel Punk, Cowboy Punk, Cyber Punk, etc., is anything goes.
If you can imagine it... it can be created.
Who says you can't do something.

~ Terry Lynn Koch

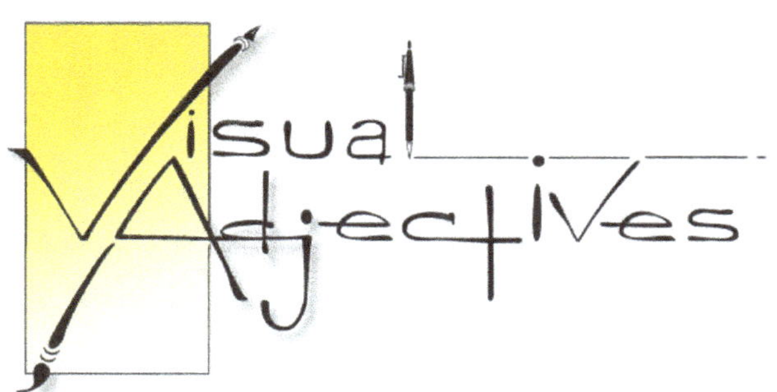

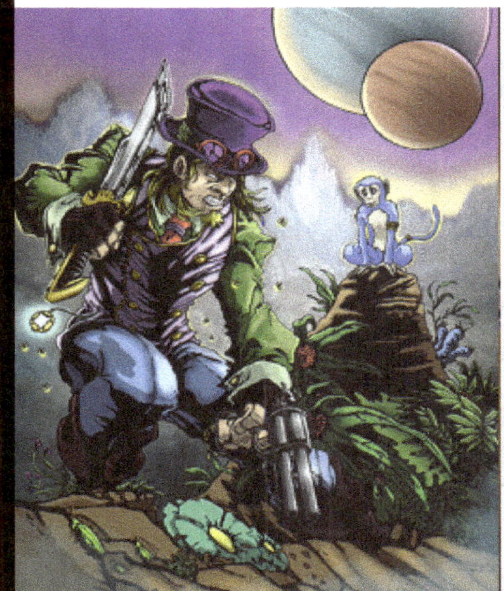

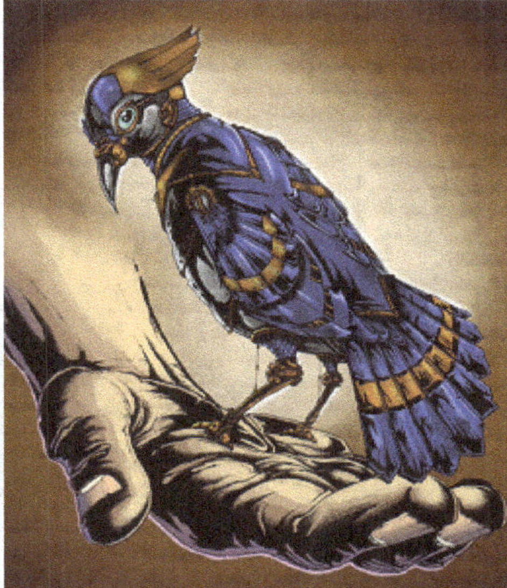

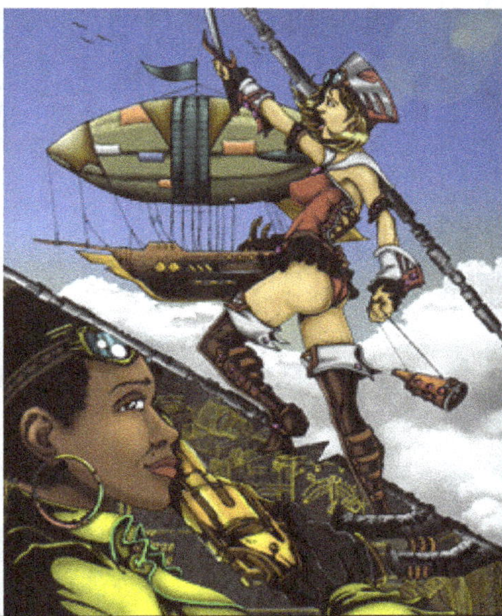

| Mercenary Edition | Engineer Edition | Captain Edition |

Visual Adjectives presents

NEW LEGENDS: MERCENARY • ENGINEER • CAPTAIN
a **Steampunk Anthology**.

With a wide variety of authors introducing their fantastic and innovative ideas into a collection of Steampunk short stories. Visual Adjectives offers a fresh take on one of the fastest growing genres and cultures!

With artwork done by "in-house" talents,
NEW LEGENDS: MERCENARY • ENGINEER • CAPTAIN
is the accumulated work of dedication and creativity.

For more information visit: **www.visualadjectives.com**
or send an email to **info@visadj.com** if you have any questions about being an author in the next anthology.

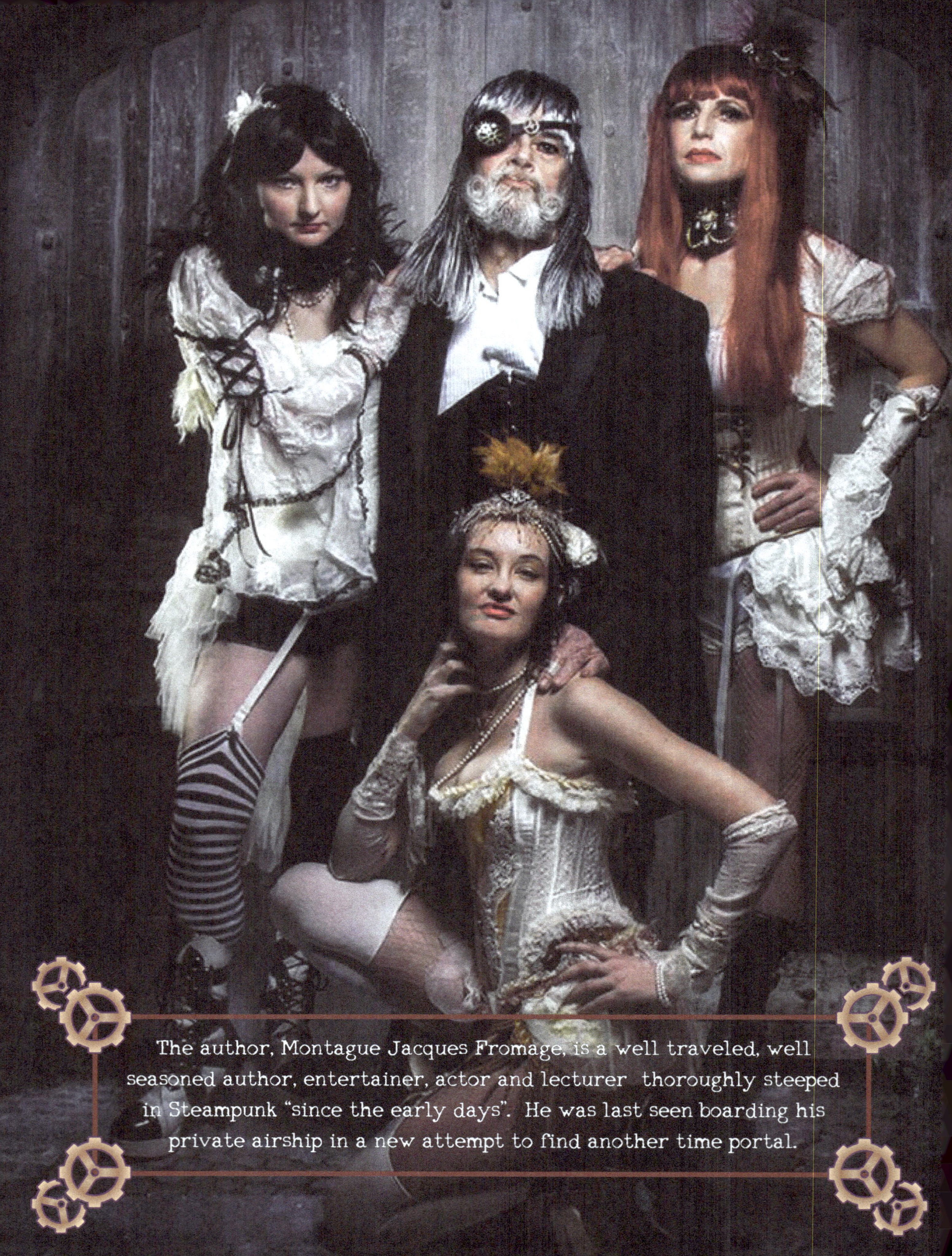

The author, Montague Jacques Fromage, is a well traveled, well seasoned author, entertainer, actor and lecturer thoroughly steeped in Steampunk "since the early days". He was last seen boarding his private airship in a new attempt to find another time portal.

WHAT STEAMPUNK ISN'T

– With Montague Jacques Fromage

STEAMPUNK is unquestionably "the" up and coming genre that is wielding its influence in media, lifestyle, literature, fashion and art. It has been hedging on the periphery for almost 25 years and is now beginning to emerge into the mainstream of everyday life. Everyone has an opinion as to what steampunk is. As with many things, perhaps a more concise method of initial analysis is to look at what steampunk isn't.

Although its roots are based in Victoriana, steampunk is not intended to be a historically accurate representation of the Victorian Era. Steampunk is in most cases not specifically "punk". It is not exclusively confined to the USA or Great Britain. It does not have a singularly representative musical style. It is not a "youth driven" genre. There is no movie or television show (yet) that is a true representation of the genre. And it most certainly is NOT going to go away in the near future.

The term steampunk surfaced in the late 1980s, coined by fantasy/sci-fi author K. W. Jeter as a tongue-in- cheek antithesis to the cyberpunk genre. The characters/society in question were based on an altered "Victorian" lifestyle. Queen Victoria reigned from 1837 to 1901. Although Queen of England, British global interests were such that the sun never set on Victoria's Empire. The Industrial Revolution, critical advances in science, medicine and technology, and most importantly, the Age of Steam all took place during her reign, taking a horse and buggy world lit by whale oil lamps to a resounding society with whirling steam powered turbines, electric lights and steam powered transportation. The entire era has become known as "Victorian". There is a general focus on the years 1880-1900 (British society in general, American Wild West and a generalized "Mad Max-post-apocalyptic" look are the three most popular variants at the moment) but couture, authors, lifestyle and the arts of the mid 1800s as well as round-the-world cultural influence are fair game for those inclined towards the steampunk genre.

There is no specific "musical style" that reflects the steampunk genre. Rock, blues, mystical, electronic as well as ethnic , folk and even rap have found their way to artists that are considered "steampunk".

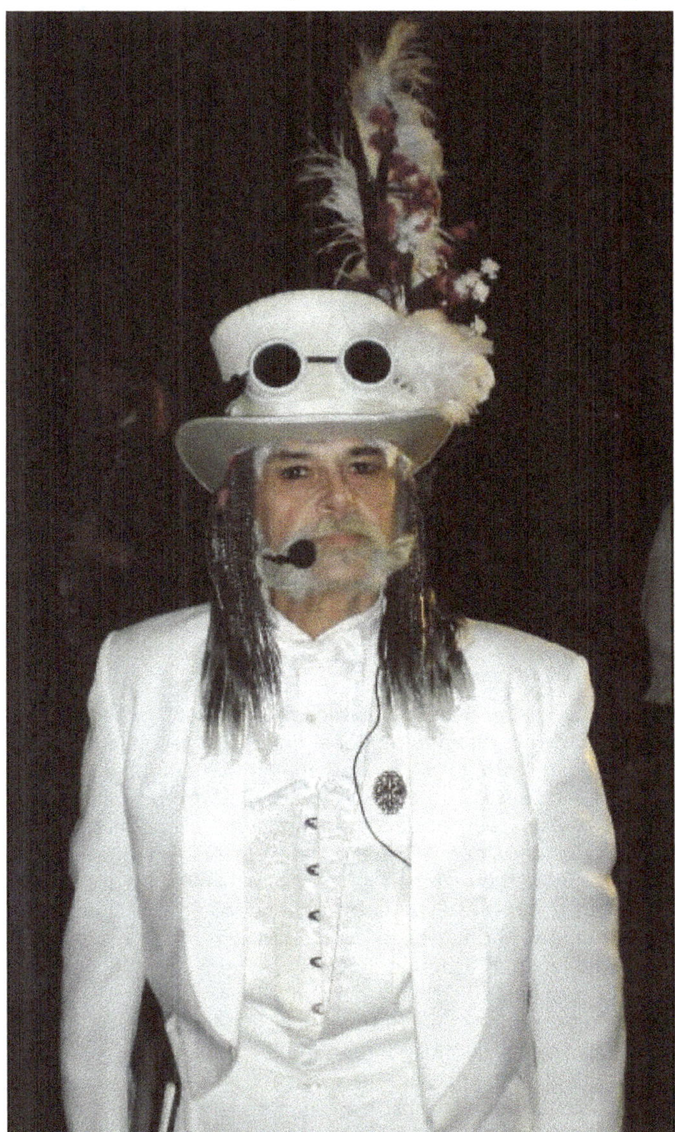

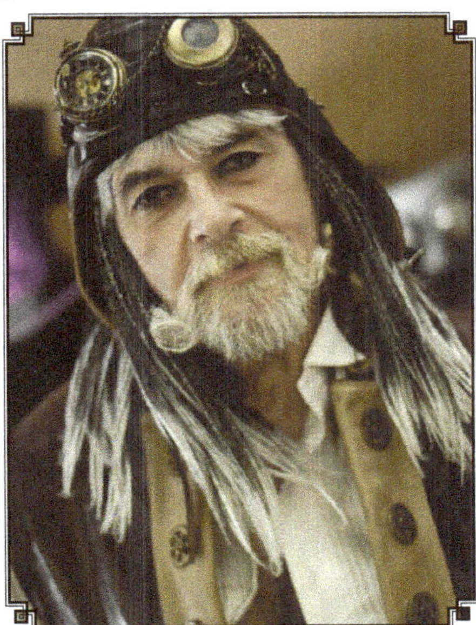

The younger generation has no specific claim to the genre. While superheroes, animae , computer game and cos-play characters abound for the 10-25 year olds, steampunk has evolved from the top-down with adults outnumbering the younger generation 5 to 1.

Recent TV shows and movies have incorporated "steampunk elements" (i.e., cogs, gears,goggles, top hats, clockworks) as well as incorporated images/machinery/inventions first put forth by H.G. Wells and Jules Verne, but none have captured the "true spirit" of the steampunk movement.

And what is the "true spirit" of steampunk? The dialogue continues in sometimes heated discussions. The jury is still out. Acknowledging that there are numerous possible definitions, it might be best to quote Sherlock Holmes: I had," he said, "come to an entirely erroneous conclusion, my dear Watson, how dangerous it always is to reason from insufficient data." (The Adventure of the Speckled Band, published 1892).

WHAT DOES STEAMPUNK MEAN TO YOU?

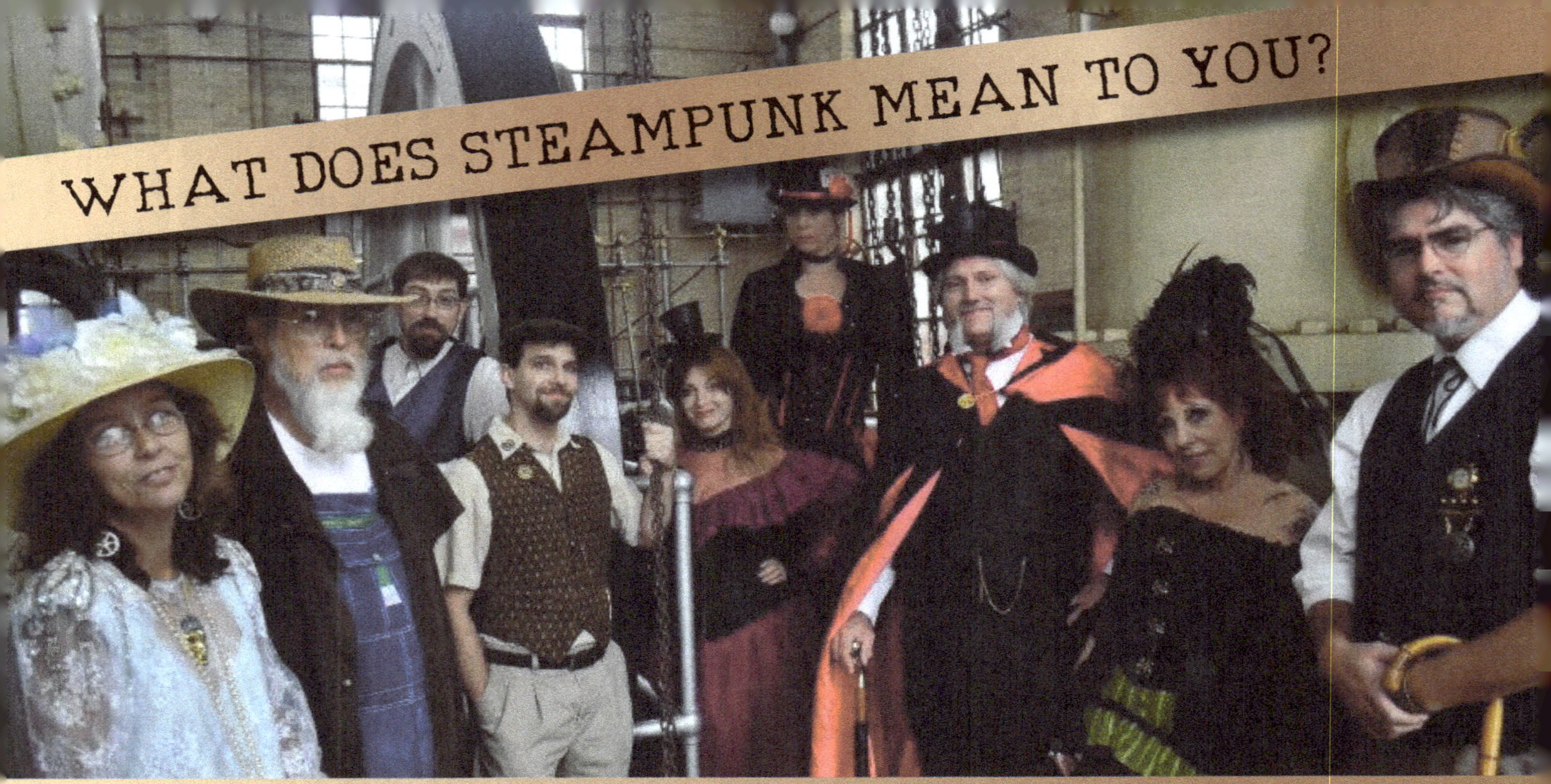

A LOOK AT STEAMPUNK CULTURE IN A SMALL SECTION OF SOUTHERN U.S.A.

In just three years, the Red River Regional Steampunk Expeditionary Society has grown to be an exceptional group that lets people come together to share their love of Steampunk and Victorian culture. It started on April 24, 2012 in a small library in Shreveport, Louisiana where "free-thinkers, adventurers, and curiosity seekers" met up and it has been history since. At first there were only members from Louisiana, but now the members range from all over the south and even from other countries. I was able to attend the first meeting when I was a young teen and have been going to the meetings on and off ever since. Being from a boring, tiny town, it was rare that neat things like this happened where I was. It was interesting to meet others that shared some of my interests. Recently, I attended a group meeting of theirs for the first time in a year and was able to talk to the founders of this group, Cassie and Carlos McDaniel.

Carlos gave me a more detailed explanation of how he created this group with his wife Cassie.

"We first started in March of 2012 as the Red River Regional Steampunk Exploratory Committee. We were trying to gauge the Shreveport/Bossier area's interest in Steampunk. We started a Facebook page and began networking; I made up a flyer and we put them out at comic stores, gaming stores, libraries, book stores and coffee shops. We networked (especially Cassie) and got the word out at the TACA Makers' Fair, then took to Facebook to announce a meeting to be held at the Hamilton/ South Shreveport branch of the Shreve Memorial Library.

Sunday, April 22nd was the day; 6:30 PM was the time. We had booked a study room at the library that could hold 16-20 people, but we were amazed to see DOZENS of people of all ages arriving (many in

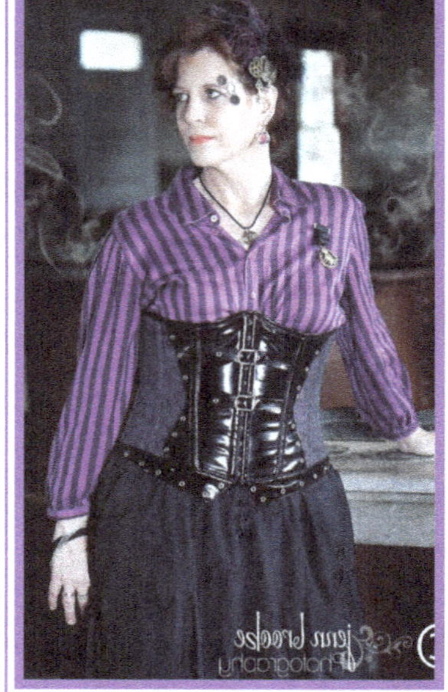

Steampunk costume) and milling about. The staff moved us to the Periodical Reading Room and still it was an overflow crowd. There were 54 people who signed the register that day and word began to spread.

We voted during that inaugural meeting to change the name to Red River Regional Expeditionary Society because the purpose of the exploratory committee had been fulfilled. The long name was in keeping with Victorian Era nomenclature (i.e. Royal Geographic Society, The North American Cosmolgical Society, etc.) and we adopted the 21st century nickname, "R3SES," pronounced "recess."

We celebrated or first anniversary on May 4th, 2013 with the event we called our Aeoliphilic Exposition and Anniversary Gala in Marshall, Texas at the Marshall Visual Arts Center. The Aeolo Expo drew Steampunks from throughout the Ark-La-Tex, South Texas, Arkansas and all of Louisiana."

"We have not done anything else quite as big: we continue to schedule expeditions to museums and historical sites and events, Steampunk photo shoots, and swap meets. Our monthly meetings are attended by a core group of about 15 local members and our social and holiday gatherings attract a larger turnout, but our membership on Facebook has grown to over 500 people from around the world. Even people in Italy, Germany, and England take an interest in, and contribute to, our discussions. Our membership ranges from teens to septuagenarians from all backgrounds.

In September of 2014, Cassie and I decided that it was time for us to step down from our positions of Benevolent Despot and Totemic Figurehead (me) and resistible Force (Cassie), and asked

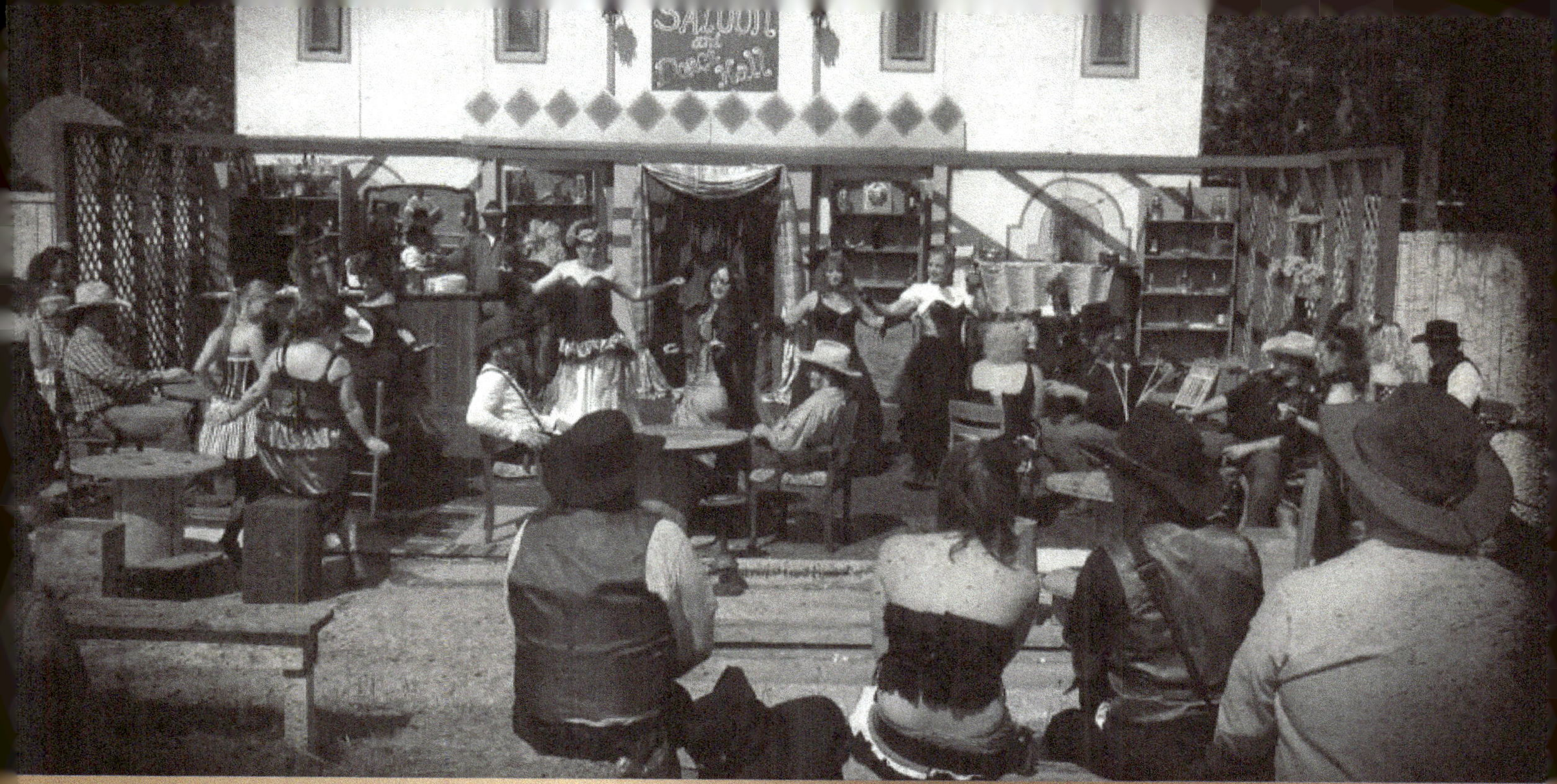

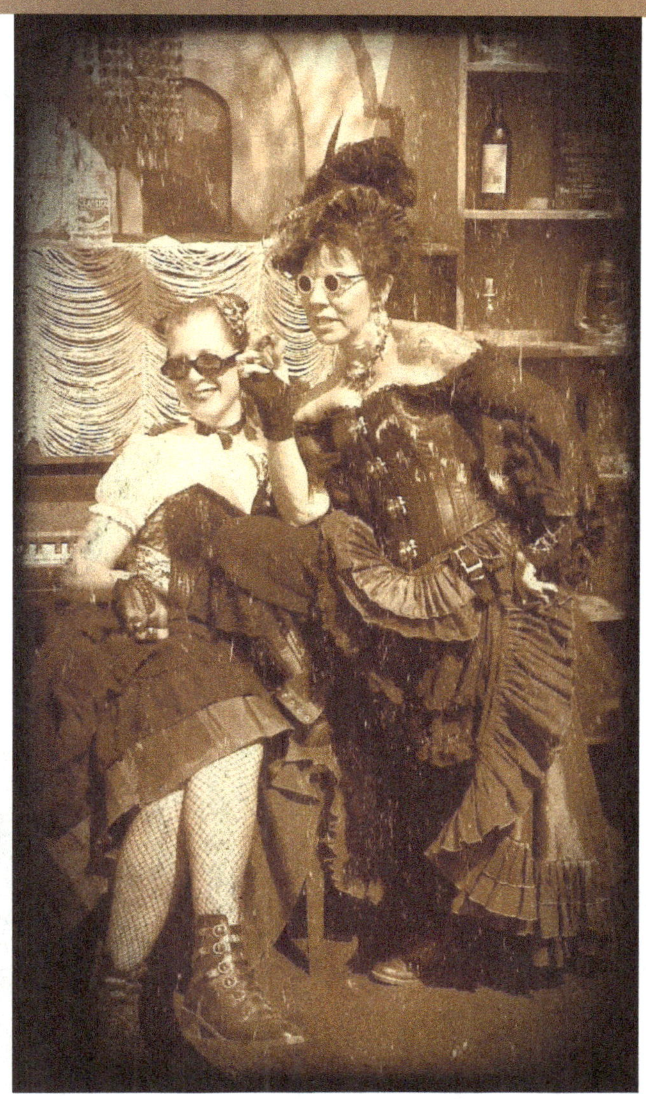

By Hyde Falkenstein

for nominations to elect a new Benevolent Despot and a leadership cadre to help carry the load. I nominated Donna Brown Smith to take my place, and she was elected by acclamation. The voting occurred during December and the inauguration was held during our Yuletide Gathering at Three Oaks Bed and Breakfast in Marshall, Texas on January 10th of this year.'

Donna has hit the ground running and has already begun to get the society involved in new and different projects. I look forward to many successful expeditions under her leadership."

Cassie gave me her explanation on what Steampunk means to her.

"It means Freedom. Freedom to explore today's society within the framework of history, freedom to imagine a brighter future through the lens of the dreamers of the past. It is the freedom to have relationships within this community that delight me and challenge me to think of things in a new way. Steampunk is a multisensory experience that awakens me to a new sense of wonder every time I encounter it."

Are you in the southern U.S.A and want to join the group and meet other Steampunkers like you? You can find them at their groups page: facebook.com/R3SESpage

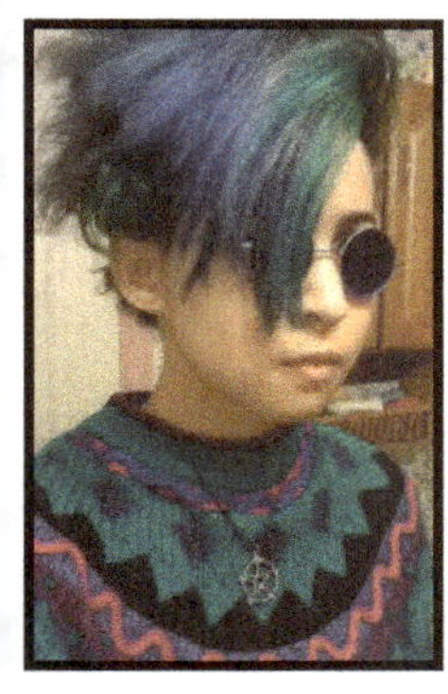

Nightfeverking is a blog started in July 2014 by Hyde, a freshman in college and an aspiring artist, writer, and film maker. It focuses on Japanese/Alternative culture and cinema. From D.I.Y tutorials, Japanese fashion, art work, film reviews, and weird things in general, it has something for everybody interested in the darker and stranger side of life.

EVOLUTION OF A STEAMPUNK

By Mary Crawley

Do you remember what first drew you into steampunk? I remember the exact image that sucked me in. It was 2007, and I had been cruising the net, I don't even remember what for, and saw that infamous picture of Kit Stolen. I'm sure you're familiar with it—a fabulously handsome post-apocalyptic Victorian gentleman in cyber dreads with goggles around his neck, his natty 3 piece powdered in a layer of dust. That's when I first read the term "Steampunk." August of that year I went to my first Burning Man, and while I was wandering through that fabulous Wonderland in the Black Rock Desert, I saw, chugging across the playa, a Victorian house on wheels. That was when I absolutely knew Steampunk was for me.

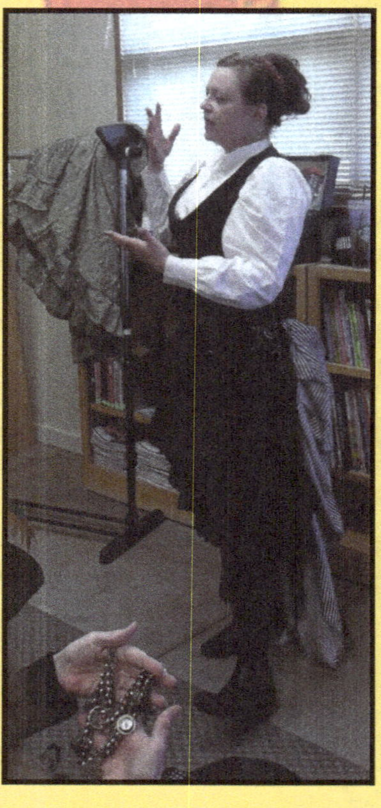

That Christmas season I attended my second Reno Santa Crawl and created my first Steampunk costume. The sewing was pretty bad, but the goggles were fabulous. They lit up at the flip of a little knife switch – and I had soldered the little light system myself! Armed with those and my Steampunk Santa Chatelaine (with handy dandy "Naughty and Nice" stamps and stamp pad concealed in a little brass box) I went boldly off into the night, asking folks to look deep into my goggles so Steampunk Santa could label them appropriately for when the real Saint Nick came around. No one knew what steampunk was, but we had fun interacting with people, including some guy named Art Mann. He said he had a cable TV show named "Art Mann Presents." I tipsily stamped him "Naughty" while my boyfriend explained my schtick. Turns out we made it onto that year's episode, and some people from Washington even recognized me at the following year's Santa Crawl. When they asked for a picture with me it made my night!

In 2008, I went to Burning Man again, this time with TWO whole steampunk outfits. Both cobbled from my closet and completed with a couple of thrift store purchases, and cool enough to wear in the daytime in the desert. It was exciting to find there were people on the playa who knew what genre I was portraying and were happy to recognize others with the same interest. Then it was Christmas and my Steampunk Santa costume that year was a teeny bit more elaborate, including a geared out flintlock that same boyfriend made and gave to me for my birthday. A few more people recognized the word "steampunk" but still not so many.

The next year was spent thrifting more, learning to sew better, and researching the Victorian era, and by the end of 2009, I found more people knew what steampunk was at the Santa Crawl. That was the year I had to learn to really read sewing directions as I moved step by step through a "Truly Victorian" polonaise pattern. The first polonaise I made (in black and white striped satin) had the flounces sewn in upside down. I shrugged to myself and wore that to the second of the three Birthdays celebrated with friends in Virginia City for our own mini Steampunk Bar Crawl. The second polonaise – with flounces sewn in right-side up this time – was part of the final iteration of Steampunk Santa.

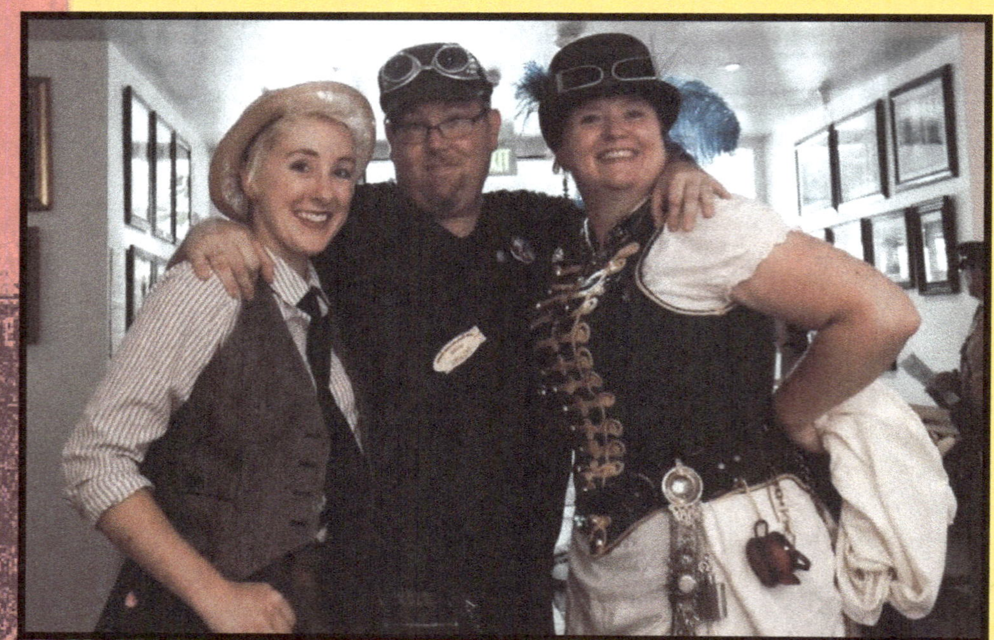

In 2010 I had completed my "go to" steampunk costume – a marvelously striped affair and between that and my final Steampunk Santa costume I was pretty satisfied. Then my friend Arthur, a military history buff, told me about a group of women called Vivandières/Cantinières, I dug into the history of these women who, starting in Napoleonic France and ending in World War I, served the military – literally. They sold brandy to the troops, serving it from tiny kegs called "tonnelets", sometimes they even served for free mid battle to keep spirits (pun intended) from flagging. These women wore weapons and fought when the lines were overrun! I looked at Vivandière clothing from around that world and created a uniform for "Vivian Dare, Battlefield Bartendress!" There was a gun made from an antique brass beer tap, a painted wooden tonnelet, teal wool, gold

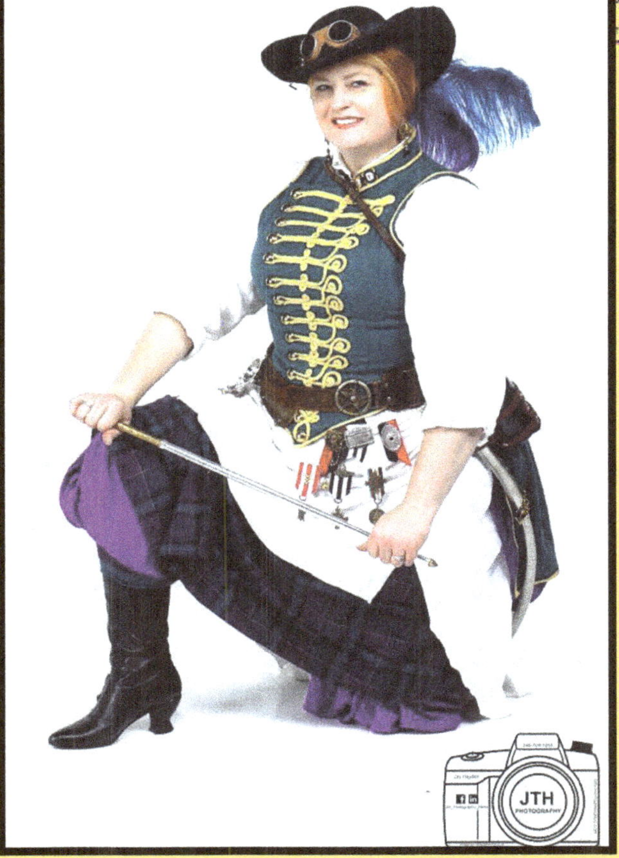

piping, purple serouel pants, and THERE WAS PLAID! Steampunk in Technicolor! It was like starting all over again, though. People knew steampunk, they just couldn't figure out what *I* was supposed to be. "Steampunk band geek?" one person asked.

By this time, I had met others with the bug at a steampunk themed Christmas Party, created as a toy drive for disadvantaged children in our community by a gentleman named Willie Puchert. In 2011, High Desert Steam was formed in response to put on the Victorian Steampunk Ball in Virginia City. We had no money, no plans, and a fairly small base at that point but Lauren Stowell said "We're doing it and it'll be at 'Piper's Opera house!'" And we did it! That summer as part of the fundraising for the ball I started to teach costuming classes, including my favorite, the "Steampunk Undress," which involves taking off my costume a piece at a time. I talk about each piece, discuss the stages of developing a costume, and talk about some of my favorite bits of Victorian clothing trivia (Since I'm wearing another costume underneath, it's only risqué if you're actually Victorian.). To make it even better, my friend David Jackson is now a part of the show to give a men's costuming perspective! For the next few years, though, my time was dedicated to helping with High Desert Steam more, and developing costume and persona less.

In 2014 I quit as an organizing member of the group to have had the chance to go back to playing more in the steam community instead of helping organize events for it. Vivian M. Dare now serves tea in battle as well, and as Tiffin Master for Tea Duels at High Desert Steam events (much gratitude to Doctor Geoff and Tinker across the pond for developing such a fabulous game for steampunks!). The uniform collects more parts – a saber from some lost fraternal organization, a bustle made of a linen tablecloth, an apron coated with medals earned in battle with every costumer's nemesis: hot glue. Currently in development is a long distance tea delivery system and tarted up tea trolly, as well as a group of other Thè (French for tea) vandières to join in the fun.

I love steampunk; I can't help it. Researching the era in world history, interacting with my fellow enthusiasts, learning how to make what I can, searching for the perfect piece for when I can't, all satisfy a deep need in me. Those enthusiasts I have met seem to have a deep love of sharing their knowledge, a delight in discovery, and a passion for learning. It is my hope that by sharing my "evolution" with you, whether you became a part of this world in the last week, or the last century, you'll be inspired to take your personal evolution or even that of your community in a direction that gives you the same joy mine has given me.

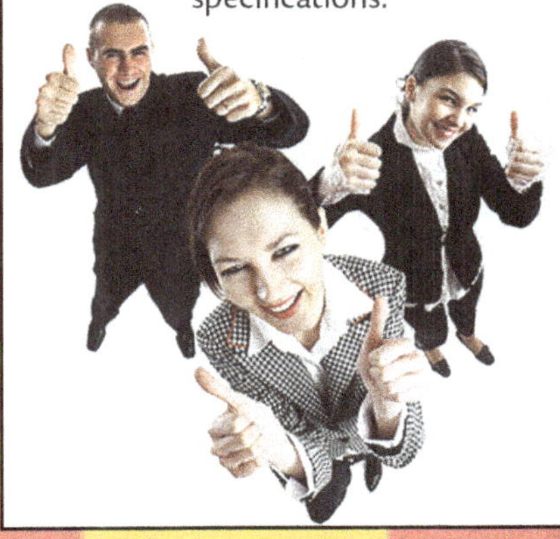

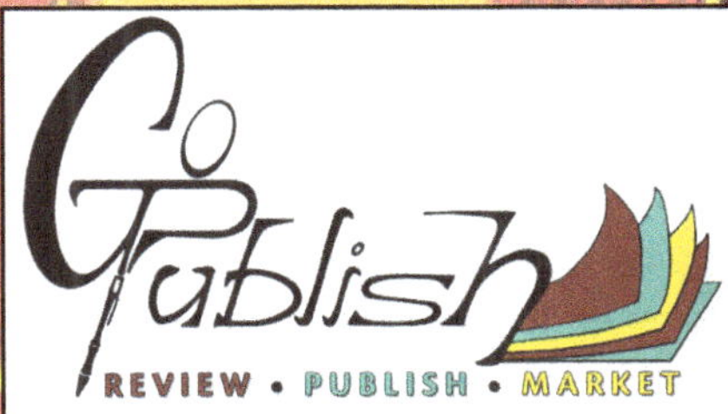

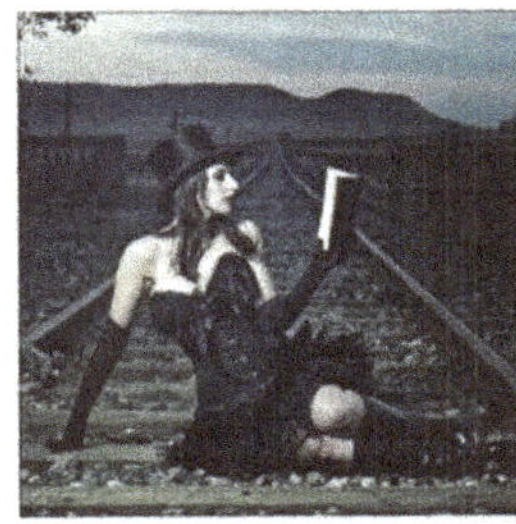

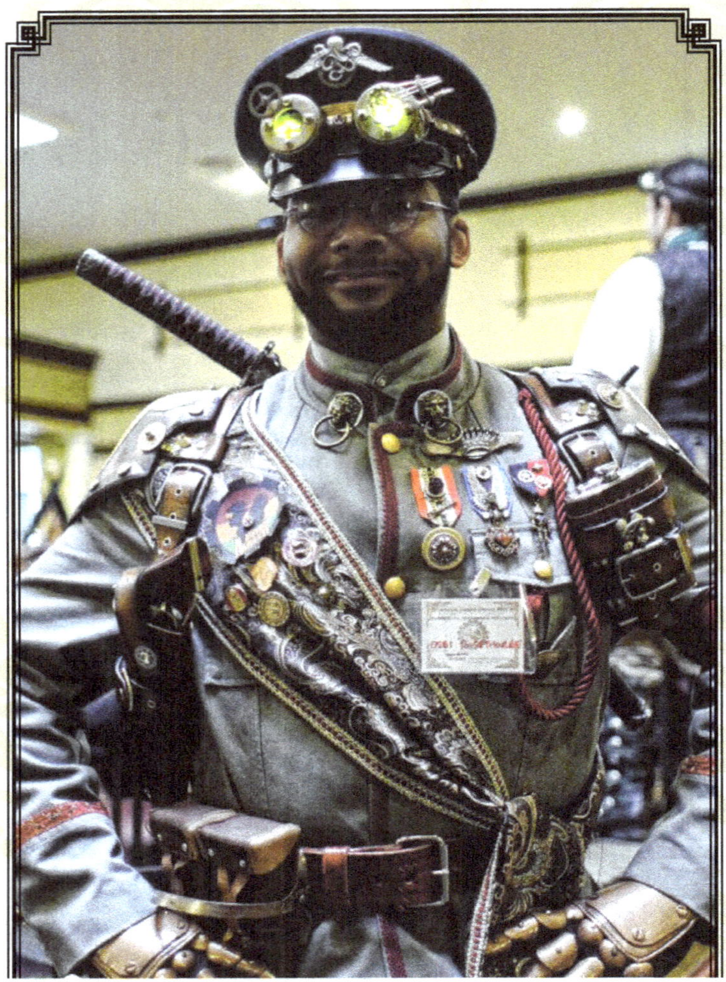
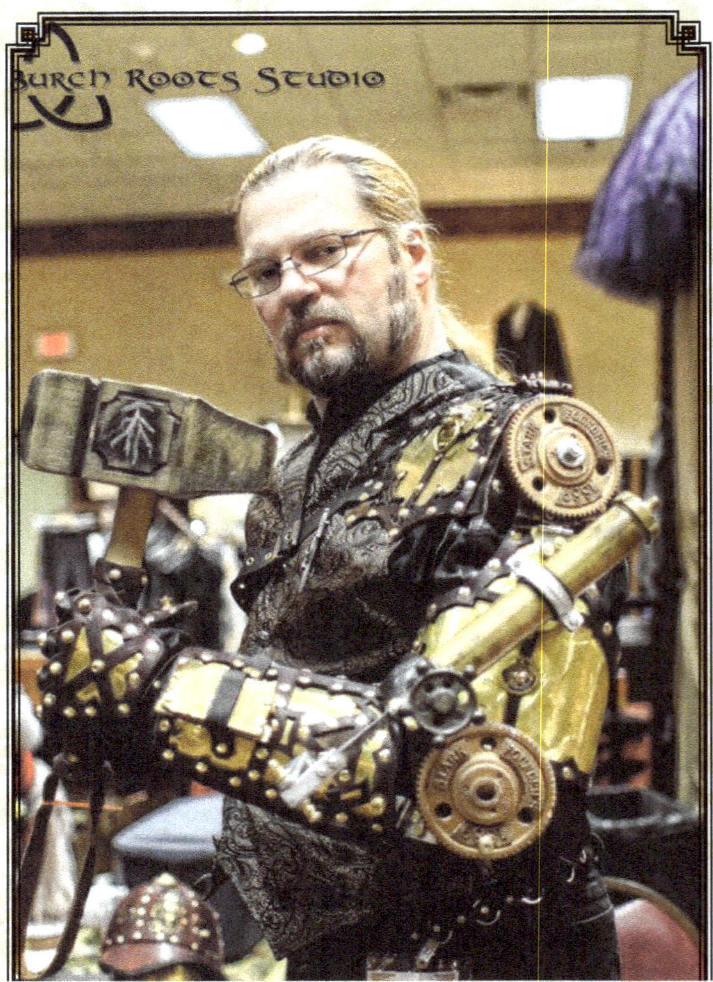

INTERNATIONAL STEAMPUNK SYMPOSIUM 2015

By Zahara

Voted "Best Steampunk Convention in the Midwest", the International Steampunk Symposium was held at the Holiday Inn Eastgate in April. This year's three-day festival was themed "Around the World in 80 Days". Special Guests included Lady Clankington (owner of Lady Clankington's Cabinet of Carnal Curiosities), Thomas Willeford (writer and maker at Brute Force Studios), Leanna Renee Hieber (award-winning author), Diana Pho (of "Beyond Victoriana" blog fame) and Mike Amend (well-known artist commissioned by Abney Park). The weekend was loaded with panels, tea parties, games, vendors and entertainment, featuring headliners Frenchy and the Punk.

Each festival has its own unique atmosphere and activities. One of the things that sets Symposium apart from other cons is that Symposium is very participant-driven and participatory. According to Aloysius Fox (Organizer), "The International Steampunk Symposium is a pioneer for interactive participatory programming, mostly in the form of the Symposium Games, which started with the first Symposium back in 2012. The Games are basically the Steampunk Olympics, [run by] someone like Willy Wonka. Attendees can compete in various eccentric challenges like mini-trike races, tea dueling, umbrella fencing, and such. The signature event is the RC Dirigible Races, in which we literally have mini-airships racing through the airspace of the convention halls. We are excited for 2016 because the "Adventures in Wonderland" theme is going to open a whole new untapped level of attendee participation that has never been seen before at a Steampunk convention."

The panels offered everything from writing to mixology, with a few adult panels on Victorian erotica and women's sexuality. This year also offered two teen panels (costuming and persona-creation), hosted by Madison Kollig. Madison and her father Brian (of Kollig Art Photography) can frequently be found at the local Steampunk events. This was her first year as a panel presenter. "I've always found there was a great amount of elegance in Victorian and Edwardian fashion and the era itself. The innovations of steam power and industrialization lead to many crowning achievements, which are still used in modern society. The brightest parts of this era are exemplified in Steampunk, and that is what draws me into it." Like most attendees, Madison and her father attend many Cons during the year, including other Steampunk expos.

According to Aloysius, the most important thing to know when coming to Symposium is that it's okay not to have a costume. "Many people hold off of attending our events, because they feel that they must have a costume to fit in. While the vast majority of attendees are in Steampunk attire, we would rather have you there in regular clothing than not there at all. Everyone needs to start somewhere, and generally, the Steampunk Community is very supportive of newcomers."

For those of us who enjoy adding to our costumes, this year's Vendors Hall was full of surprises. I especially enjoyed the leather ensembles by Shop Troll (www. shoptroll.net). They offer off-the-shelf and custom pieces that are perfect for Ren Festivals, Steampunk, and much more. And the best part of their designs are… the pockets! The attention to detail and leather-work is incredible, plus there are fully-functional pockets hidden in every piece, eliminating the need to carry a bulky bag with you during festival season. I was also mesmerized by the hats at The Blonde Swan (http://www.theblondeswan.etsy.com/). These stunning, well-crafted toppers span many subcultures, and custom pieces are also available. I especially enjoyed the hats inspired by Dr. Who and "The Nightmare Before Christmas". According to both vendors, you can stay updated on their latest creations and photographs by "liking" their Facebook pages.

Another favorite was War Pony Candy Forge (http://warponyforge.com/). The talented woman behind War Pony is known for her sweater coats, and she's also been vending her homemade candies at various indoor conventions. She offers samples of nearly everything she sells, and the 4-salt caramel she makes is amazing! The flavors in her infused hard candies and chocolates are very subtle, and there's no overwhelming, artificially sweet nonsense in any of her goodies.

The expanding list of vendors is just one reason Symposium outgrows its venue every couple of years. Outgrowing the host hotel is a good problem to have, but does create extra work and long-range planning for the organizers. The 2015 and 2016 events will be in the same location, but the 2017 festival is being wooed by four different counties in the area. Aloysius notes, "It's nice to be popular!"

For those of you (especially teenagers) who want to get involved in Steampunk, Madison offers this advice. "Try and get your friends into it. Look up information about what events might be happening that are age appropriate on Facebook pages, and find a way to get there. Have a friend who can drive take you and themselves to an event, and from there it only goes up. People are generally friendly to newcomers and want to know who you are and talk with you, because you are one of them. You went out of your way to go to an event [and] to get into Steampunk because you like it, and the people are there for the same reason. They enjoy it, too!"

The 2016 International Steampunk Symposium will offer new surprises and puzzles, as inspired by the "Adventures in Wonderland" theme. And attendees are promised a dramatic reveal at closing ceremonies!

Mark your calendars for April 7-10, 2016, and visit http://thepandorasociety.com/2016-events/symposium/ for more details.

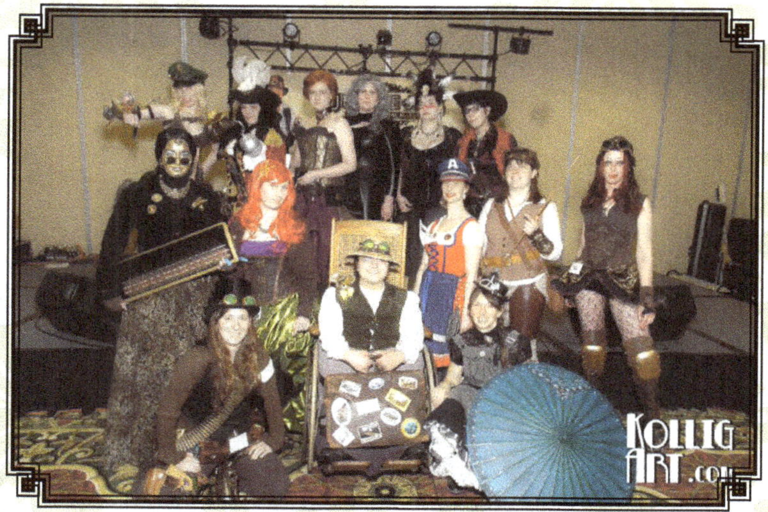

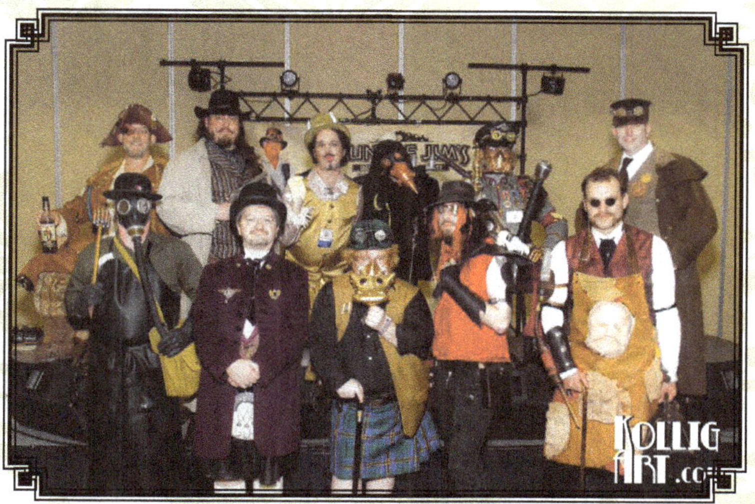

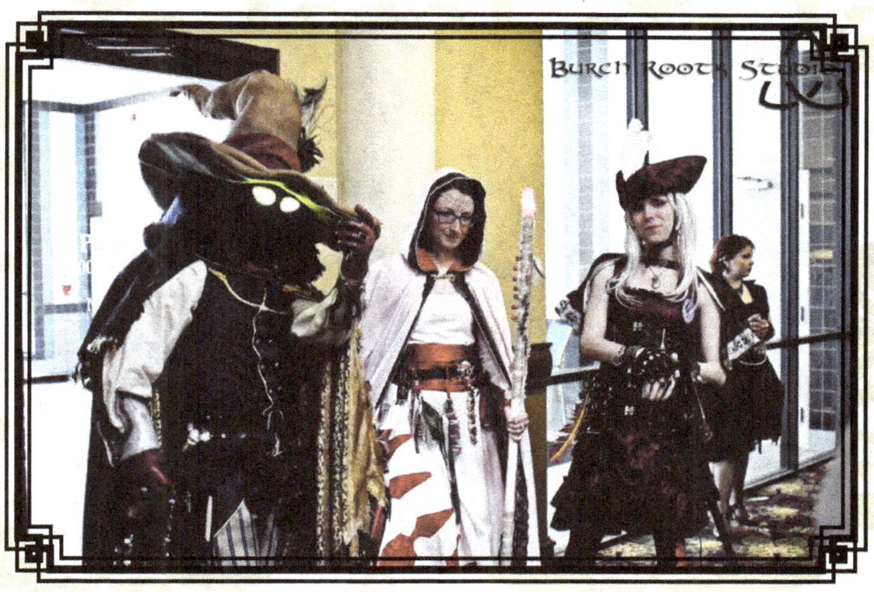

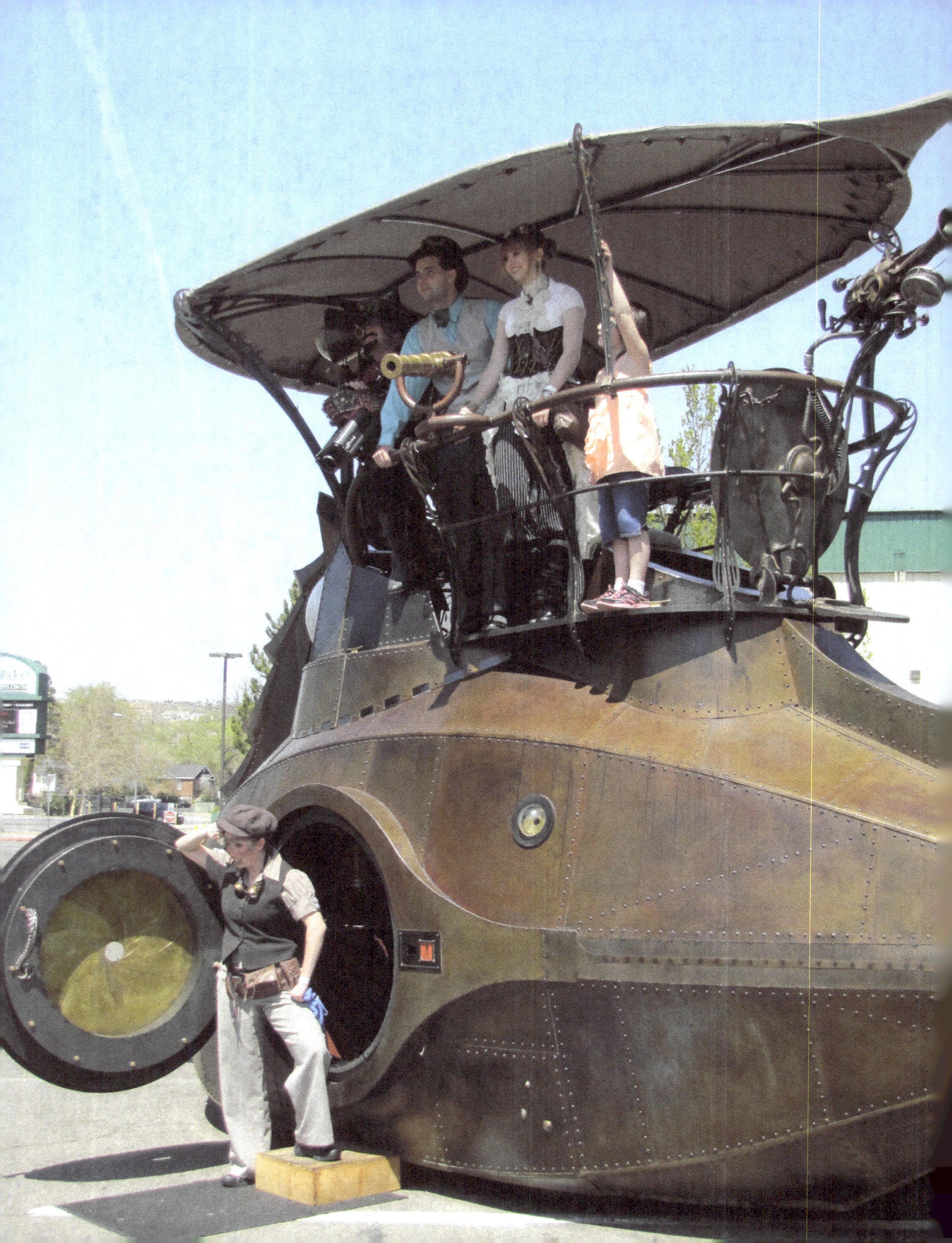

STEAMPUNK EXPO - RENO, NAVADA

By Kathleen Sharkey

I am extremely fond of the Steampunk movement that is now sweeping the world over. I have always loved the esthetic quality of Victorian era garb, even if I am not fond of some of its more restrictive clothing and gender concepts. So when I found out that our local Steampunk group was putting on their annual Expo I knew I would be going. This year the venue had been large enough to take over the Livestock Event Center's Exhibit hall, having over 40 vendors and numerous local performance groups.

Outside of the event were some amazing art cars on display. Most of the art cars that come our way travel through Reno around the end of August for the Burning man festival, however one of these vehicles makes its pilgrimage more often to Reno, The Nautilove (http://nautilove.com/). This re-creation of Captain Nemo's massive mythical ship, from Jules Verne's 20,000 Leagues Under the Sea, is a marvel unto itself. With brass shells adorning its magnificent hull, tentacles for door handles and portals with working irises, this vehicular feat is a spectacular adornment to any Steampunk event. Also on display at the Expo was the monster hunting vehicle "Monstrosity", a double decker vehicle adorned with all of the accoutrements necessary for a Miskatonik battle, including amazing speakers which kept onlookers entertained while checking out its amenities.

Inside of the 20,000 square foot exhibit hall the vendors and exhibitors were given enough space, relieving any problems with crowding. So it was truly easy to shop at each booth and see all of the wares offered. Centrally located was the exhibition stage. Set with a few rows of chairs one could see what was happening on the stage at any point in the room. With the help of the Aether Brigade to announce each performance we could even hear what was happening on the stage from anywhere in the exhibit hall.

The Aether Brigade is a fantastic Time Traveling Comedy troop, and were the "hosts" of the Expo. They put on a one hour show each day while also announcing and interacting with all of the other performances at the expo. Comprised of the crew of the Time ship Simultaneous, this band of intrepid adventurers are not only wonderfully funny and entertaining they are also the perfect group to give a Steampunk event the perfect flavor. The Aether Brigade is a group of storytelling, improv actors with fabulous talent and amazing props. http://aetherbrigade.com/ .

Other performances included a Tea Duel, hosted by High Desert Steam's own Vivian M Dare, BBPE, DOTB. This fun concept arose as an alternate to stabbing pointy things at one another because of some perceived, or misperceived insult. Started by two gentlemen from England, Dr. Geof and Tinker, it is quite the fun and challenging game to play at any Steampunk event. For rules and regulations see the original website at http://teaduel.yolasite.com/.

Also on the stage we were able to see two fabulous dance presentations by Asha and the World Dancers, local Belly dance troupes. These women danced to both modern and traditional music and kept the audience enthralled with hip flash, excited grins and an immense amount of talent.

As I travelled amongst the various vendors I came upon a display of photos shot during the making of what could only be a Steampunk style movie. Upon watching the video presentation, and getting to talk to the attendants at the booth, I was delighted to see I was right. If any of our readers are like me you are probably a little irritated by the lack of new ideas being turned into movies. The "remake" has become the norm and I for one am a little disgusted. So when I heard that some amazingly talented movie makers, producers, cinematographers and artists were getting together to make a Steampunk Movie for Steampunk people with a brand new concept I was really excited. With Drew Hall ("Convergence", "Nigel and Oscar Versus the Sasquatch"), Horst Sarubin ("The Hobbit Trilogy", "Iron Man 3", "Furious 7") and numerous other talent laden names Aether appear to be a pretty spectacular movie. Though talent laden, the crew of Aether is still trying to get the larger studios to pick up and understand their vision and so they are looking for public support so that they can prove that people are really interested in the concept. Take a look on their website http://wwwweareskyborne.com or Facebook page https://www.facebook.com/AetherMovie, I know the idea has really got me excited.

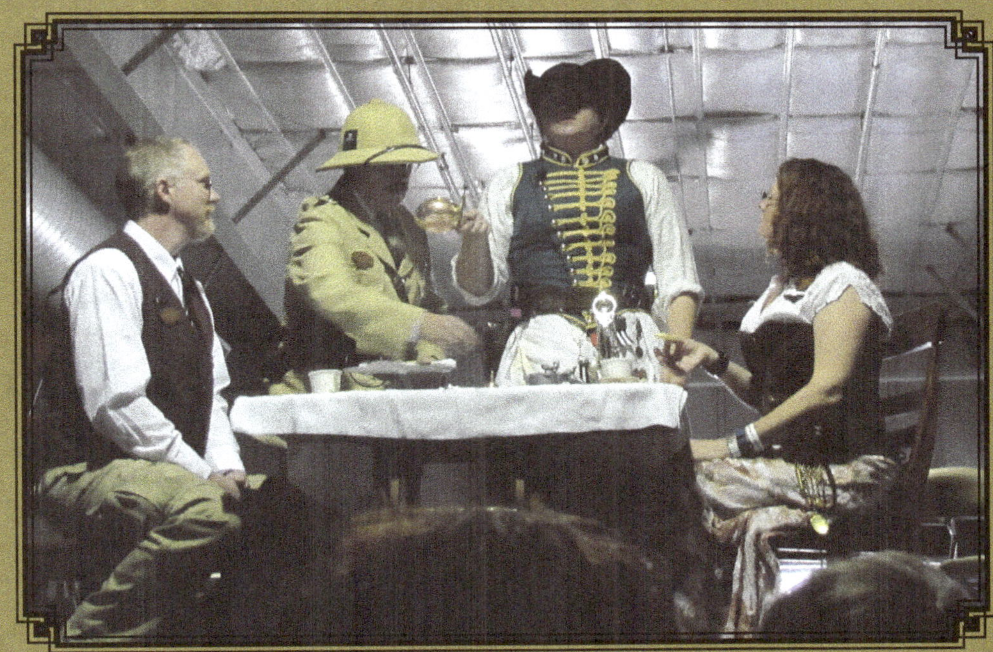

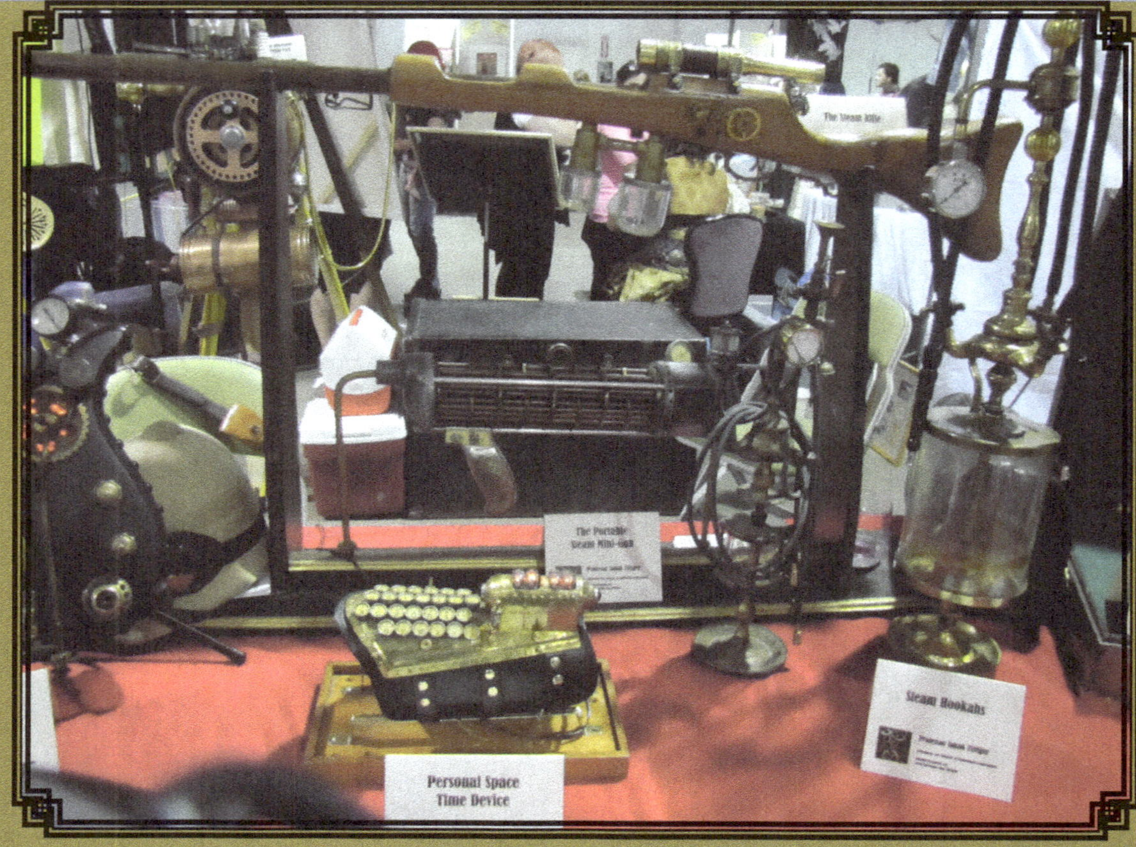

Amongst the other booths were amazing wares, costume pieces, hats, lights, writing utensils and a beautiful art display containing examples from photography and moquettes to drawings and paintings. Everything was well appointed and drew me in. Then there were the smells. From cupcakes at Buttercream Bliss (www.buttercreambliss.blogspot.com) to the Teas, they perfumed the air with scented ambiance more gratifying then gear oil and mechanical machinations. Other vendors had amazing concepts wrapped in Victorian flare like High Desert Botanicals' bitters kits which look to be a kind of kit for the mad scientist, and Gear Oils perfectly decorated pure oils with capped scents of the bygone Victorian era.

None of this would have been truly possible without the direction and production of our local steampunk organization High Desert Steam http://www.highdesertsteam.org/. This group has managed over the years to put on not only a yearly Steampunk expo but also, a Steampunk Ball in the beautiful Virginia City NV, a Steam Crawl through downtown Reno's bars and pubs, and a variety of other events to bring Steampunk into the public. If you ever happen to be in the Reno area, or are coming to the next Burning man event, make sure to take a look at High Desert's events list they are guaranteed to be fun for all.

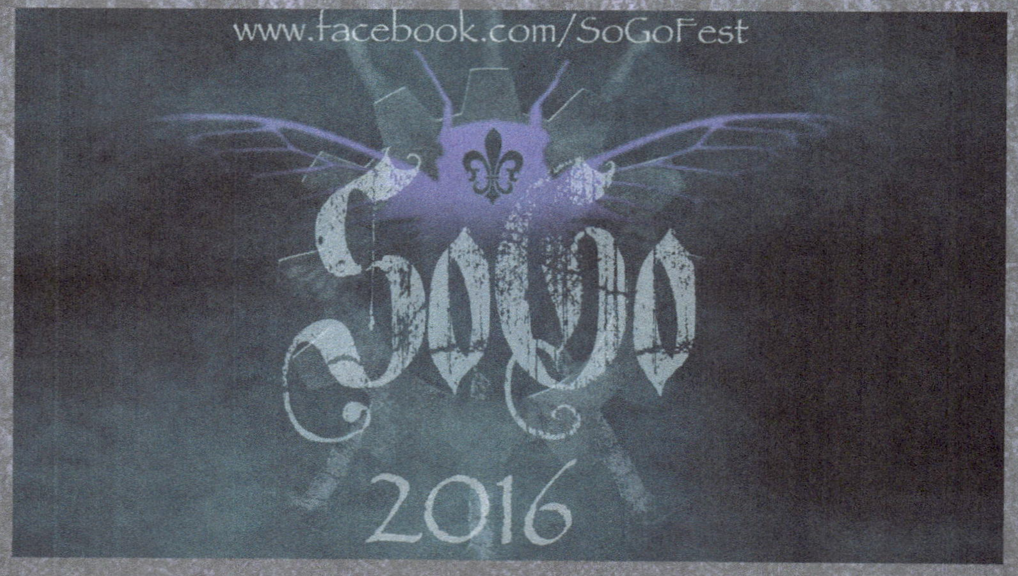

11 STEAMPUNK-INSPIRED FILMS AND ANIMATIONS

By Ethicus

1. Wild Wild West (1999)

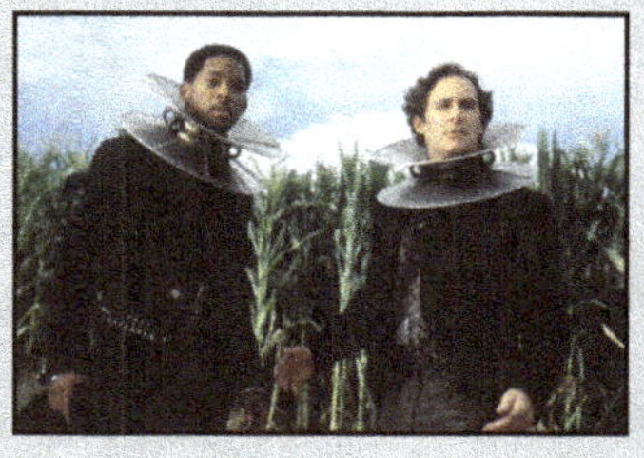

A classic that is a fantastic and imaginative movie. It acts as a true foundation of what Steampunk can be in wild western civilization. With plenty of fun to be had between the characters and their gadgets and gizmos, Wild Wild West is a joyride.

2. The Golden Compass (2007)

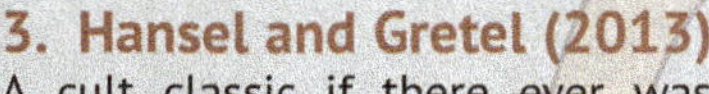

Set in an alternate universe; magic, armored polar bears, airships are abounded. Whirling, whirring, and wonderful technology are throughout the story. For the sheer expanse of the visual aspect, it's worth the watch.

3. Hansel and Gretel (2013)

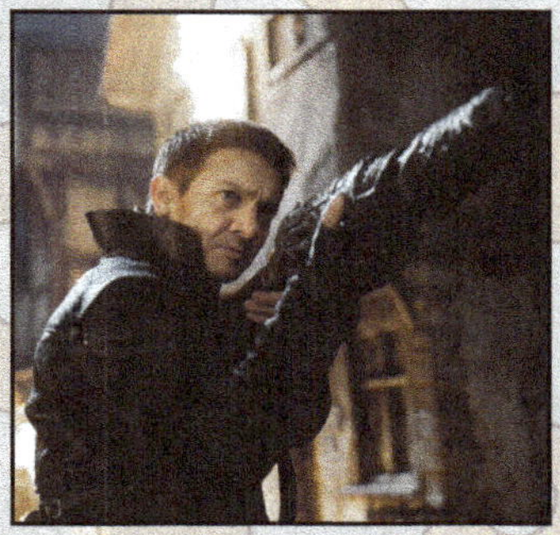

A cult classic if there ever was one. Hansel and Gretel go on Witch Hunts in a style and tone similar to the dark and gritty world of Van Helsing. Hansel and Gretel does a spectacular job of reimagining classic stories into a modern telling, that then, throws on a grim and dark action packed adventure along the way.

4. Tai Chi Hero (2012)

A Chinese martial arts film of a prodigal fighter. An epic adventure spanning two movies, (and a planned 3rd movie) western technology is introduced through a plot that means to destroy the town and build a railway through it. Steam powered war machines and gorgeously designed mechanisms battle against traditional martial artists as the villagers try to combat the power of gunpowder and cannons.

5. The Time Machine (2002)

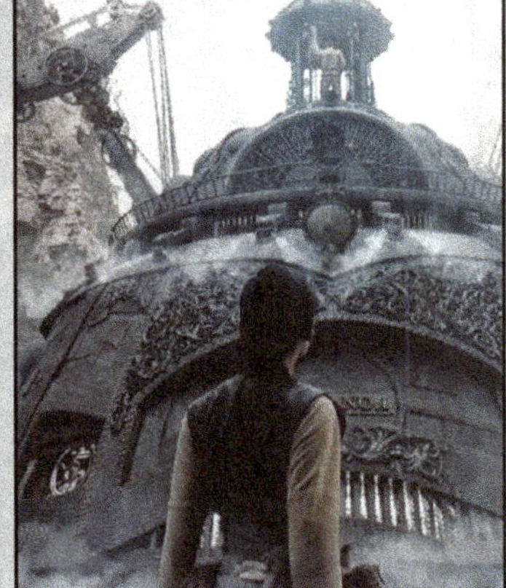

An adventure through time with an eccentric chronologist. What's not to appreciate. Though some may compare and contrast it to its older ancestor, both provide a unique narrative that will make you consider truly traversing time and space.

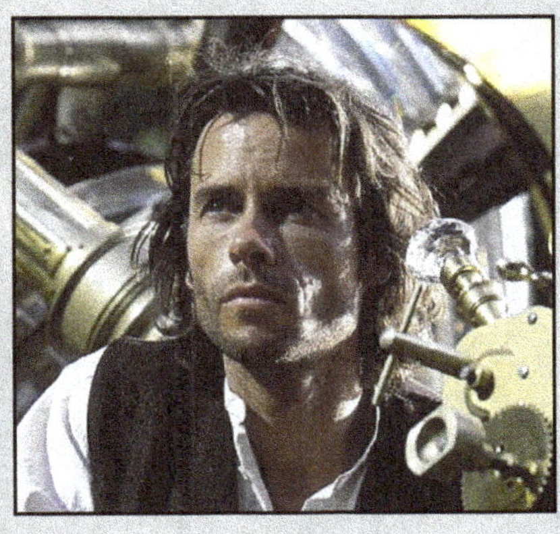

6. Steamboy (2004)

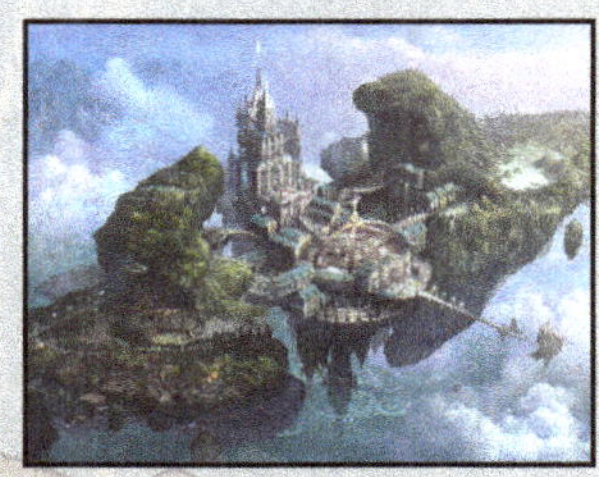

The primary focus and popularity of Steamboy comes from its detailed and dynamic inventions all centered on the power of harnessing steam. Creating a device that condenses steam to such a degree that it holds and produces a near infinite amount of steam. Power struggles occur between inventors to utilize the true power of steam.

7. Nausicaä of the Valley of the Wind (1984)

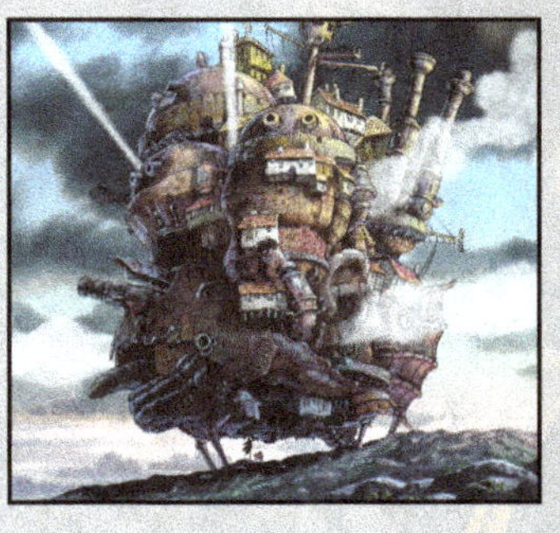

8. Castle in the Sky (1986)

9. Howls Moving Castle (2004)

Hayao Miyazaki – Known for master crafted artwork illustrating genius written stories, Miyazaki often uses steampunk-like technology in his fantastical worlds. This technology allows for unique plethora of aesthetic features in each movie that make each stand-alone from one another, yet still provide an enthralling adventure through each unique world of Miyazaki.

Only a few of Miyazaki's expansive work, these are all near perfect animated movies. Each is completely unique form one another in concept, execution, and drama. Though, each utilizes their own form of intricately imagined technology to effectively guide the viewer through the adventure alongside the strong-built protagonist in each story.

10. The Legend of Korra

Following the fantastic world and adventures of the "Avatar: The Last Airbender" series, "Avatar: The Legend of Korra" thrusts the unique world of Avatar into a revolutionary industrial era where steampunk acts as the aesthetic. With bending as the all-time premise of the story, the writers and artists of the series make steampunk seamlessly fit into the many aspects of the series.

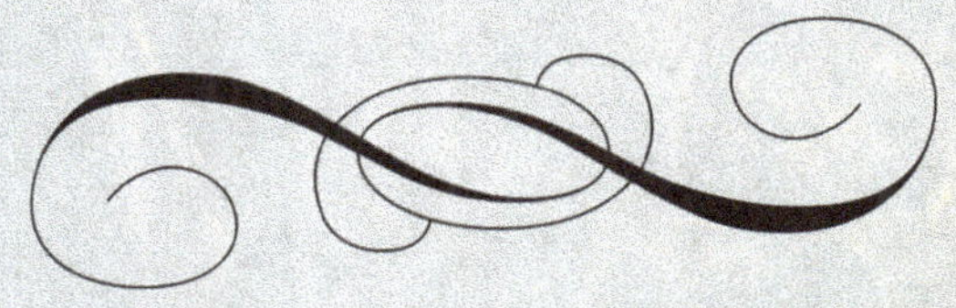

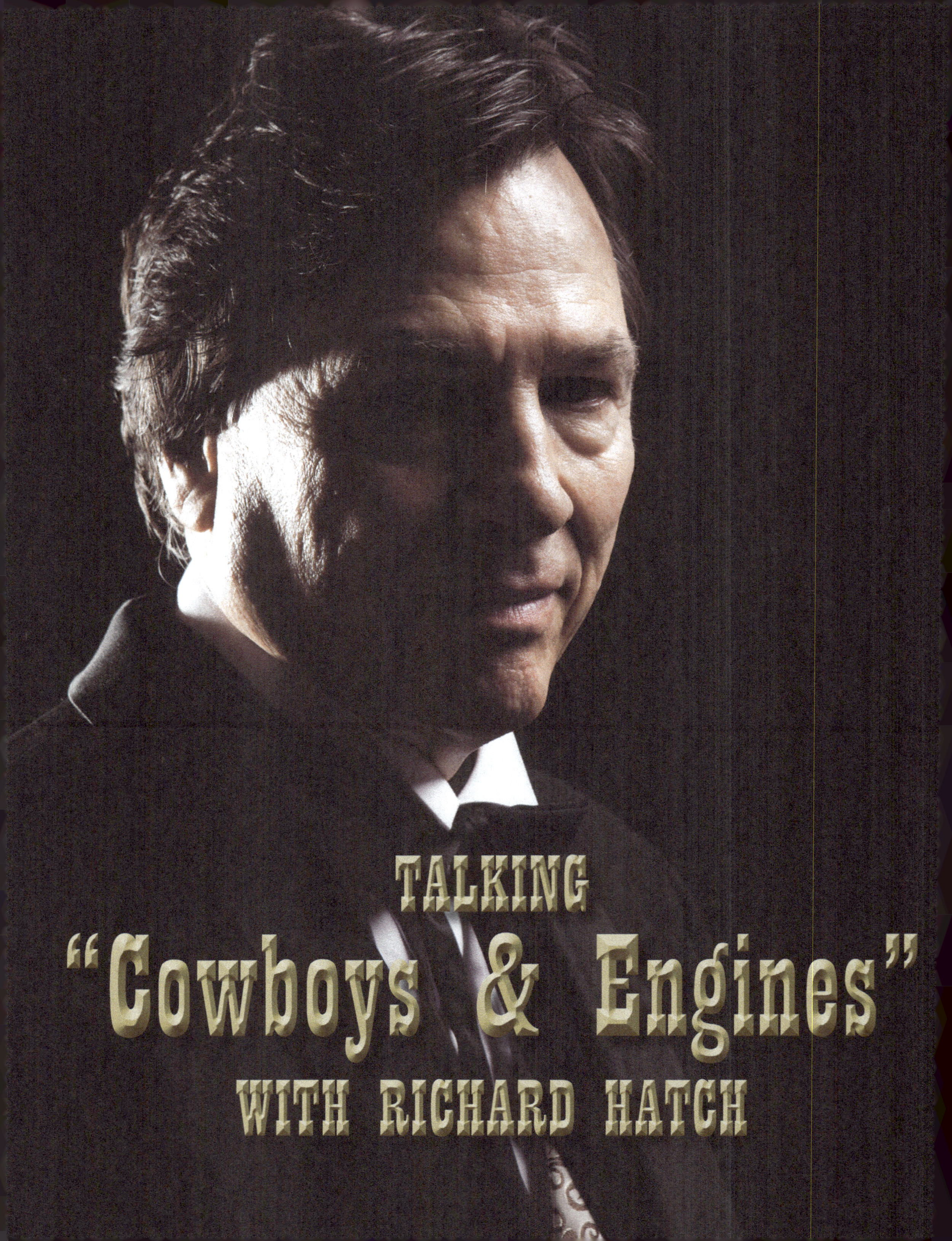

TALKING

"Cowboys & Engines"

WITH RICHARD HATCH

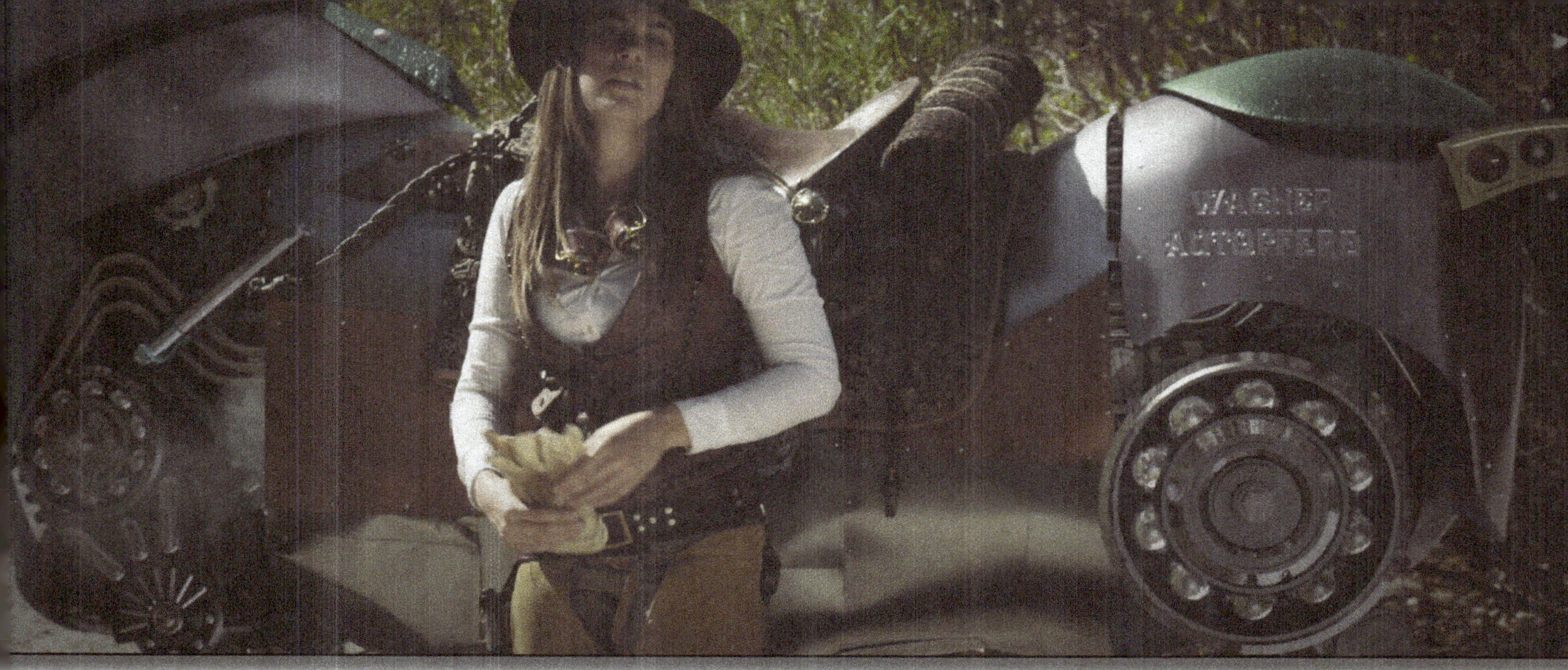

By Mr. Dark

I recently had the opportunity to sit down with Richard Hatch (Battlestar Galactica, Star Trek: Axanar, All My Children) to discuss an exciting new feature-length entry to the steampunk genre, Cowboys & Engines, which bills itself as an ambitious futuristic adventure. Cowboys & Engines follows the conflicted Cade Ballard (Hatch) as he and his captivating accomplice, Guinevere Wheeler (Libby Letlow), try to stop the tyrannical Dr. Clay (Malcolm McDowell) from destroying San Francisco.

"I was going to play the villain originally and then we were able to get Malcolm McDowell for the part." Hatch said.

"I have read that playing the villain is the most fun for actors because you can go over-the-top with the role. Is this true?" I asked.

"Yes, there are less restrictions in playing an over-the-top character." Hatch answered.

Hatch, who is also a renowned acting coach, has made a name for himself in recent years by performing in fan films and lower-budget projects. When interviewed, Hatch remarked that in Cowboys & Engines, he and his co-star often found themselves lost in the steampunk world portrayed in the film. This is what any serious actor seeks in a performance, but sadly these moments are often rare. Hatch relayed, "I finally had one of those special moments with my co-star of Cowboys & Engines. We just forgot everything and had a total immersion in the role."

From the exclusive photographs provided by Hatch, it is clear that Cowboys & Engines succeeds in bringing together a futuristic blend of the Victorian Era past, classic western films, and a post-apocalyptic future. Even if Warner Brother's Wild Wild West failed to incite interest in steampunk westerns, Cowboys & Engines, with Malcolm McDowell hamming it up as the villain, stands a chance of reinvigorating audience interest in this quirky, but appealing genre.

Unfortunately, there are really very few futuristic steampunk westerns available. Full Moon Pictures' Oblivion (1994) is an excellent example, though the film only contains reference to steampunk and mostly relies on its futuristic details. Conversely, Cowboys & Engines seeks to explore the genre in-depth and further define the steampunk western.

As a fan, I am looking forward to seeing Cowboys & Engines it in its entirety. Whether you 're a fan of the genre, or just a curious inquisitor, be sure to keep your eyes on this production.

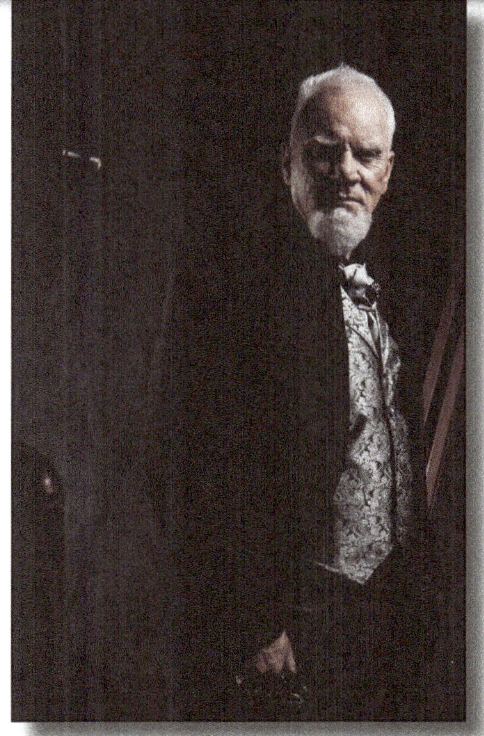

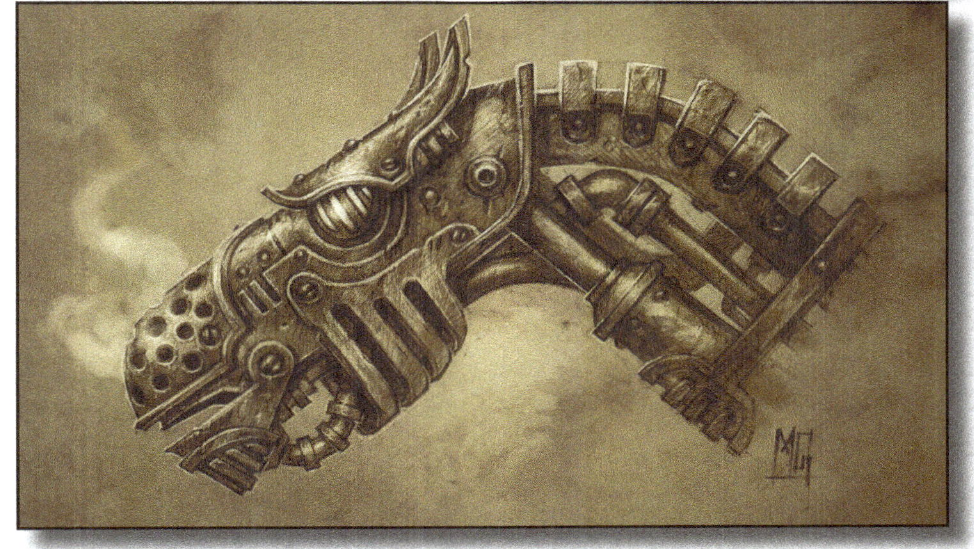

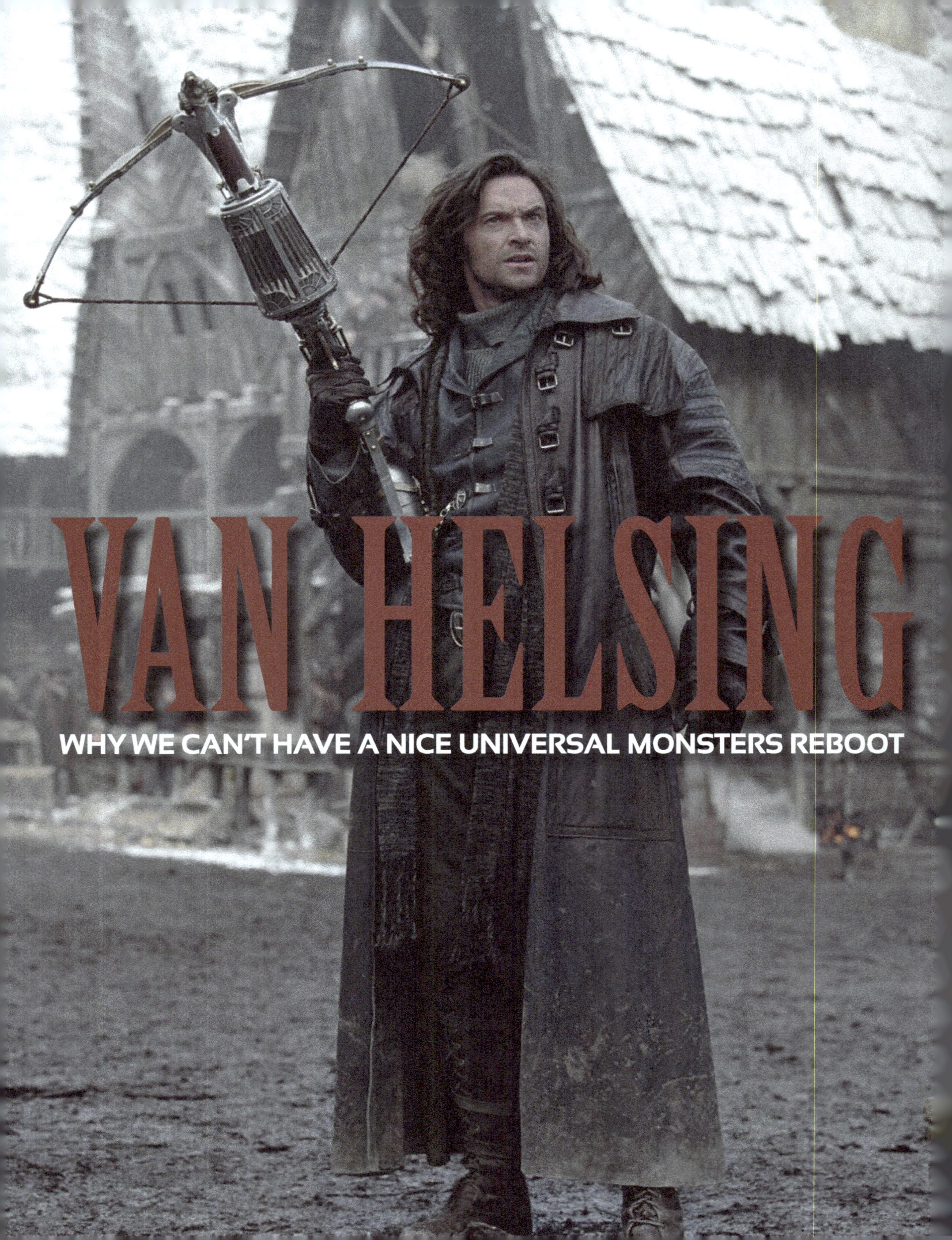

VAN HELSING
WHY WE CAN'T HAVE A NICE UNIVERSAL MONSTERS REBOOT

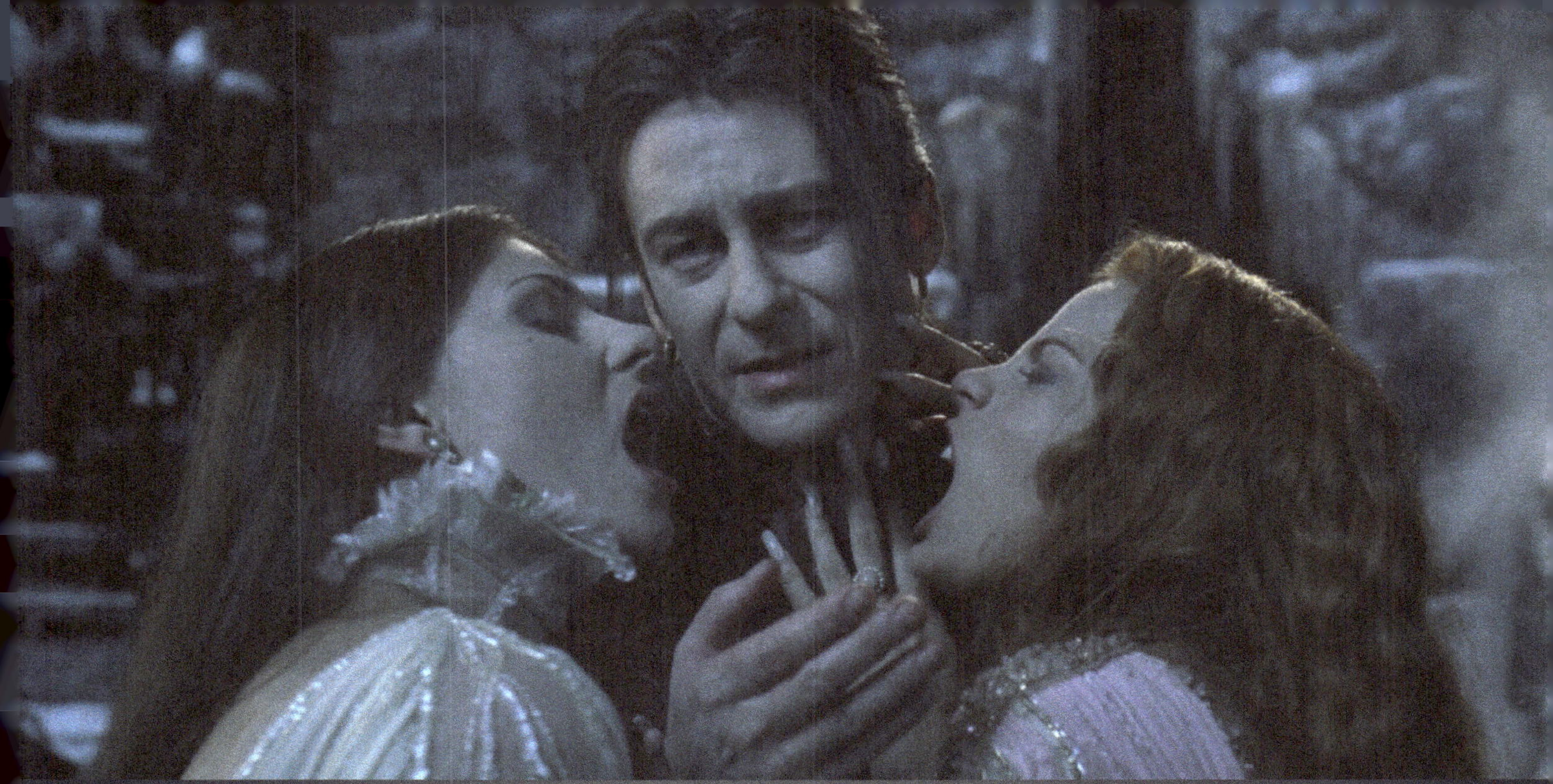

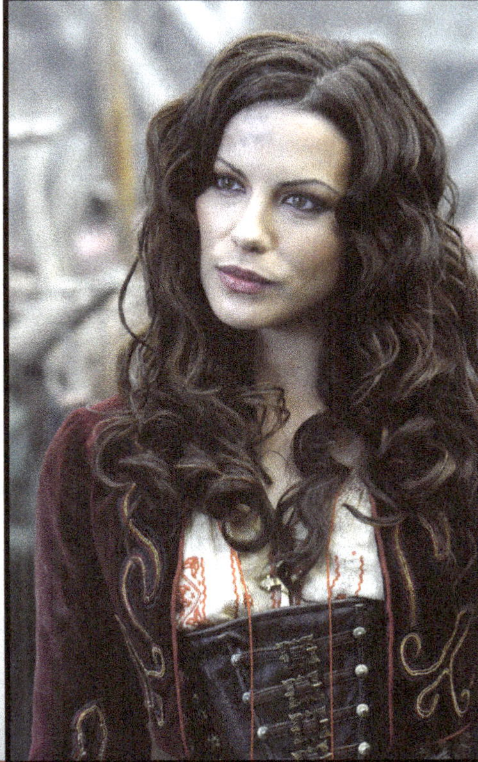

By KA Morris

The 00s were full of horror films that weren't exactly horror films, but were instead a valiant effort at pretending to be horror films because of the inclusion of characters based in horror mythology. Van Helsing is a painful addition to this group; I say painful here due to that fact that it really tried to be amazing, managed to pull together an fantastic cast, but still somehow failed on almost every level. Interestingly enough, Van Helsing crossed some similar story lines as The League of Extraordinary Gentlemen, but more on that later.

The story: Altered from his professorial roots and re-imagined as Gabriel Van Helsing (Hugh Jackman), the titular character is now a notorious monster hunter sent to Transylvania to stop Count Dracula (Richard Roxburgh), who is using research stolen from Dr. Frankenstein's experiments to achieve an almost impossible goal. The addition of a werewolf complicates matters just a bit.

Writer/director Stephen Sommers turned the scholarly character of Abraham Van Helsing from Bram Stoker's Dracula into Gabriel Van Helsing, a Vatican foundling who is a sort of James Bond of the clergy… stay with me. His very own Q is a long-suffering friar named Carl (David Wenham), dragged along on Van Helsing's most recent adventure into the wilds of Romania, where Van Helsing's mission is to save the last tattered remnants of a "Warriors for Christ" family - the Valerious clan, from extinction. The Valerious family has pledged their souls to damnation until they can defeat heir ancient enemy, Count Dracula.

The film opens on the capture/accidental death of Dr. Jekyll/Mr. Hyde in Saint Michel, Paris, and Van Helsing's subsequent flight from justice. Vatican enforcers are above the law, and Gabriel has bigger things on his mind. Van Helsing is a complicated soul and he's not exactly a fan of his current monster-busting lifestyle.

Against his will, Van Helsing and Carl are sent to Romania on one final mission for the church: Rescue the last remaining members of the Valerious family from extinction, and maybe find a way to kill Count Dracula while he's at it. Over in Romania, in a small village that is stereotypically small, Anna and Velkan Valerious protect the people of the village from the random attacks of Count Dracula, his vicious wives and a werewolf; a new addition to the "don't move here" brochure. Above the attacks of the Valerious clan, Dracula has other problems to deal with, namely his three wives who are desperate to have children. Sadly for them, through some convenient quirk of mythology, they are unable to breed - but Dracula has learned that by harnessing the power of the research and science of Dr. Frankenstein that their precious offspring will survive their monstrous (and they are) births.

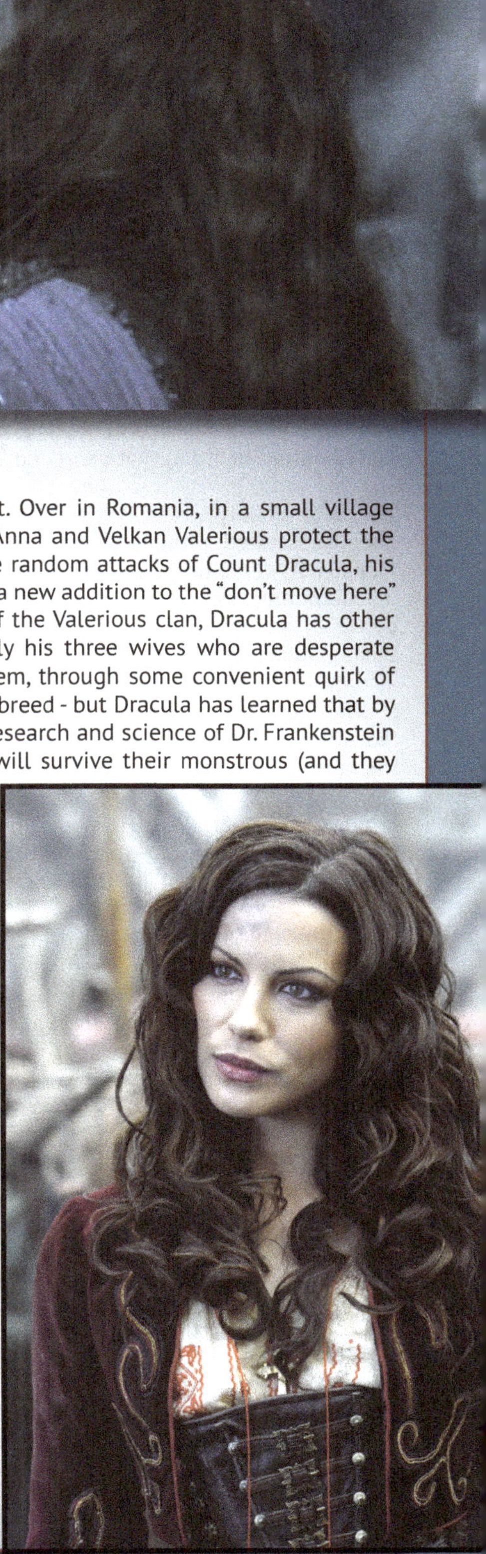

One avenue where Van Helsing and LoEG meet, is the re-awakening of literary characters and characters from cinematic history to create a backdrop for the film. Van Helsing features Dr. Frankenstein, Frankenstein's Monster, Igor, Dracula and his wives, and a Werewolf - all existing in the same timeline. However, in the vein of Steampunk films, I would actually hesitate to grade Van Helsing as such. Timeline wise, it's correct enough, but only because of the characters utilized within the story. The weapons used by Van Helsing are a very basic form of Steampunk, in that they use elaborate metallic gear and pulley systems

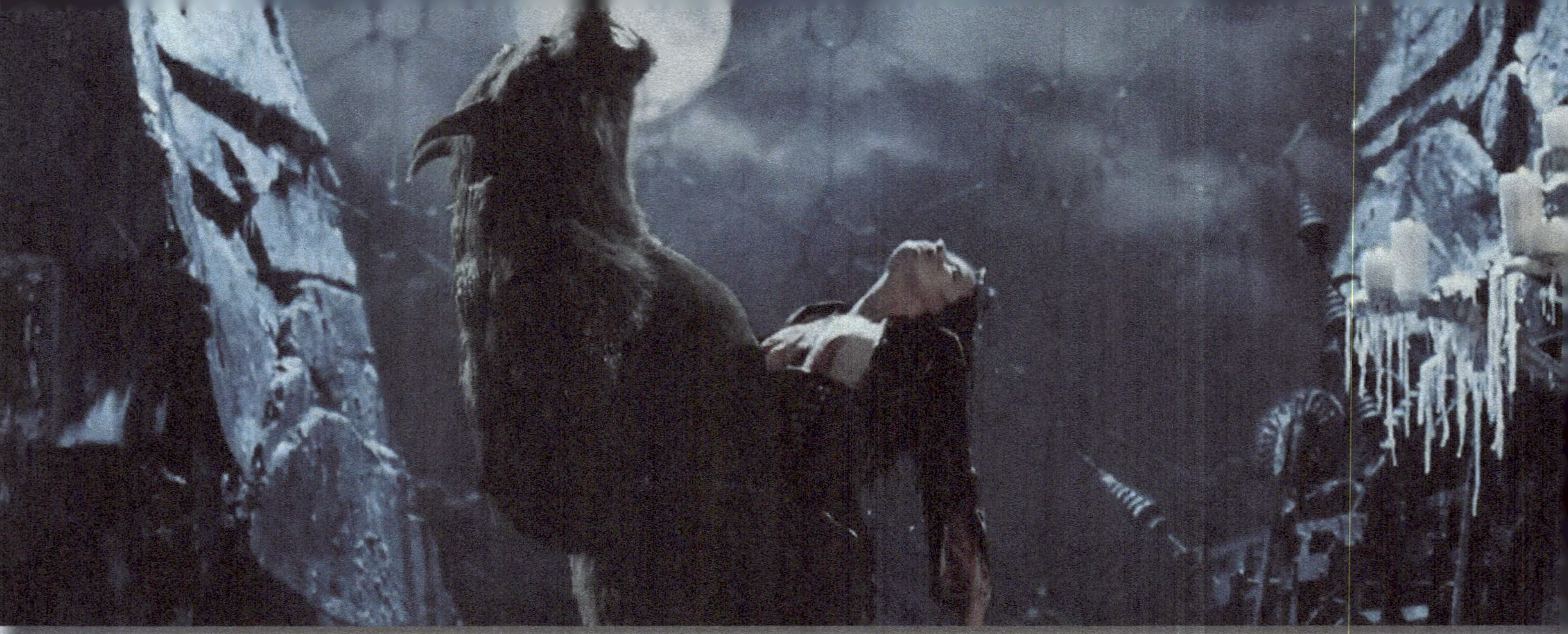

with wooden components, but are otherwise unworthy of note. The wardrobe of Anna Valerious, most notable for the corset that Beckinsale has stated she despised, could only be considered vaguely Steampunk for its shining of traditional female dress norms of the period, in that she wears leather breeches. Shocking Personally, I see Van Helsing as more of a Gothic tale than anything, as it utilizes scenery, wardrobe, and literature befitting that genre more closely.

The most notably Steampunk element of the film is a visual one, and it's encapsulated within the laboratory of Dr. Frankenstein and his Monster. Powered by the uncontrollable forces of electricity, the lab is a beautiful mess of antique equipment (purchased on eBay by the set dec team) and snapping Tesla coils. The Monster himself is a study in Steampunk elements as he is not only an amalgamation of man, but also of man and machine - a proto-Borg if you will. With a brainpan churning with visible electricity to a steam-powered leg, Frankenstein's Monster, while acting as the key to unlock all of Dracula's desires, is the most unique element of the entire film.

From the outset, Van Helsing is a misguided mess, however, with closer scrutiny, it's plain that the intentions of a film such as this are noble enough. Uniting the Universal monsters in their first "serious" ensemble film since the later 1930s, Van Helsing is an honest attempt at refreshing modern interest in this almost forgotten arm of Hollywood filmmaking.

Coming off of a disappointing experience in LoEG, Roxburgh is an exceptional leading man, and his Dracula is charming, threatening, and highly entertaining despite the forced accent. Beckinsale plays Anna Valerious the same way she plays Seline in Underworld, which was filming at the same time, but it works well here. Jackman's world-weary hunter, Van Helsing, is wise cracking and very similar to his Wolverine –

a franchise which was also in production during the filming of Van Helsing. Where Van Helsing ultimately falls flat is in the execution of its lofty CGI goals. The blatant use of CGI at every available opportunity is a slap in the face to its noble attempts at honoring the golden age of Universal Monsters.

The verdict: 2.5 coffins measured to fit out of 5. While an entertaining film, Van Helsing's shortcomings as it races to a predictable conclusion are painfully obvious. Also clear as are its issues with blending too many distinct story lines, which collide and leave the viewer confused, or at best, blissfully unaware as to what they've actually just watched.

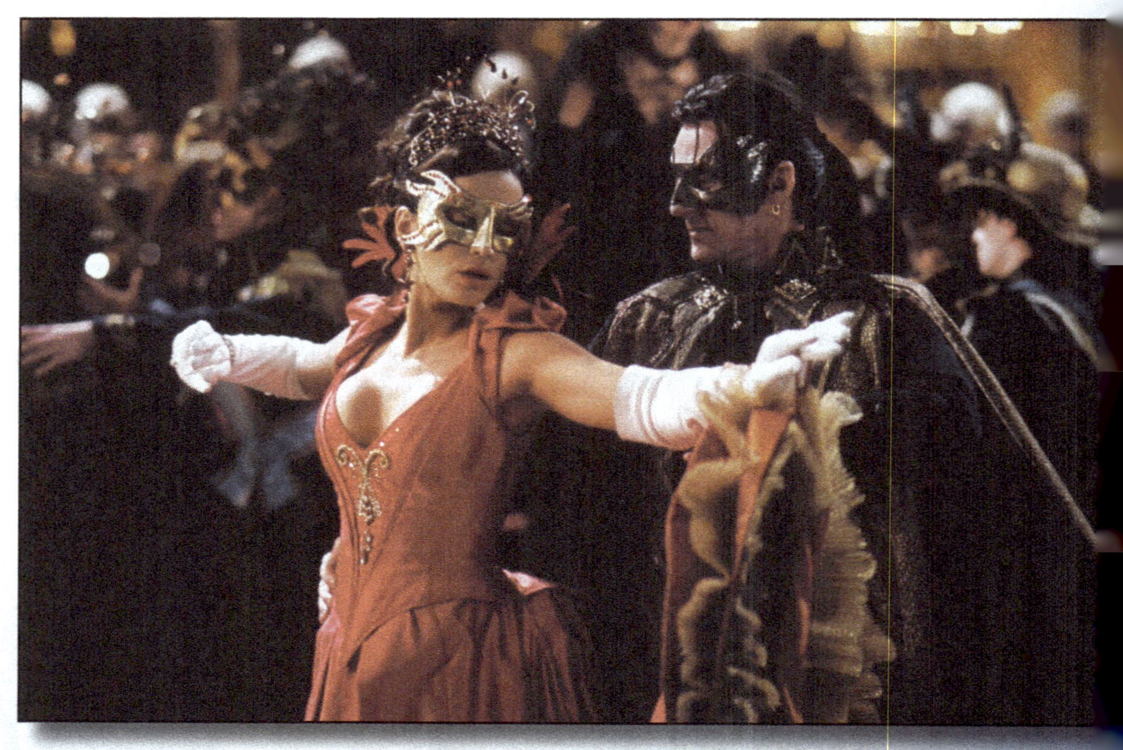

MAGIC & MISDIRECTION
WATCHING CLOSELY IN THE PRESTIGE

By Katie McKensie

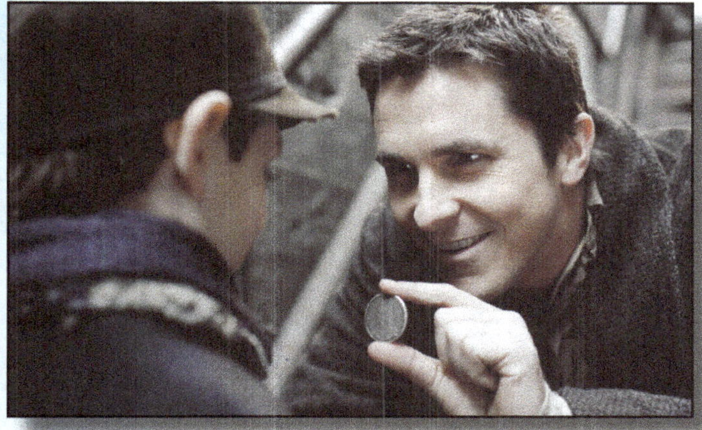

"Are you watching closely?" The first line in Christopher Nolan's 2006 magic-imbued mystery The Prestige is a provocative invitation to look, but not a promise that you'll see anything of significance if you do. Based on a 1995 novel by sci-fi/fantasy writer Christopher Priest, the film is a circuitous odyssey into the world of stage magicians in Victorian-era England, focusing on two highly ambitious yet troubled illusionists: Hugh Jackman as Robert Angier and Christian Bale as Alfred Borden. Looking closely is a challenge aimed directly at the viewer, but also serves a thematic purpose for Angier and Borden's inability to reconcile the dichotomy between their private and public selves. The closer one looks, the more one loses perspective on the bigger picture and looks for something that just isn't there – when the simplest explanation is often the correct one. The enigmatic nature of magic is right at home in Nolan's late-19th century setting, where enlightenment about the truth behind an illusion is as thought-provoking as the newly-minted electric technology of the era.

The opening question of The Prestige, spoken by Borden, is accompanied by a brief, uncontextualized shot that will later be a key to unlocking one of the film's central mysteries – proof that Nolan's sleight-of-hand as a filmmaker is immediate and persistent throughout the entirety of the film. As dueling magicians in an age when fascination with the art of illusion was at an all-time high, Angier and Borden are driven to come up with acts that meet the growing demands of an audience seeking increasingly dangerous and mystifying tricks. From elaborate feats of escape to bullet catches, Angier and Borden engage in career-spanning acts of sabotage and one-upmanship that ultimately devastate both their personal and professional lives.

The "turn" portion of the film arrives when Borden unveils his "Transported Man" trick – a bewildering act in which he is able to enter a cabinet on one side of the stage and emerge from another on the opposite side a moment later. The rest of Angier's life is devoted to uncovering the mystery behind the Transported Man – and by duplicating and improving upon it, achieving his own fame and notoriety in the world of performative magic. His obsession leads him to seek out real-life inventor Nikola Tesla, played in an inspired bit of casting by Ziggy Stardust himself, David Bowie. Tesla's highly secretive experiments with electricity may provide Angier with a working device to accomplish his own Transported Man trick, but his ensuing success is also burdened with tragic consequences.

Nolan's adaptation of Priest's novel is a striking meditation on the nature of duality – not only in how characters see themselves in contrast to one another, but also in the bifurcation of one's self. As professional foils, Angier and Borden make formidable opponents; even more interesting is how each man grapples with the dueling desires within himself. Borden surrenders so completely to the art of his craft that he must settle for a life only half-lived when he's offstage. Conversely, Angier runs from his life of privilege to seek out a new onstage identity, reinventing himself as "The Great Danton" in an effort to achieve renown outside the confines of his family name. Nolan reinforces this theme with repeated dyadic imagery – the horrible truth behind the disappearing/reappearing dove trick immediately comes to mind – as well as the cyclical nature of the film's timeline. Like Nolan's previous work Memento, the resolution to the mysteries within The Prestige reveal themselves in due time by recalling previously-shown events once the audience is privy to newly uncovered information. Revisiting these moments places greater emphasis on things that may have been overlooked the first time around, following through on the film's early invitation to "watch closely."

The concept of "The Prestige" as described in the film – the awe that follows when you've produced a transformed object at the end of a magic trick – is what Angier and Borden wish to achieve, albeit for a different purpose. In magic as well as in film, revealing the methods behind the trick can quickly deflate any sense of wonder the act held in the first place. As one character in the film puts it, "Now you're looking for the secret… but you won't find it, because of course you're not really looking. You don't really want to know. You want to be fooled." Not only does the film explicitly tell us to watch closely and repeatedly shows us its cards, so to speak, but the denouement still manages to surprise, making it a treat for repeated viewings to see how many clues you can pull out of each frame. When Nolan finally reveals his hand, it's mind-blowing solely for how prosaic the answer truly was all along – and it is for pulling off this great magic trick that he deserves a special kind of prestige all his own.

Rating: ****

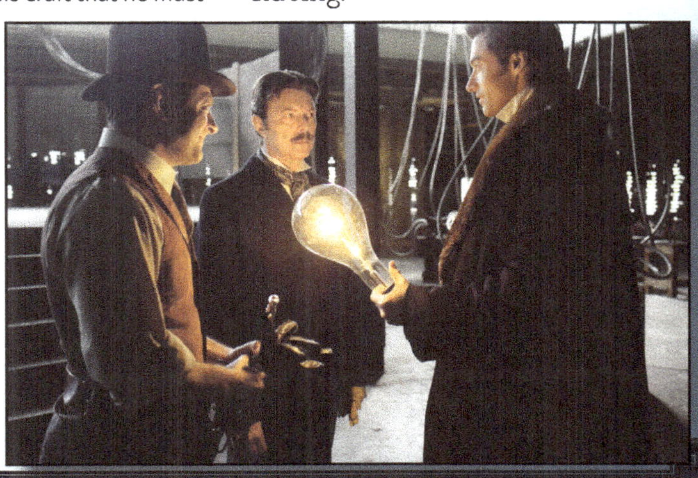

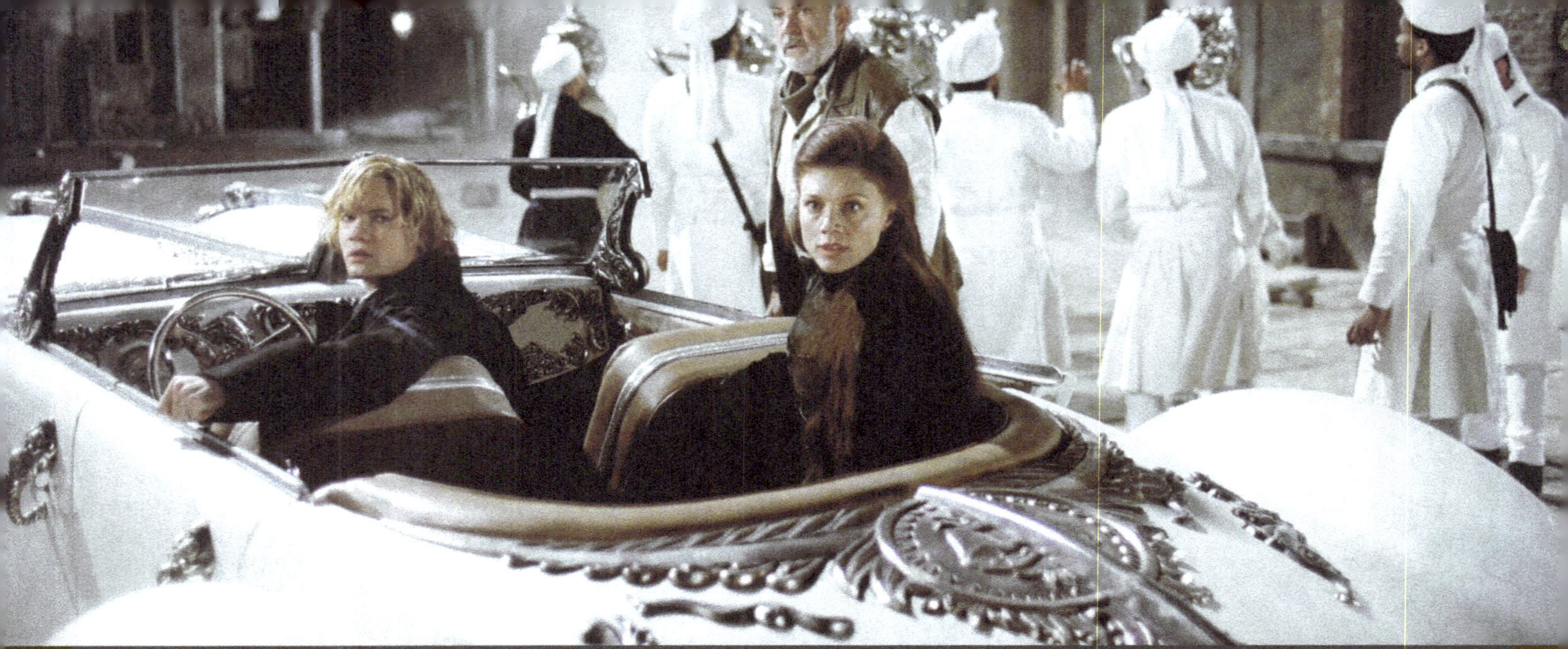

MEMBERSHIP CLOSED:

OVERTHINKING "THE LEAGUE OF EXTRAORDINARY GENTLEMEN"

By KA Morris

While it would never normally cross my mind to call a piece of popcorn cinema cerebral, The League of Extraordinary Gentlemen is exactly that. However, it is also a film that was so fraught with controversy and bad blood that it caused multiple problems for cast, crew, and collaborators and resulted in the retirement of both the director and the star of the film.

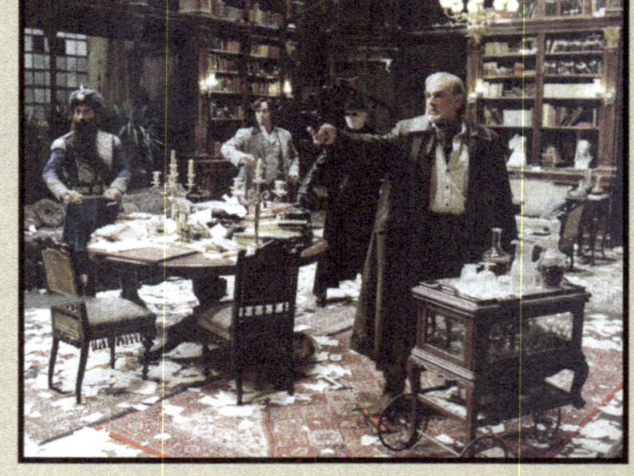

The story: In an alternate Victorian Age, a group of famous contemporary fantasy, Science Fiction, and adventure characters from Victorian literature team up on a secret mission to save the world from the plot of an evil madman.

Massive in its scope, LoEG takes place in a world before modern warfare, in which the characters from some of the most beloved and revered works of literature act as a team of heroes who are tasked with completing insurmountable feats in order to save the world from total war. Taking place in 1899, when the world was on the threshold of a new millennium, modern warfare was a dream bound for reality in only a few short years. In a time where hand-cranked machine guns were a devastating weapon, and only 40 years earlier, men were still charging into battle on horseback, the machines of war that would become a reality in 1914 would have been a terrifying sight.

In LoEG, this is where the Steampunk elements of the script come out to play. Using "modern" technology with antique sensibilities, LoEG is a film that makes its Steampunk impressions visual using bulky, functional war machines like tanks and dirigibles balanced with the grace and elegance of the Nautilus submarine and the most gorgeous automobile ever. True to time period, much of the scenery is dark and grimy, and we are very seldom given a view of the cities visited in the daylight, which adds to the gothic feel of the film. The scenes with the most light don't come until the end of the film, and by the time they do, you'll recall how much you love the darkness and dimly gas-lit ambiance of 1899 London.

The literary characters at play come from some of the best examples of Victorian literature available. Heavy hitters like mythical adventurer Allan Quatermain (Sean Connery), Science Fiction's Captain Nemo (Naseeruddin Shah), Gothic flavor with Dr. Jekyll/Mr. Hyde (Jason Flemyng), Dorian Gray (Stuart Townsend) and Mina Harker (Peta Wilson) are introduced, and some unexpected American bravado is added with the addition of Tom Sawyer (a young Shane West). Quartermain is the leader of the group, which is a deviation from the graphic novel, in which Mrs. Harker was the head of the League. Richard Roxburgh's "M" is a role that you would expect from the enigmatic Roxburgh, and he plays it with smarmy grace.

As with any superhero movie, LoEG begins with the collection of the members of the League. Thankfully, only Quartermain and Jekyll are located outside of England, so the sequence, while valuable in providing backstory for the characters (admittedly one of my favorite parts of any film) is mercifully short, and is completed on team's journey to Venice. This is where they hope to meet their enemy, known only as The Phantom, who is threatening the world with "Total War" face to face.

Along their journey, certain "innocuous" occurrences lead the group to believe that they are being sabotaged by one of their own, namely a common thief by the name of Skinner (Tony Curran) who has accidentally acquired the ability to be invisible. Unable to secure the rights to the character of The Invisible Man, the character was altered to suit the purposes of the film, and Skinner adds a lowbrow touch to the group that would otherwise be missing, such that even

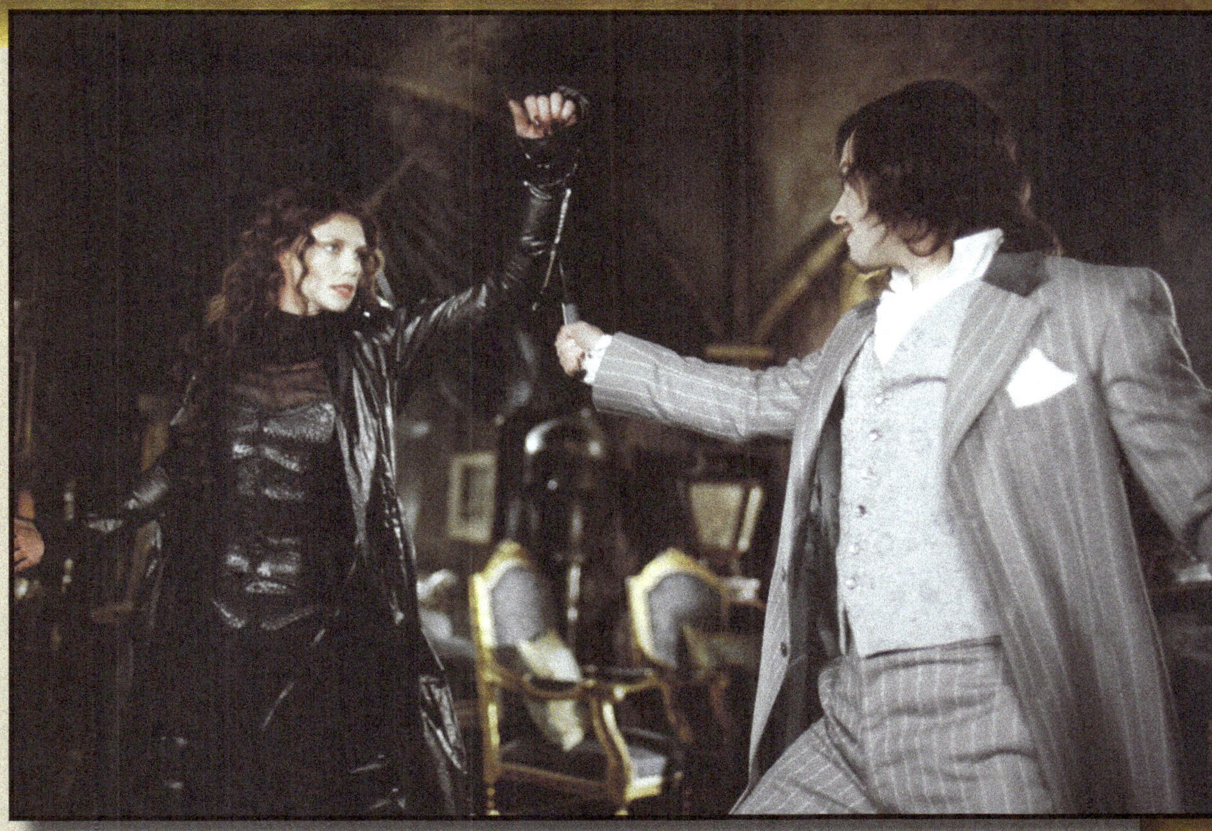

Sawyer comes off as cultured "in a colonial way" when compared with Skinner. Suffice to say that by the time the League reaches their destination, every member has had something very important, and very personal, stolen from them. When under attack from The Phantom's henchmen, the guilty party escapes the Nautilus in a beautifully rendered mini-submarine and attempts to cripple the ship at the same time. This is also the point in the film where things fall apart, and the action and story become irredeemably muddled. The original point of the quest is lost, and any attempts to rescue the storyline and character development are essentially thrown to the proverbial wind.

After picking up the pieces in a somewhat haphazard fashion, the League follows the pod to the outer reaches of Mongolia/ somewhere frozen to The Phantom's lair, and where the final battle will be held. Continuing the disappointing messiness of the second act, the final action of the film is depressingly predictable. The powers of the League are used for nefarious means, and personal demons are battled in a literal and physical sense by all of the characters in one form or another.

While not a truly great film, LoEG is extraordinarily entertaining and delivers action, and thrilling content that is expected of a summer release date film. While most won't take the time to dig deeper into the more cerebral aspects of the movie, my own appreciation for LoEG is deeply rooted in the Victorian and Gothic literature that is the backbone of the story. The importance of the time period is also something that cannot be ignored, and the stunning background and sets add a richer level to an otherwise predictable and lackluster superhero story.

Worth noting: Alan Moore, creator of the graphic novel series, is unhappy with this adaptation of his work, and has distanced himself from the project, as he has with other adaptations like Watchmen.

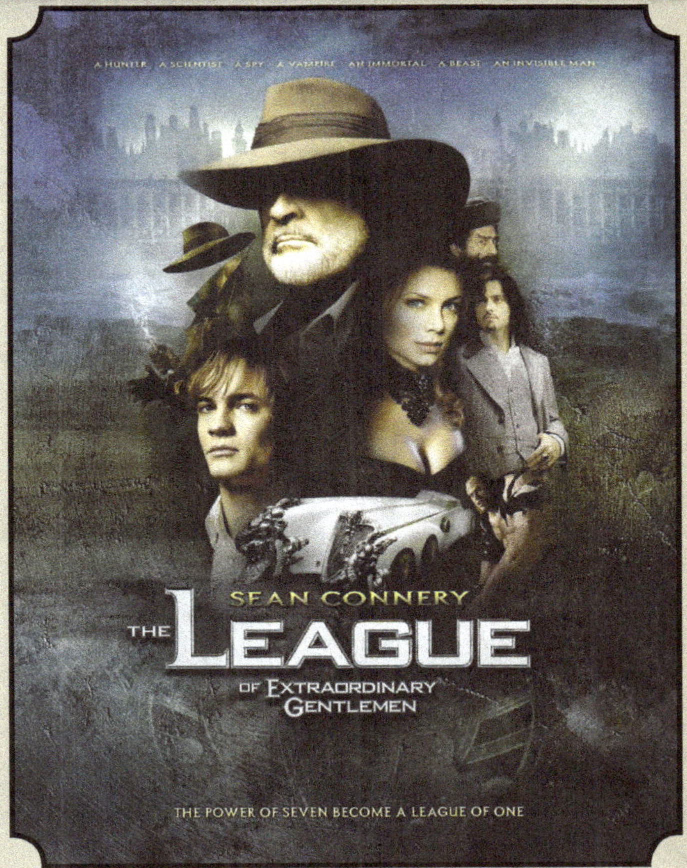

Verdict: 3 aging superheroes out of 5 – LoEG is entertaining, but don't overthink it…

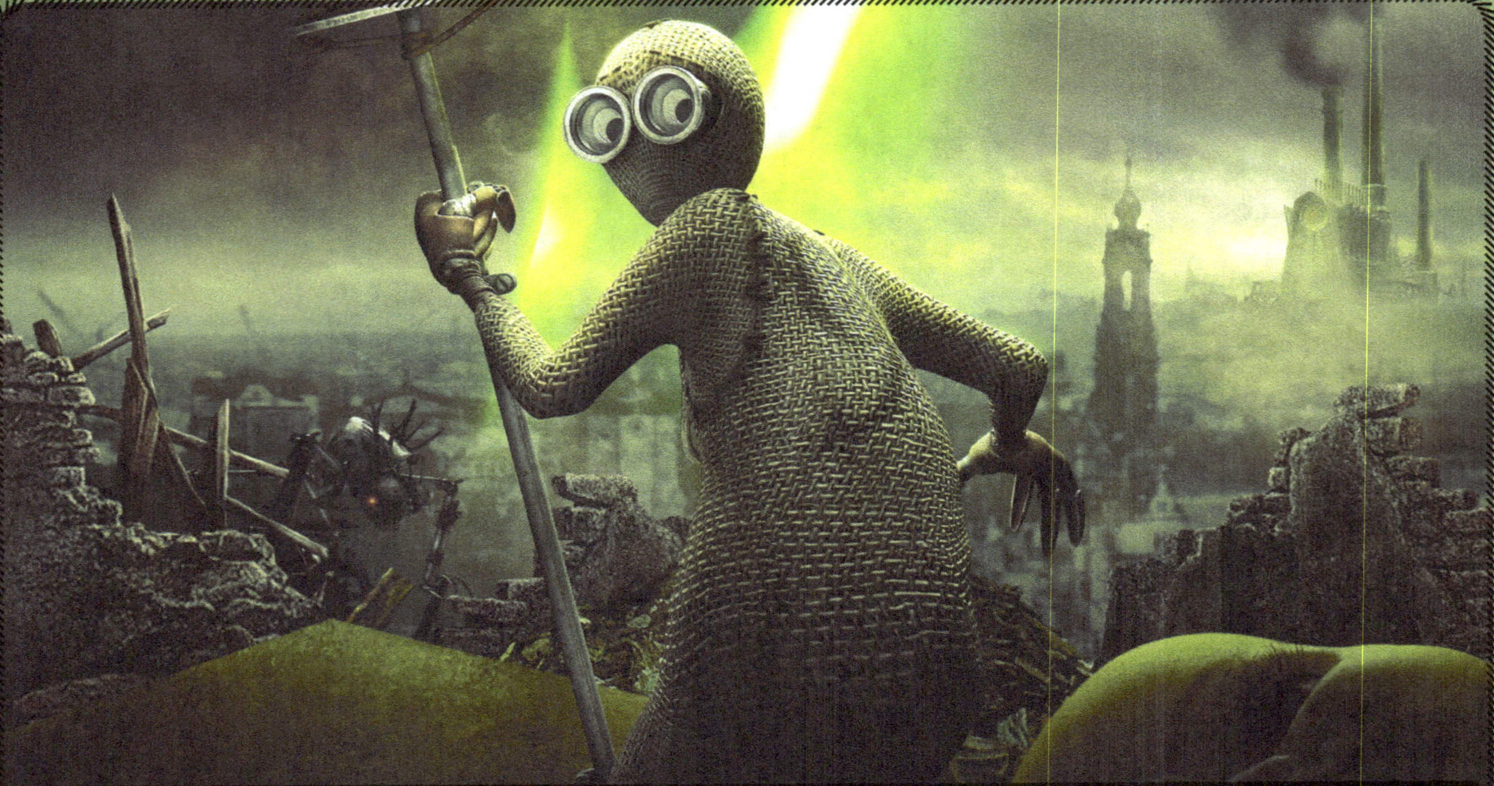

THE PICTORIAL POETRY OF SHANE ACKER'S "9"

By Katie McKensie

Released on 09/09/09 (clever), Shane Acker's 9 – based on the Oscar-nominated short film of the same name – was able to see the light of day as a feature-length production thanks to the personal investment of the short's biggest fan, Tim Burton. As a producer of 9, a credit featured prominently on the film's official poster, Burton lends a built-in fan base of filmgoers drawn to the dark side to the post-apocalyptic world of Acker's tale. Set in a future age where machines have annihilated every living thing on the planet, only a handful of semi-humanoid beings have survived: nine rag dolls, each imbued with a fraction of the soul of their alchemist creator. The rag dolls, also known as "Stitchpunks," are assigned a number as well as a defining characteristic that makes up the whole spectrum of human emotion; the film's hero

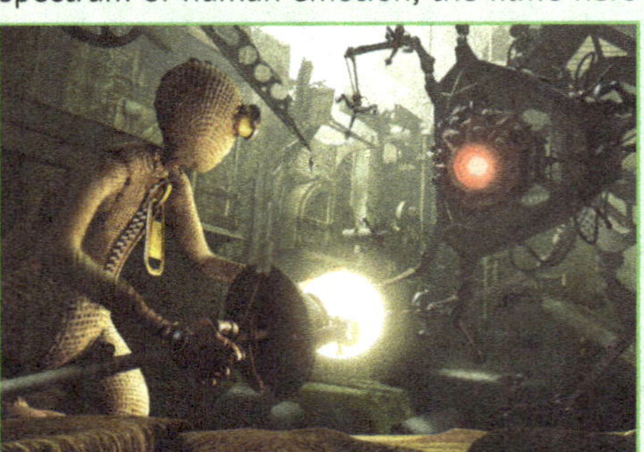

is rag doll number 9 (voiced by Elijah Wood), the most thoughtful and empathetic of them all. Together the Stitchpunks must defeat an industrious and aggressive device known as the Fabrication Machine, the leader of all the instruments of war that wiped out mankind.

Machines make up a great deal of what is visually compelling about this film, and it is in that sense that 9 doesn't disappoint. The Fabrication Machine is a looming hulk of metal, glowering menacingly with a giant red beam for an eye; the 'Winged Beast' swoops down on prey with pterodactyl-like wings and claws; and the 'Seamstress,' endowed with mechanical appendages that wield sharp sewing tools, was designed to create but reprogrammed to kill. The nuts-and-bolts of these mechanized robots are a striking contrast to the soft stitches of the burlap rag dolls, dotted with buttons and zippers, their curious eyes peeking out from behind aviator goggles. Acker's flair for the chromatics of light and darkness are beautifully evident in shots of the film's murky industrial wasteland. An especially nostalgic touch is visible in Stitchpunks 3 and 4, who cast light into the shadows by projecting films from the fluttering bulbs of their eyes.

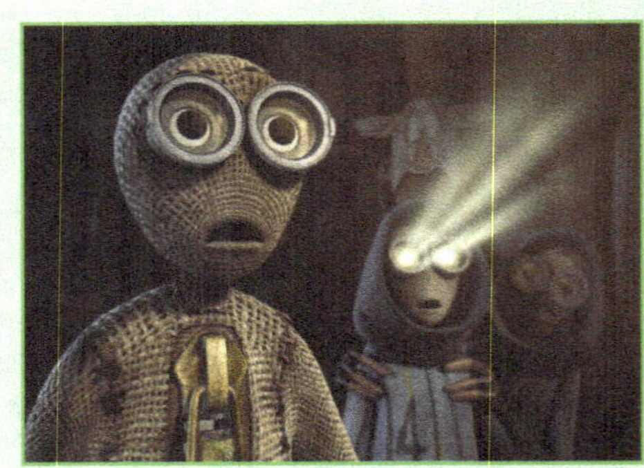

Though 9 is a visual marvel, the film struggles with adapting the story from the short on which it's based into feature-length material. Clocking in at an abbreviated 79 minutes, more of the film's runtime is devoted to showy action set pieces than conflict between the Stitchpunks and the inner discord within their group. Without a significant emotional foundation for the larger and more immediate threat of the Fabrication Machine, there's even less for the audience to feel invested in. Part of the problem is that the film opens with the character of 9 waking up after the Fabrication Machine's destruction has taken place, so he is filled in on these cataclysmic

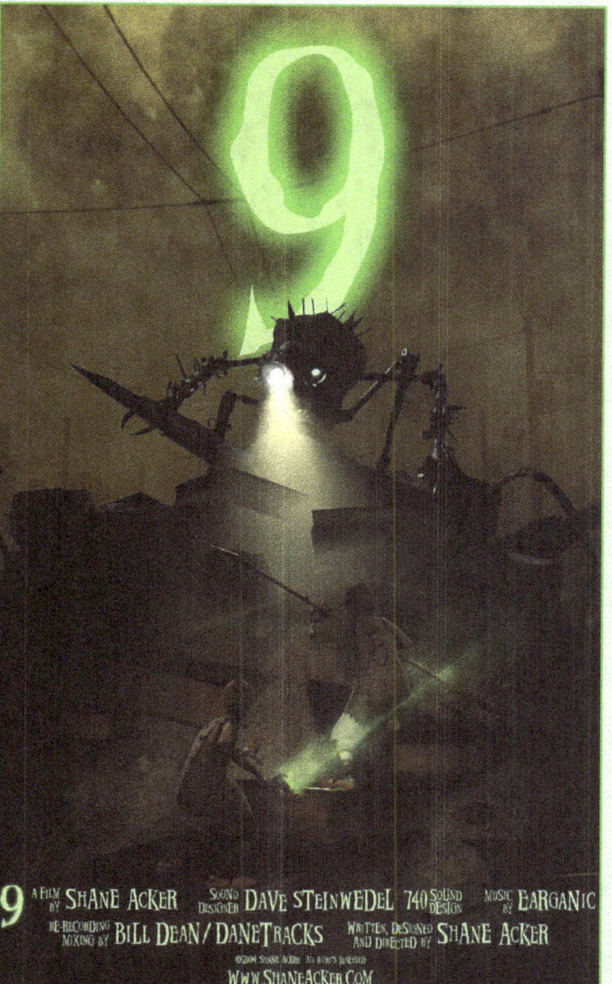

events via newscast. For the filmmakers, this is a way to sneak in some exposition while circumventing the expense and time it takes to fully develop these sequences; but for the audience, it renders us less mindful of what's at stake. If the film had spent more time on the events prior to 9's awakening and included more scenes with the Stitchpunk's scientist creator, there might be greater impetus to see these rag dolls as multifaceted humanoid characters – not just objects identified by a number and a singular personality trait.

While Burton's unique milieu is a noticeable influence on Acker's work, perhaps a loftier comparison can be drawn to a filmmaker whose work is sometimes incorrectly attributed to Burton: The Nightmare Before Christmas director Henry Selick. Arriving in theaters six months before 9 made its feature-length debut, Selick's Coraline shares 9's aesthetic sensibility in the realm of stop-motion animation, backed by a solid story that deepens its emotional resonance. If Shane Acker took a cue from Selick and expanded the inner world of his characters rather than just the physical one, he might have a near-perfect addition to the dystopian film canon. Instead, 9 remains a visually engrossing though ultimately hollow animated apocalypse.

Rating: ***1/2

11 QUOTES YOU HEAR ONLY AT A STEAMPUNK CONVENTION

By Lisa Walker England

An annual steampunk convention or festival is one of the best places to fashion retro-inspired memories. Besides the wonders you'll see or experience, you also might be amazed at the comments you overhear: things no one would say anywhere else on the planet.

I've often wished I could carry a secret recorder to capture the delightful repartee. But since my steampunk persona only dreams of being a spy, I keep her ears pricked the old-fashioned way and write down the juiciest morsels.

11. "I love corsets. I don't care how much they hurt."
   (It's like I always say, darling: "No pain, no gain.")

10. "Oh no! A stray gear!"
   (Perhaps it needs to find its mother?)

9. "Did you time travel here to find one of Santa's reindeer?"
   (As long as you brought the airship I need to haul it home.)

8. "We're protesting that most vile substance, absinthe."
   (So you're the guy with the "Got Absinthe?" bumper sticker.)

7. "Kilts do not equal consent."
   (For all those times I've been harassed by a highland warrior, clearly.)

6. "I'm aghast at how much my legs are showing right now."
   (Trust me; everyone else is, too.)

5. "We only had one fight at the convention: two guys, arguing over an energy source."
   (So was this about powering their airships—or their laptops?)

4. "Airships are not feasible. Mother Nature likes to eat them."
   (Apparently Mother Nature is not a vegetarian.)

3. "If I find one more reference to Tesla in a steampunk novel, I'm going to scream."
   (Tesla probably would, as well.)

2. "A steampunk convention is the only place where saying 'My, you've got a big butt!' is actually a compliment."
   (We do so love to turn social conventions on their head.)

1. "Steampunks don't owe a film studio or comic company anything, because we are the ones who make our fandom.
   (And that, if for no other reason, is why I absolutely love this community!)

THE DREAMS OF CHILDREN...
THE MIND OF A MADMAN...

JEAN PIERRE JEUNET'S "THE CITY OF LOST CHILDREN"

By LinnieSarah

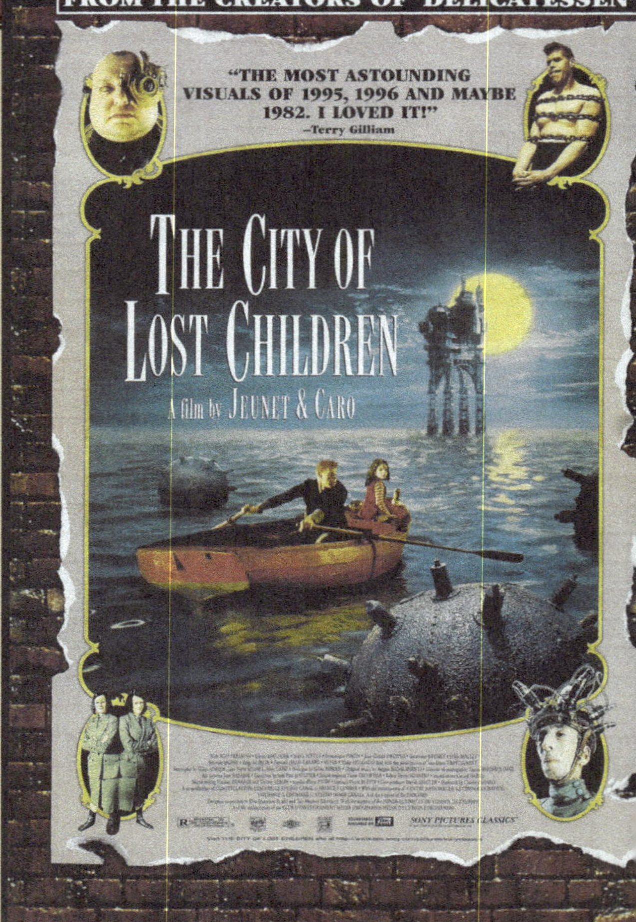

The films of visionary director Jean Pierre Jeunet have always been spectacular combinations of the fantastic, the horrific, and the beautiful. Best known for works such as Amélie and Delicatessen, Jeunet's movies are best described as fairy tales for grownups, films that showcase both the best and worst of life through the kinetic colors of a Esther Williams musical. One of his most enduring movies has been La cité des enfants perdus, or The City of Lost Children, and its steampunk aesthetic has gone on to inspire countless filmmakers in the years since its 1995 release.

The Story: In a world where everything gives off the appearance of a collapsing carnival, mad scientist Krank (Daniel Emilfork) begins kidnapping children in an attempt to steal their dreams. He believes that while he can't dream for himself, the dreams of the children will make him young again. But when he steals the adopted little brother of street-performing strong man, One (Ron Perlman), he and precocious orphan Miette (Judith Vittet) embark on a perilous journey to rescue not just One's brother, but all the stolen children of the city. Surrounded by a madcap cast of clones (Dominique Pinon), the evil conjoined Octopus sisters (Geneviéve Brunet and Odile Mallet), a loquacious brain in a tank (voiced by Jean-Louis Trintignant) and a Steampunk Cyclops (Serge Merlin), The City of Lost Children is a beautifully dark exploration of the lengths men will go to in order to cling to their youth.

Co-directed by Jeunet and Marc Caro, the world created in The City of Lost Children is so expansive in style and vision that it is hard to believe this was only Jeunet's second film. Loaded to the brim with steampunk-themed mainstays such as submarines, strange and frightening machines, and huge metallurgic cities run by water and fire, the art direction in City is practically a character unto itself. Every tiny detail is so carefully thought out, no matter how many times you watch the film, you will always find something new to look at.

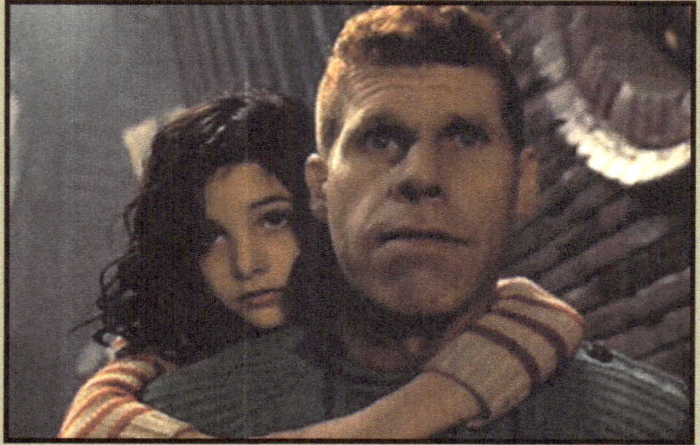

The cast performances are also spectacular, especially from Perlman, who didn't speak any French prior to beginning his work on the film. As One, Perlman speaks in shortened sentences that he learned phonetically over the course of filming, but the limited dialogue so perfectly fits the character that it is barely even noticeable. Jeunet regular Dominique Pinon is equally fantastic in multiple roles, playing Krank's cloned children, all with different personalities. He also appears later as a diver who aids Miette, and who may have a special connection to the clones. The true standout, however, is Vittet as Miette, a little girl with the attitude and spirit to survive not only living as a pickpocket under the thumbs of the horrible Octopus, but also to help One find his little brother. The relationship between One and Miette is the cornerstone of the film and it is equal parts touching and nerve-racking when things go south.

The City of Lost Children is the kind of film that only gets better with repeated viewings, and no matter how many times you watch, you will always find yourself entranced by Jeunet and Caro's fairytale. Lovely, terrifying, and twisted, The City of Lost Children is a movie well worth adding to your collection.

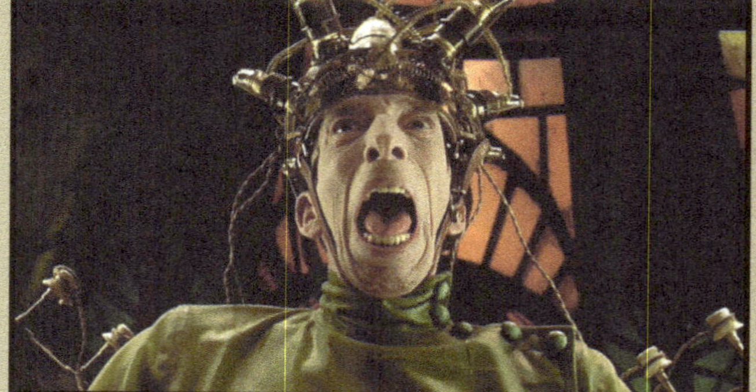

Rating: 5 Trained Fleas out of 5

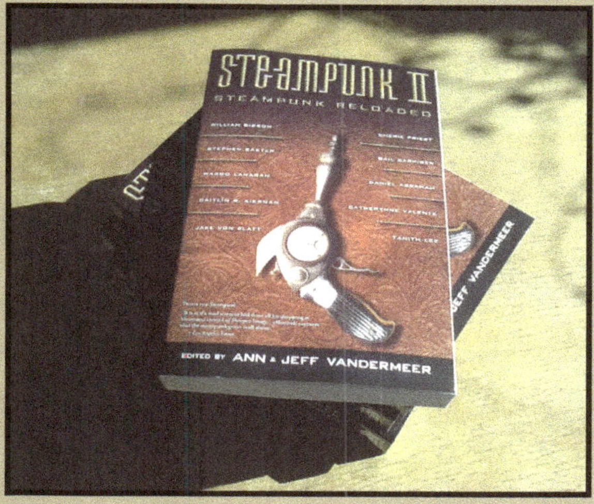

Steampunk II: Steampunk Reloaded
Editors: Ann & Jeff Vandermeer
Publisher: Tachyon
Released: 2010

By Mark Hickman

Steampunk Reloaded is the second of three anthology volumes edited by Ann & Jeff Vandermeer. As I have not read the other two installments, I can't compare this book to them but after reading, I would definitely be interested in checking them out.e

The anthology begins with an introduction by the two editors and is followed by the main body of the book – a collection of different stories written by various authors. Overall there are twenty-three short stories, each one written by a different author. And a short non-fiction section covers the last section of the book. A personal favorite of my mine would be the second story, Great Breakthroughs in Darkness by Marc Laidlaw, which I thought was both funny and disturbing. It really goes to show how far a mad scientist can go when he's completely blind to the consequences of his own actions.

Of course, as this is an anthology the book, it will most likely feature stories of various interests. So while some stories may grab your attention, you may find yourself skipping over others. It will depend on what type of stories you enjoy reading. Fortunately, the book contains a nice variety of story types ranging from erotic, to mad science, western, and more.

I also wanted to point out on the really fantastic graphic art by Ramona Szczerba. Her pieces really capture that weird and bizarre side of steampunk visuals. One particular piece I was really impressed with was the portrait of Obadiah Theremin early in the book. There are also some art pieces by Eric Orchard, Ivica Stevanvoic, and John Coulthat, which are equally intriguing.

Overall, Steampunk II is an interesting compilation that I would recommend checking out to find the steampunk-themed story that interests you most!

Final Score: 7.5/10

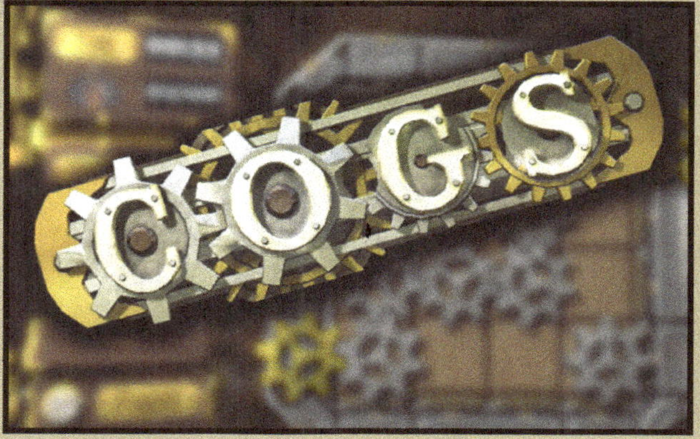

Throwback Game Preview: COGS

By Miss Bella Blitz

I don't know about you, but growing up we had Friendly's and Cracker Barrels around every corner. And, within these "family-friendly" eateries were table-games; small wooden puzzles meant to entertain - or keep quiet - restless kids and make adults feel nostalgia for the simpler things before video games.

These days, with everyone and their mother on some sort of technical device, you might be hard-pressed to find anyone playing with table games at restaurants anymore. Or, would you be?

COGS is an awarding winning, steampunk, puzzle game for PC/Mac, iPhone, Android, iPad and netbook. With stunning visual design, COGS utilizes steampunk engineering to allow the player to slide tiles and build a variety of machines. With over 50 levels and three gameplay modes you could literally sit at your favorite restaurant through breakfast, lunch, and dinner.

Playing COGS is almost relaxing. The background music is soothing and the repetitive motion of sliding tiles to reroute steam or make gears rotate is addicting. COGS also succeeds in tapping into the brain exercise of increasingly difficult puzzles combined with the intricacies of steampunk mechanics and design.

It's a more than suitable substitute for a table game, and it will never be missing a peg or a tile.

You can download a demo, or buy the full game Lazy 8 Studios at cogsgame.com.

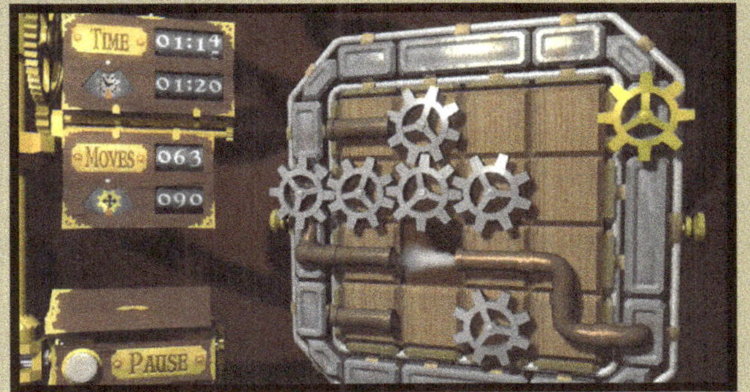

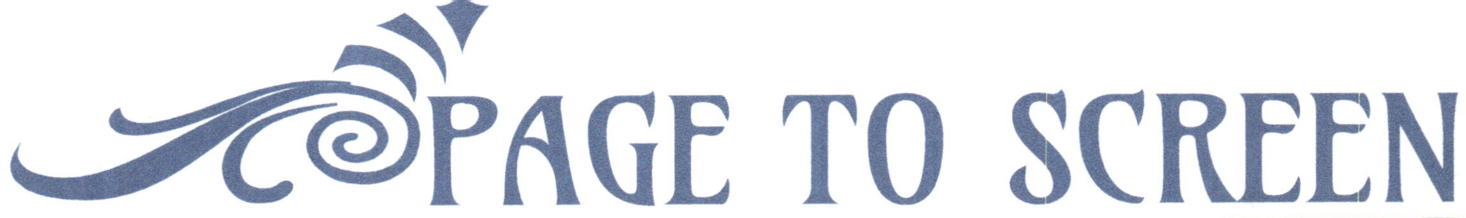

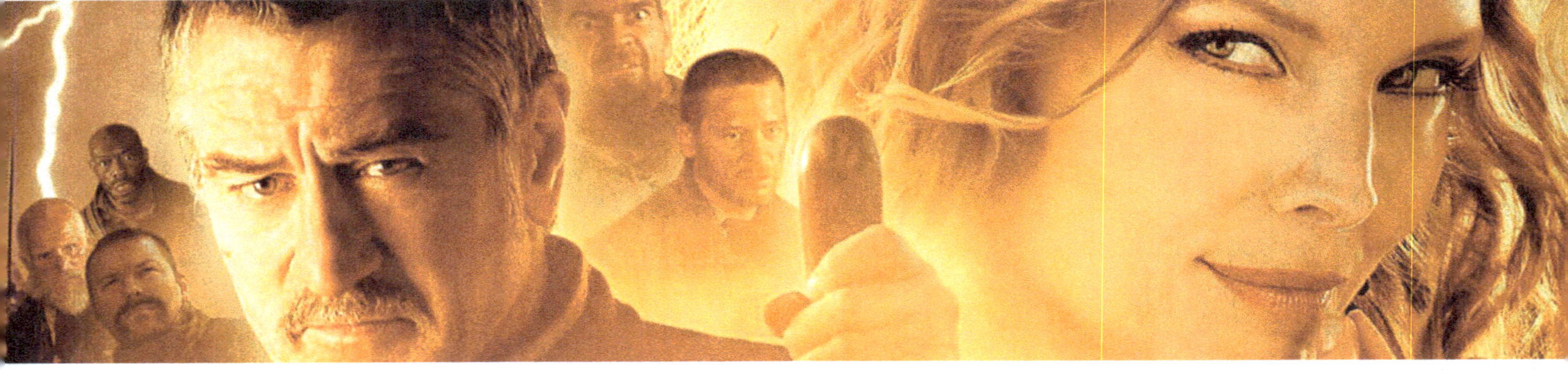

STARDUST

By Miss Bella Blitz

As a self-proclaimed creepy kid, growing up I relied heavily on my own imagination to create the macabre, magical, and fantastical worlds I wished to inhabit. The books that were available to me were either too adult in content for my impressionable self or too childish for my snobby teen wiles. It wasn't until I became a self-proclaimed creepy "adult" that I found a happy balance between the pages; when I was introduced to the writings of Neil Gaiman.

My introduction to Gaiman was with the Sandman series. I blew through each trade faster than the one before it, soaking up the mythology and magic of it all. My greedy hands reached next for American Gods and then Neverwhere and then Smoke & Mirrors and on and on. Snuggling in and preparing for a day in a murky world of mysticism and mayhem is high on my list of joys. Gaiman creates the perfect balance of dark against light in his stories and they just suck me right in.

Stardust was absolutely no different.

Although written with a different tone and style than Gaiman's typical prose fiction, Stardust still balances the dark with the light; the magic with the mechanical; and the humorous with the dramatic. Stardust tells the story of a young, half-Faerie man, Tristran, from the village of Wall, which borders a magical land - aptly named Faerie.

Every nine years the villagers of Wall and the inhabitants of Faerie come together for The Faerie Market. One year this union brings to life Tristran, who is raised by his father in Wall, without knowledge of his Faerie blood. Tristran falls in love with the most beautiful girl in all of Wall and proclaims his love to her, right as a star falls from the sky. The heartless girl promises her love to Tristran only if he can collect for her that fallen star. And so, Tristran begins his quest for the star in the magical realm of Faerie. But, Tristran is not the sole seeker of this star; and the star is hardly a mere rock.

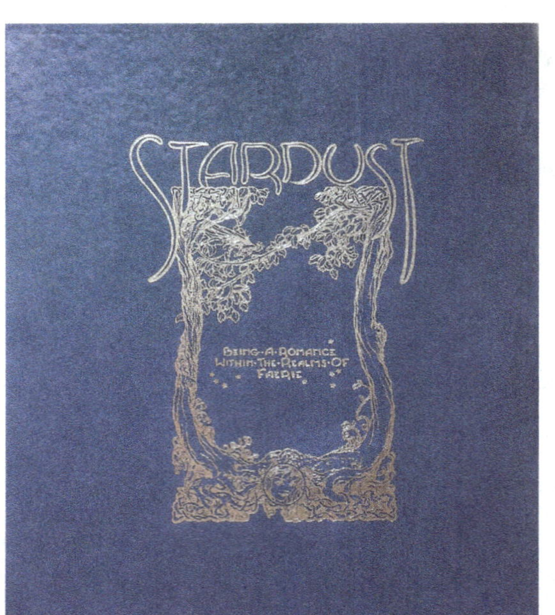

Clearly, Stardust is a fairytale. If this is a turn-off for you, keep in mind that it is told masterfully by Gaiman. Having done his research this fairytale includes seedy sex, gruesome back-stabbing, evil witches, sky-pirates, and happily-for-a-while endings - all paying homage to what pre-Disney fairytales actually were. And, all of this is accomplished while maintaining focus on Tristran's adventure for love.

Stardust flits in and out of your literary life, much like you would imagine real stardust to do. You embed yourself into this world and when the story is over, it is a shiny memory. So, what could be even shinier than rereading this engrossing fairytale? Watching it, of course. Stardust was adapted from it's pages in 2007 into a feature length film.

Now, while I enjoy Stardust (the movie), it left me wanting.

Comparing a book to its movie counterpart is often like comparing oranges to tangerines; there are just enough differences to be noticeable and affect your pallet. Luckily for me, I enjoy oranges and tangerines. Although, I do prefer oranges, and I feel that the novel Stardust is definitely an orange.

Stardust, while leaps and bounds above Neverwhere's mini-series adaptation, is still a cheesy iteration of an elegantly pieced together story. The narrative is similar - so the story doesn't change too much - but the execution is more silly than magical. This is something that I find to be a disappointment in most of Gaiman's adaptations, whether he works on the screenplays or not. There is something lost in translation, and that something always seems to be the darkness that creeps into his pages and gives his stories the shadows I so love to hide in.

While Stardust seems to down-play the evil within the mystical from the novel, it does successfully play up the humor. This comes mostly from the sky-pirate scenes with Robert De Niro as the transvestite

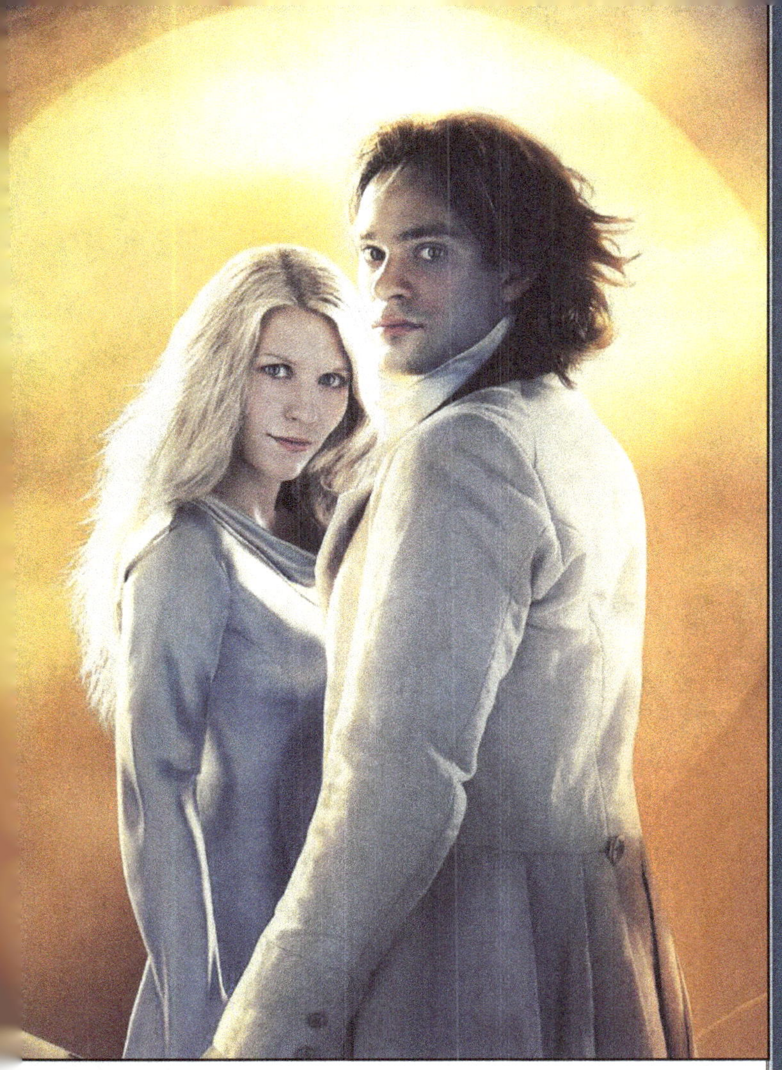

Captain Shakespeare. Even the Fates-inspired witches are laughable, although who doesn't want to see Michelle Pfeiffer chew scenery as an increasingly haggard witch on the hunt? This humor laden screen adaptation almost pulls you out of the fairytale - but of course, not entirely. Just by bringing Gaiman's world to life Stardust succeeds at building the fantasy around you.

The difference in scenes between the novel and the film are hardly worth debate. They are fun and stand out in their moments. Just as with the novel, poof, they are gone - leaving you with only a shining memory. The story remains intact, but I would be remiss if I didn't comment about the change in tone. Stardust is a romantic, adventure movie more focused on having fun than that of magic.

All in all both are enjoyable - if for entirely different reasons. Gaiman's story always remains a coming of age tale about love, and the people/things and customs Trist(r)an encounters while adventuring towards it. Both the novel and the film read/show like short stories, or vignettes; one-off tales of our hero's journey. Each is replete with the mystical elements of a world that Gaiman intricately designed - one darker than the other - but still fantastic in their own way.

Stardust (novel) 4.5/5
Stardust (movie) 3.5/5

A DAILY DOSE OF MAGIC

By Lisa Walker England

Sometimes, even as a fantasy writer, I find my daily life isn't very magical.

Endless deadlines. Complex commitments. If it's not my day job weighing me down, it's an after-hours novel draft that just won't behave. The reasons are varied, of course. But whatever they might be, I often find myself in desperate need of a quick trip to an alternate dimension.

Luckily, there's this thing called "afternoon tea."

Every day in my cubicle—usually when "The Afternoon Slump" hits, and I'm headed into my tenth phone meeting of the day—I stop everything. I open the drawer of my desk and take out a beautiful porcelain teacup inscribed with the word "friend." It was a wedding gift from my quirky landlady, who admonished me to sip from it by the light of the hurricane lamp which she had also bought. (Too bad my office has a policy against open flames. Sorry, Connie!)

I took to heart the other half of her instructions, however. With that cup proudly balanced on its saucer, I walk all the way through the maze of cubicles to a hot water dispenser in the break room. It's a short trip indeed. In a few minutes, I'm back at work with piping hot and very proper loose-leaf tea. And if I've chosen to have a standing desk that day, you might even call it a new form of "High Tea!"

In an office as hectic as mine, this ritual tends to mystify my colleagues. People stare at my cup as I'm walking past. I get asked all the time where it came from, and if that's real tea inside, and do I really do this every day?

I just smile and nod, "Yes, indeed. Every day." And then I take another sip.

Because if there's any magic to be found in daily life, I often find it in the small things. In simple routines and old-fashioned pleasures. Those touches of an "alternate dimension" that defy the tyranny of today and remind me this, too, will soon be Yesterday.

Tea is my daily dose of magic.

What's yours?

The Well-Dressed Steampunk Bookshelf

By Michele Combs

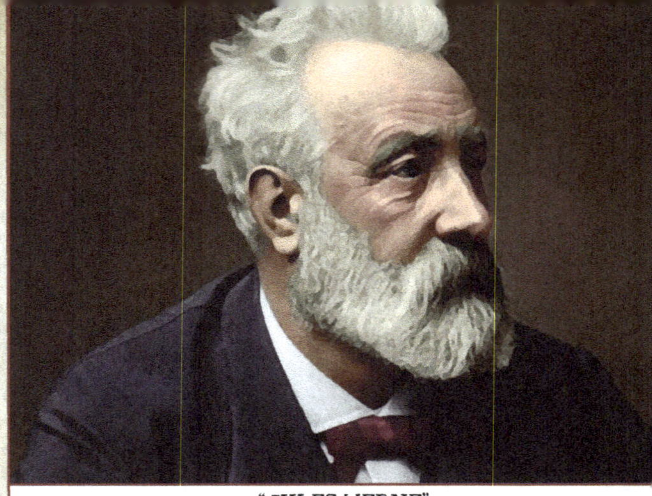

"JULES VERNE"

It's always good to remember where you come from and celebrate it. To remember where you come from is part of where you're going.
– Anthony Burgess

Whether you read, write, live or simply love steampunk, there are certain books with which the well-read gentleperson is likely to be familiar. These are the ur-texts of the genre, what G. D. Falksen calls "proto-steampunk," which introduce themes, events and ideas that have been adopted, adapted, expanded, and re-imagined by today's authors. The most famous are the French poet and novelist Jules Verne (1828-1905) and the English man of letters H. G. Wells (1866-1946), but these were preceded by and intermingled with a number of other authors, equally worthy of note but less well-known, to whom this essay shall introduce you.[1]

Although the first tale involving alien life-forms and outer space travel was written in the 2d century AD (True Fictions, Lucius of Samosata), it cannot properly be called "science fiction" since it did not extrapolate from existing science – or, as it was known then, natural philosophy – but rather sprang purely from its author's imagination. As such, it is more properly classed as fantasy. The first true science fiction came in the 17th century when, drawing on new discoveries in celestial mechanics, a cluster of lunar travelogues were published. Among these were Somnium (1608) by the German astronomer Johannes Kepler, the first to speculate on how the Earth would appear from the moon; The Discovery of a World in the Moone (1638) by English clergyman and natural philosopher John Wilkins, one of the first to theorize about life on other planets; and L'Autre monde ou les états et empires de la Lune (1657) by the French playwright Cyrano de

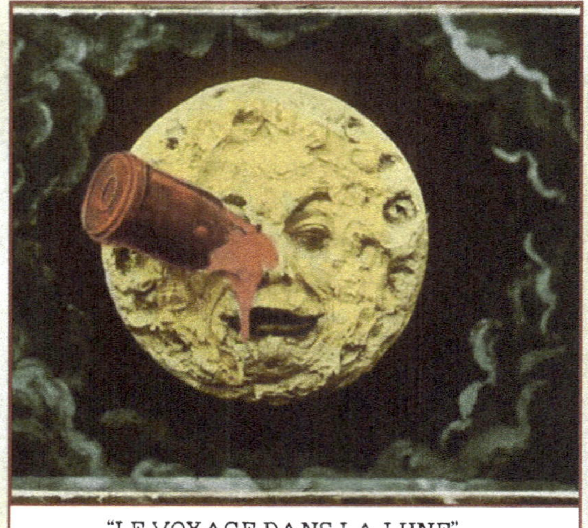

"LE VOYAGE DANS LA LUNE"

Bergerac, marking the earliest appearances of rocket-powered flight, the ramjet engine, and the use of solar power. Some fifty years later the French philosopher Francois-Marie Arouet, better known as Voltaire, wrote Micromegas (1752), the story of visitors from Saturn and from a planet circling the star Sirius, while his fellow countryman Louis-Sébastien Mercier theorized about the 25th century in The Year 2440 (1770), wherein he "fore[saw] a marvelous society that worships science, with the telescope and the microscope central to each youth's first communion." The novel went through 25 editions.[2]

It was the Industrial Revolution, however, with its advances in steam power – including the portable "table engine" – that proved the most fertile for such ruminations on the future of science and technology. These "proto-steampunk" tales provide a window into how those living in the 19th century perceived their science, what they believed it was capable of and to what they speculated it might lead.

In the summer of 1835 the New York Sun published a series of six articles, attributed to noted astronomer Sir John Herschel and allegedly reprinted from the Edinburgh Journal of Science, announcing "GREAT ASTRONOMICAL DISCOVERIES LATELY MADE" by viewing the moon through an enormously powerful new telescope fitted with "hydro-oxygen magnifiers" and various lenses. Among these lunar observations were bipedal tailless beavers that built huts, huge veins of gold hanging from open cliffs, and intelligent copper-furred winged humanoids. The articles were quickly revealed to be fictitious and are collectively known as "The Great Moon Hoax," but they boosted circulation of the newspaper considerably! Two months earlier Edgar Allen Poe, better known today for his gothic tales of murder and madness, had published the first installment of "The Unparalleled Adventure of One Hans Pfaall" (Southern Literary Messenger, June 1835) detailing the nineteen-day journey of a German nobleman, Baron Pfaall, to the moon in an airship; Poe had intended to continue his aristocratic aeronaut's adventures but the exposure of the Great Moon Hoax prevented this.

Turning from the macrocosm to the microcosm, The Diamond Lens (1858) by Irish author Fitz-James O'Brien tells of the inventor of a supernaturally powerful microscope who discovers a world in a drop of water, complete with forests, inorganic life, and a beautiful female whom he names Animalcula. Meanwhile, in a brash young country across the Atlantic, American authors were imagining giant steam-powered robots (The Steam Man of the Prairies, 1868), Earth-orbiting satellites complete with resident astronauts (The Brick Moon, 1869), faster-than-light rockets, cyborgs and time travel years before H. G. Wells (the novels of Edward Page Mitchell).

---

1   The 19th century also saw the publication of fiction involving such "scientific" theories as mesmerism and occultism, as well as social criticism in the form of utopian novels and "soft" science fiction. However, for this essay we shall focus on fiction with a basis in a device, innovation, or discovery pertaining to "hard science."

2   "Science Fiction: The Early History," H. Bruce Franklin, http://andromeda.rutgers.edu/~hbf/sfhist.html

Although most authors of the day focused on the potential benefits offered by contemporary advancements in science and technology, a few were less sanguine, predicting dire outcomes. The publication in 1859 of Thomas Darwin's On the Origin of Species threw much of Victorian society into a furor, and a mere four years later it resulted in what is perhaps the first expression of trepidation over the technological singularity. In 1863 the English novelist Samuel Butler (1835-1902) wrote a letter to a daily newspaper in Christchurch, New Zealand, which the paper published under the title "Darwin Among the Machines." In the letter, Butler warns that

> *In the course of ages...man will have become to the machine what the horse and the dog are to man. He will continue to exist, nay even to improve, and will be probably better off in his state of domestication under the beneficent rule of the machines than he is in his present wild state...Our opinion is that war to the death should be instantly proclaimed against them. Every machine of every sort should be destroyed.*

Butler expanded this idea a few years later in his book Erewhon (1872), in which a utopian society has destroyed all their machines because they had become self-replicating and "were ultimately destined to supplant the race of man, and to become instinct with a vitality as different from, and superior to, that of animals, as animal to vegetable life."[3]

Other Victorian authors viewed the entire idea of mechanization with suspicion. John Ruskin, social thinker and philanthropist, had this to say:

> *Change must come; but it is ours to determine whether change of growth; or change of death. Shall the Parthenon be in ruins on its rock, and Bolton priory in its meadow, but these mills of yours be the consummation of the buildings of the earth, and their wheels be as the wheels of eternity? Think you that 'men may come, and men may go,' but-mills-go on for ever? Not so; out of these, better or worse shall come; and it is for you to choose which.[4]*

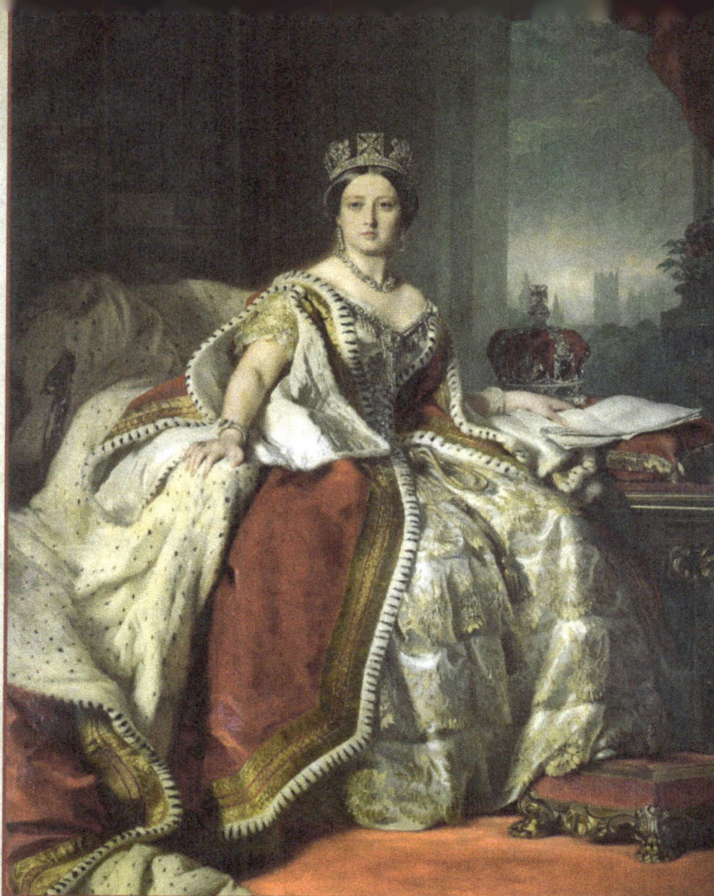

"QUEEN VICTORIA"

Influenced perhaps by Ruskin, the English naturalist Richard Jeffries wrote one of the first post-apocalyptic novels, After London, or, Wild England, imagining an England where a long-ago catastrophe had left machines to fade into myth and legend. William Morris (1834-1896), known for his energetic efforts to revive traditional arts and crafts, remarked in his soft science fiction News from Nowhere that it was "the allowing of machines to be our masters and not our servants that so injures the beauty of life nowadays."

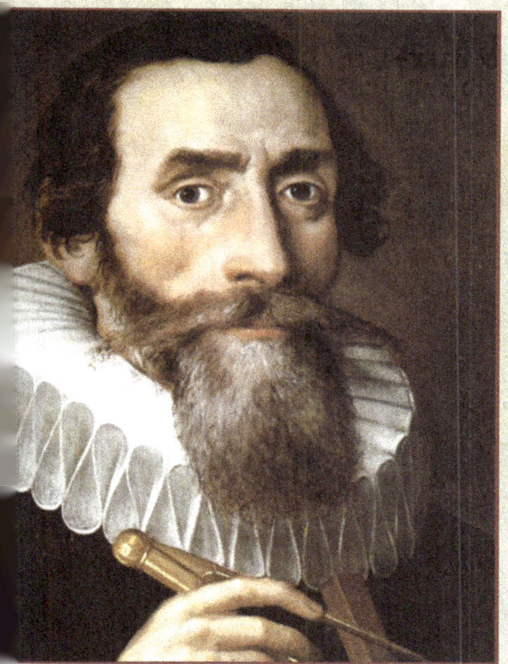

"JOHANNES KEPLER"

These were the exceptions, however. The vast majority of authors embraced the new world of steam-power and machines with cheerful gusto. The most epic of these adventures are probably the early space operas Angel of the Revolution (George Griffith, 1893) and Edison's Conquest of Mars (Garrett P. Serviss, 1898).   In Angel, set in the near-future of 1903, a group of nihilists build a fleet of airships which they then use to impose world peace: "Let every man's person and property be respected, and let the penalty of all violence be death. Those who have plotted against the public welfare will be dealt with in due course, and yonder air-ship will be despatched with our message to the Tsar at sundown. Long live the Federation!" (283)

Edison's Conquest offers up a rollicking space opera, pitting Thomas Edison – joined by a celebrity ensemble cast including William Roentgen, Lord Kelvin, President William McKinley, Kaiser Wilhelm, and even Queen Victoria herself – against a fleet of invading Martians. The intrepid Earthlings battle the Martians in space before finally defeating them on Mars itself; along the way they invent spacesuits, asteroid mining, and a disintegration ray.

Although H. G. Wells and Jules Verne are indisputably the best-known of the "proto-steampunk" authors, they were by no means alone in their fascination with the potential – and indeed the beauty – of the machines rapidly multiplying around them. Like interlocking gears, they drew from and energized others, creating a complex apparatus whose power is still felt today.

Many of the titles mentioned above are freely available online through Project Gutenberg (http://gutenberg.org). An excellent assortment may also be found in Sam Moskowitz's Science Fiction by Gaslight: A History and Anthology of Science Fiction in the Popular Magazines, 1891-1911 (Hyperion, 1974). Those desiring a more scholarly investigation may wish to consult Darko Suvin's Victorian Science Fiction in the UK: The Discourses of Knowledge and of Power (G.K. Hall, 1983).

---

3   Erewhon, chapter 9.
4   John Ruskin, The Crown of Wild Olive, p. 173.

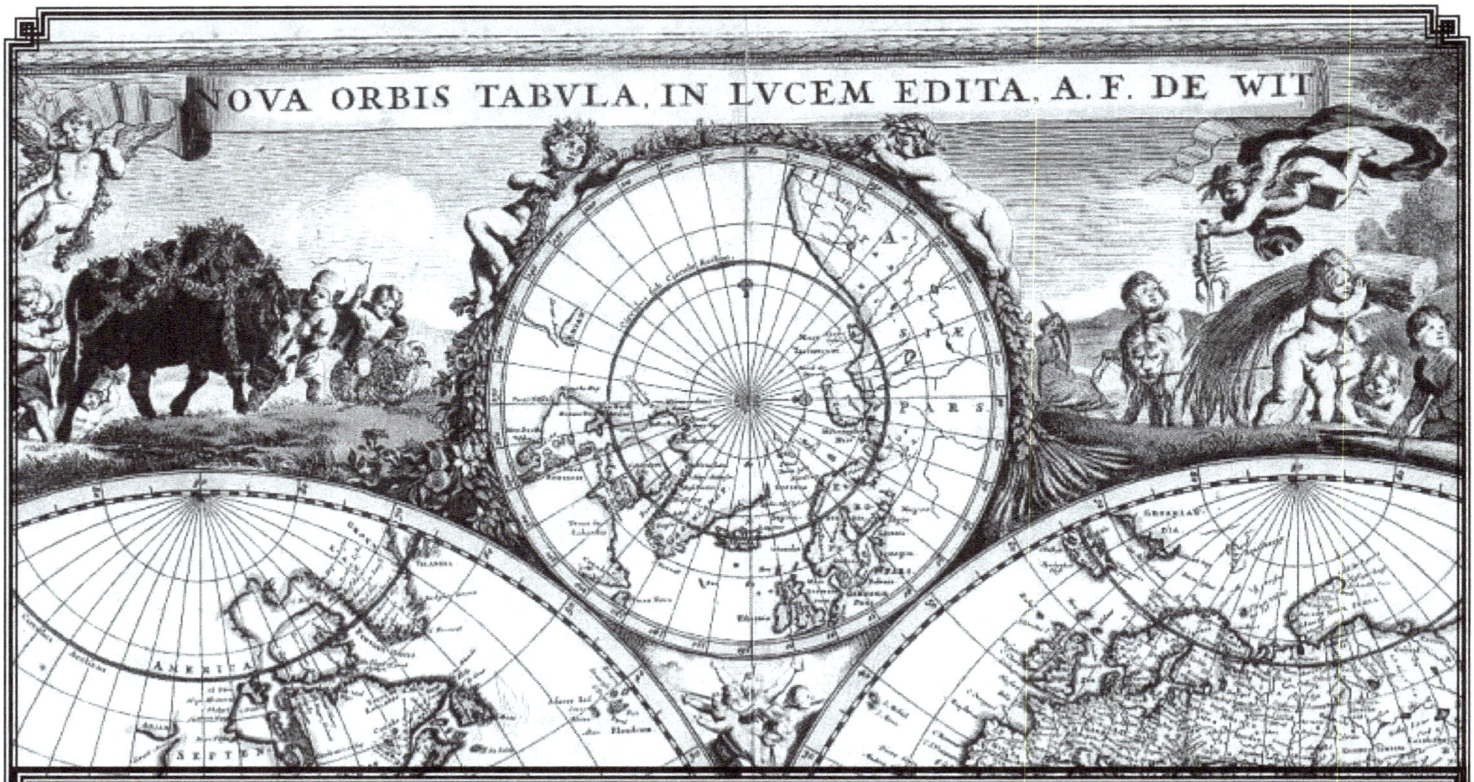

STEAM-POWERING THE WORLD

By Michael Jack

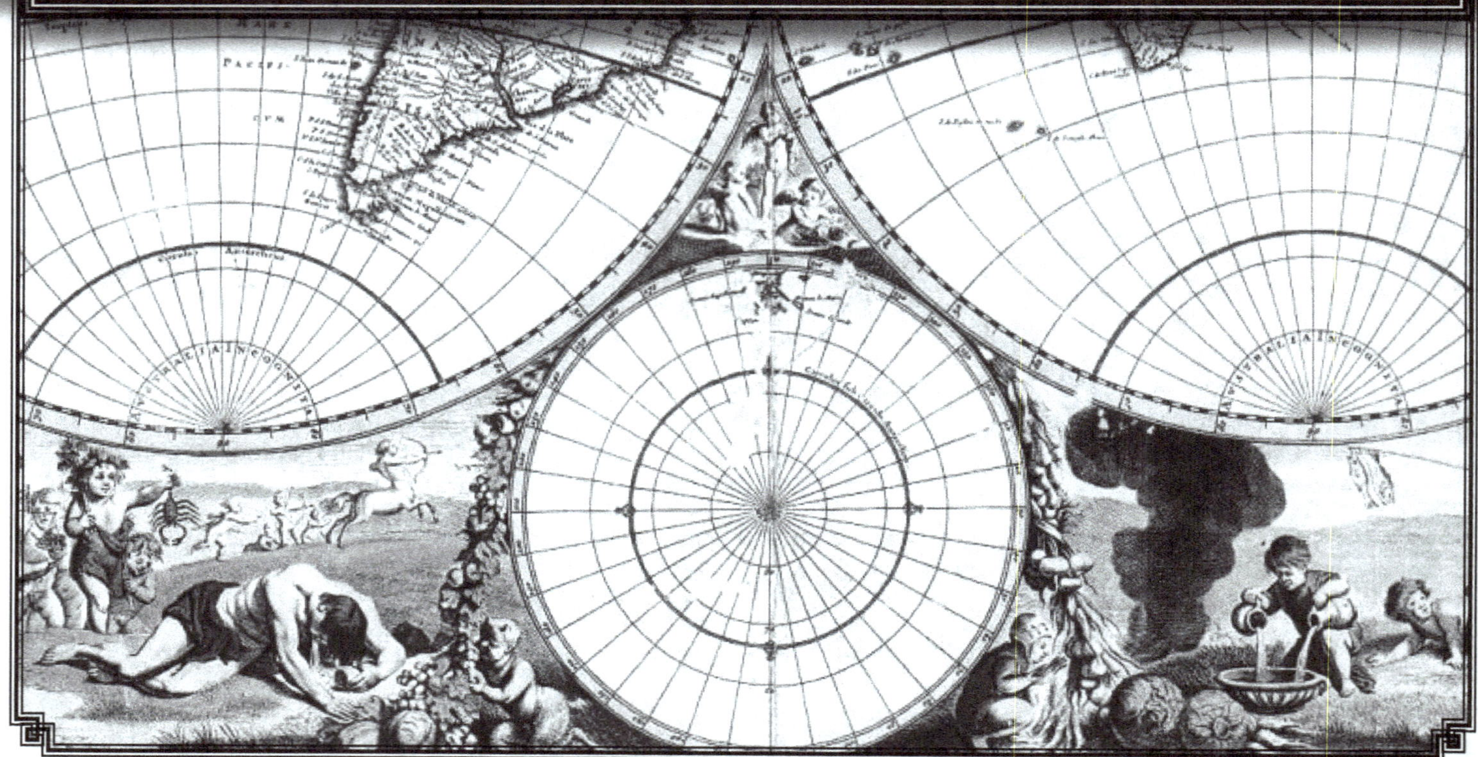

When we talk music, Steampunk is a relatively new genre to the game. Barely more than a decade old, it has entrenched itself in the imaginations of a growing subculture throughout North America, England, and is now spreading throughout Europe. The curious thing, Steampunk doesn't have any real defining characteristics besides a theme...a future that might have been. The music itself can be folk, ragtime, use grand orchestral arrangements, rock, or many other things not even closely related to the ones I just mentioned. I think the most important classification is Steampunk fans like it. And it's growing. Worldwide. Beyond the borders of lands we normally associate with Steam. In this article, I would like to briefly introduce some bands from around the globe that are helping to fuel the train, and turn Steampunk into a global phenomenon.

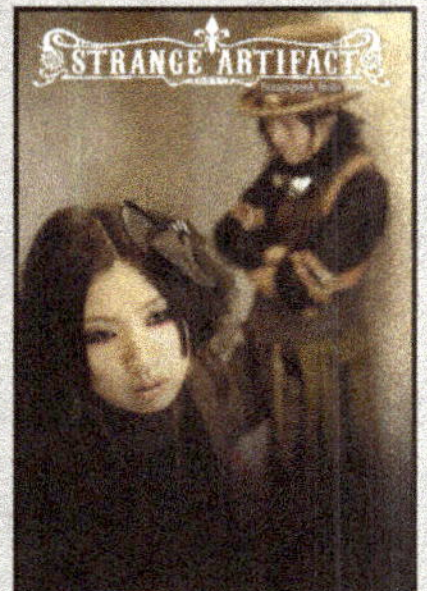

Strange Artifact -- Japan

Japan has a long history of underground scenes. Metal, Punk, and Goth all thrive within this society. It was only a matter of time before Steampunk reached the land of the Red Sun, and Strange Artifact has the prestigious honor of being Japan's first Steampunk band. With DIY apparel and accessories, vocalist MaRy and musical mastermind 130JET are blazing the path for future bands to follow. Their sound is similar to J-Rock, but they combine strong elements of engine inspired industrial sounds, and hints of Victorian pianos. Their sound is considered by many to be infectious, and they are beginning to gain international attention.

Artefactum Vapore -- Chile

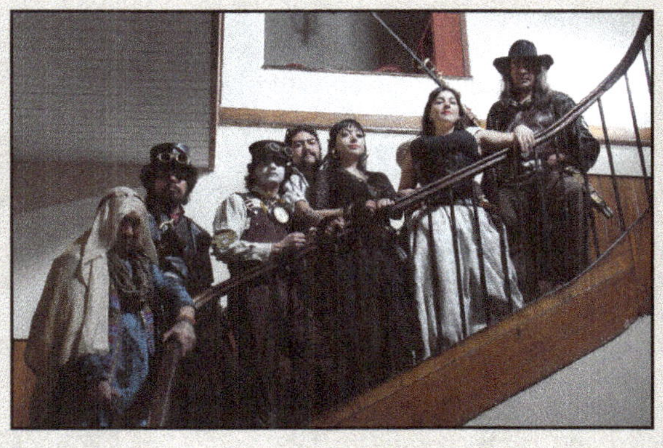

Steampunk is alive and well on the western southern strip of South America. Not only is the culture growing in Chile, they have several Facebook pages dedicated to Chilean Steampunk with thousands of likes. Artefactum Vapore hails from this land, and are quickly gaining popularity. Their music is more traditional turn of the century ragtime. They forgo the electrical instruments, and go straight for the violin, piano, and stand up bass. Artefactum Vapore are prone to comedy, and fully embrace the more whimsical side of Steampunk...the Vaudeville.

Alex the Kid -- New Zealand

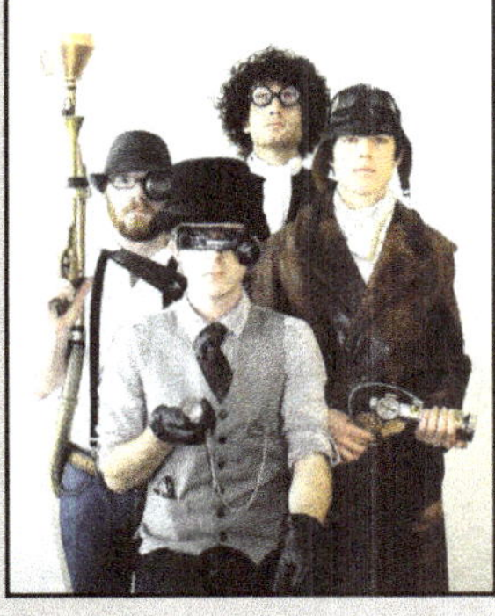

This Auckland band fully embraces the futuristic themes of technology and robotics. Their style can be considered more Electro-Punk. They use a combination of vocoders, synthesizers, guitars, and sequencing to create an infectious sound many new wave bands would be proud of. Steampunk is rapidly growing in the neighboring island to the land down under, and Alex the Kid is helping to lead the way. If you want to spend an evening of post-apocalyptic fun with a twist, definitely check this band out.

Sunday Driver -- India

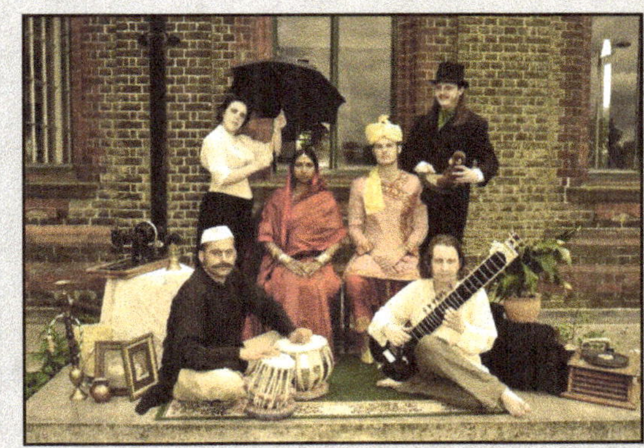

If you are familiar with the band Sunday Driver and are reading this, you are probably shouting, "They are not from India!" You would be correct. Sunday Driver is a unique blend of Steampunk themed Victorian rock, British folk, and traditional western music. They use instruments like the sitar, tabla, and clarinet to create a sound that can most be compared to World Music. Sunday Driver's members reflect their style, and are a blend of Indian ancestry and Anglo-Saxon British. Although this band is from the UK, they are quickly catching fire in other parts of the globe, especially in their fusion inspired country of India. When you can expand the culture of Steampunk in a land that represents almost one seventh of the world's population, you deserve a mention in this article.

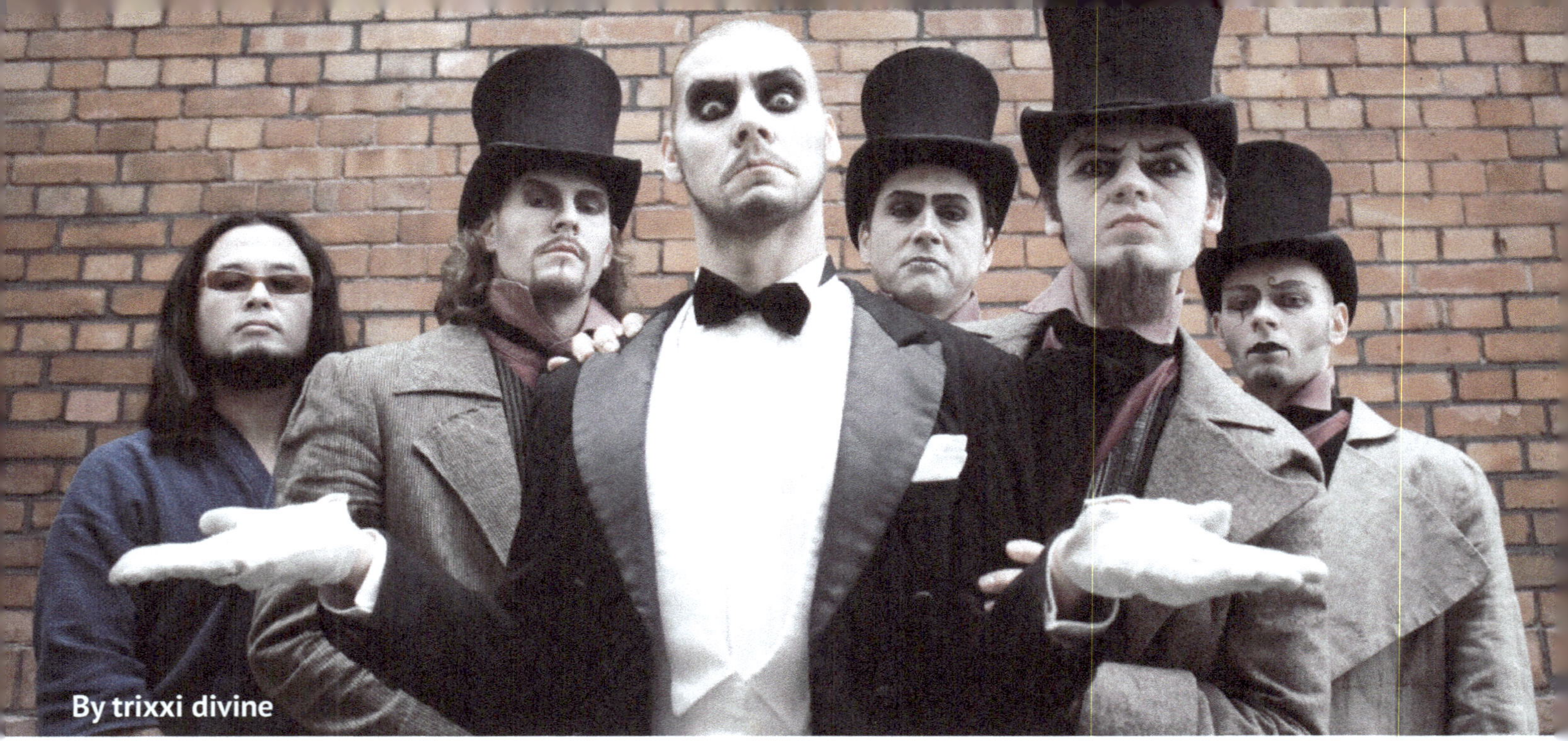

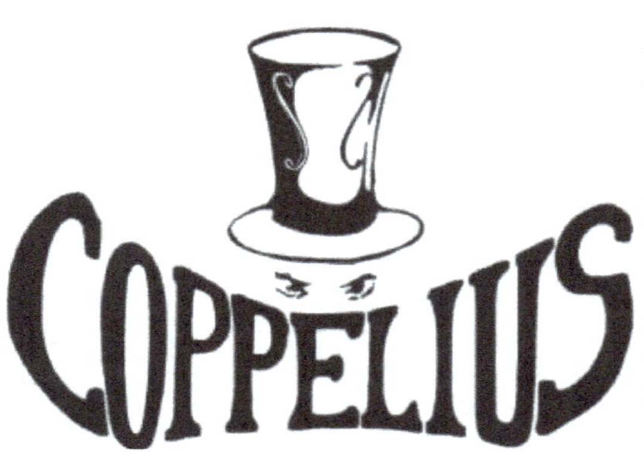

By trixxi divine

Coppelius is an obscure German Steampunk band with a cult following who perform metal on drums, double bass, cello and clarinet. Nothing particular is known of this mysterious band from Berlin, however they are currently wrapping up an extensive tour throughout their native Germany in support of their latest CD release, and have also graced the stages of many of the larger known festivals throughout Europe. The bands members are: Max Coppella (clarinet and vocals), Comte Caspar (clarinet, vocals, and harpsichord), Graf Lindorf (cello, vocals), Sissy Voss (double bass), Nobusama (drums) and Bastille (Butler, vocals). Often they are accompanied by Prof. Mosch Terpin (technician and harpsichord). On stage and for videos, these gentlemen are gallantly styled in formal clockwork couture inspired mainly by the Victorian era as are many of their songs. Their fans are well-known for writing lyrics and prose on their bodies and faces whilst attending Coppelius' shows. Ironically, they have a strong following in Japan.

Coppelius formed in 2007 and have been recording with the F.A.M.E. label. Their most recent of five successful LPs, HERTZMASCHINE, was released in January. I have spent extensive time listening to various tracks from the full discography, in German, and appreciate the talent and musicianship of these enigmatic performers. Each song is unique and melodic in its own right; others are metal as f@ck! [As an aside, I had to translate many but don't let this detail affect your decision in giving them a fair listen; this band is adept in their ability to compose and master their instruments respectively. The musical content and collective vocals may even be motivation to quickly learn the language]. If one were to transport themselves back to Victorian era of Imperial Germany, Coppelius would assuredly be performing for the Royal Courts. And in the upcoming autumn season, they will be performing the world's first Steampunk Opera in their mother land, "Steampunk-Oper mit Coppelius". Fasten your pantaloons and tighten those corsets, these dandies seriously rock!

DISCOGRAPHY:

2007 - Time-Zeit
2009 - Tumult
2010 - Zinnober
2013 - Extrablatt
2015 - Hertzmaschine

http://www.coppelius.eu/

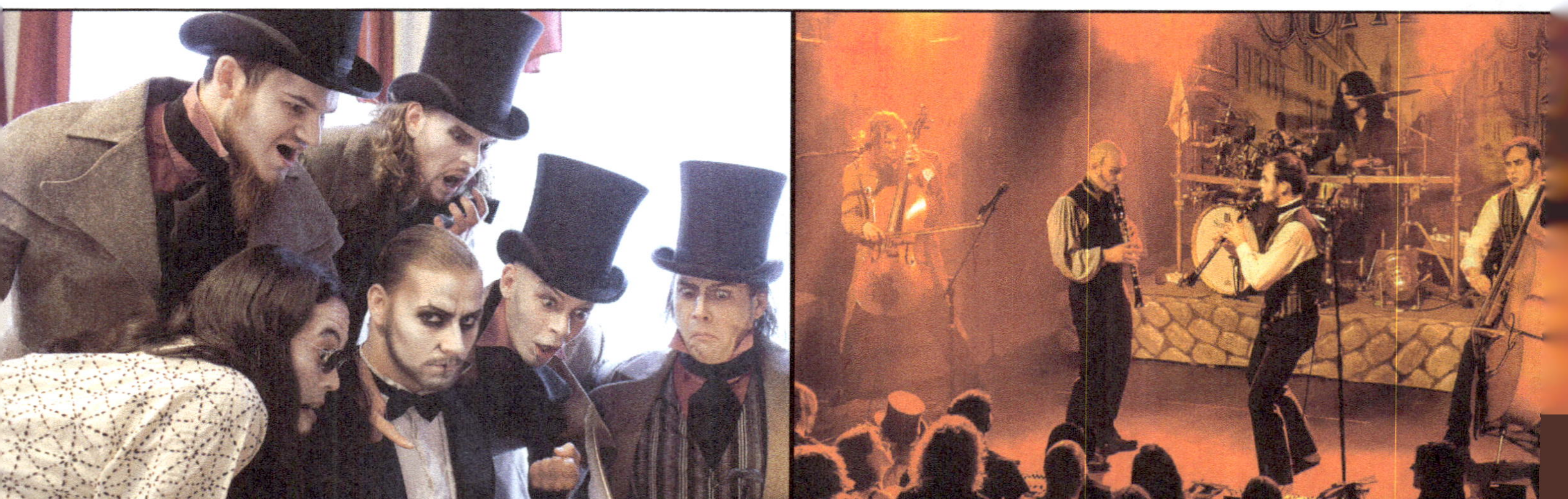

MERRY MISCHIEF

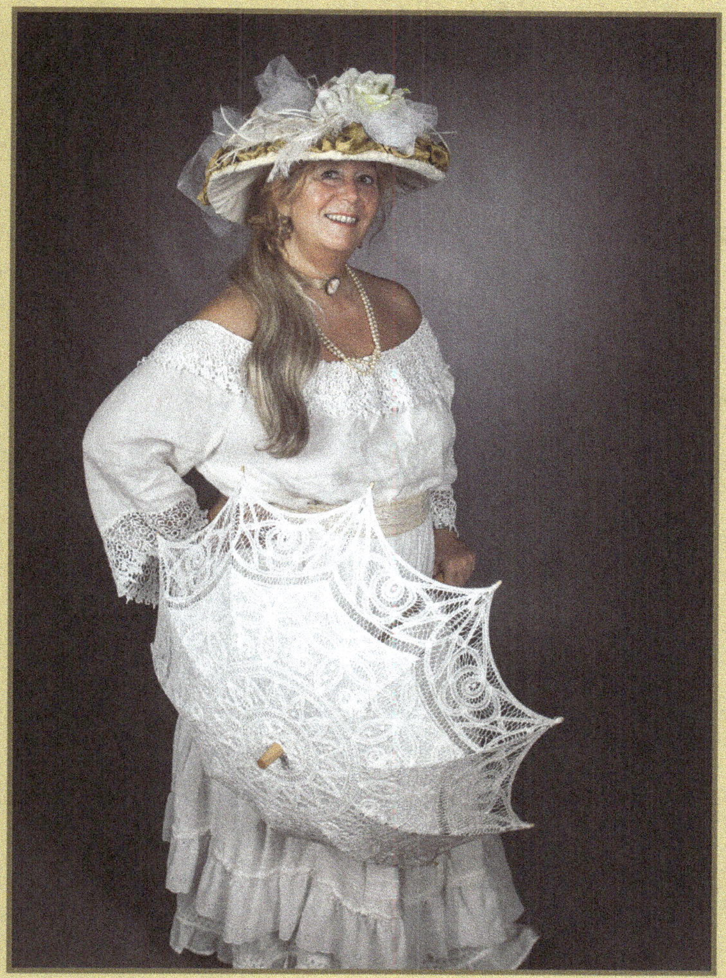

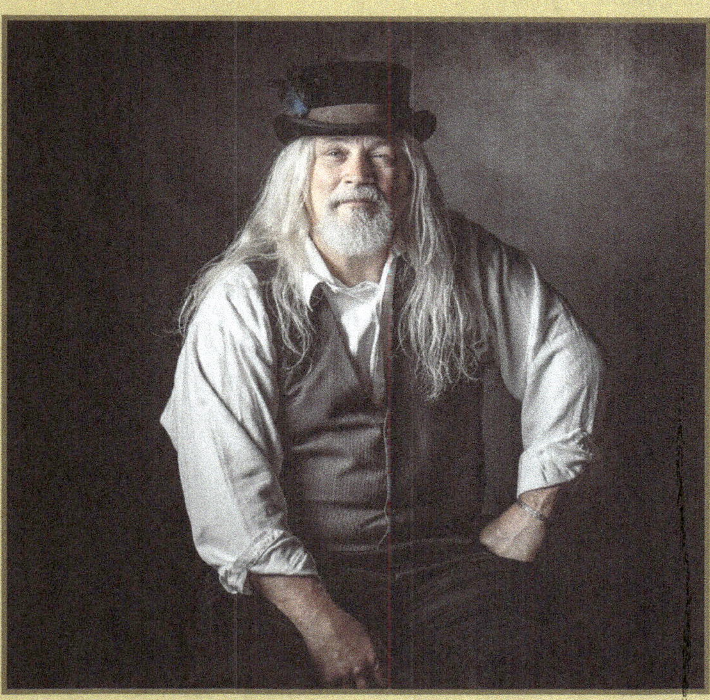

Lock 51 is home for "Merry Mischief" - a traditional, theatrical music duo (Merlyn & Harry) who enjoy bringing history to life! Tunes along the Towpath are shared by Merry Mischief along with a heaping helping of harmony and humorous factoids. Water floated the boats, and whiskey floated the spirits on the Erie Canal. When Clinton dug the canal, it was said that it couldn't be done. Not only was it done, but it was designed by amateurs, put folks to work, the project came in under budget and came in on time, and paid for itself in the first year! How's that for a mule and packet story?

But don't stop there. Merlyn and Harry enjoy the fashions and music of many years from the Renaissance to the Erie Canal and Civil War era, to Pirates and Celts. They've even played and sang as Vikings! "Steampunk was just the next logical step" said Merlyn. "It gives us an opportunity to time travel and play music from our eclectic repertoire. Also, it's fun to play in the garb rack."

Working within many genres: Steampunk, Erie Canal, to Renaissance music and combining wondrous harmonies of Merlyn's alto voice and rhythm 12-string guitar, to Harry's tenor voice and picking 6-string guitar, they will take you to days gone by. Living on the old Erie Canal really sparked an interest in this music and they added many of those songs and folklore to their arsenal of ditties.

Their CD, "Evening on the Erie" was nominated for a SAMMY award when released. It features old timey tunes and the feel of the canal. "We've played on packet boats, houseboats, trains, wagons, historic venues through many of the waterways of New York State...363 miles of canal through 83 locks from Albany to Buffalo and the Fingerlakes. Unique style finger picking and a variety of instruments are featured along with some amazing old home harmonies.

Of course, it wouldn't be "Merry Mischief", without some mischief! Antics, silly anecdotes, goofball limericks and knee slapping jokes will keep you amused and wondering what will happen next. Catch Merry Mischief some time and let them take you back to days of sitting by the camp fire or the woodstove. Merlyn and Harry can go from bawdy to ballad in a swish of a mule's tail.

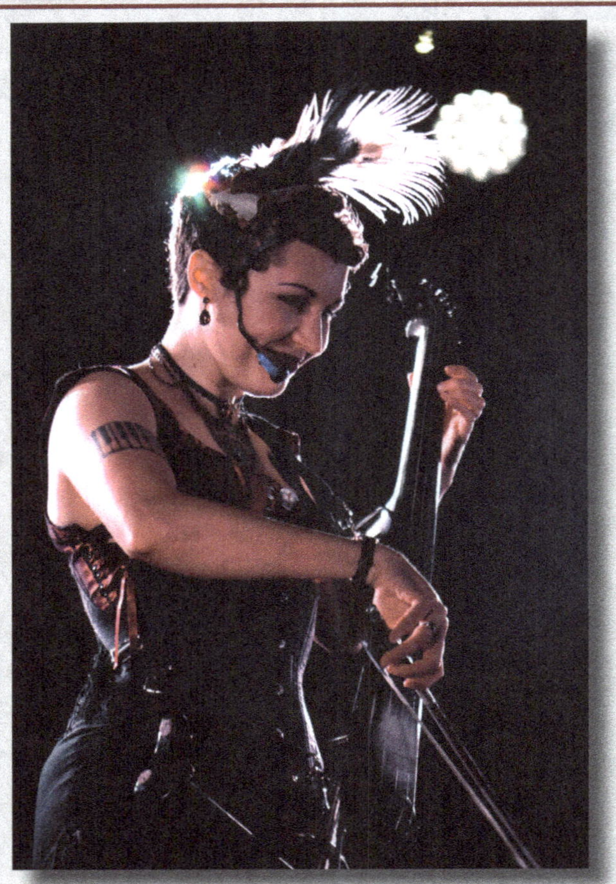

Interview with Erika Mulkey (Unwoman)

By Kathleen Sharkey

In 2011 I was able to attend the Science Fiction Convention in Reno. I was fortunate enough to get to meet a beautiful and talented young woman from San Francisco and do a review on her one woman band, Unwoman. I have always loved her very individual musical style and I am very happy to see that she is still as musically prolific today. With three more albums, numerous shows and more on the way I was extremely grateful to get to talk to her about her music.

[Carpe Nocturne] First could you introduce yourself to our readers?

[Unwoman] I'm Unwoman, a solo singer-cellist-performer. I play a lot of steampunk conventions and produce all my own music. I've been active since 2001 and a full-time artist since 2010.

[CN] Where does the name Unwoman come from? How does it describe how you perform?

[Unwoman] The name comes from Margaret Atwood's The Handmaid's Tale. I don't know that it describes how I perform -- but it is related to the fact that I eschew prescribed gender roles as a female performer by insisting I own my own image, publishing, and production at all times.

[CN] You are classically trained in numerous instruments (cello, piano, banjo and Theremin). How do you translate the traditional sounds of these instruments into the amazing modern music you create?

[Unwoman] I'm also trained in composition and electronic music production. One important thing for me in studying music was the ability to take influences from various places and make the most of them. For my earlier works, blending cello with other tracks was more of a challenge, but over fifteen years of producing made me better at that.

[CN] Do you think your classical background gives you a different perspective of music in general?

[Unwoman] It helps in a few ways, I think. It makes composing and harmonizing simple pop songs, and improving cello parts to other artists' music really easy. And it gives me tools to write songs that sound different from each other; one problem I notice a lot of popular artists have is they keep writing the same song over and over. While that may be commercially viable, it would bore me to tears! But there are also artists with no classical training who have a deeper understanding of other popular genres (jazz, folk, hip hop, etc.) than I do and they have strengths I don't, of course.

[CN] You seem to do pretty much every step of releasing an album by yourself, what have you found difficult about doing everything by yourself?

[Unwoman] I do! I do everything myself except mastering, photography, and mailing. The most difficult thing is probably that I don't have anyone to tell me when to stop working obsessively on some particular portion of the process. I rely on deadlines, mainly self-imposed -- and I'm great at making them but I'm basically never early!

[CN] Is there anything about "Self Releasing" your albums you find more liberating?

[Unwoman] I don't have anything to compare it to, as I've never done an album on a label, but when I've considered trying to do an album on a label, I've never

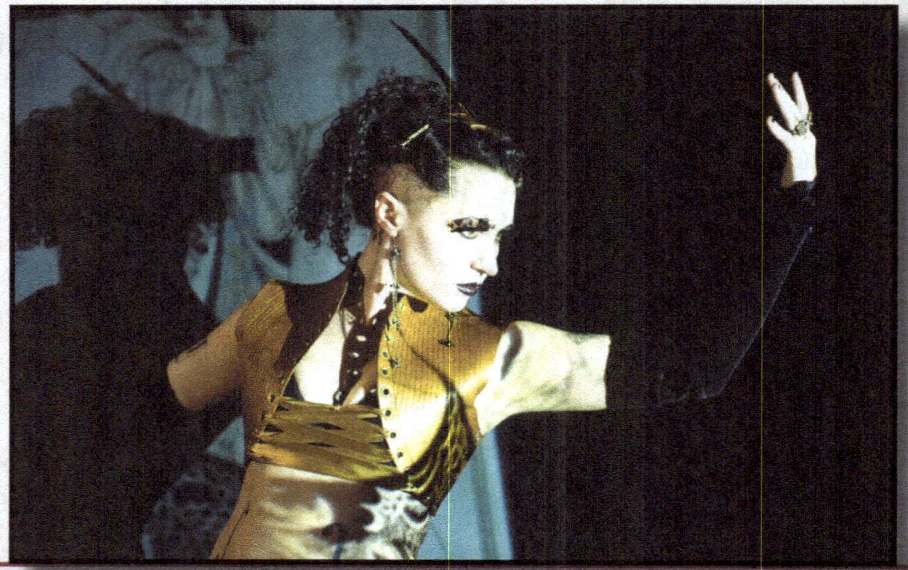

found it appealing -- for example, I love that all the sales I make when I play live, I get to keep all the money, which is often the only thing that makes traveling to perform affordable at all. And of course, the fact that no one is telling me what I can and can't say on my albums is critical to my songwriting.

[CN] How has the popularity of sites like Patreon effected your ability to "self-release"?

[Unwoman] I've always been self-releasing, since long before Bandcamp and Kickstarter, and later Patreon existed, but now there are certainly a lot more tools that savvy and well-loved artists can used to get funding for their projects and their time. Kickstarter came along just in time for me to quit my day job, actually, so I started financing album projects directly with fan's money rather than corporate money, and I have more time to create and am much more prolific now.

[CN] You have gotten to perform with some other amazing artists like Voltaire, Abney Park and Amanda Palmer, to name a few, and you have gotten to perform at some amazing events. Do you have any favorite performances you have been a part of that you would like to share with us? Are there any events or places where you would like to perform in the future?

[Unwoman] my favorite live collaboration ever was probably the very last time i played with rasputina, in new orleans. i knew it was probably my last time ever playing with them, and we rocked super hard. i played with amanda palmer for 1200 people on my birthday a couple of years ago, and she led the entire audience in happy birthday for my! abney park in australia, really every time i have played with them, was also amazing. and touring with voltaire and his band was a grand adventure.

I'm hoping to get to continental Europe one of these years, but I don't have the time or energy to put work into booking a European tour, at the moment.

[CN] All of your album covers (and your website photos) are like fashion shoots, have you ever considered a modeling career?

[Unwoman] Hah, thanks! I did a little amateur modeling in my very early twenties, but it wasn't for me. It was actually really challenging, and the photographers were not very fun to work with, and I never liked doing shoots I wasn't at least co-directing, I prefer to have some control over my image.

[CN] Do you enjoy putting together the costumes for your performances as much as we, your audience, loves seeing them?

[Unwoman] Oh yes! I love costuming! I'm working on a steampunk Princess Leia costume right now, as well as a Rococo Goth look with a black Madame du Pompadour wig. We'll see which one is ready first.

[CN] You have a collaboration with Matt Fanale (Caustic) coming out this spring can you tell us a little about it?

[Unwoman] Sure! Beauty Queen Autopsy's debut album, Lotharia, is coming out June 30. Matt does the songwriting and production on this and I sing. It's a really fun project for me -- Matt somehow magically writes songs I relate to really well, with a bit of a goth party-girl persona (only a shade different from my actual life, really -- my Sasha Fierce, if you will.)

[CN] What is your take on the Steampunk culture?

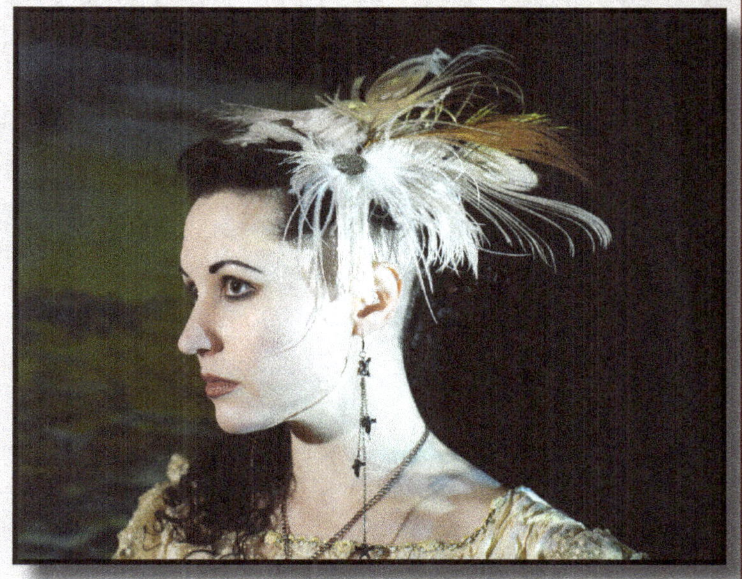

[Unwoman] I find a lot of inspiration in steampunk, and get a ton of support from steampunks. I didn't feel my music had any place at all before I found it in 2009 -- though I don't think my music is explicitly steampunk. I am too anti-cliche and too unusually orchestrated to fit any actual genres, and too pop and anti-academic-art-music to call myself classical.

[CN] Is there anything else you would like to share with our readers?

[Unwoman] I'm really, really excited about the covers I'm making for my Patreon patrons. I just finished this Hozier cover. Only Patreon and Bandcamp subscribers can download it, but anyone can stream it here: https://soundcloud.com/unwoman/take-me-to-church-4-30-15

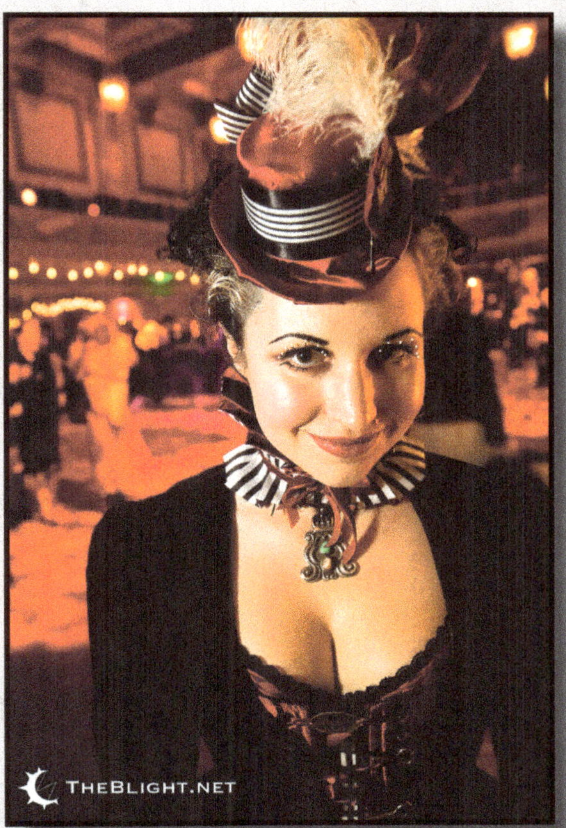

Aurelio Voltaire

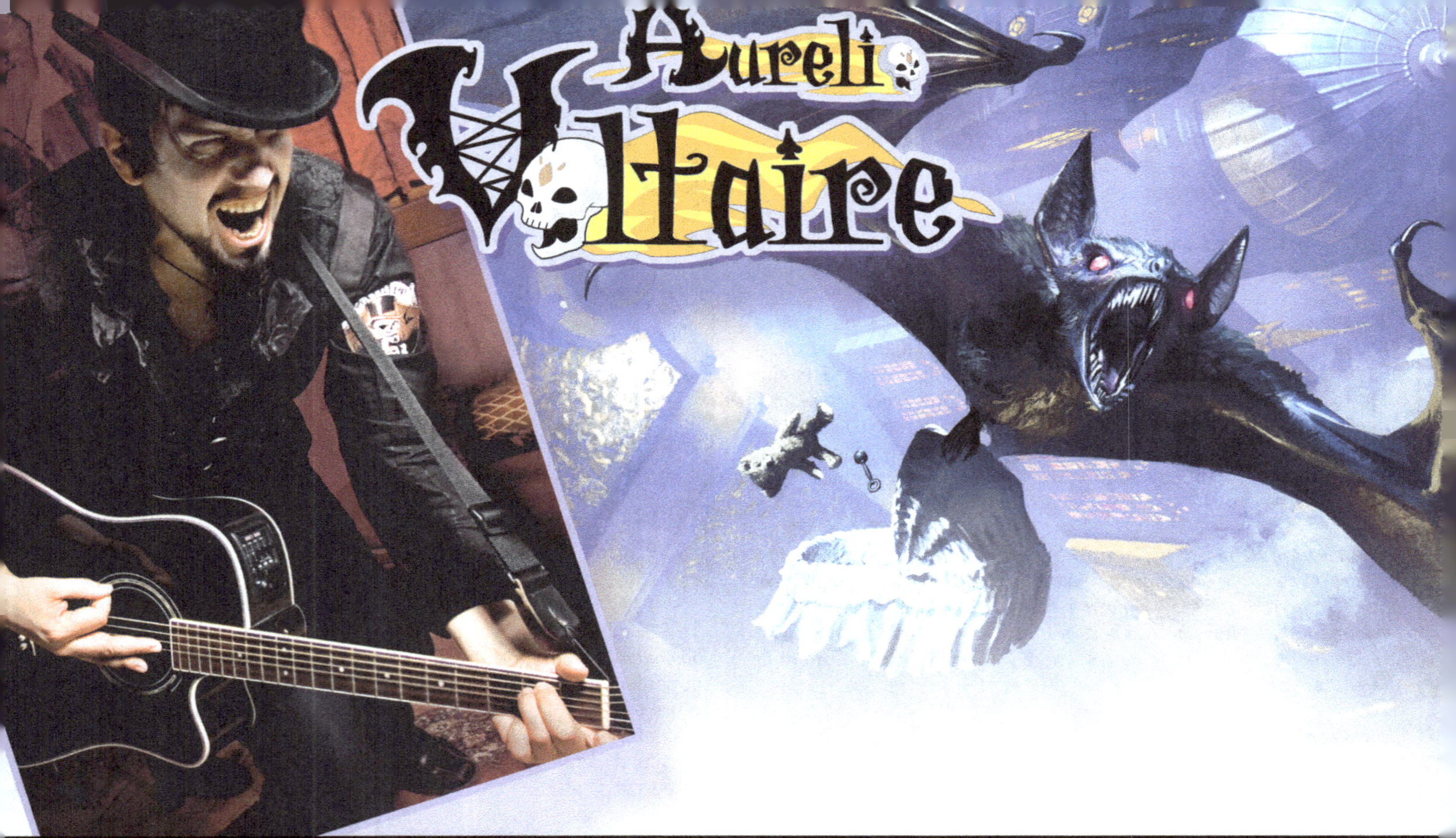

By Asylum Attendant

Versatility and devilish charm come to mind when thinking about musician, animator, writer and top hat wearer **Aurelio Voltaire**. His music takes you straight to a Victorian graveyard where skeletons play the violin and zombies are a roaring good time. Voltaire's sound defies classification, ranging from dark cabaret to gothic rock to country to children's music depending on the album. What always remains, however, is Voltaire's lyrical wit and humor that take the dark culture and transform it into one big spooky shindig. I dare listeners not to laugh their corsets off to songs about vampires with snaggleteeth and murdering ones' ex lover's lover. The sarcasm is always rich for those light-hearted Goths that recognize how ridiculously silly (and awesome) the culture can be. Just add comedian to Voltaire's growing list of talents.

While Voltaire's music is what most fans know him for, he actually started out as a director and stop-motion animator of commercials for Kellogg's, Parker Brothers and Budweiser. I particularly love Voltaire's 1988 stop-motion MTV station ID inspired by Flemish painter Hieronymus Bosch's "The Garden of Earthly Delights" triptych. Who wouldn't want to see Bosch's monstrous, corpse-eating "Prince of Hell" come to life with some eerie music playing in the background? Then, there are Voltaire's myriad of toys, books, comics, merchandise and television appearances. He's a busy man trying to take over the world, one ignorant small-towner at a time.

Now that that lengthy introduction is out of the way, let's delve into Voltaire's music. His first album, The Devil's Bris, was released by Projekt Records in 1998. "The Man Upstairs" will resonate with anyone who's ever had annoying or strange neighbors they'd like to do away with. Those who embrace their inner villain will relate to the prideful, wicked lyrics of "When You're Evil". The Devil's Bris is full of antique strings and dynamic drums with modern pop song structures and entertaining lyrics. Voltaire's serious and sarcastic personas exist in harmony along with timeless instrumentation.

Voltaire wears his black heart on his sleeve with 2002's Boo Hoo. It's a break up record, yet Voltaire still maintains his comic relief. Both "I'm Sorry" and "See You In Hell" explain the dissolution of love through lush violin solos and a gentler sarcasm. The song "Bachelor(ette)", a cover of Icelandic songstress Bjork's poetic gem, flips the lyrics to a male point of view. Voltaire's cabaret production style makes for a nice twist on an eccentric female love song.

The undead are given free rein to party hard to Voltaire's Ooky Spooky album. This one is super random with prominent brassy

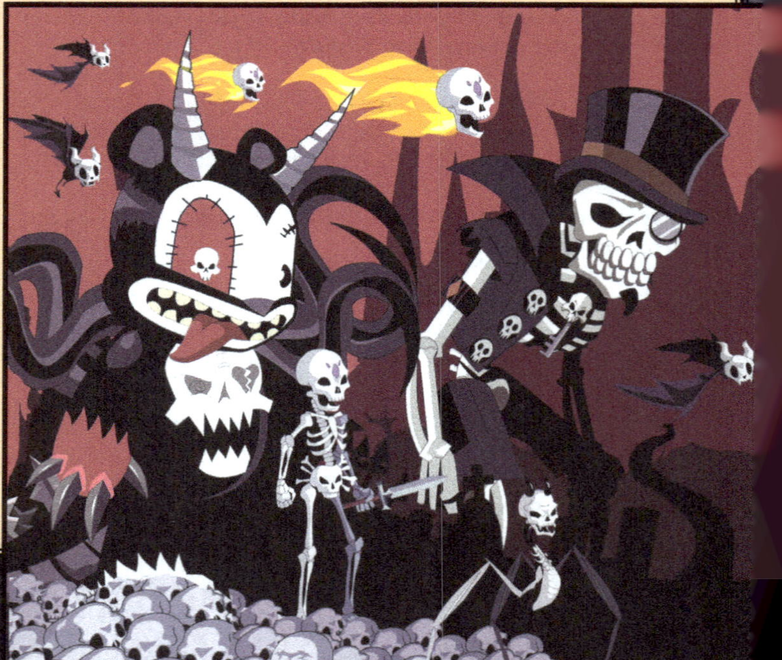

horns and would be the perfect accompanying music to a Halloween gathering. "Bomb New Jersey" is pretty easy to figure out. I'm going to take a stab in the dark and guess that Voltaire wasn't an avid watcher of The Jersey Shore. The duet with Amanda Palmer of The Dresden Dolls entitled "Stuck With You" is a creepy cute tune about a love/hate romantic relationship. Amanda's humor meshes seamlessly with Voltaire's. Take a mariachi band and damn them to Hell; that's Ooky Spooky.

Any country music fans out there? Regardless, I urge you to listen to Voltaire's authentic country album Hate Lives in a Small Town. I think any Goth can relate to that title. The title track features a bluesy harmonica and the contradictions that exist in so-called perfect towns. Voltaire's engaging storytelling abilities really shine in a genre known for its simplicity and straightforwardness.

Released in 2014, Raised by Bats is Voltaire's newest album and his first in the Gothic genre. The album was actually crowdfunded by his loyal fans. Raised by Bats features collaborations with tons of other artists, like My Chemical Romance, Rasputina, Chibi of The Birthday Massacre and Ego Likeness. "The Conqueror Worm" is Voltaire's musical version of Edgar Allan Poe's famous poem about how life is like a play on a stage in which death is unavoidable. With harpsichords, organs, accordions, synths, guitars and more, Voltaire's gothic rock debut sounds refined and completely natural for this Renaissance man. I give him the gothy seal of approval.

Music aside, Voltaire's books are equally amusing. He wrote an anti-bullying children's book called The Legend of Candy Claws. The book features a large, heroic bat named Hargoyle who brings Halloween candy to good children on Christmas Eve. The lovely, whimsical illustrations by Shamine King make this the perfect book for any Goth parent to share with

their children. Paint it Black: A Guide to Gothic Homemaking and What is Goth? will help readers classify all kinds of gothy types, decorate like Tim Burton and more. Goths young and old can learn a thing or two from Voltaire's morbid musings.

Voltaire even crafted his very own toy named Deady, an evil teddy bear imposter. He's created many graphic novels and web comics featuring the nefarious adventures of Deady. There are many Deady toy variations to collect, including collaborations with Skelanimals and Disney. All of Voltaire's merchandise is sure to cause a passerby's blood to run cold.

Pirates, gypsies, deathrockers, steampunkers and creepy kids from every corner of the world revel in Voltaire's shadowy folk tunes. So what are you waiting for? Enter the Lair of Voltaire today...

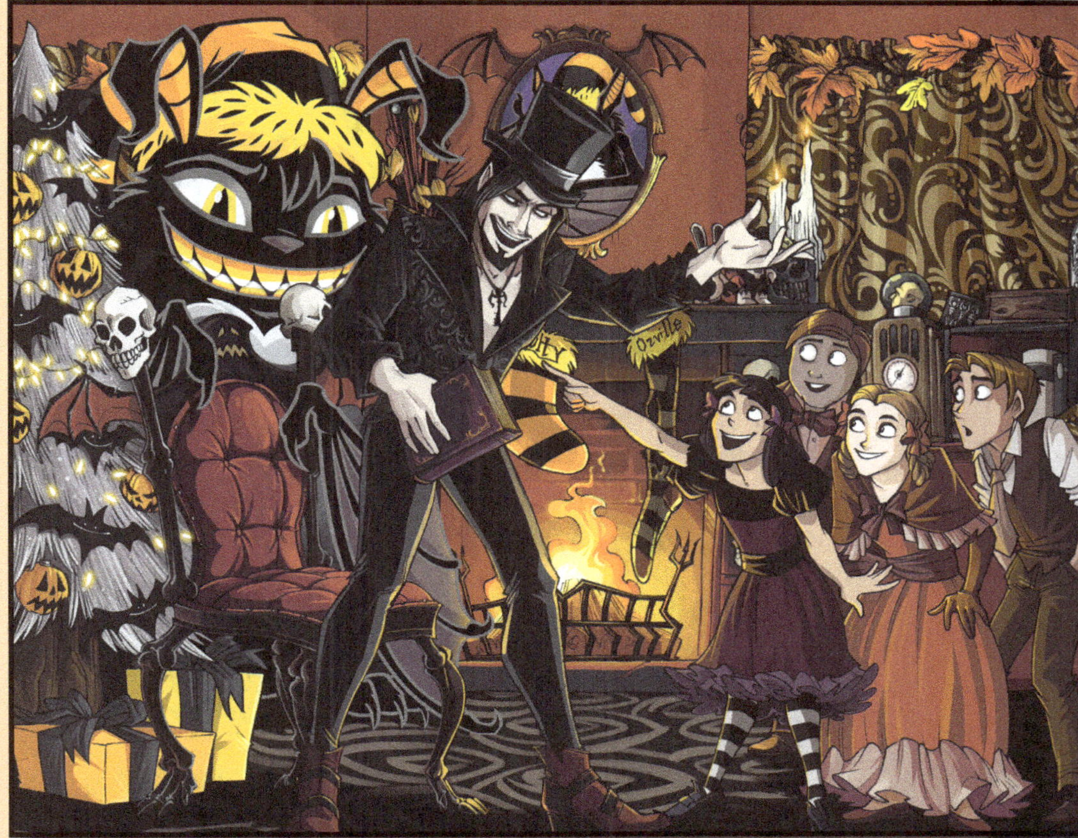

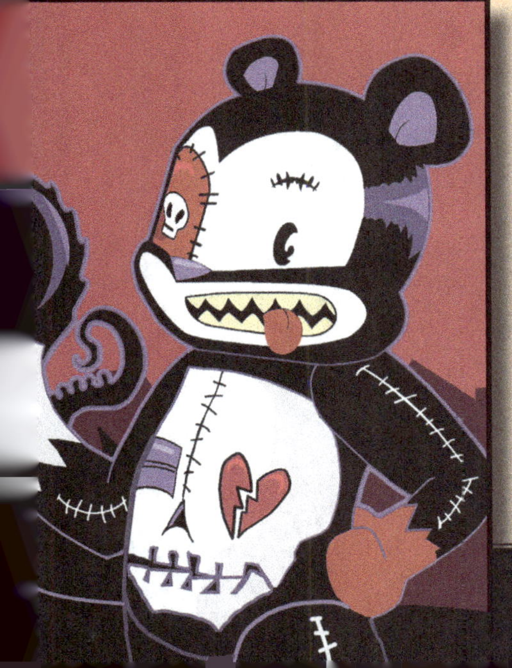

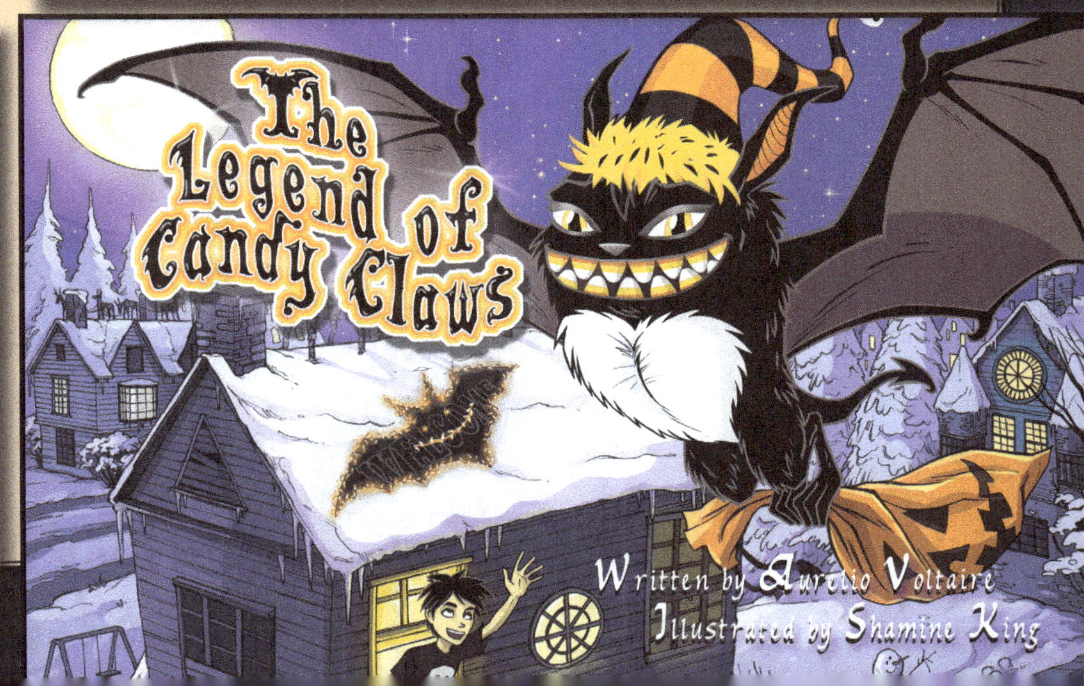

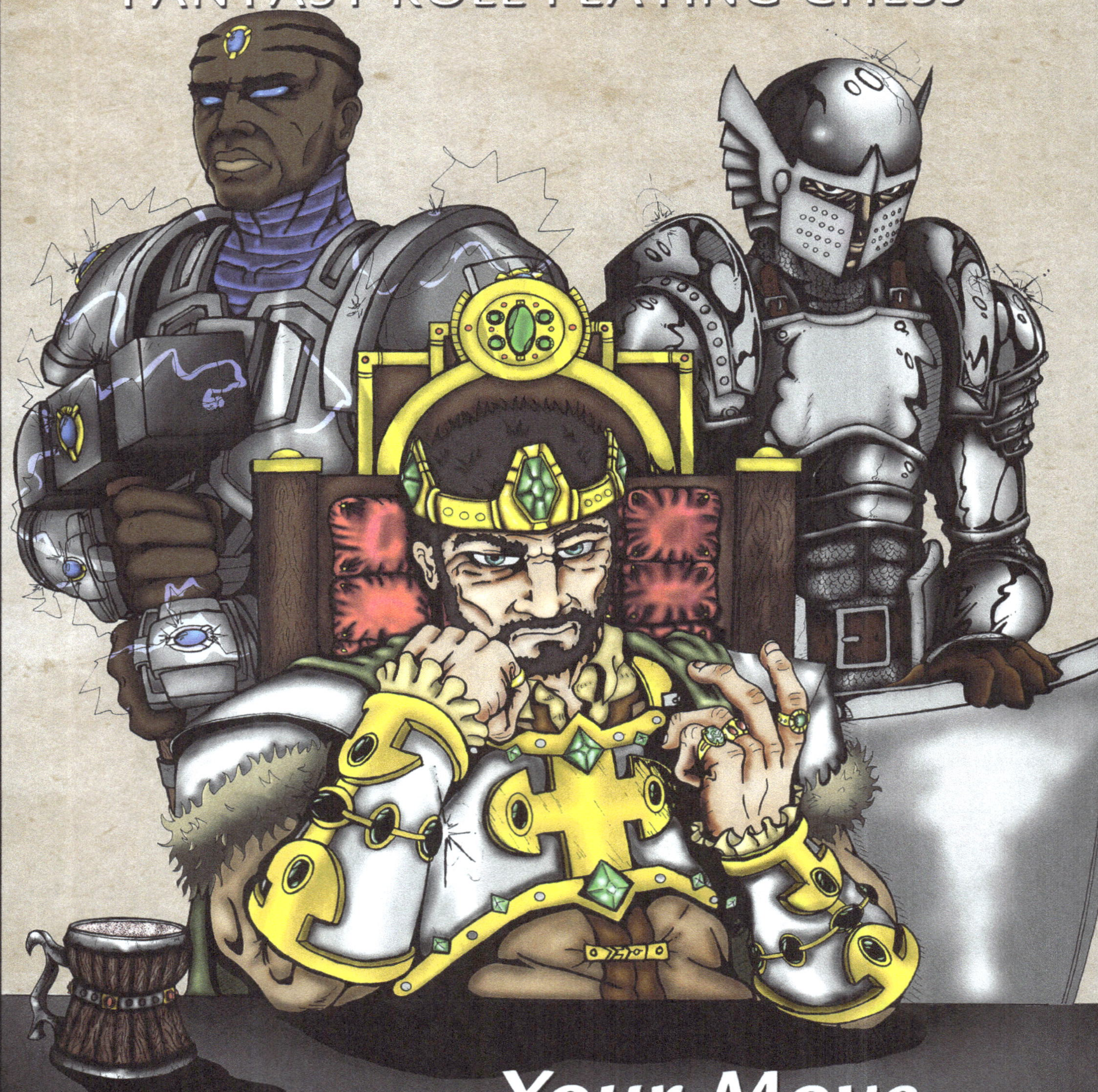
Cathedr'l
FANTASY ROLE PLAYING CHESS
Your Move . . .
FACEBOOK.COM/CATHEDRL
CATHEDRL.COM

The Incredible Adventures of Van Helsing is a real-time action RPG, a game of action and theatrics, larger-than-life heroism and snappy dialogues, with wry humor and various twists on the well-known gothic clichés.

by Omen

From beginning to end, everything about this games breathes the stench of oil, muck, and steam. It is engulfed by political dismay, presented by the conflict between technology and magic – they are both arcane, feared, and integrated into this fictional culture. How often can one speak of a ghost with the sexiness of a 'nickel-worth' stripper, the wit to win an Oscar, and the wrath to slay a wave of foes, as easy as a blacksmith tying his apron? She, Katarina, was the angelic protection to our protagonist, Van Helsing, acting as his satirical aspect of a conscious.

Here's the notable thing about, not only this game, but somewhat, its purpose… *The Incredible Adventures of Van Helsing* is a reluctant glue the ties the subcultures of Goth and Steampunk together as family, while defining each of their dispositions. This game is Goth with a noir approach presented by Gothic architecture, in a fictional era between the end of a dark age and the reluctant approach to a technological renaissance which is viewed as an evil. The prodding theme of Steampunk acts as the glue to bring everything together! The turn of a cog and twist of a vial are presented as seamless as breathing and walking. A fireball is as natural as a ghost, a gun, and a shield all being seen as casual resources for adventuring. This game is brutally cool!

I can't say enough about it, mainly because it reminded me of Blizzard's Diablo, done right! While Diablo was a fantasy RPG, focused on increasing the speed of action by making it hack-and-slash… Van Helsing delivered a different experience by introducing a new, twisted world with a sick form and relatability that damn near made it feel like 'home'.

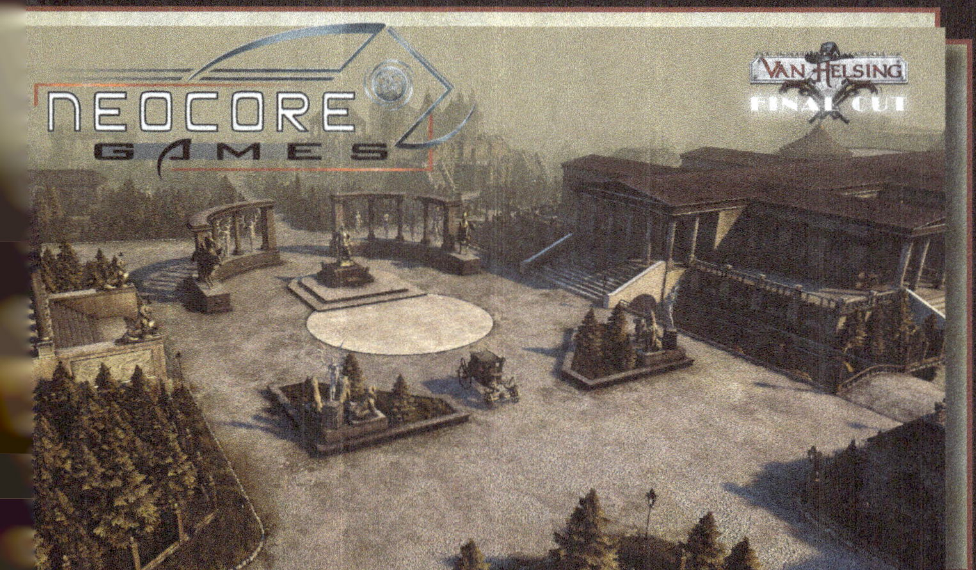

We reached out to the creators of *The Incredible Adventures of Van Helsing*, NEOCORE GAMES and were greeted with not only a quick response, but a welcoming impression. As players of the game, we had questions of our own and to answer them we have Julia Inzsol, *PR and Social Media Manager* and Viktor Juhasz, *Lead Writer* to share with our readers.

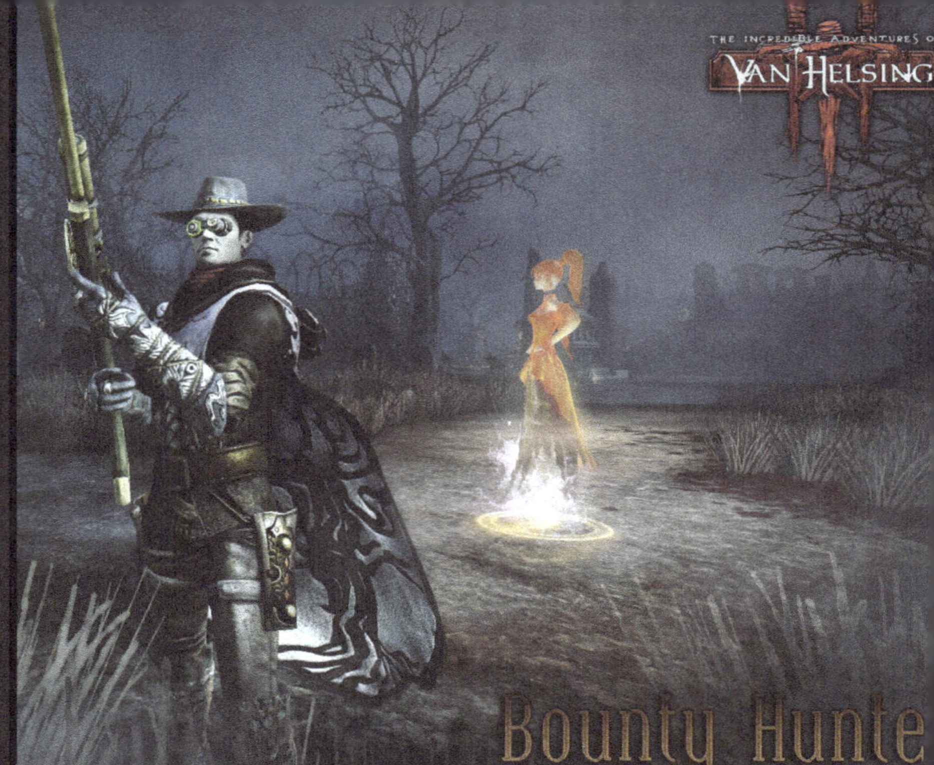

*≈ **Carpe Nocturne** ≈ There are very few videogames in which a single person can be identified as the creator. Is there a certain person that can be attributed with the creation of this fictional version of the Van Helsing's universe (Abraham Van Helsing)?*

≈ **Neocore Games** ≈ The core concept and the idea for the background and the atmosphere came from Viktor Juhasz, our Lead writer/Narrative designer. Fleshing out the universe, on the other hand, was a colossal teamwork of the narrative designer, concept artists and all the designers. We think that if you can find the right people to work together on one idea is the best. We're lucky because we found them.

≈ CN ≈ When the development of this game began, what was the initial vision as to how this was intended to be received? Did this vision change as the game evolved? If so how and why?

≈ **NG** ≈ One of these fundamental changes was the transformation of the originally pitched Van Helsing – a young kid with a much less grim attitude – into the tough monster hunter specialist you can encounter in the final game. When we introduced our protagonist in a teaser trailer, our audience they didn't react too positively to the character. We didn't have anything to lose, so we changed it, we created three different characters, put them into a funny casting video and asked the community to vote for the best one. That's how our character came to life. From the very first moment we've been developing the game with the help of the community feedback, that's why we decided to try to build a trilogy. Give something to the community and listen to their feedback so the next game can be even better. Of course we couldn't have make the second part unless the audience liked and bought the first one. Luckily the success of the first part was much greater than we thought, high above our expectations.

≈ CN ≈ What went into developing the storyline?

≈ **NG** ≈ Countless hours of brainstorming on behalf of the narrative designer, who used various Gothic novels, classical silent horror movies, a tremendous amount of pulp fiction, tons of pop cultural references and vats of strong coffee as inspiration.

≈ CN ≈ Why was the Top-Down approach chosen to deliver this adventure instead of first-person or third-person perspectives? Was this decided initially or was there debate on the choice of delivery? How did this viewpoint affect the focus of the game?

≈ **NG** ≈ It's not a secret that we love Diablo. For us this was the right approach to choose for this kind of game. It is that simple. It was always a fixed element of the game. It affected everything visually, the way we designed levels and created the world. It had an impact on the mechanics and the models as well.

≈ CN≈ What do you have to say to those who immediately speak of Diablo when describing your game?

≈ **NG** ≈ Firstly we have to say that we love Diablo. It's not a bad thing that our game reminds the community to Diablo. At the same time, there are several Diablo like games and they are all different so just because they are the same genre it doesn't make them clones.

≈ CN≈ What influences for character design were there for this game?

≈ **NG** ≈ Classical pulp and gothic and noir influences: we wanted to create various incarnations of the well-known monster hunter tropes and make them playable.

≈ CN≈ Will we ever get to learn Katarina's full background and story?

≈ **NG** ≈ In the final part of the trilogy Katarina has her own chapter where she tells the whole story of how she died and why has she been bound to the Van Helsing family. This was something that our community was wanting for so of course in Van Helsing III we gave it to them. (That is actually my favorite part of the game.)

≈ CN≈ How did you decide on the music score for your games? Who was responsible for the music score and what influenced the choices made (music genre, historic era, etc.)?

≈ **NG** ≈ We are really proud of the music in the game. Our composer, Gergely Buttinger is responsible for it.

≈ CN≈ The Steampunk influence into this gothic world has created an impact in the gaming community. Was this intended? Was steampunk a recognized aspect of this game during the development?

≈ **NG** ≈ Steampunk was always an influence, but we didn't want to get stuck at steampunk. Van Helsing incorporates all kinds of weird, mad scientist-type influences, way beyond steam engines: sizzling electricity, colossal doomsday devices, Frankenstein-like reanimated creatures and so on. Our narrative designer tends to call this genre "Mad-Scientistpunk".

≈ **CN** ≈ The release of Van Helsing 3, while great, was met with a volley of issues and complaints. It has not been overlooked as to how well the response has been from your team to address the issues. What impact has this had on the team and its processes?

≈ **NG** ≈ We've released several patches soon after the release of the game and we always keep our eyes on it. We had to make some choices with Van Helsing II that was not so popular among the community. The second part of the game had tons of new features in it – according to our fans' feedback a wishes. With the final part we couldn't do the same because the game was about to become too hectic, we had to reduce the numbers. We put new character classes in the game and put an emphasis on the story since this was the final part of the trilogy. We do understand the complaints and where they come from but we had to do this. Also Van Helsing: Final Cut is coming and it's going to have everything in it what our community missed from the games. We're releasing Final Cut for our fans who have supported us over the years – it's going to be free for everyone who owns all three games – and we're relesing Final Cut for everyone who have never heard of the franchise before. For them t's going to be as polished as it can be with the help of our supportive community to whom we're very grateful.

≈ **CN** ≈ What was your most challenging game to develop? If so, why?

≈ **NG** ≈ Our most challenging game development is happening right now. We've learned a lot about RPGs during the development of the Van Helsing series and now we're working on a big title. Obviously it's a challenge to make a great game to a community that expects a lot from you.

≈ **CN** ≈ Is there the possibility of a book series based on any of the games?

≈ **NG** ≈ In the early stages we actually discussed this possibility, but for various reasons it never happened, mostly because the games tell the whole story in an interactive way, so there wouldn't be much sense in telling the same story in prose. But who knows what the future holds?

≈

Concluding our Q&A, we can't forget to mention and recommend Neocore Games' other titles. Be sure to check them out at www.neocoregames.com

≈

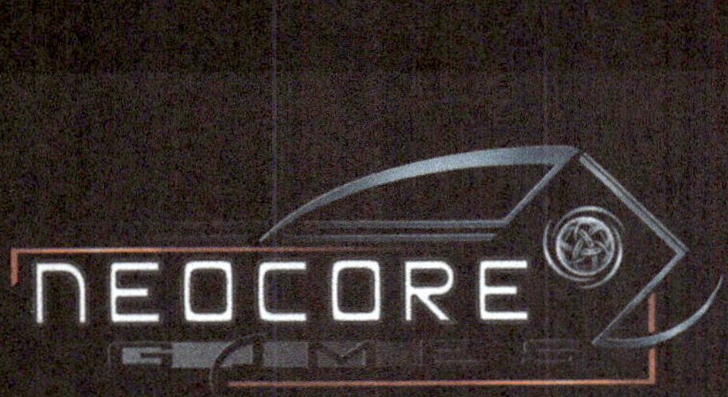

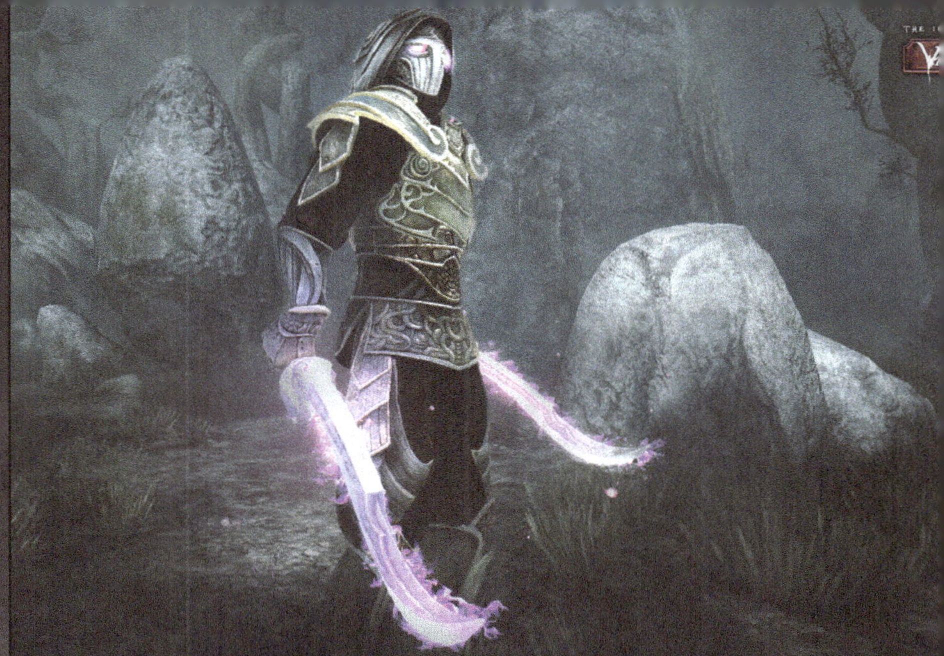

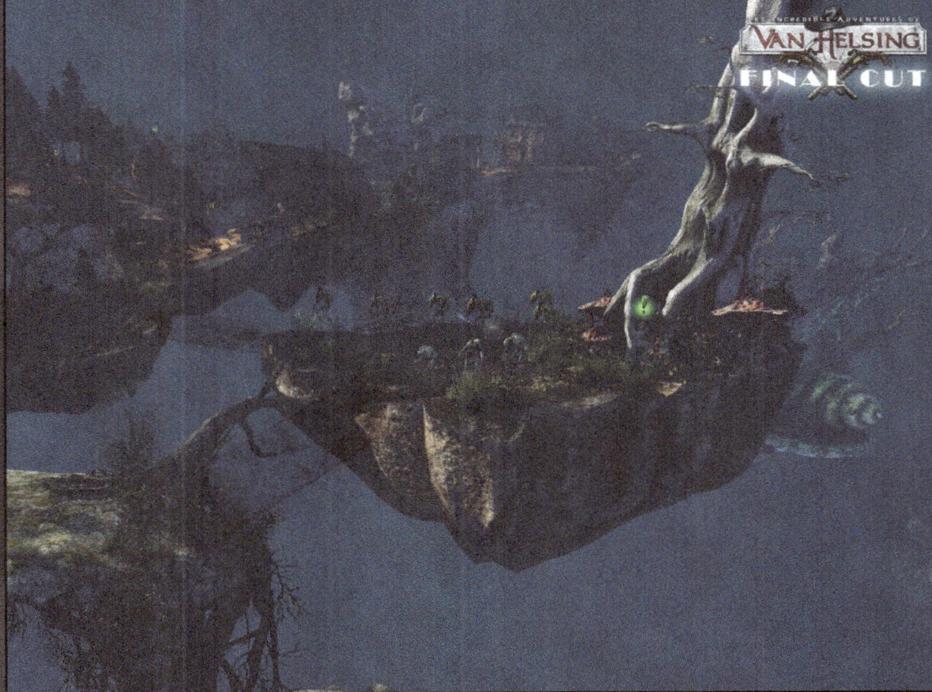

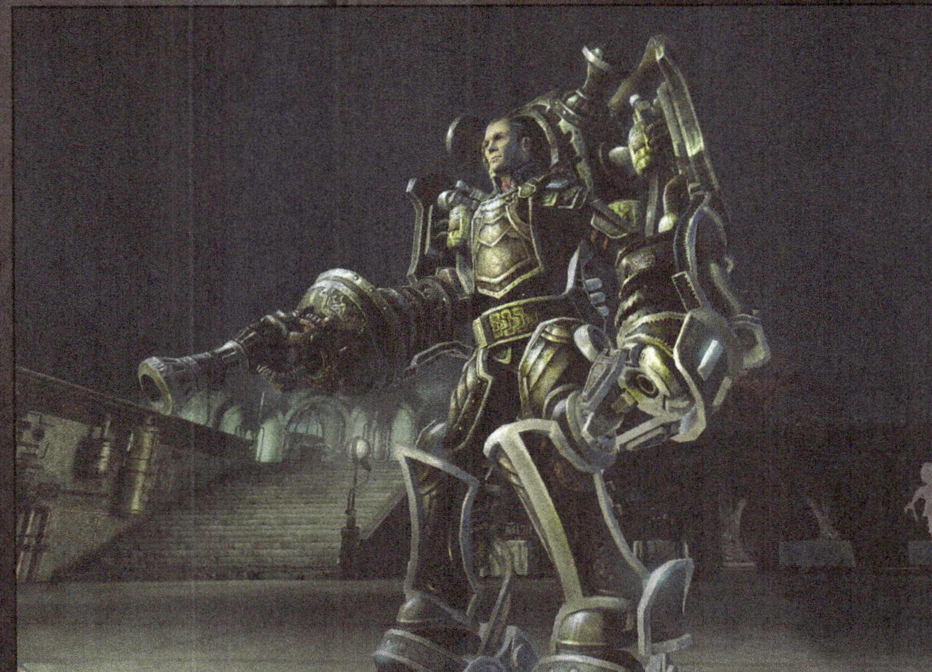

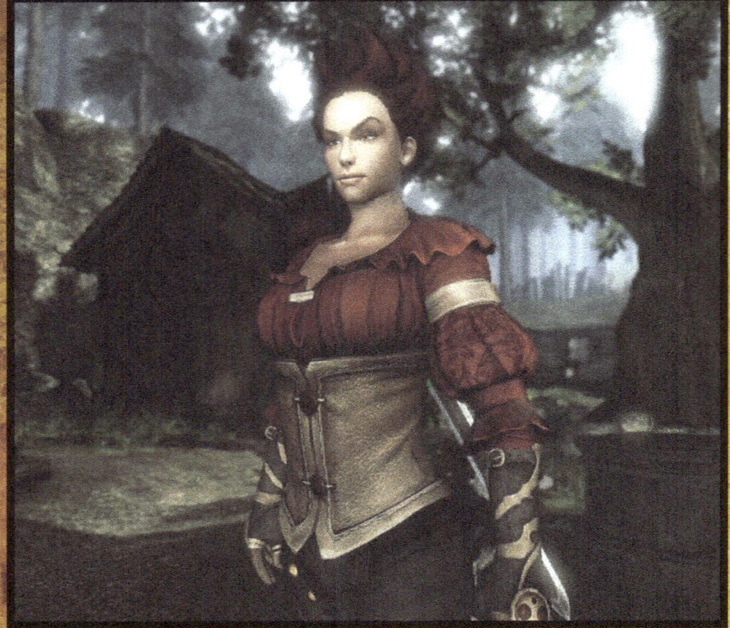

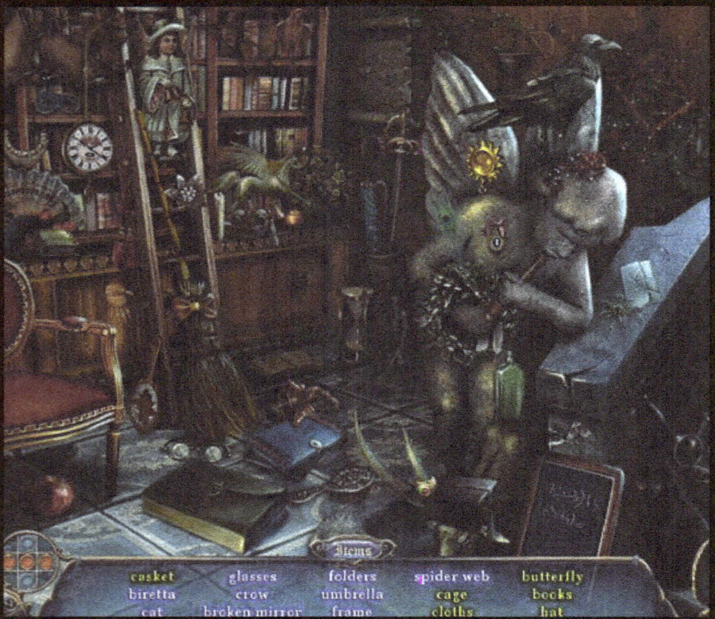

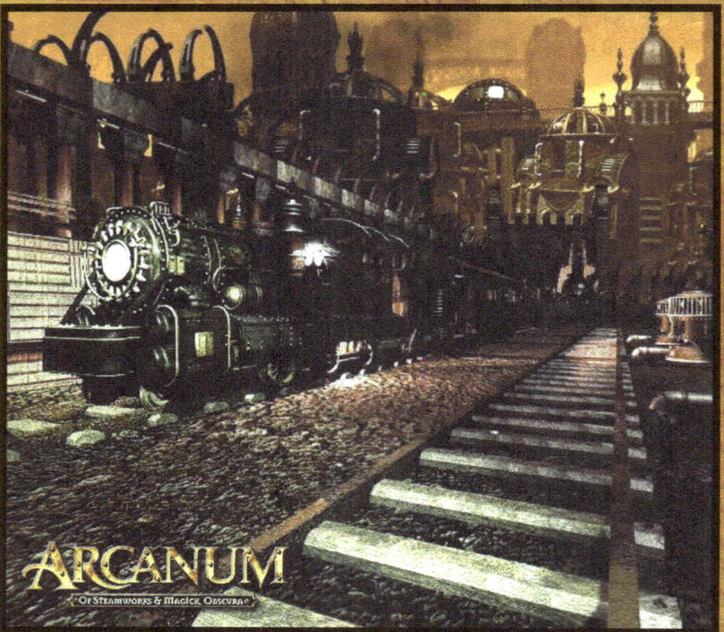

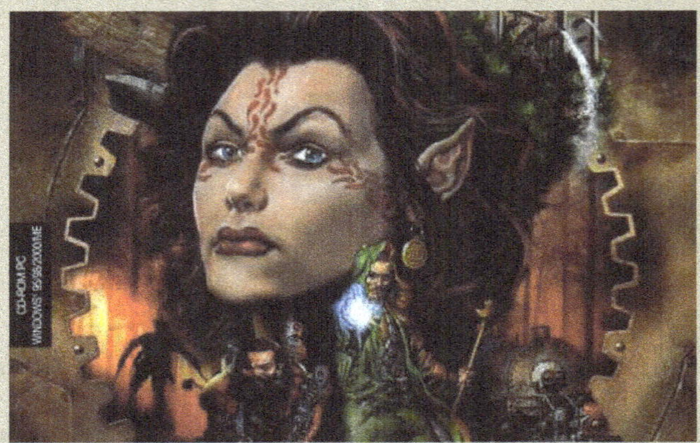

Arcanum: Of Steamworks and Magick Obscura

Developed: Troika Games

Published: Sierra Entertainment

Released: August 21st, 2001

By Mark Hickman

Created by the team who developed the original Fallout, Arcanum, at first glance looks similar to said game. However, Arcanum is grounded within an original fantasy setting and boasts a strong steampunk aesthetic.

The most exceptional part of the game is the massive world for the player to explore and numerous quests for them to undertake. Before the game starts, the player will need to create their character. The character creation screen has a large amount of options for the player to choose from, so it is easy to fashion many unique characters for each play-through. Sadly, not all character builds will have much to do. In fact, some prove to be completely useless. But since this is a video game and not a tabletop game, it is understandable why this ends up being the case.

The weakest aspect of the game would have to be the interface layout. At first glance, the layout is not clear and without a guide, walkthrough, or spending an inordinate amount of time with the interface, you may get exhausted trying to ascertain what element does what. For me, I had difficulty switching between the world map and area map. But after several hours of playing, you will likely get used to the layout.

The game does have a multiplayer feature, however given the game's age, chances are you won't find anyone to play with. Retail copies also came with software that allows users to create their own custom content for the game. Sadly, digital versions of Arcanum don't include this add-on.

Arcanum is a special game that, unfortunately, isn't as well-remembered as the Fallout titles. Hopefully, those who haven't played it in a long time can find their copy and brush off the dust to have some more fun with it. Likewise, for those who have never played or heard of Arcanum, I recommend checking it out. Despite the off-putting interface, the gameplay itself will bring hours of entertaining role-playing fun.

Final Score: 8/10

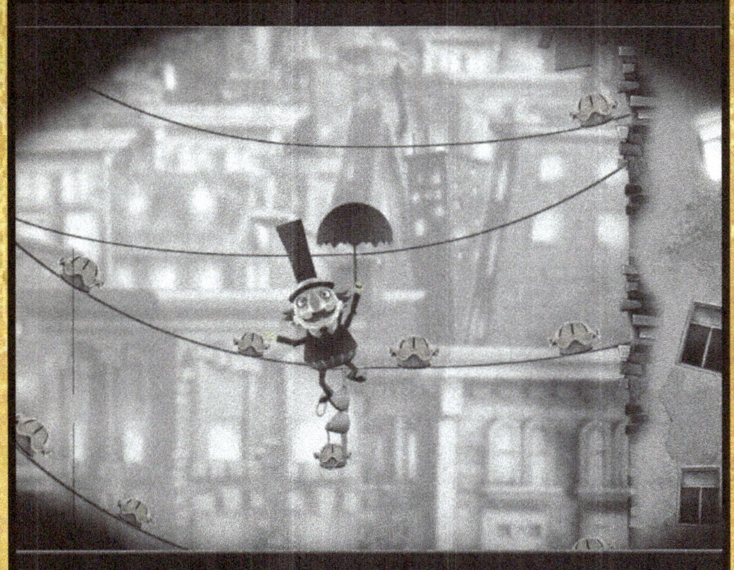

It's not over 'til you've gobbled each and every cobbler.

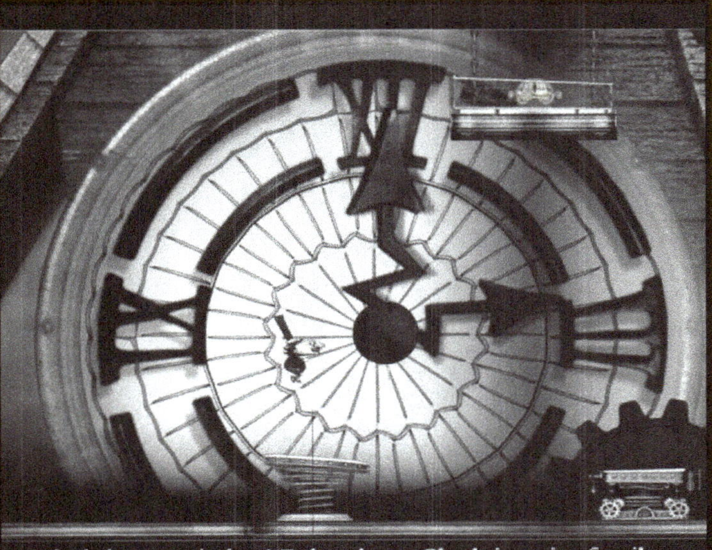

Mind those switches! Bakersburg Clock is quite fragile...

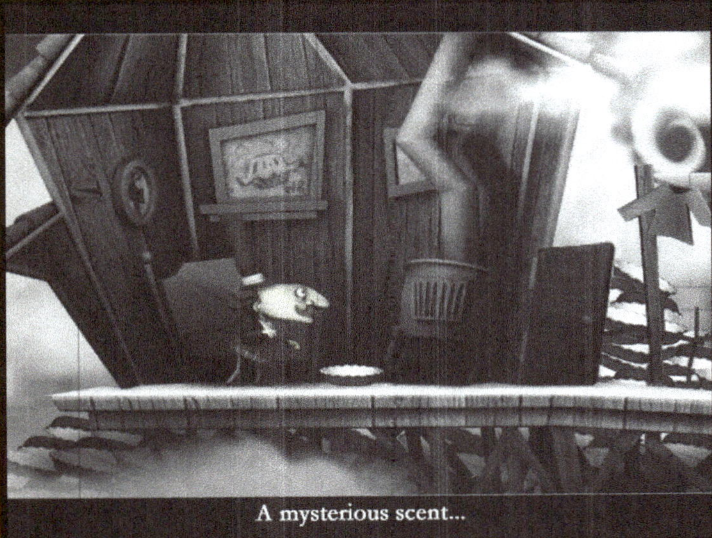

A mysterious scent...

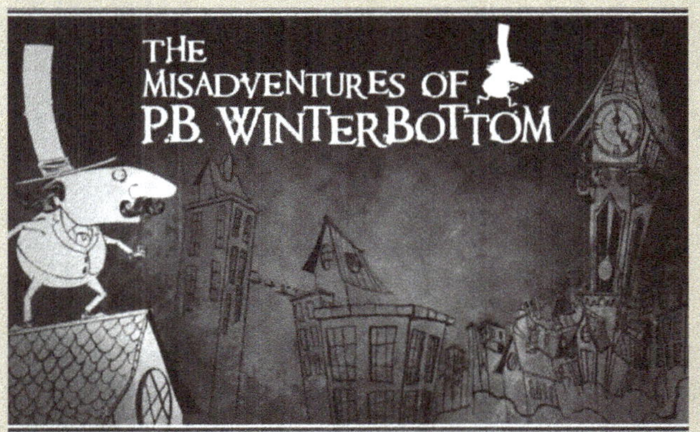

Throwback Game Preview:
The Misadventures of P.B. Winterbottom

By Miss Bella Blitz

Let me ask you a question: Do you like pie? How about steam-powered mechanisms? Time travel? And, what about title cards? If you answered "yes" to any of these questions, then please, let me introduce you Mr. P.B. Winterbottom. A villainous character, P.B. Winterbottom travels through a macabre and comedic silent film world, harnessing the power of time travel to nab all the pies he can. Sounds delightful, yes?

P.B. Winterbottom floats into your life on his umbrella, not unlike Mary Poppins. But, unlike Mary Poppins, Winterbottom's adventures are full of mischief and mayhem. Using clones to manipulate time paradoxes, The Misadventures of P.B. Winterbottom plays like a simpler, more humorous version of Braid. The art style, music, and silent film inspired title cards lend a creepy/cute vibe to the game play that you don't want to escape.

Misadventures is more than just a platforming puzzle game, it's a story of dastardly deeds and the consequences of manipulating time for your own just desserts. Because: Pie. With increasingly difficult puzzles and levels that change the mechanics of your time clones Misadventures keeps things interesting and dark. It may also keep you hungry. The Misadventures of P.B. Winterbottom was developed by The Odd Gentlemen and can be purchased on XBox Live Arcade and Steam.

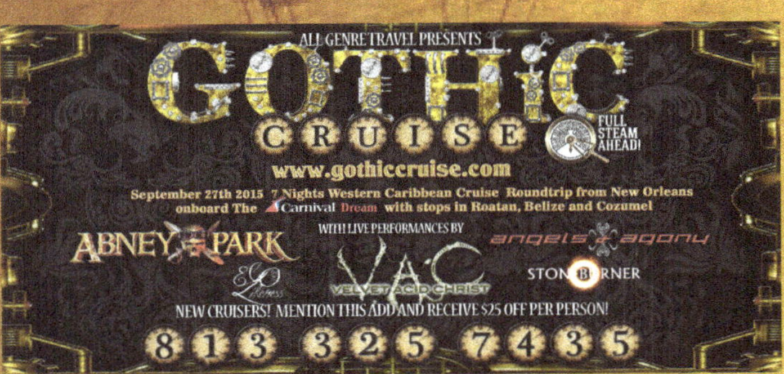

THE HIDDEN TREASURES OF

By Dannette Tillery

Do you have a love for Steampunk? Do you have a love for video games? Ever wish you could have both put together? Well it has been done and you may have just missed out on a few great titles that are steampunk based. Here are a few hidden gems in the Video game world that are worthy "Steampunk" based masterpieces. If you have not tried them or heard of them, then you are in for a treat.

Blood Omen 2

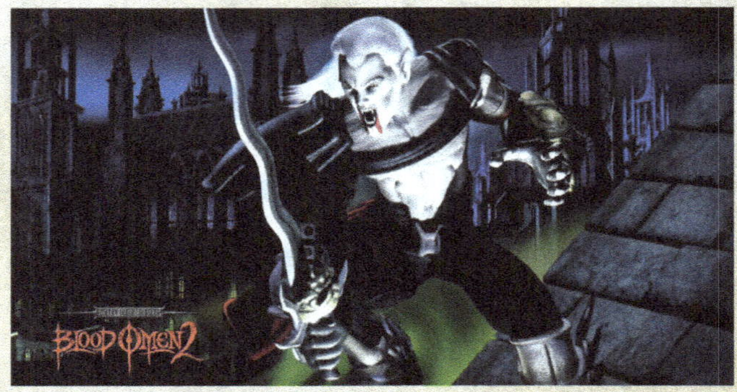

Blood Omen 2 was released on Ps2, GameCube, Xbox, & PC in 2002; It's the sequel to the "Legacy of Kain." It Continues the story of Kain the Vampire four hundred years after the events of the first game. The opening cinema shows Kain's defeat at the hands of a Demon general. Left for dead, he awakes years later in the presence of a mysterious female vampire, telling him he is to help her group of rebel vampires retake Nosgoth from the enemy scourge....and so begins our game. The game takes place in Nosgoth during Its Industrial Period. Essentially, the most steampunk setting it could be, with its steam powered lifts, doors & other devices. The game's landscapes are sewers and Gothic mansions set in 17th century London. It creates a world of Steampunk Vampiric fun.

Damnation

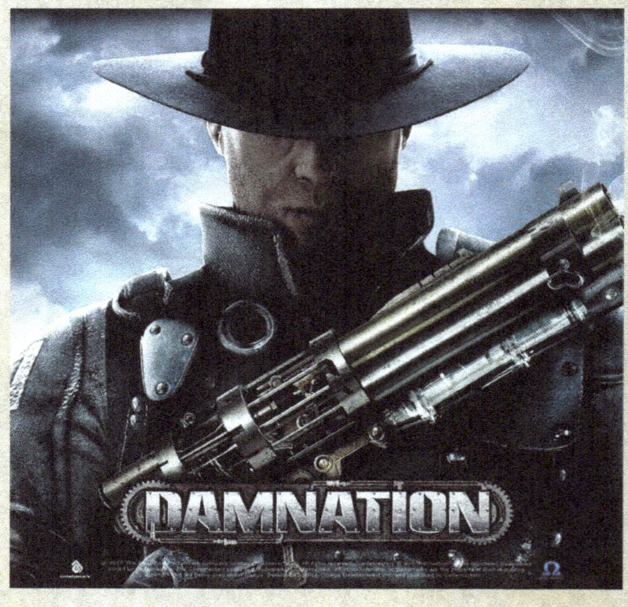

Released in 2009, for Ps3, Xbox360, & PC, Damnation is a Third person steampunk shooter. It is set in an alternate 19th century where the tech is far more advanced than is possible for now, let alone two hundred years ago. Like most shooters, the game starts with you in the middle of the action. You Play as Hamilton Rourke, an ex-Cowboy Soldier with a storied past, who leads a group of freedom fighters against an evil corporation named Prescott (XD). The corporation's intent is to rule the world, and this band of would be rebels are the only thing standing in their way. The steampunk aspects of the game add to the overall ambience of this storied shooter. With steam powered motorbikes, trains, aircrafts, and weaponry, the game has a nice premise at its core. The clothing is also rich in design, and touch's the heart of any steampunk fan who's played or seen the game. Its steampunk aesthetics are "Damnation's" best feature without a doubt.

The Order: 1886

This Third-person cover shooter was released earlier this year exclusively on the Ps4. You play the role of Sir Galahad, an immortal knight in the order of the roundtable. Granted, he's not the original Sir Galahad. The names of the knights are passed down in succession to brave warriors throughout the ages. The game begins with you awaking in a prison being tortured by your jailers. You manage to break free from your captors (through a few quicktime events), killing them, and trying to make your escape. While in the halls of the prison, you encounter a few more guards on your way to freedom. Along the way, Sir Galahad is corned on a tower bridge by the rest of the order. They tell him to give himself up, to which he replies, "I'm already damned anyways." Sir Galahad jumps off of the bridge, and so the game begins.

The order is set in an Alternate 19th century London being terrorized by Vampires and Werewolves. With steam powered weapons, aircrafts, and the like, The Order's world is a beautiful blend of Gothic and Steampunk imagery. For me, that is a dream come true. With all of its gears, levers, and steampunk attire, it'll make you cry in joy.

STEAMPUNK IN VIDEO GAMES

Alice: The Madness Returns

Released in 2011 For the Ps3, Xbox 360 & PC, Alice the Madness Returns is a Gothic psychological horror action-adventure game set in a steampunk world. The story takes place in a twisted retelling of the Alice in wonderland tale. This game occurs years after the first. Now Alice is a young woman dealing with her twisted adventures in wonderland and the deaths of her family. She's now seeing a psychologist who's trying to help her deal with these tragic events……or so it seems. Somehow, she keeps getting sucked back into that demented place, and so the game begins. With a full clockworks world, with clockwork knights, trains, towers, slimes and monsters around all corners ready to jump out and kill you in the best ways you can image, this game is Steampunk at its finest. Alice's costumes are beautiful in a Gothic Steampunk fusion we all love so much. They have to be seen to truly appreciate them in all of their glorious twisted beauty.

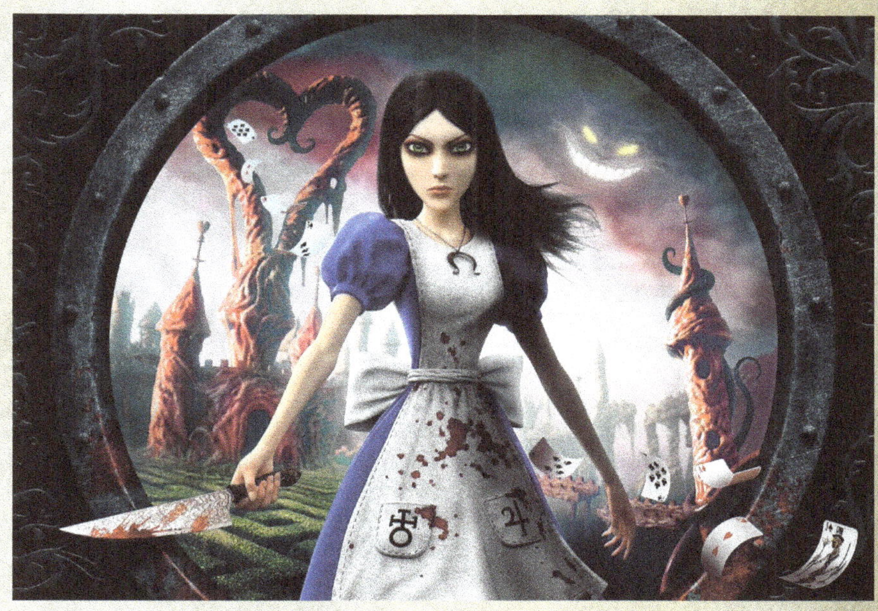

Bloodrayne

Launched in 2002 for Xbox, 2003 for GameCube & 2004 for Ps2, Bloodrayne is a Character Action game set in 1930's Louisiana, Argentina, & Germany. You Play as Rayne, a young dhampir Vampire hunter, new to the job, out to rid the world of vampires once and for all. She soon learns her enemies' grip on the world far exceeds what she originally believed. Rayne Punches, kicks and slashes her way through three acts of Zombies, Vampire Nazis, and other supernatural creatures, all to get to the bottom of this conspiracy. The game's aesthetics range from very Gothic to extraordinarily Steampunk, and Rayne's outfits follow suit. The game has a very tongue and cheek atmosphere which will give most gamers a good laugh at the very least.

There is more where those came from, do a search online to find more, check out these games to get your gears cranking.

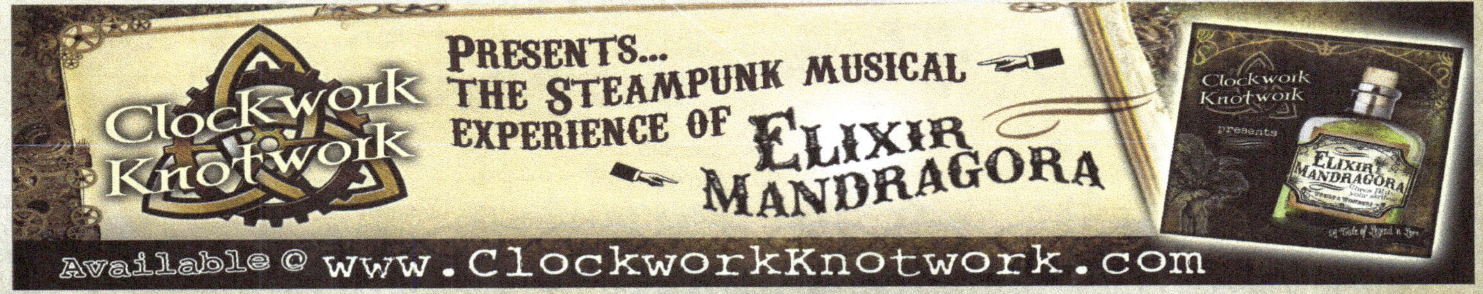

AFTERNOON TEA:

A STEAMPUNK GATHERING IN THREE COURSES

Text by Lisa Walker England
Photos by Kathy Berger

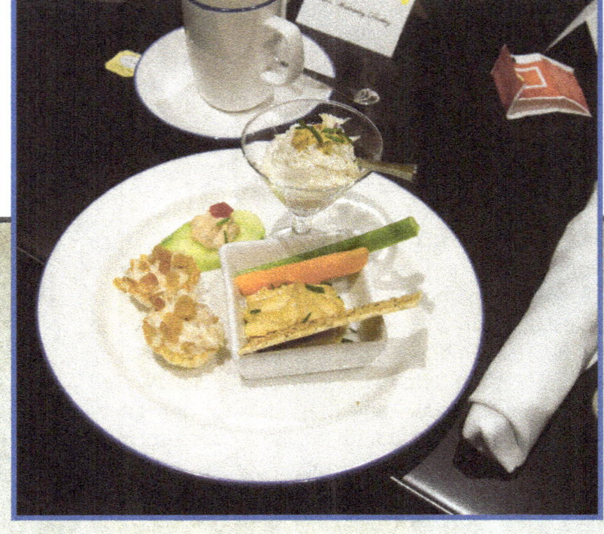

If there's anything steampunks love to do, it's get together for tea. High tea. Low tea. Every tea in between. Name a venue that offers elegant service and real china cups, and we've probably been there. Or at least have it on the calendar.

In fact, you might say that if the steampunk community hasn't yet sampled a particular high tea, the venue in question hasn't proven itself yet. Take for example a tearoom that opened last year in my town. Recently, I joined several local steampunk groups in full regalia to test its offerings against our appetite for elegance.

Our hosts for the afternoon were no less than a local duke and duchess, known and loved by all. And the rest of the guest list was no less distinguished. Nobility, gentlefolk, sky pirates, sea-faring captains, even a few maverick wanderers (such as myself) descended upon the venue at 1 PM for a three-course spread and all the tea a well-corseted stomach could hold.

For those who may not be initiated, high and low tea are very different. The terms even mean different things to British people than to Americans! To avoid the inevitable hairsplitting, I'll call our spread at the venue simple "afternoon tea." Our group enjoyed a smorgasbord of small sandwiches, savory snacks, and finger desserts with a few twists on the usual. For example, this was the first time I'd seen vegetable spring rolls on a tea menu!

And that was not the only sight to behold.

Sometimes the most amusing aspect of these outings is watching the venue staff react to our costumes. Most have never hosted a group quite so well-frocked. (As one waiter put it, "Ma'am, when most people come to high tea they wear jeans and a t-shirt.")

In these cases, the small accommodations that make a cosplay event more successful—such as cranking the air conditioning early in the day—go unattended; that is, until the staff set eyes on our five-layered frocks and three-piece wool suits. Steampunk garb traps heat like nothing else I know!

But steampunks are used to these minor hiccups. In my experience, we tend to handle them with a good humor that, for many of us, was no doubt one of our first attractions to the community.

Where else, after all, will you shout "Huzzah!" on cue or practice your British accent without feeling silly? Not to mention wear ten pounds of jangling brass gear and feathers that stand a full foot off your head?

With as many high teas as I've been to over the years, I've spent considerable time trying to figure out what attracts us to these regular gatherings. After all, they offer few surprises. We all know the sort of food we will eat, the beverage we'll drink, and what we're likely to converse about at table. We wear the same general types of fashions. We expect the same kinds of toasts. And in a community this small and tight-knit, we know exactly who we'll meet.

I would imagine that's actually part of the attraction.

In a world that has lost sight of the power of ritual, afternoon tea offers a welcome sanctuary of ceremony and old-fashioned decorum. It's a social dance, previously agreed-upon, that we all sign up to play: one that ties us to the people of the past and provides a sort of anchor in the midst of our chaotic modern lives. Either that, or we really just like those little cucumber sandwiches.

Of course, I can't speak for everyone in the steampunk community. But for me, rituals like tea are one of the reasons I keep coming back to steampunk events each year. These events are my chance to be with people who share my love for the past and my obsession with hand-crafted things. People who also share my appreciation for ritual and order.

I can relax over china and silver, in my best starched frock, precisely because I know what's going to happen next.

We'll nibble and sip. We'll laugh. We'll practice our accents. We'll expand our steampunk personas and make memories for our modern selves in the old-fashioned way. All the while, we'll assemble new futures for ourselves using the odd pieces (or in this case, utensils) of a cast-off past.

At the end of the day, our new tea venue met our approval. Each high tea has its strengths, and this one proved its particular merits. Enough to warrant receiving our group again next year.

Thanks, local steampunk group, for another fantastic afternoon. Thank you to the duke and duchess for hosting us. Thank you to my table mates for sharing both stories and costuming advice. Thank you also to the venue for welcoming us into your lovely space.

And thank you most of all, steampunk community, for being an oasis of ceremony in an often-unceremonious world.

Here's a big "huzzah" to you!

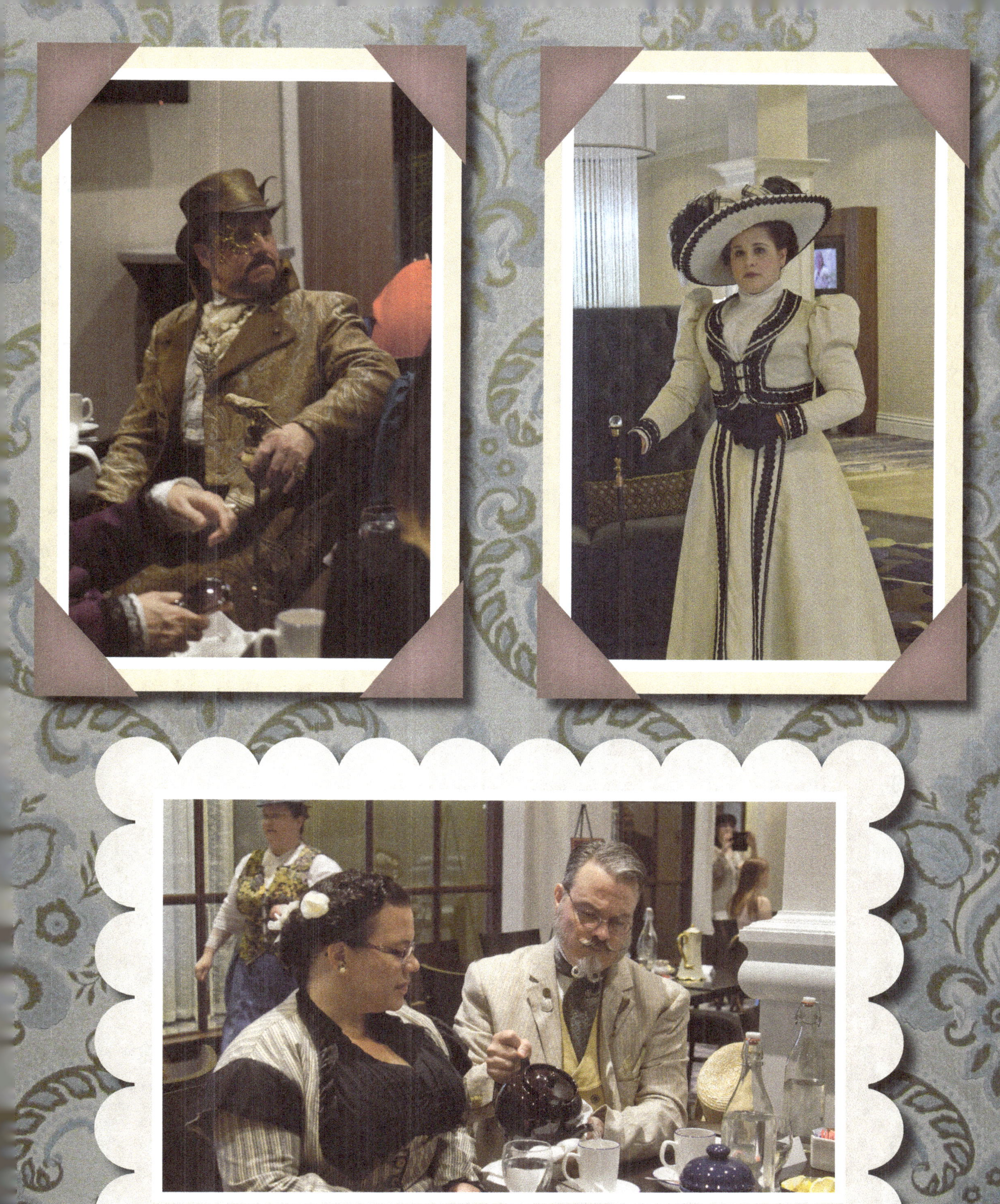

DEVLISH DETAILS AND WISPS OF WHIMSY

By Zahara

Cincinnati hosts the International Steampunk Symposium every spring, and while shopping for some new costuming pieces, my eyes fell on some beautiful Steampunk posters. They had a stained-glass quality about them. I was unfamiliar with Seth Lyons and his drawings, but I was fascinated by his unique mix of Steampunk elements, whimsy and elaborate detailing. Not only was this was his first time at Symposium, but it was his first time ever vending at a Steampunk convention. I had the opportunity to speak with Seth about his artistic journey into the Steampunk realm.

[Zahara] Let's start at the beginning... how would you describe your evolution as an artist, and what media do you enjoy using the most?

[Seth] My favorite media is easily pen and ink on Bristol or illustration board. The evolution of my work is a little harder to answer. Over the past few years, my work has became more intricate and detailed. If there's a grommet or texture to the material, I'll compulsively render

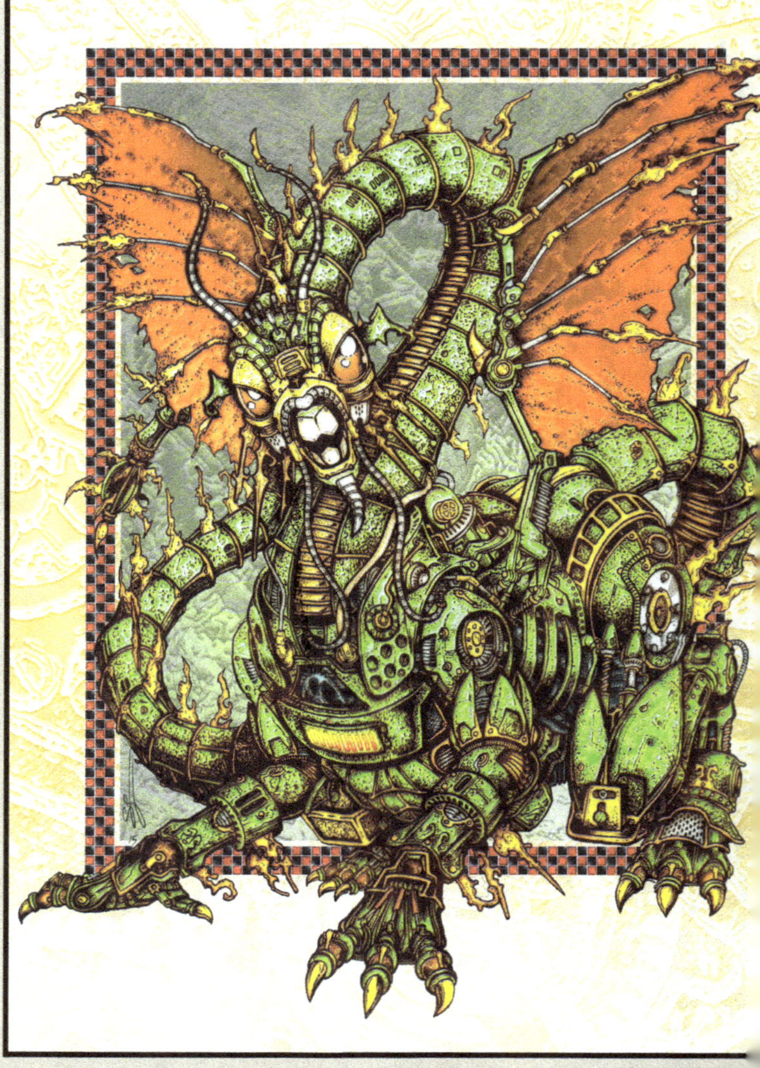

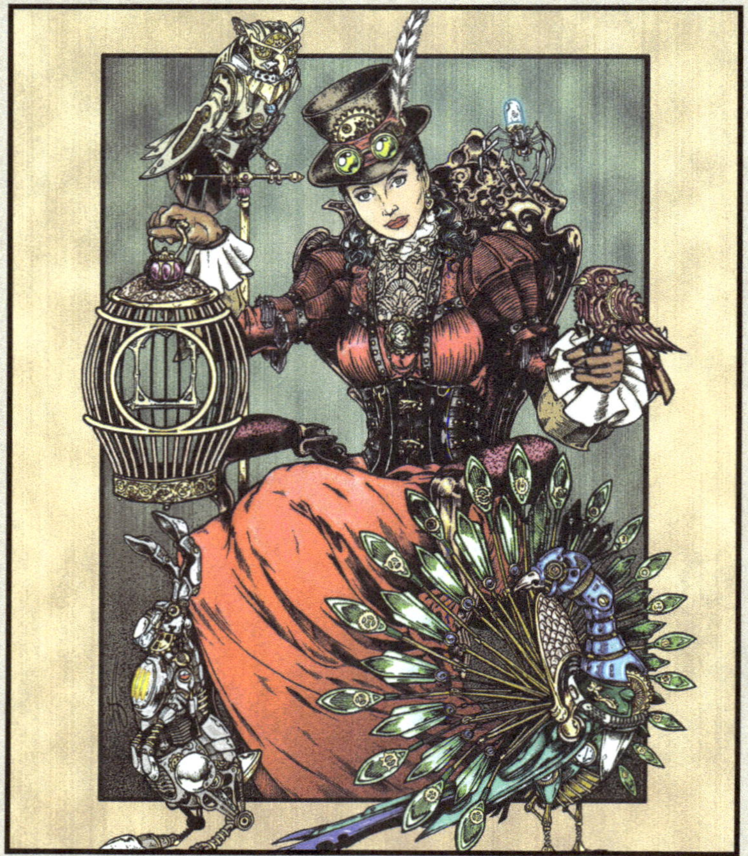

it. Sometimes I sketch and re-sketch certain details as I go before inking them, but once the pen hits the paper, there's no going back. I do prefer to color digitally just for the degree of control you have; but I'm trying to step back from that and do more coloring by hand again, using whatever medium I need to achieve the marks I want. Aesthetically, I feel my Steampunk designs are a universe removed from the standard look. I like adding different cultural or fantasy elements to my designs that you don't typically see. I feel like the Steampunk world should expand further than just Victorian England, but still be recognizable as Steampunk.

[Z] Could you describe how you first began creating Steampunk art?

[S] If I had to pinpoint the turning moment that had me creating my Steampunk art, it would be my piece entitled "Steampunk Menagerie". She is a very much based on a traditional Steampunk design with the top hat, goggles, Victorian dress and surrounded by a menagerie of clockwork animals. I have a love of old black-and-white movies, and this particular model is loosely based on Audrey Hepburn from "My Fair Lady", which I used as reference material.

What led me to even create this piece was a chance meeting with the proprietor of The Alley Vintage and Costumes in Dublin, Ohio. Without going into the long-winded story of our entire exchange, I ended up showing her a piece I had recently finished called "Oz Reimagined", which had some Steampunk-style elements such as the Wizard and Flying Monkeys. This lead to being asked if I had other Steampunk art, with the potential that it could be sold on consignment through the store. I felt I had to seize the opportunity, so I produced "Steampunk Menagerie". I did not want to do the same type of designs over and over, so I have tried putting my own spin on it while keeping some of the Steampunk aesthetic. I have done a series of elementals, mythical beasts (the dragon being one of my most popular pieces), as well as fairies, an angel and a unique spin on Wonderland.

[Z] You have a beautiful array of work. Aside from your Steampunk pieces, what are your favorite scenes to create and why?

[S] I also do a lot of comic illustrations, and I always have fun with big collage pieces or scenes with multiple characters; my record is 655 characters on one piece. I enjoy creating these massively intricate pieces, because people have to really look to find out what is going in my work. I'll hide things for the viewer to find. A lot of the comic-related pieces I've done recently have been more nostalgic in nature, so I guess their appeal to me is just a return to my childhood.

[Z] Do you work on commissioned pieces? If so, please describe one of your favorites and why you agreed to do the piece.

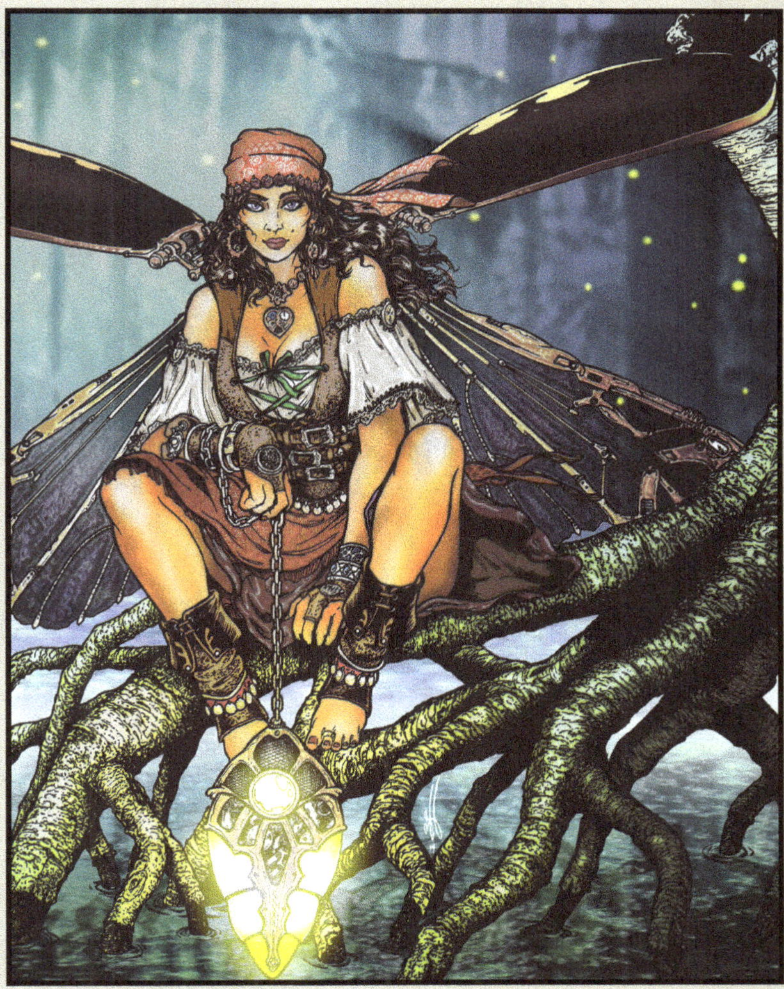

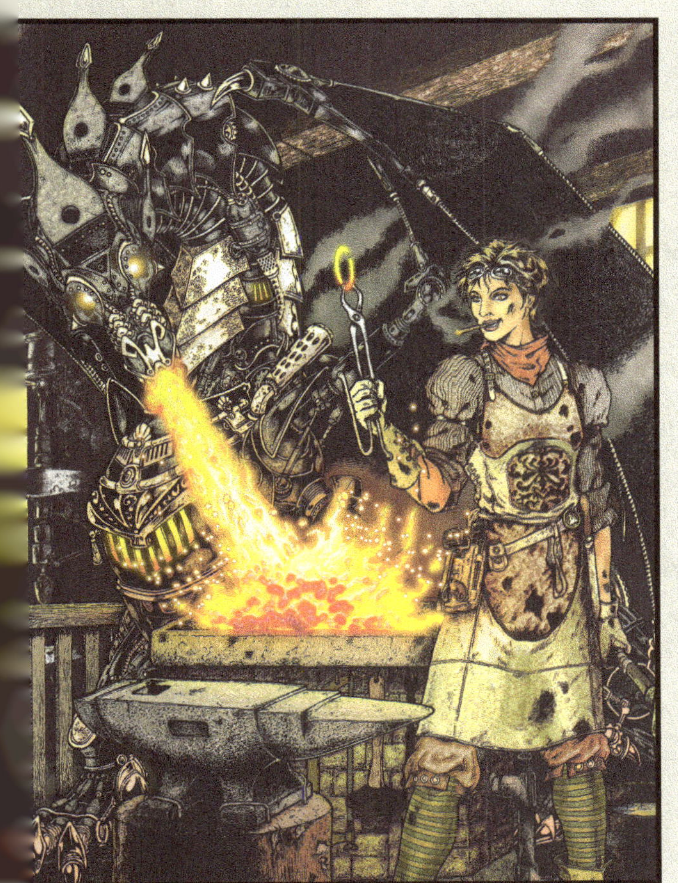

[S] I do work on commission pieces. I find it easier to work on a commissioned piece when there is a personal connection to the buyer. It seems those works that have an emotional element to them resonate more for me while creating them. I've done some illustrations for literary conventions that have a wide array of contrasting imagery and themes, so it's a real challenge developing a cohesive image; however, the end results are very rewarding when you feel like you've finally succeeded. My favorites are still the ones that have individual appeal rather than universal. A cancer charity piece I did for my best friend's brother-in-law comes to mind. The imagery for that piece was chaotic and meaningless, unless you knew who the piece was representing. All his friends and family, to whom I was a stranger to most, were awed by how much the illustration personified his character, interests and history. Unfortunately, that memory is bittersweet, considering he lost his battle with cancer shortly afterwards. Now that illustration serves as a unique reminder of a lost friend and brother.

[Z] Where can we see and purchase your art? Where will you be vending again in this year?

[S] You can see my work in progress on Facebook most of the time. Whenever I'm working on an illustration, I like to show my progress as a piece comes together. My work is also available at my online store: http://sethlyonsgallery.storenvy. com/ or at The Alley Vintage and Costumes at 3502 W. Dublin Granville Road in Columbus, Ohio. I currently only have one more upcoming show this year, where I'll be at Tricon Columbus on August 22nd, so look out for new artwork this summer!

POOPBIRD MEETS PIRATES

By Miss Bella Blitz

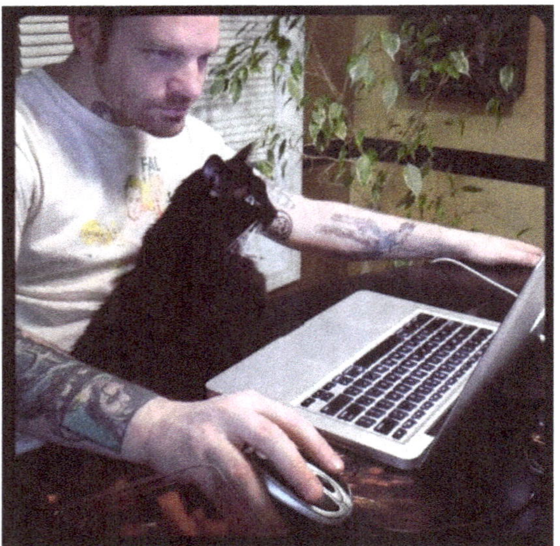

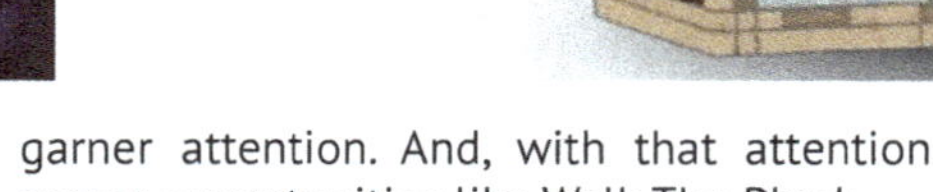

When most people think of tattoo artists they think of intimidating men, listening to death metal, with gruesome tattoos on their throats. It's a stereotype that we, as a society, are hard-pressed to get away from. But, as a community that embraces the tattoo art-form and body modification, it's a stereotype we can laugh at; knowing full well that some of our tattoo artists are just geeky guys, listening to They Might Be Giants, with beautiful (artists name) tattooed on their neck.

Meet Mike Groves (aka Poopbird) a self-proclaimed nerd, well-known artist, and famous tattoo artist now turned game art designer. Having had the opportunity to see Mike's art up close and personal, and having played a good many video games and board games with him, I'm excited about his turn as a game art designer. Mike's style, while ranging from the ridiculously cute to the gloriously creepy, is always unique to his hand. With touches of watercolor or full-blown vibrancy, combined with dots and splatters, the art of Poopbird never fails to

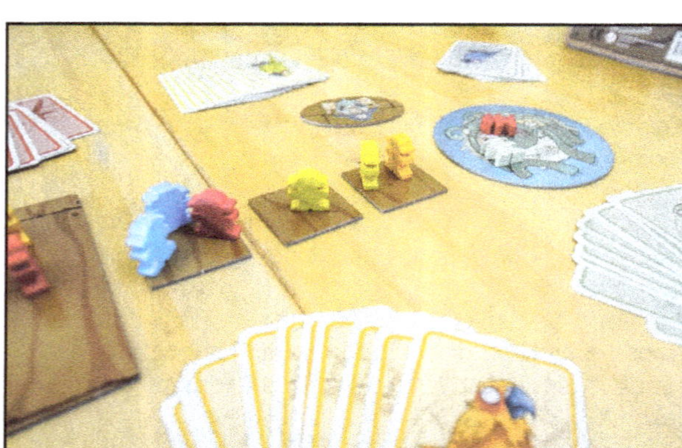

garner attention. And, with that attention comes opportunities like Walk The Plank.

Whether you've been a fan of Mike's work for a while, or just recently looked through his portfolio, you know that pitting him against mutaneous pirates in a pseudo-Munchkin inspired card/board game just seems like the right thing to do. I had an opportunity to sit down with the man known as Poopbird to get a little insight into the game art design and the game itself.

[Carpe Nocturne] *Can you tell us a little bit about Walk The Plank?*

[Moike Groves] It's a super fast, easy to learn pirate game. Every player is trying to force the other players off the end of the plank, while [at the same time] trying to keep your crew members safely out of harms way. The BoardGameGeek.com entry sums it best: "In Walk the Plank!, players represent the worst pirates in a captain's crew. The captain has rounded you all up because you're all lazy and stupid and simply not worth the rum and loot you get paid. That said, the captain has decided he's willing to keep two of you in his crew. To prove you're worthy, you will fight amongst yourselves, trying to shove other players' pirates off the end of the plank while keeping yours alive!"

[CN] *How did you get involved with the creators of the game to become the designer/illustrator?*

[MG] Max Holiday was working for MayDay games and lived in SLC at the time. I was there for a tattoo convention and Max was wandering around looking for new artists for some projects he had on the table. It was smart to do some headhunting at the tattoo show; there is a crazy amount of talent there that companies often overlook. Anyway, he made his way to my table and we briefly talked about gaming. I'm sure my love for boardgames became very clear very fast. Even if he hadn't liked my work, I was so insistent he pretty much had no choice. Not long after that, he was sending me details for his lil pirate game.

[CN] *What was it like working with the creators and being on the production end of a game? How many times did you stop in the creative process to actually play the game instead?*

[MG] This title was super easy! Somehow we were all on the same page pretty quickly. The only big change was [originally] I had a siren with huge boobs calling the sailors off the edge of the plank to their doom. I didn't understand how wide an audience this thing would have and we swapped out the girl for the less-sexy kraken image. Other than that, I only had to change little random things here and there. My card colors were very similar and they showed me how to fix that so it wouldn't be a problem for someone with colorblindness. I never would have considered that, and I was more than happy to make those changes.

I actually didn't play the game until it came out during GenCon where i had to demo it for folks.

It's such a simple concept they just needed to give me the rules and the number of different cards they needed. It's pretty easy to figure out what was happening even without playing it.

[CN] *I know you to be an avid gamer - how quickly did you jump at the opportunity to become a board game art designer?*

[MG] I really did jump. I was super excited and thankful for the opportunity. I was also a bit spoiled by how easily it came together and how well it did on kickstarter. It was a nice introduction into that world - even if it doesn't always work that well.

[CN] *As a fairly well-established artist (working the convention circuit, a good stint designing for J!NX, and your tattoo career) were you given any artistic direction or were you left to your own devices?*

[MG] It felt like they just let me do what i wanted. The truth is, i probably just got lucky, and my first designs happened to fall in line with everyone's vision for the game.

[CN] *What influence for this game design did you derive from your other work, if any? Has this game design influenced any of your other art?*

[MG] It was actually very different than how I normally approach other projects. Whenever I was working I would have cards from other games nearby - mostly to remind me that these illustrations were going to be printed reeeeally small. I often get crazy and do a bunch of tiny details and textures that you sometimes can't even see. It would have been very true on these game pieces, so I had to constantly remind myself to pull back a bit.

[CN] *This is one of the first game art designs under your belt, are you looking forward to more? If you have any other games in the works - can you tell us about them?*

[MG] I've worked on three games now. I've had a handful of other opportunities too, but my tattoo job requires the bulk of my attention. However, I do have another title I'm going to start on soon. Max has a game ready to go and wants me to have complete creative control over the look of it. I get to do pretty much anything I want with it - and that's both exciting and a bit overwhelming. I actually can't wait to get started. We hope to have the kickstarter up and running before the end of the year.

Walk the Plank is available now on MaydayGames.com and Amazon.com.

You can find Mike Groves online at Poobird.com. He's social via Facebook, Twitter, Tumblr and Instagram.

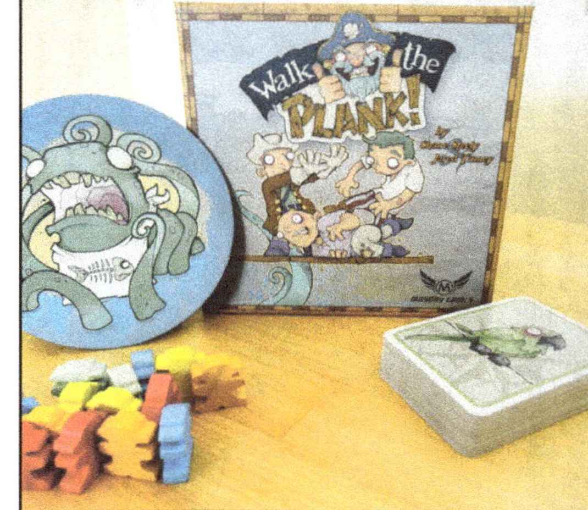

FORGET IT JAKE... IT'S L.A. NOIRE: A GAMING REVIEW

By Linnie Sarah

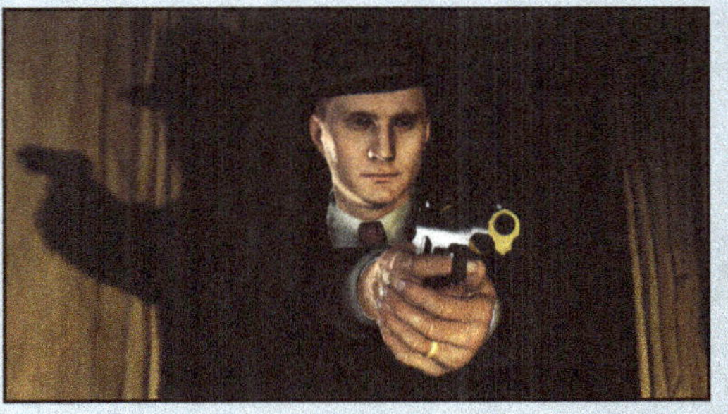

Despite a serious love of gaming, it takes a special game to entice me away from my work and keep me engaged for hours on end, days at time, without the slightest hint of guilt. Rockstar Games's L.A. Noire achieved this rare feat by presenting as the perfect action adventure game: gorgeous, detailed, brilliantly written, and utterly devastating. And when it was over... I shed a tear over both the game's emotional conclusion, and the fact there was no L.A. Noire left to play.

So join me, budding detectives, as we explore Los Angeles in the 40s, take on police corruption, battle the reign of Mickey Cohen, and fall in love with a mysterious dame with a voice like velvet and a body for sin.

The Story: You play the majority of L.A. Noire as Cole Phelps, a former soldier making his way from street cop to detective in the LAPD. You investigate a series of cases, from the Black Dahlia murder tp a morphine smuggling operation, all while navigating your increasingly complicated personal life. While you eventually finish out the game as Private Investigator Jack Kelso, Phelps is your man for the majority of L.A. Noire and as you hunt clues, interrogate witnesses, and close cases, you will inevitably become attached to this flawed and flawlessly performed gumshoe.

The first element you will notice about L.A. Noire is the absolutely stellar motion capture performances from an array of well-known actors. Aaron Staton (Preservation) stars as Phelps and his performance is wonderful, worthy of any 40s noir film. Genre stars such as Greg Grunberg, John Noble, Courtney Gains, Brian Krause, Vincent Kartheiser, and more, are instantly recognizable thanks to the game's ground-breaking MotionScan technology, which gives the whole affair a distinctly cinematic look. Add to that L.A. Noire's painstaking attention to historical detail and you are left playing a game that could easily pass for a film.

The story behind L.A. Noire is just as engaging as the game's graphics, keeping you not only mildly obsessed with solving the crimes, but totally enthralled by the genius cutaways. Multiple stories intertwine with the solving of cases, covering everything from World War II flashbacks to the inner workings of Los Angeles mob. The plots are so seamless woven together that you can't help but get lost in the story, occasionally to the detriment of police work. For me, L.A. Noire's version of the Black Dahlia murder was utterly engrossing, and one of the more plausible theories of the crime that I've seen in any form.

Overall, L.A. Noire is far and away one of the most entertaining and beautifully crafted gaming experiences I've ever had. If you haven't delved into this spectacular world yet, now is the time. You won't regret it.

Rating: 4 Corrupt Business Men out of 5

LAUNCHING BELLY DANCE IN AMERICA
THE CHICAGO WORLD'S FAIR OF 1893

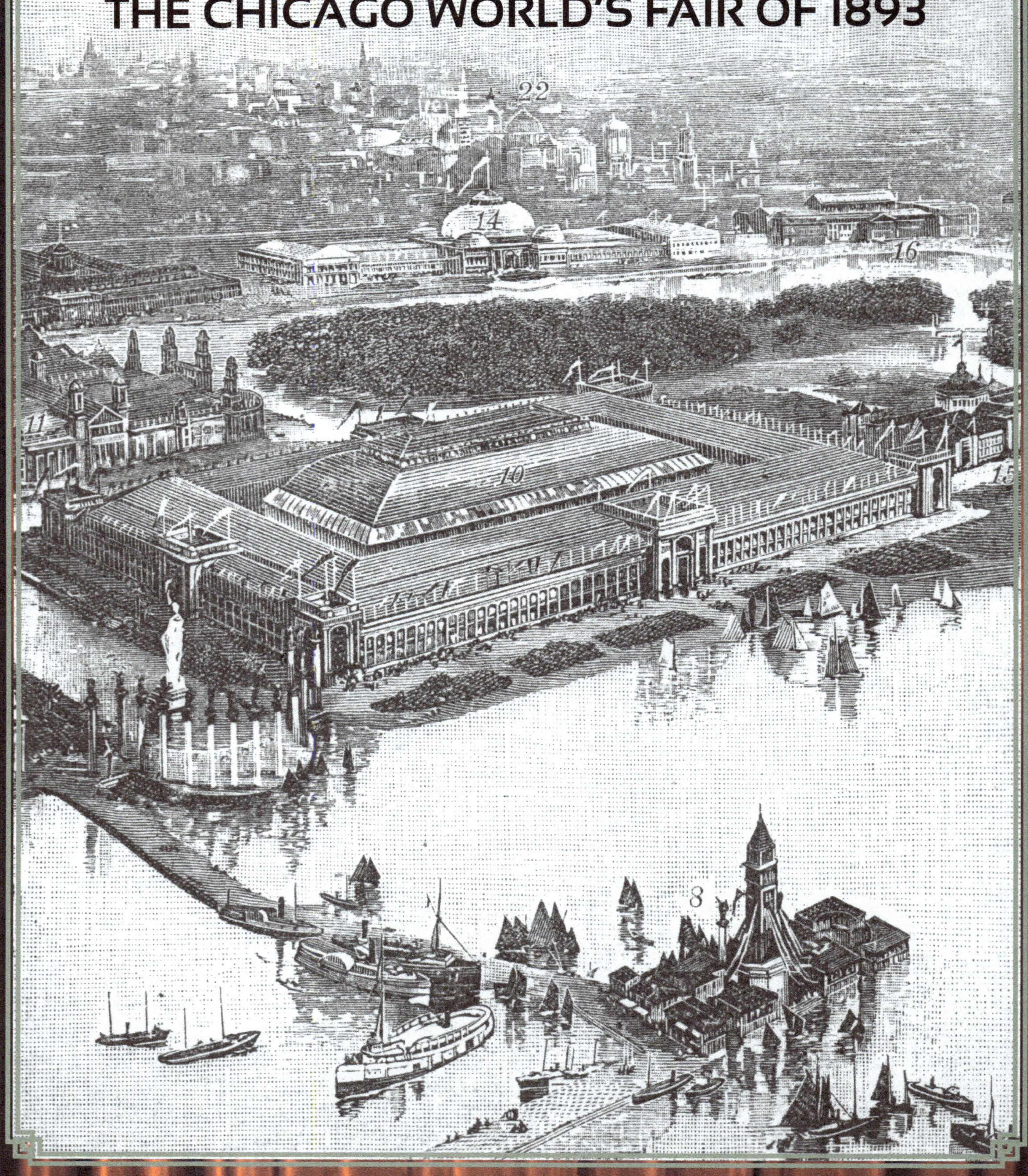

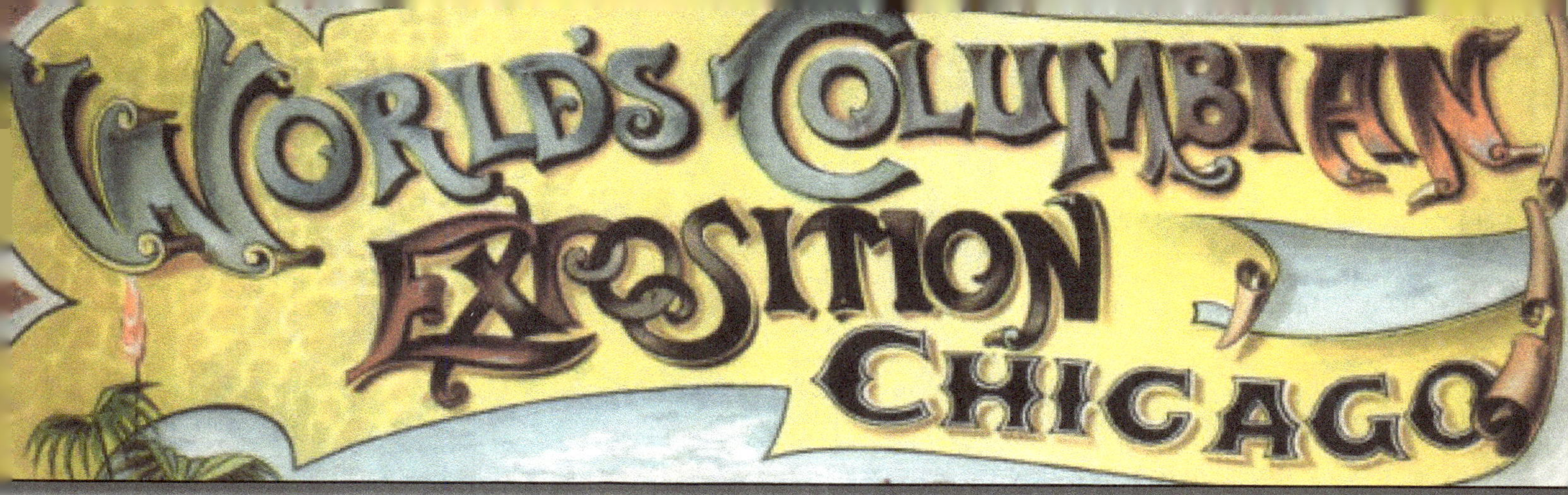

By Jezibell Anat

Come boys, let's away to the Midway Plaisance,
There are visions of loveliness there to behold
Oh, the lithe Moorish maidens with bangles of gold
And eyes that will set you afire at a glance...

And hush, we will see that Algerian dance –
Come boys, let's away to the Midway Plaisance.

Eugene Fields

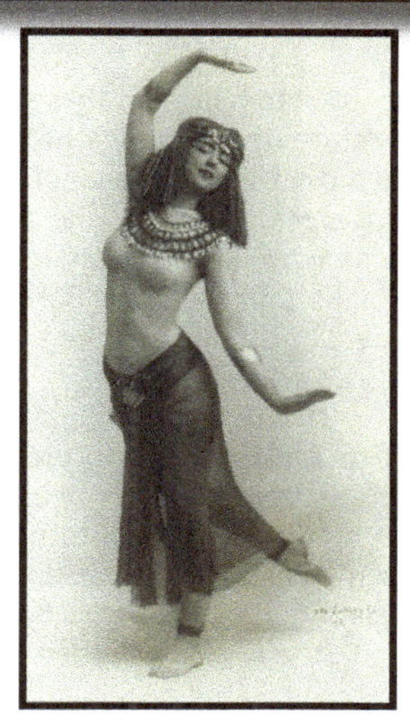

I first learned about the Middle Eastern dancers of the Chicago World's Fair of 1893 in the history section of a classic instructional book, The Serena Technique of Belly Dancing by the renowned teacher and performer Serena. To my modern American eye, these dancers looked pretty tame, even a little boring, but for their time, they were a game-changer for the controversial art that would become known as belly dance.

With the internet and the abundance of information we can now access through Google, it is easy to forget how difficult communication used to be and how little people knew of the world in the nineteenth century. One global link was the series of international expositions known as World's Fairs that provided large-scale displays of culture, history, craftsmanship, and science to a cosmopolitan audience from 1880 to World War I.

These Fairs highlighted the industrial and technological revolution. They presented the development of the steam engine, telephone, typewriter, and other advances that would become the basis of modern life. Fair exhibits brought people together, stimulated trade and influenced styles in fashion, art and architecture.

When Chicago won the right to stage the 1893 World's Fair, it was similar in prestige and publicity to a city being the host of the Olympics today. But instead of bringing in crowds for a few days, the Fair lasted for six months, opening on May 1 and continuing until October 30. This particular event was also known as the Columbian Exposition, celebrating four hundred years since Columbus arrived in America. With forty-six nations participating, it was probably the most spectacular of all the World's Fairs. Chicago at the time was most known for its slaughterhouses, so hosting the Fair was a chance to improve its image.

Seeking to outdo its predecessors, Chicago's Expo featured art galleries, halls of science, and "native villages." These ethnic exhibits were meant to show the "primitive" way of life in Africa, Asia, and the Pacific Islands, and to demonstrate the progress of civilization leading to its culmination in the West. This Expo attracted a wide audience - approximately 1 out of 4 people in the United States came to see it, and it provided both an economic boost and a cultural awakening. Here, America witnessed the new wonder of electricity for the first time.

> ***Expecting to be refused he demanded a thousand dollars a week, which was more than the President of the United States.***

The Fair was designed to be a dazzling panorama, consisting of a vast garden layout, spread over 600 acres. The structures housing the exhibitions were built with classical facades, white-plastered pillars and porticoes, along the shores of Lake Michigan, forming a grand complex which became known as the "White City". This fabulous White City led to a resurgence in neo-classical architecture and became the inspiration for the design of the Emerald City in Frank L. Baum's The Wizard of Oz."

Despite all the erudition and refinement of the White City's high-minded displays, the main profits for the Expo came from the noisy, lively Midway Plaisance, a mile-long entertainment zone with amusements for the working-class patrons. Among the acts were a young Harry Houdini. The Midway introduced hamburgers, carbonated soft drinks and the Ferris wheel, as well as exotic animals, but it is most famous for the jugglers, acrobats, magicians, and the female performers who became known as belly dancers. This Midway and its entertainment became so popular that it became a staple of American carnivals.

Although the Oriental dancer had been a frequent subject of art, only upper class travelers from Europe and America had ever been able to see them in their countries of origin. The 1893 World's Fair brought the dance to audiences of all classes through promoter Sol Bloom (1870 - 1949). Bloom had made a reputation for his advertising and organization abilities in the New York theatre world, and he had visited the Paris International Exposition of 1889.

The Paris Expo was most famous for building the signature structure the Eiffel Tower, but it also featured many representations of global culture. Among the most popular entertainments were the sinuous dancers from the French colonies of North Africa, who were able to undulate their midsections in what was called the danse du ventre (literally, "dance of the stomach").

Bloom acquired the contract to represent these Algerian performers in the New World. Upon returning to America, he found that the Chicago organizers were bogged down in their goal of creating a refined and dignified concept for the Midway, which he described as "about as intelligent a decision as it would be today to make Albert Einstein the manager of the Ringling Brothers and Barnum and Bailey Circus." Bloom was under no pedantic delusions - he knew that people would rather be entertained than edified.

So Bloom headed off to San Francisco to promote boxing matches. The Expo's organizers realized that they needed someone with his business acumen, and they asked Bloom to name his own salary to become manager of the Midway Plaisance. Expecting to be refused, he demanded a thousand dollars a week, which was more than the President of the United States. Instead, they gave it to him, and he proved to be worth it.

Bloom moved his family to Chicago and began the business of recruitment, importing dancers from Algeria, Tunisia, Egypt, Syria, Turkey, and what was then called Palestine. His next step was marketing, and the dance needed a name. Americans knew enough French to translate the danse du ventre into belly dance, but that was not a term that could be used in polite society of the time. In underground word play, "belly" was also a reference to the notorious San Francisco dance hall, the Bella Union, which offered racy entertainment to male customers from the 1840's Gold Rush through the 1906 earthquake. This play on words immediately gave the dance a suggestive reputation.

Through venues on the Midway such as the Algerian Theatre and the Persian Palace, these enticing performances were touted as "Houri's

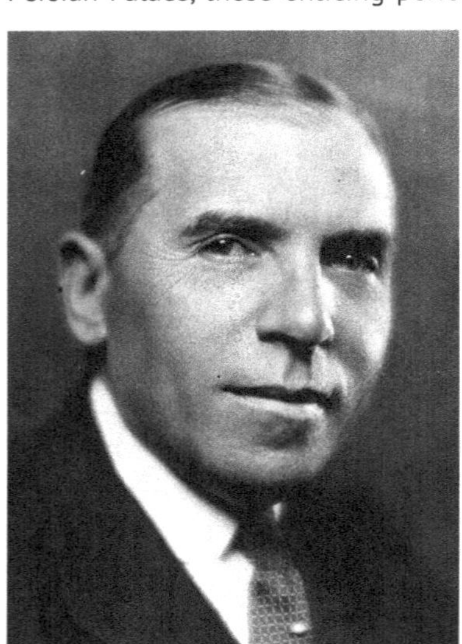

Dance," "Moorish Dance," and "Nautch Dance." Except for the geographical name Moorish, these terms also had sexual overtones. In Islam, the houri are the beautiful maidens who awaited the devout in Paradise, and the Nautch were a class of professional female dancers of northern India who performed primarily for men.

Another less flattering label for them was "Hootchy Kootchy," a term borrowed from contemporary descriptions of the sharp movements in the dances of African-Americans. Some of the shimmies and

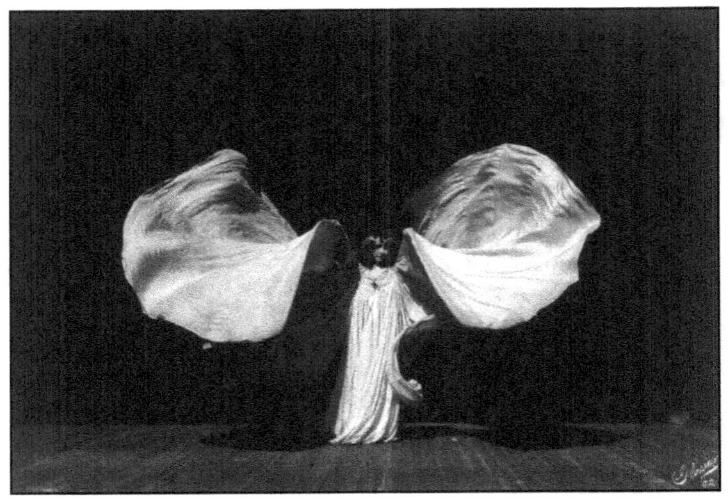

linear movements of Middle Eastern dance appeared jerky and awkward to the American eye.

When the Fair first opened, business was stagnant, until a Chicago minister saw fit to denounce "that dance," and then attendance soared. Bloom later wrote in his memoirs, "It is regrettable -- of, if anyone should choose to disagree, it is at least a fact -- that more people remember the reputation of the danse du ventre than the dance itself. This is very understandable. When the public learned that the literal translation was "belly dance" they delightedly concluded that it must be salacious and immoral. The crowds poured in. I had a gold mine."

The common assumption is this dance was perceived as scandalous because of the lack of clothing, but the dancers' torsos were covered. Part of that perception was simply the difference in the styles of dance. In general Western dance is based in footwork, while Middle Eastern dance employs the full range of the torso.

But the greatest shock to Victorian audiences was that these dancers' bodies were not confined and that they enjoyed so much freedom of movement. While Western women were heavily corseted and crinolined in layers of fabric, these foreign dancing girls in flowing skirts and beads were easily stretching and circling their arms, hips and shoulders.

As Sol Bloom later wrote: "As a matter of strict fact, the danse du ventre, while sensuous and exciting, was a masterpiece of rhythm and beauty; it was choreographed perfection and it was so recognized by even the most untutored spectators. Whatever they had hoped to see they were enchanted by the entertainment actually placed before them."

Almost at once this dance was imitated in amusement parks all over the country. As it became debased and vulgarized it began to acquire the reputation that survives today – that of a crude, suggestive dance known as "The Hootchy-Kootchy."

Until the Fair, the belly dance was considered a titillation for men, but in Chicago the dance aroused a great response among the women, as well. Some were horrified - the Board of Lady Managers complained, but the dance was too popular to be shut down. Other women were challenged and encouraged. The fluidity, sensuality and strength of these exotic dancers provided an obvious contrast to the rigidly respectable ladies of America, who were expected to be delicate and demure.

These dancers also had an economic impact, for they were compensated well for their work. The most popular dancer became known as "Little Egypt." Her real name was Fahreda Mazar Spyropoulos (c. 1871 - 1937), and she was Syrian, the wife of a Greek-born Chicago restauranteur. She and other dancers, including some Western imitators, went on to perform at parties, carnivals and fairs. So many of them claimed to be Little Egypt that this name became identified with belly dancers in general. But Fahreda was recognized as the original, and she danced as Little Egypt in 1933 at Chicago's Century of Progress Fair.

The dancers at the 1893 Expo expanded awareness of the Oriental influence that had been filtering into more respectable entertainment as well. Its most familiar manifestation in theatre and opera was in the biblical story of Salome. Though her actual name is not mentioned in the New Testament, Salome is thought to be the young daughter of Queen Herodias, whose dance so pleased King Herod that he offered to give her whatever she asked, up to half his kingdom. Herodias told the girl to ask for the head of John the Baptist, and Herod reluctantly complied.

There is nothing in the Biblical account indicating a sexual aspect to her dance. Given the literary and historical context, the girl's dance was probably the Levantine equivalent of a charming and naive Shirley Temple rather than a lustful seductress. However, the Salome story has been interpreted in many ways and forms, ranging from spiritual revelation to languid debauchery.

One of the first versions of Salome was performed by modern dancer Loie Fuller, who was known for her theatrical manipulations of flowing fabric in her shows. Her work may have inspired the flamboyant Irish author Oscar Wilde to write what is probably the world's most famous stage direction, "Salome dances the dance of the seven veils" in his play Salome, which premiered in 1896. This play inspired the opera of the same name by Richard Strauss in 1905.

Wilde's term "Dance of the Seven Veils" led to the extensive drapings, operations, and removals of the veil in Oriental-inspired dancing. The many Little Egypt copycats began devising their own performances of the "Dance of the Seven Veils," in which the term became a synonym for striptease.

However, this "Salomania" craze was not limited to entertainment for men. Florenz Ziegfeld also included Salome numbers in his lavish vaudeville revue, the Follies. Further, the roles of women were changing with the century, and the idea of the free, sensual, and powerful dancer became an inspiration. Many women were fascinated by the Salome story, and in 1908, the New York Times described a women's only Salome party where the ladies dressed as Salome and imitated her dance.

Surprisingly, Strauss' operatic version of Salome could still scandalize an audience in Chicago in 1910. In this production, Scottish-born soprano Mary Garden (1874 - 1967) appeared in a flesh-covered body stocking and kissed the head of John the Baptist. In describing her dance, Police Chief Roy T. Steward said, ``It was disgusting. Miss Garden wallowed around like a cat in a bed of catnip." But this performance made her a household name, and despite her wallowing in catnip, she later became Director of the Chicago Opera.

Continuing and developing the Oriental influence in modern dance was Ruth St. Denis (1879 – 1968). She began her career as a vaudeville skirt dancer, but, while sipping a soda in a drugstore, she became intrigued by a poster for Egyptian Deity cigarettes that portrayed the Goddess Isis. She persuaded the clerk to give her the poster, and it led her to study the

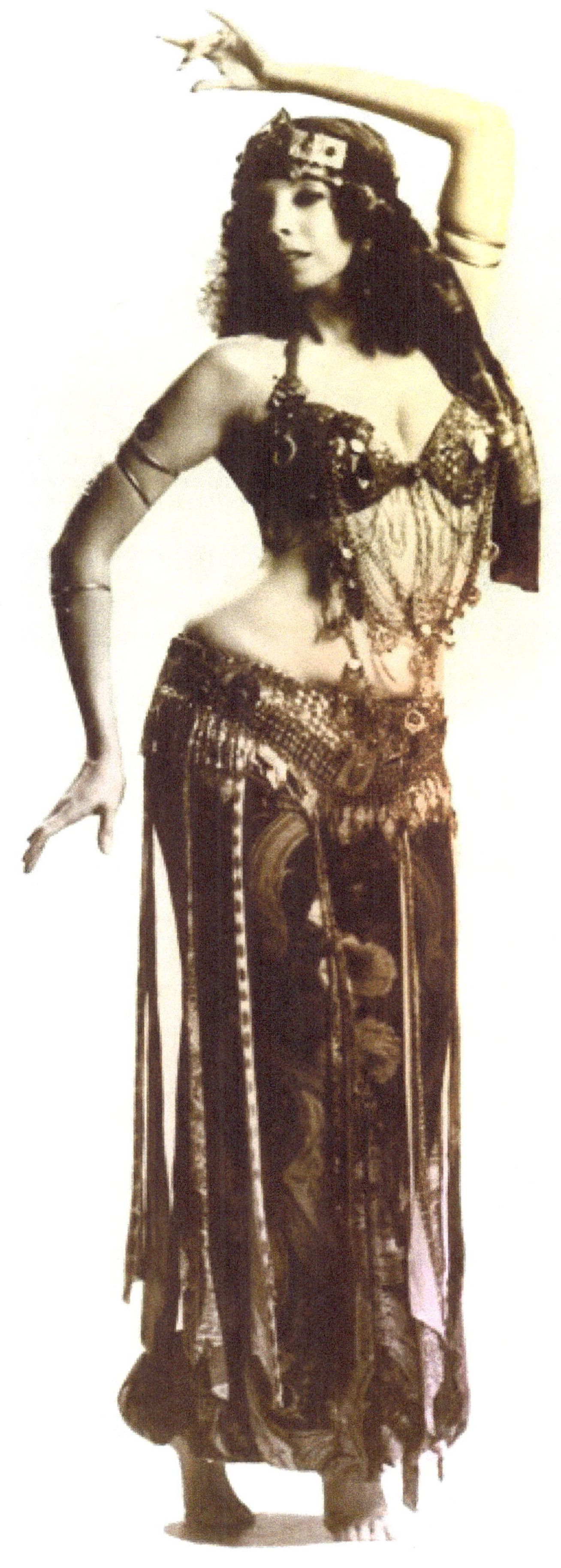

Serena

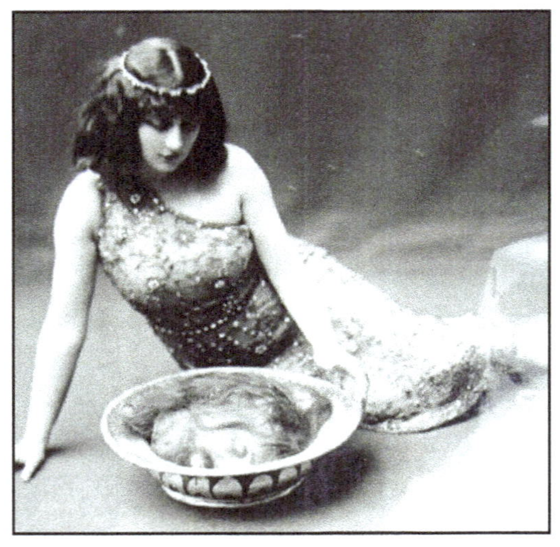

spiritual aspects of Eastern dance. Working with Indian immigrants in New York, she created her own interpretations of Egyptian and Hindu dance, bringing Oriental mysticism into Western art.

She also taught many dancers, and one of her last students was the young Serena Wilson (born

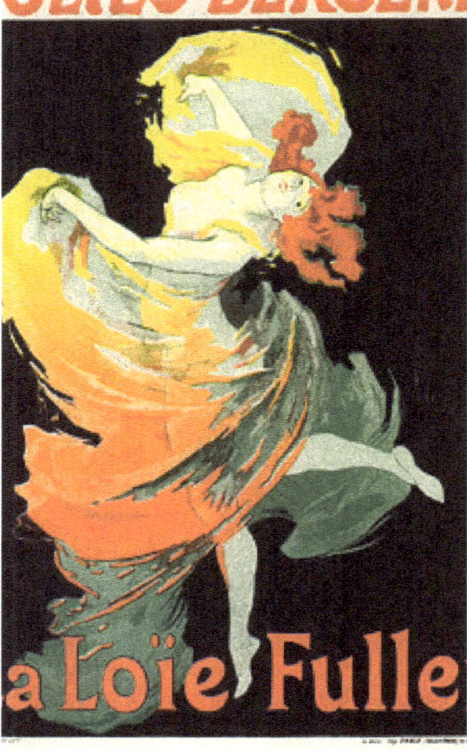

Serene Blake, 1933 - 2007), who grew up to become one of the iconic first generation New York City belly dance performers and instructors. Serena was born into a vaudeville family, Blake & Blake, and she often appeared onstage with her parents. They provided her with an artistic and eclectic education which included Russian ballet, sculpture and fashion, but one of Serena's main inspirations was Ruth St. Denis, and thus she described her lessons:

Ruth St. Denis was seated on a couch that was draped with a silk fabric brilliantly patterned with flowers. She sat throughout the entire lesson, and only dealt with movement of the arms. After I had taken a

"Miss Garden wallowed around like a cat in a bed of catnip!"

few classes with her, Miss St. Denis presented my mother with a copy of her book, An Unfinished Life. In it she had inscribed, 'To my youngest student at this time, Serene Blake, whose future I watch with great affection'.

Serena became a top performer in the Manhattan nightclub circuit, and she also choreographed elaborate shows for the Serena Dance Theatre. Her style was interpretive belly dance, and she was renowned for her poise, sophistication, and personal approach to the dance. However, she never forgot her roots in vaudeville. One of her signature dances was an homage called "Kootch", in which she portrayed a statue of a carnival dancer who comes to life, discovering movement as she plays her zils, then returning to her pedestal.

Serena's book first came out in 1972 and went through several reprints. It was one of the earliest books on belly dance for a mainstream audience, and her focus was on the fitness and health aspects of this style of dance for women. When I lived in New York, I had the privilege of studying extensively with Serena, and I also taught and performed with her studio. She also led us on trips to Egypt, Morocco and Turkey where we could see the traditional dancers and buy locally crafted costumes. One time, she even put me in a black wig to portray Little Egypt in a history of belly dance revue.

Belly dance has gone through several phases of popularity, and now, with increasing research and study, we have discovered a great deal more about the authentic dances and cultures of the Middle East than we ever could have known in the twentieth century. But belly dance in America has always been a mix of fantasy and folklore, and, unbound by more repressive societies, we are willing to be creative.

We know that the presentation of the dancers at the World's Fair was not an accurate representation of Middle Eastern culture. It was a

romanticized portrayal of the exotic other. But even an overlay of Arabian Nights fantasy with silly cliches of sultans and harem girls provided a more appealing image of the Middle East than our current association with terrorism and fundamentalist religion.

Serena herself never claimed to be an ethnographer. She would view regional dances and choose the most interesting aspects to form her choreographies. Unlike a lot of belly dancers, she did not deny the connection to vaudeville and even high-class burlesque. I even saw her play a washboard! Also, most belly dancers in the 1960's wore extremely revealing costumes for their lucrative nightclub shows.

Once, Serena told us that she had opened for strippers as a belly dancer. She was always careful to remind us that these were the days in which strippers did not take everything off, and that their performance was the classy theatrical act of reveal and conceal, a dance that is gaining popularity again as neo-burlesque. Like Sol Bloom, she knew people would rather be entertained than educated.

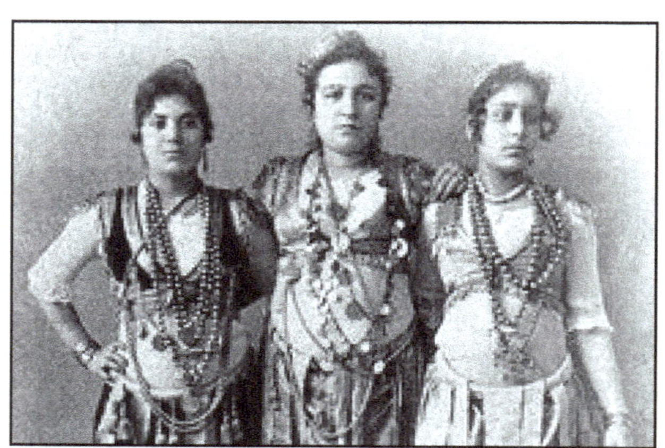

How To Develop A Daily Art Ritual:

By Zahara

By talking to various dancers and artists around the world, I often hear the same item mentioned when it comes to continually improving at their craft. That is the task of daily practice. Whether you aspire to become a professional artist, or you simply enjoy creating as a hobby (or cathartic outpouring), you will gain much more from your endeavors if you do a little bit every day.

If you find this idea to be daunting, keep in mind that you set the guidelines. I've found that creating a ritual around my artistic time has made a huge difference in my focus and commitment to writing and dancing every day.

Some artists go into their favorite space (studio, library, etc.) and expect to simply fall into being "creative". While this does work for some people, most of time, we find ourselves distracted and overwhelmed with the possibilities of what we could/should be doing. Creating a ritual around your art that is easy to follow will help solve these problems.

Here are a few guidelines to keep in mind when developing your artistic ritual.

Here's a sample of one of my old writing "opening rituals":

- Brew coffee
- Mentally set the intention for today's writing and bring that intention into my writing space
- Put on music
- Light three candles
- Burn incense
- Sit in comfortable chair
- Set favorite pencil and journal on desk
- Set purple cards off to the side for capturing ideas and inspirations
- Close my eyes and energetically join the space by taking three deep breaths
- State my intention (silently or softly) for today's practice
- Open my eyes and compose!

DURATION: Rather than setting a goal that may be unreasonable to keep (such as one hour), start by setting the minimum amount of time you can definitely devote to your art on a daily basis. Even if you can only commit 15 minutes every day, it's a starting point. In my opinion, it's better to start with a shorter duration each day, knowing that you're going to spend more time whenever possible, than to refuse to do anything artistic for an entire day because you cannot spend a large amount of time to the practice.

LOCATION: This should be a space you enjoy and one that makes you feel uninhibited and inspired. If you find the space to be claustrophobic, distracting, cluttered or frustrating, then you may need to spend time establishing a more conducive space. If you feel most inspired in your living room or at the kitchen table, so be it!

TIMING: The majority of my friends are night owls, who find they're wide awake and ready to create after midnight. I personally enjoy very early morning hours, when it's quiet and dark in my home, and I feel most alive, invigorated and refreshed. Perhaps you find a burst of creative energy in the afternoon, right after school or work. Everyone's creative timing is different, and you'll find that it's best to tap into your own time signature.

FOCUS: I try to choose one creative task before entering my space. It can be as specific as continuing or completing a particular project, or as unspecified as doodling. The point is to pick something ahead of time, which will keep you from getting distracted.

Once you've defined the items above, you can set about developing more specific steps in your ritual. Consider how you want your daily practice to begin and end, how to engage all your senses, and how to handle flashes of inspiration.

If I can simply enter this sacred space, then I'll be there as long as possible. We typically talk ourselves out of being creative, so just taking the first step is a major accomplishment. And artists are often their own worst critics. If we listen to the negative voices, we'll never get started. This process has provided me with a process for following my muse, as well as handling the frustrations, anger and stress of daily life. Imagine how much better you'll be at your craft and how much more inspired you'll feel by simply doing a little every day, following your own rituals.

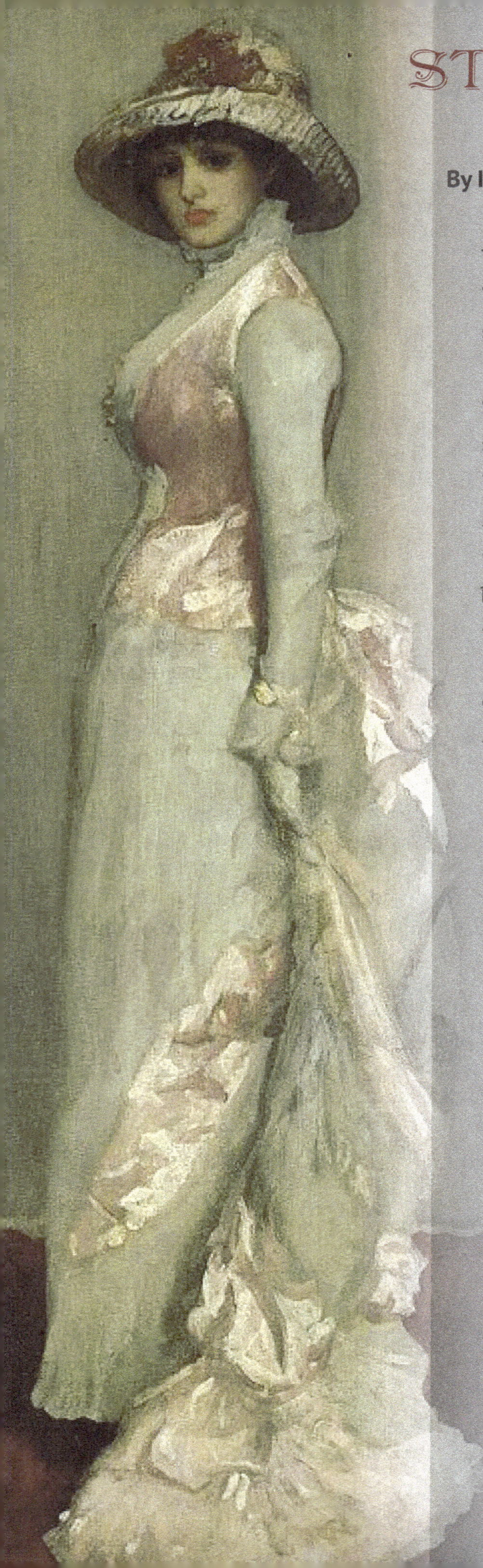

STEAMPUNK INSPIRED MAKEUP

By Isolde De Mortimer

When it comes to Steampunk makeup, there is no real standard. Try a quick internet search, and you'll see a vast variety of styles and ideas come up for "steampunk makeup".

Steampunk by definition has a Victorian/Edwardian fashion sense, yet when one pictures Victorian or Edwardian makeup, "very little" is what comes to mind. The simple concealer, foundation, a little blush, groomed brows, mascara, and lip balm will create an era-appropriate look, but isn't very fun. And being bellydancers and performers, the "no makeup" look isn't our typical style.

So while you're free to be creative, here are a few popular interpretive options to use as your guide and inspire your vision:

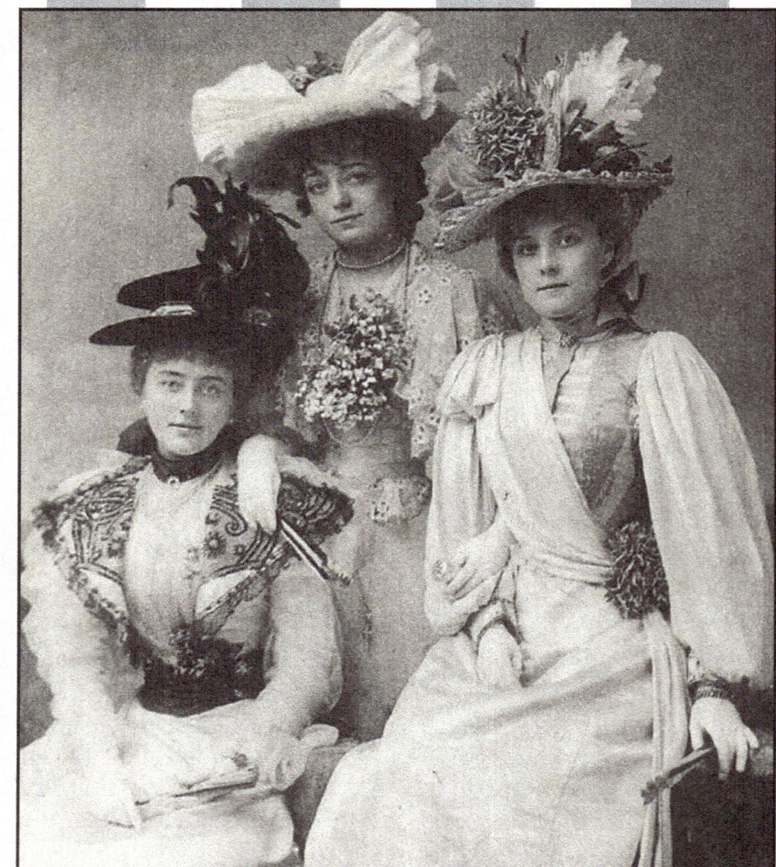

Working Girl

She's smart and tough and been hard at work repairing machinery, so she is smeared with grease and ash-covered. Use blacks and deep charcoal greys that mimic grease, dust, and grime. Apply dark smudges to your face and body. Keep your application simple yet bold, so that it will read properly for your audience from a distance.

Glamour

She's an Edwardian woman with a kick. Try a nude cut-crease eye in earthy colors and flesh tones paired with bold, winged liner. Fill in your brows and exaggerate your arch to really define them. You can add plenty of lashes with loads of mascara or falsies. Top it off with fiery red lips.

Dancehall

The American Wild West is encompassed in the Victorian timeframe, so for this look, think old west saloon girl with smoky eyes and nude lips. Colors to use include bronze, gold, and copper; warm metallics that bring brassy machinery to mind. Maybe even add a little beauty spot at the corner of one eye. All the emphasis is on the eyes so use a lighter, more natural shade of lip color to not detract from or compete with your facial focal point.

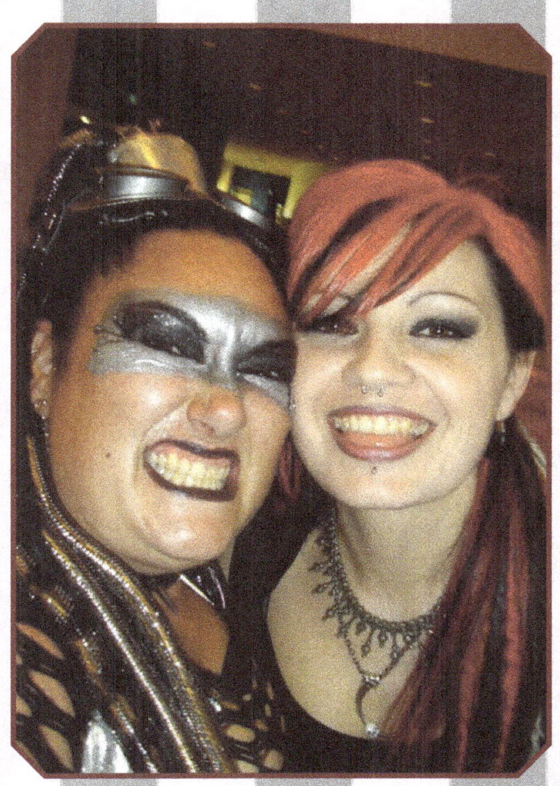

Edgy

Cogs, gears, etc. used in fun fantasy. Craft shops and hardware stores will have small, lightweight metallic bits and pieces you can adhere with eyelash or body glue. Apply them over your eyebrows, at the corners of your eyes, on your décolletage area, whatever you can come up with to combine machinery parts into your makeup. These accents could also be drawn or painted on with liner pencils or loose pigment and fixative. Because skin is so pliable, if you're going to use actual pieces glued onto your skin, be certain to practice in full makeup to make sure nothing is going to pop off while you're shimmying.

Since there are no real Steampunk makeup rules, you're free to be wildly innovative. Take your venue and costume into consideration when finalizing your makeup plans. For example, if you'll be wearing goggles, there's no need for elaborate eye makeup or if your venue is large, small makeup details like a daintily drawn on beauty mark, will be missed by your audience, so don't waste your product or time on them.

Above all, do what makes you feel in character and beautiful

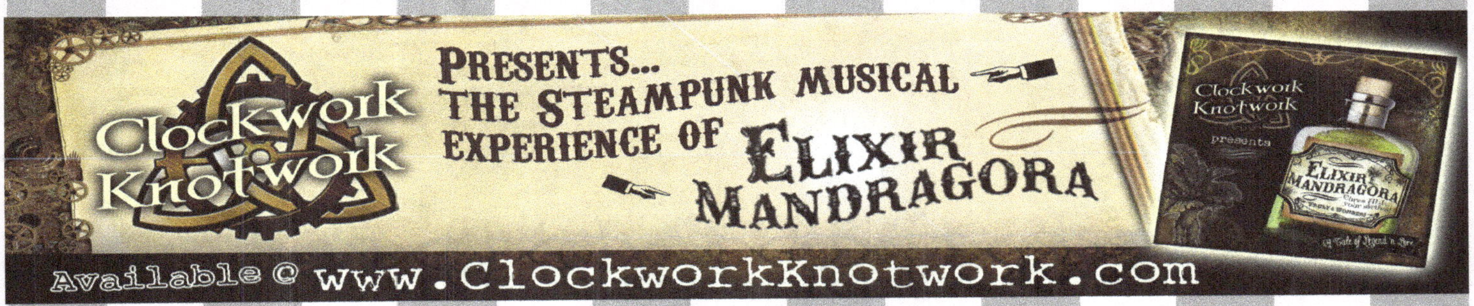

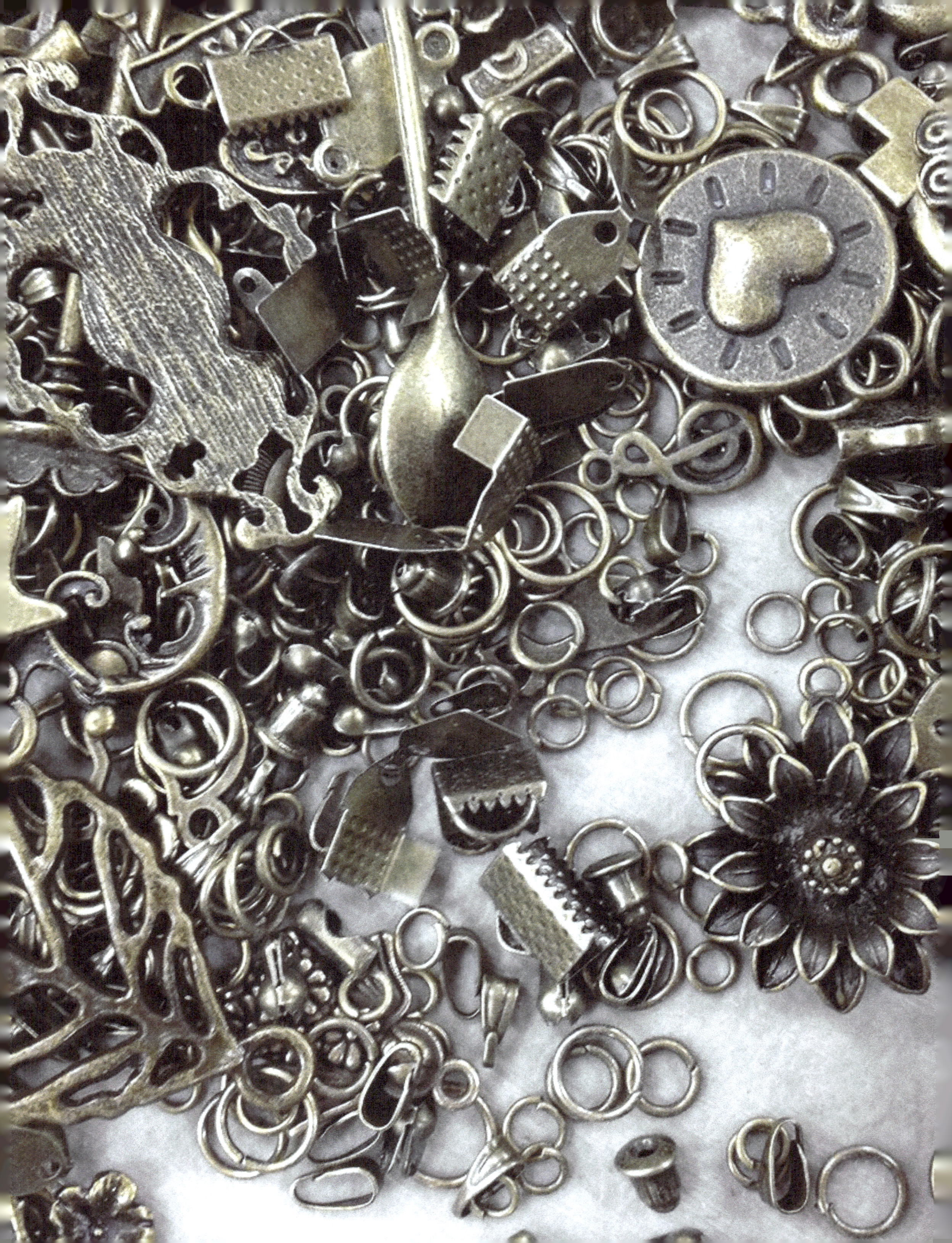

STEAM UP MY BELLYDANCE

JEWELRY FOR YOUR BELLYDANCE

By Yasaman Vrd'dhi

Are you ready to spice up and steam up your belly dance jewelry and embellishments? Well, this is the article for you. There are many ways to bring Steampunk into your belly dance. Jewelry is one and embellishments for your costuming is another. With jewelry, you can either get crafty and create your own, or search the web and local events and purchase some. If you are crafty, but don't know where to start or understand how to make Steampunk-based jewelry, then please read on.

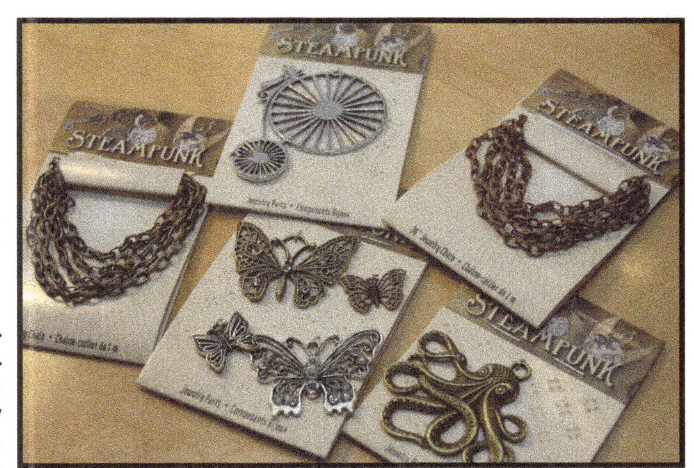

I recommend going to your local A.C. Moore, Joann, or even Walmart. Also, if you are an online shopper, then that opens even more doors. Just going to a local store, you can see and feel the textures of the items until you become familiar with them by look. A.C. Moore has a very nice line of Steampunk pieces, pre-made pieces and embellishments for jewelry making. If you are super crafty and want pieces that are unique, then you can use things like old antique jewelry, old watches, old skeleton keys, gears, chains and things along those lines.

Next thing is your glue. There are different ways to put your jewelry together, depending on what materials you are using. For example, for things like leather and cotton, you can use "Mighty Mendit." For pipe, metal and coppers, use "Copper Bond" and for plastics to metal, use "Gorilla Glue" or "Super Glue Epoxy." If you are a beginner (or on a budget), you can use a hot glue gun, but this could result in pieces falling off and repairs being needed. A way to help with that is to scuff the back side of the pieces you intend to use in your design. This will give the glue a surface to set in, helping it stay longer. There are more skills you can learn for making Steampunk jewelry, such as soldering (which you should look into, if this is something you would like to do on a regular basis).

Embellishments are used the same way, and for Steampunk are the same things used in making your jewelry (gears, keys, copper, etc.). If you are embellishing your costume, you can use hot glue, since fabric will be your base. Note again, if your fabric is leather or cotton, use Mighty Mendit as your adhesive onto which you will be applying the embellishments. Some embellishment pieces can be sewn on, if there are small holes on the embellishment, although hot glue is faster and works very well.

So get designing or buying. Good luck.

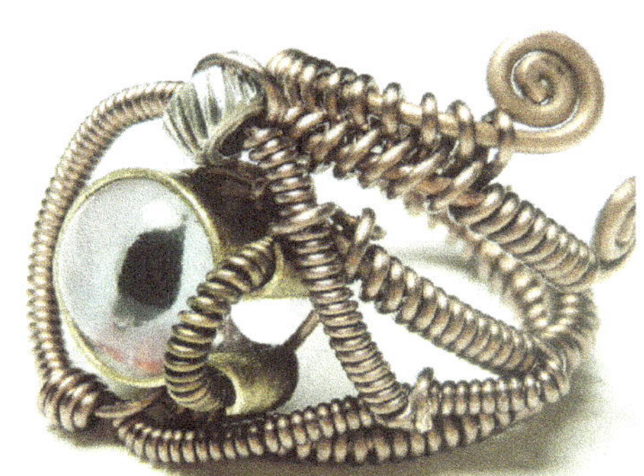

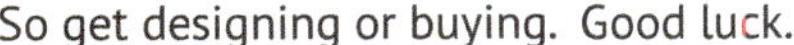

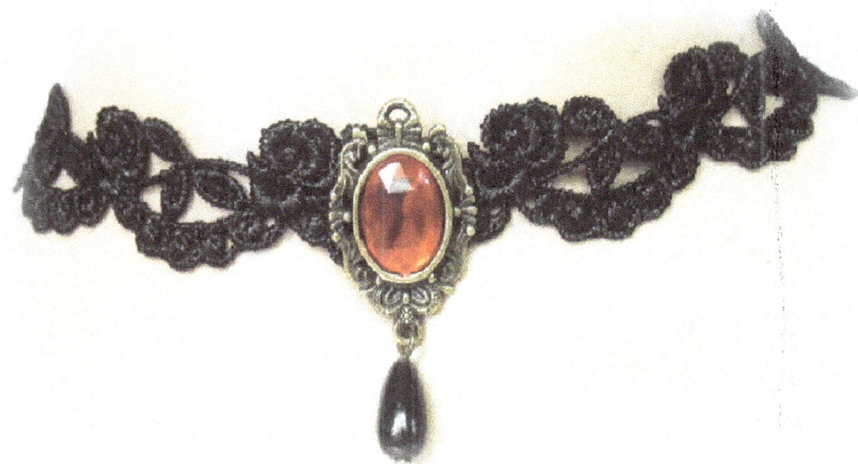

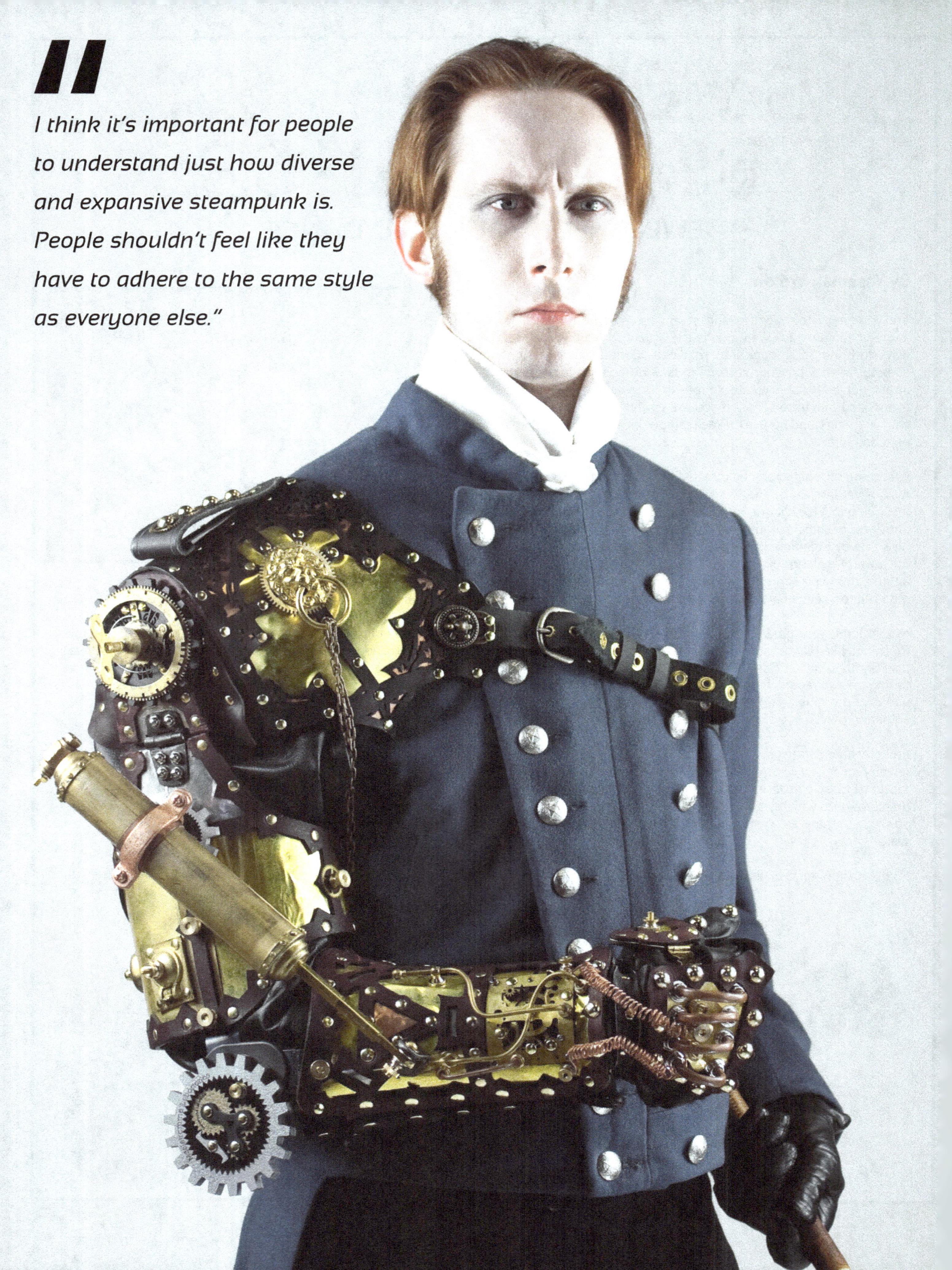

"

I think it's important for people to understand just how diverse and expansive steampunk is. People shouldn't feel like they have to adhere to the same style as everyone else."

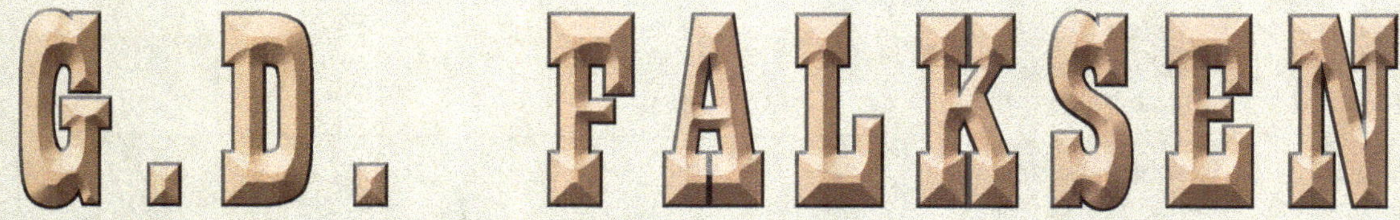

G.D. FALKSEN

NOTED WRITER AND STEAMPUNK FASHION AUTHORITY

By Kathleen Sharkey

Described as one of the foremost authorities on Steampunk GD Falksen has been one of the strongest proponents of the steampunk movement. As a fiction writer and blogger, not to mention he looks amazing in Steampunk costumes, Mr. Falksen has been a go to guy for all things Steampunk. So I was terribly excited when he agreed to take time out of his busy schedule and talk about the fashion of Steampunk.

[Carpe Nocturne] *First and foremost can you introduce yourself?*

[G. D. Falksen] My name is G. D. Falksen. I am the author of several books and short stories, including The Ouroboros Cycle series and a forthcoming YA book being released by Soho Teen in 2016.

[Carpe Nocturne] *Can you define Steampunk Fashion for our readers?*

[G.D.F] Steampunk fashion is simply fashion inspired by steampunk fiction and the steampunk aesthetic, essentially the sort of thing that you might find someone wearing in a steampunk novel or film. It's a diverse and varied style that combines the elegance of the 19th century with tremendous creativity and imagination.

[CN] *Since Steampunk Fashion is based off of Victorian élan does the variety of Victorian fashion across the world fit in (ie. The American West during the Victorian era, Asian acculturation during the time period) or does the fashion have to be based upon British/European Victoriana?*

[G.D.F] High Victorian styles are often the most seen in steampunk (which is likely the result of late 19th century Britain's visibility in our modern popular culture), but in fact steampunk and steampunk fashion draw upon influences from the whole of the 19th century (and the 20th century up to the First World War) and from the entire world during that time period. Historically, the technological advancements of the period allowed for an unprecedented level of interaction between people across the world, and logically the even greater level of technology in steampunk would only increase this. In short, any culture or civilization that existed during the 19th century has an equal and valid role to play in steampunk fiction and fashion.

[CN] *Aside from the obvious are there any stand out differences between women's and men's Steampunk fashions? Are these differences due to the historical time frame constraints or has the fact that Steampunk is a modern fashion trend created other differences/or lack thereof?*

[G.D.F] In a broad sense, men's and women's steampunk fashions would be influenced by the styles of the culture and time period they are drawing on (which, as I mentioned previously, is a very diverse topic that spans more than 100 years and the entire globe), but being a modern construction it allows for much greater freedom (it would

have been taboo for a woman to wear a suit in the Victorian era; that is obviously no longer the case today). Really, steampunk fashion is about choice, options, and personal expression. It's about people drawing upon a historical period to help express their own personal style.

[CN] *How would a Steampunk newcomer go about starting his or her own costume?*

[G.D.F] One of the great things about steampunk fashion is that it's about clothing rather than costumes, which often makes it easier to put an outfit together. Certainly, clothes from the 19th century can be difficult to locate (and those that can be found are antiques and

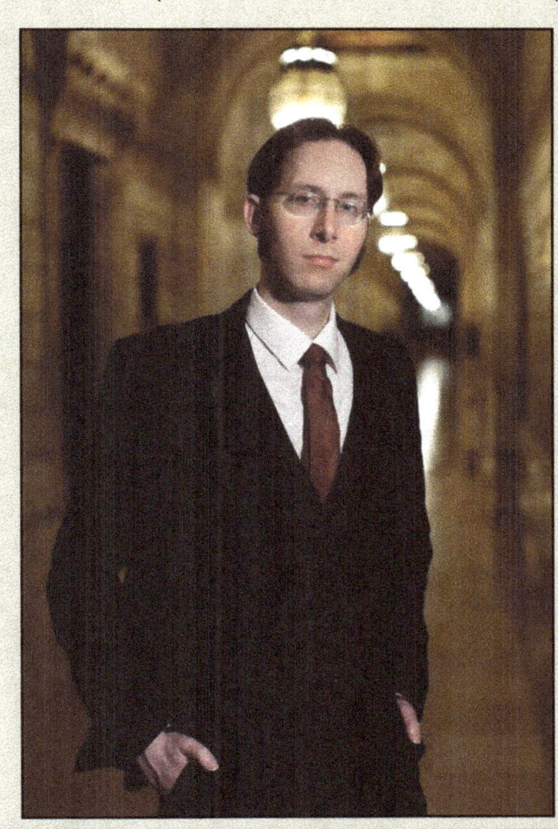

better preserved than worn) but for a person interested in sewing, most fabric shops have at least one or two patterns for recreating 19th century styles. And furthermore, for a person just starting out, the modern three piece suit is descended from Victorian men's casual wear, while an easy Edwardian women's outfit is simply an ankle-length skirt with a blouse, all of which are easy to find in thrift stores (assuming you don't have the pieces in your closet already). From those two simple bases, you can then accessorize or add to your heart's content.

[CN] *Are there some must haves when putting together a great Steampunk Costume?*

[G.D.F] I like to say "start historical and then add" for ease of assembly, but aside from that basic guideline there really isn't anything mandatory. It's all about drawing upon a mixture of period style and one's own imagination for personal expression.

[CN] *How does Dieselpunk and Steampunk differentiate in your opinion?*

[G.D.F] What's sometimes referred to as "dieselpunk" (alternatively you may be more familiar with the term "pulp adventure" or "pulp sci-fi") is a style of retrofuturist fiction and aesthetics based on the early and mid 20th century. It picks up where steampunk leaves off (at the end of the First World War) and continues on until shortly after the Second World War (I find it's easiest to say it covers from about 1920 to about 1950). Whereas steampunk takes the technology of the Victorian era (the steam engine and the various advancements it made possible) and says "what if?", pulp or "dieselpunk" does the same thing with technology in its time period (petroleum fuel, electricity, early generation computers, etc).

[CN] *What are some of your favorite Steampunk concepts?*

[G.D.F] I'm generally fascinated by the history of technology, so I especially enjoy the way that steampunk translates modern concepts or capabilities into a 19th century industrial context. A computer revolution growing from Babbage's Difference Engine and Analytical Engine, for example, or the use of the telegraph to simulate the modern Internet. It's all extremely interesting from both a fictional and a historical point of view.

[CN] *What concepts would you love to see done with a Steampunk twist?*

[G.D.F] I'm a big fan of spy-fi so I really enjoy seeing well done Victorian espionage, especially drawing on parallels to the Cold War.

[CN] *What would you like people to understand about Steampunk culture?*

[G.D.F] I think it's important for people to understand just how diverse and expansive steampunk is. People shouldn't feel like they have to adhere to the same style as everyone else. It's about personal expression coupled with a love of history, and I think it really is big enough to offer something to just about everyone.

[CN] *Are there any other things you would like to touch on about Steampunk fashion?*

[G.D.F] Above all, be yourself. All fashion is about expressing your own tastes and interests, so if you like 19th century fashion (and that's a really big topic) I say embrace it and use it to channel your own personal style.

http://www.gdfalksen.com
https://www.facebook.com/pages/G-D-Falksen

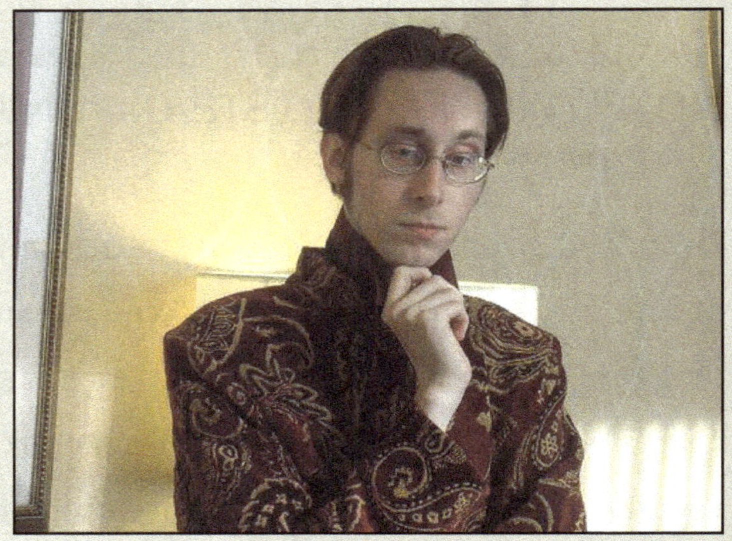

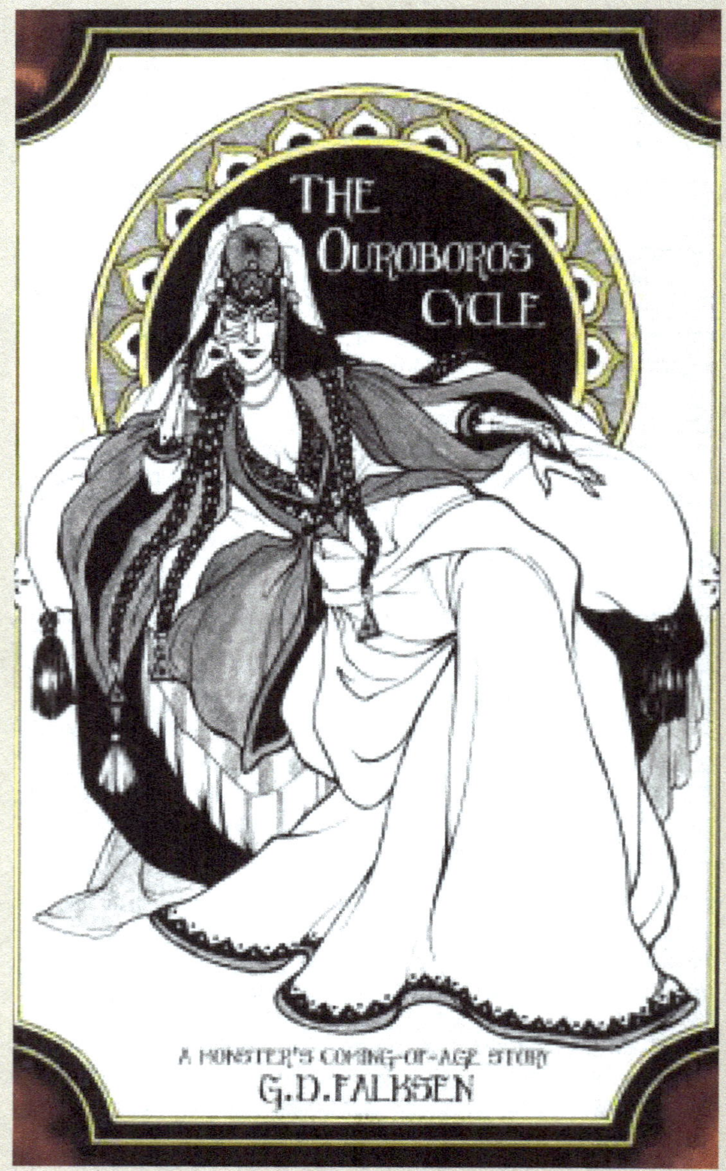

THE CREATIVE DREAMLANDS OF ARATHIN

By Asylum Attendant

I first stumbled upon the stunning Swedish alternative fetish model Arathin whilst blogging on Wordpress. Her fierce poses in corsets and latex ranging from gothic to fairy tale themes truly captivated me. Years later, I finally have the opportunity to share her entrancing work with the world. I got the chance to go in depth with Arathin and learned she's much more than a fiery model with a love of high heels.

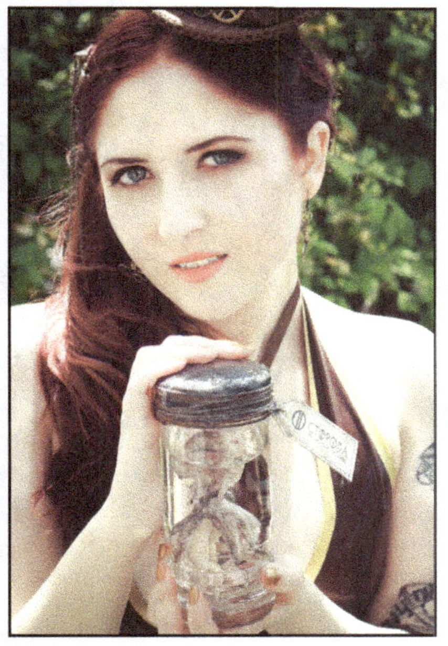

[Asylum Attendant] *What is the meaning behind the name Arathin and why did you decide on it as your model name?*

[Arathin] I came up with the name many years ago when I was going to participate in a fantasy LARP (live action role play, for those of you who don't know the term), although I can't for the life of me remember what character I was going to play. The event was unfortunately cancelled, but somehow the name stuck in my head. It's like something out of a fantasy novel with a bit of an edge to it, which fits my aesthetics perfectly. Today I can't think of a better artist name to go by.

[AA] *Your positive body image is refreshing and inspiring. How do you maintain a healthy sense of self-esteem in an appearance-based industry?*

[Arathin] It's all about knowing that you're worth more than just your looks, that you have other qualities that make you badass. I know I'm intelligent, hard-working and really good at what I do and that helps me feel good about myself. Yes, having a good/unique look is pretty important in this business. But I'm a firm believer in that if you are creative enough and that creativity shows, your inner beauty will shine through. Of course, even I have my bad days when it's really hard to keep this up. But that's usually fixed with some tea, chocolate and some sleep. Spending time with my friends also works, or to talk with the models from The Alternative Model Directory, that I'm also a part of. We're like a family and we always have each other's backs no matter what. And that's a really good feeling to have.

[AA] *Who are your favorite Steampunk fashion designers or clothing companies?*

[Arathin] Oh there are so many to choose from! But some of my favorites are Morrigan, Clockwork Couture, Rosies Art, Retroscope Fashions and Steampunk Couture. However, I'm a huge accessory freak and that's what I really love to look for. In that department my favorites are MADmoiselle Méli H (who's also a very talented model), Catherinette Rings, Brute Force Studios, Tom Banwell, Hysteria Machine and Tragically Adorned. I love taxidermy jewelry as well and for that I mostly turn to Lady Locks Creations. I'm currently collecting her tentacle jewelry, being the octopus lover that I am. And I have to mention corset designer Viola Lahger, who has made nearly all of my corsets – including my custom made Steampunk one.

[AA] *I've seen that you make some of your own jewelry, clothing and accessories for your photo shoots. How important is it to possess a do-it-yourself spirit as a model?*

[Arathin] I think it's pretty important. For me, it helps to keep the creativity alive whenever I'm not shooting. It doesn't have to be making your own clothes and props. Basic things like putting

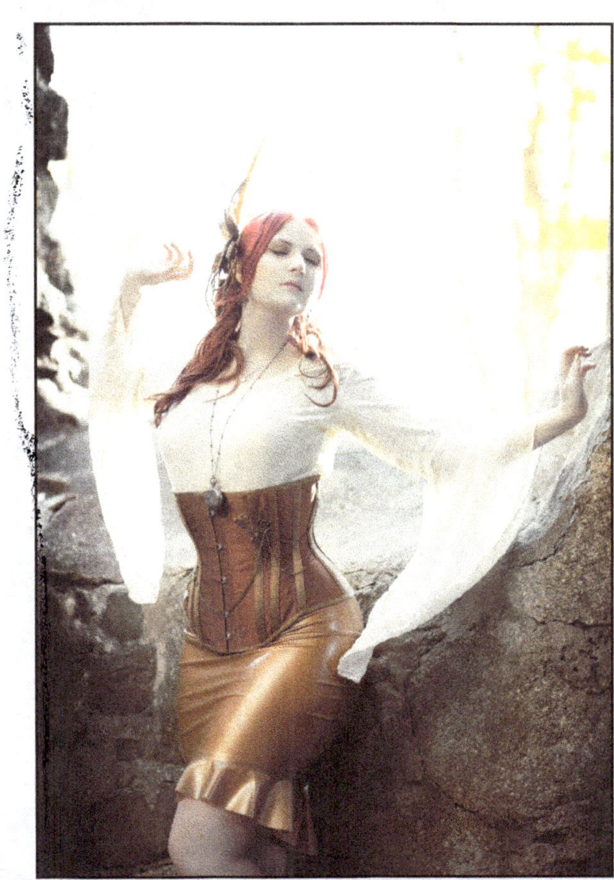

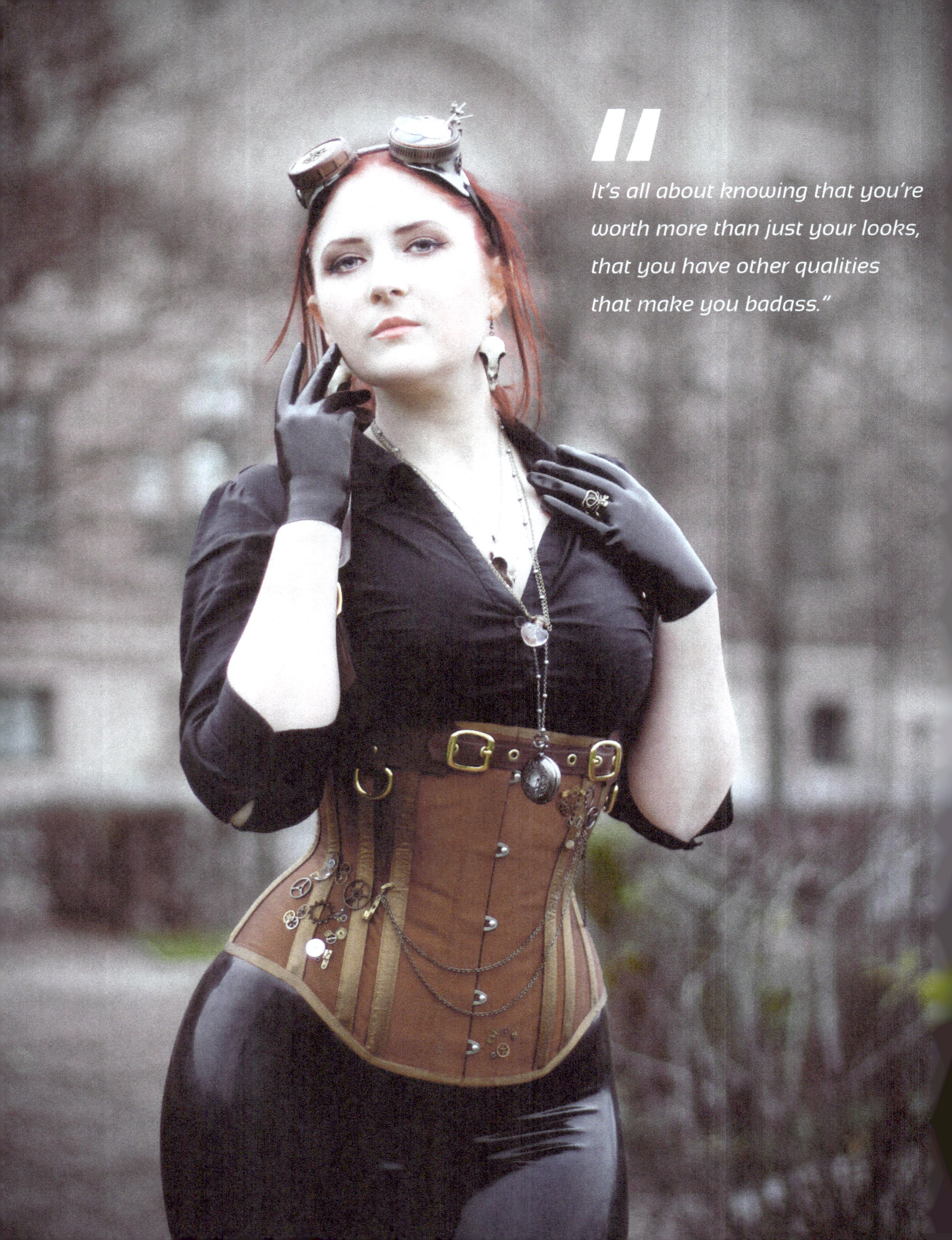
It's all about knowing that you're worth more than just your looks, that you have other qualities that make you badass."

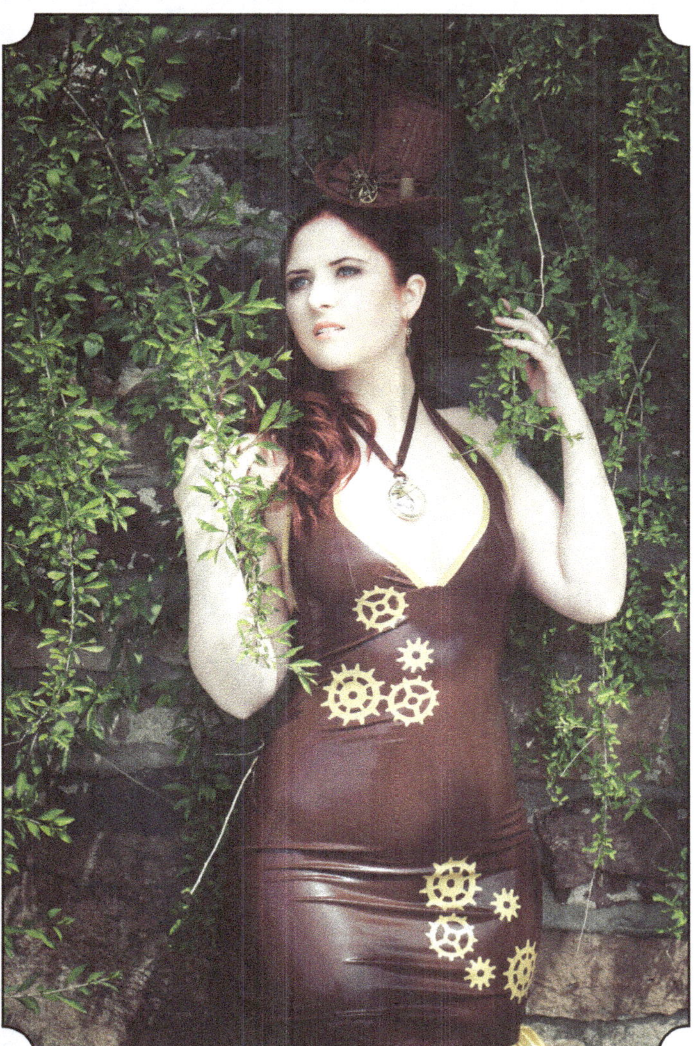

together the entire outfit, as well as knowing how to do the perfect makeup and hairstyling for the planned shoot are just as important and equally creative.

[AA] *Describe your unique spin on the Steampunk look.*

[Arathin] I have a tendency to mix traditional Steampunk with unconventional materials, like latex. Even though I love the traditional Victorian look, I mainly use it for inspiration. I don't like to do things "by the book"; it just doesn't work for me or help my creativity. I like to mix things up, to add things that originally aren't considered Steampunk and put them in a Steampunk context. So far I've gone from fairy tale/fantasy based Steampunk, to fetish oriented, to Gothic and Dieselpunk inspired. Mind you, I still haven't done a proper Victorian Steampunk shoot yet so that's one of the things still on my Steampunk To-Do List. I'm still learning about this whole subculture though, so I can't say that I have perfected my take on it yet.

[AA] *You make latex clothing look quite classy and elegant. What would you say to people who are hesitant to try wearing latex?*

[Arathin] First of all, thank you! But to answer your question, you want to start off small. Don't buy a catsuit the first thing you do, because if you realize you don't like it then you will have spent lots of money on something you will never use. Start with a pair of gloves or a basic skirt (if you're a woman, that is) or a top, and make sure you've read up on how to treat it properly. It might seem a strange material at first but once you're used to it you will find that it hugs your shape perfectly, feels smooth against the skin and has a lovely shine.

[AA] *I hear that you love to drink tea. What are some of your other hobbies besides modeling?*

[Arathin] I love reading and watching movies, mostly science fiction, horror, fantasy and fairy tales. I'm also a huge science geek and enjoy reading as well as watching documentaries on space, astrophysics and theoretical physics. I also collect octopuses and anything Lovecraft related, from books to stuffed animals. Alongside of all this I also love to solve crossword puzzles and cook. Seriously, food is my second passion apart from modeling. I love eating, cooking and learning about food, food chemistry and techniques.

[AA] *I think your stance to not pose nude is admirable. Do you feel a lot of pressure to pose nude as a fetish model?*

[Arathin] Of course there's a pressure, but I don't feel that affected by it. I have my personal reasons for not doing nudes, and they have nothing to do with the aesthetics of lingerie/nude modeling. I prefer to keep my clothes on and will leave the nude modeling to the beautiful ladies who do it best. I suppose there are some who think that to be a fetish model you have to pose nude, but I disagree. Fetish does not equal nudity in my world.

[AA] *Tea Time, the lovely alternative model and Ashbury Heights band member, is one of your biggest inspirations. Why do you look up to her so much?*

[Arathin] Tea Time is a very close friend of mine and she's also one of the people who got me back into modeling after a period of doubting myself as a model as well as my place in this business. I've learned a lot from helping her during shoots and also by watching her perform on stage during the years we have known each other. She's one of the most down to earth people I know and incredibly creative.

[AA] *Why did you choose alternative modeling over a more traditional modeling career? Does it give you more freedom to be yourself?*

[Arathin] It does give me more freedom but it wasn't really a question for me which direction I wanted to go in. I don't fit the standards of the traditional fashion model. I don't have the right shape and was also too old when I started out at 22. Alternative modeling allows me to be myself. I don't have to change radically to fit into any mold. And honestly, it's a lot more fun and creative.

[AA] *What's next to come from the Creative Dreamlands of Arathin?*

[Arathin] Next up are some more Steampunk and gothic shoots, hopefully I will be able to do a Lovecraft inspired one this year that I have been working on for quite some time. I'm also working on a few Cosplay shoots. I'm not really a Cosplay kind of girl, but these are characters that are very close to my heart so it feels like a good idea to bring them to life like this. I will probably put a little spin on them though and not make the outfits all that traditional. And of course there will be latex and corsets, I just can't go one year without shooting some of the traditional fetish attributes.

SPOTLIGHT FEATURE

There are a lot of truly talented people out there, especially in our culture. Some use this talent simply for passing the time and personal growth, while others develop their talent to create services, works and objects for others to enjoy. Some post their creations on their website and never try to sell their works, while others use their talents to supplement or create their income. Carpe Nocturne Magazine admires, respects, and supports YOUR TALENT!

Whether you are creating to sell or only for personal enjoyment, LET THE WORLD SEE WHAT YOU'VE GOT!
There is NEVER A CHARGE to be Spotlighted or Featured!

The feature within Carpe Nocturne Magazine spotlights artists, designers, photographers, crafters and others with a creative side.

Does your work relate to the subject matter of this publication. Whether you do what you do for self-enjoyment or to sell your craft, we support you.

Contact: art@CarpeNocturne.net
Subject Line: Spotlight Feature

ARTISTS • COSPLAYERS • CRAFTERS • DESIGNERS • MODELS • MUSICIAN • PHOTOGRAPHER

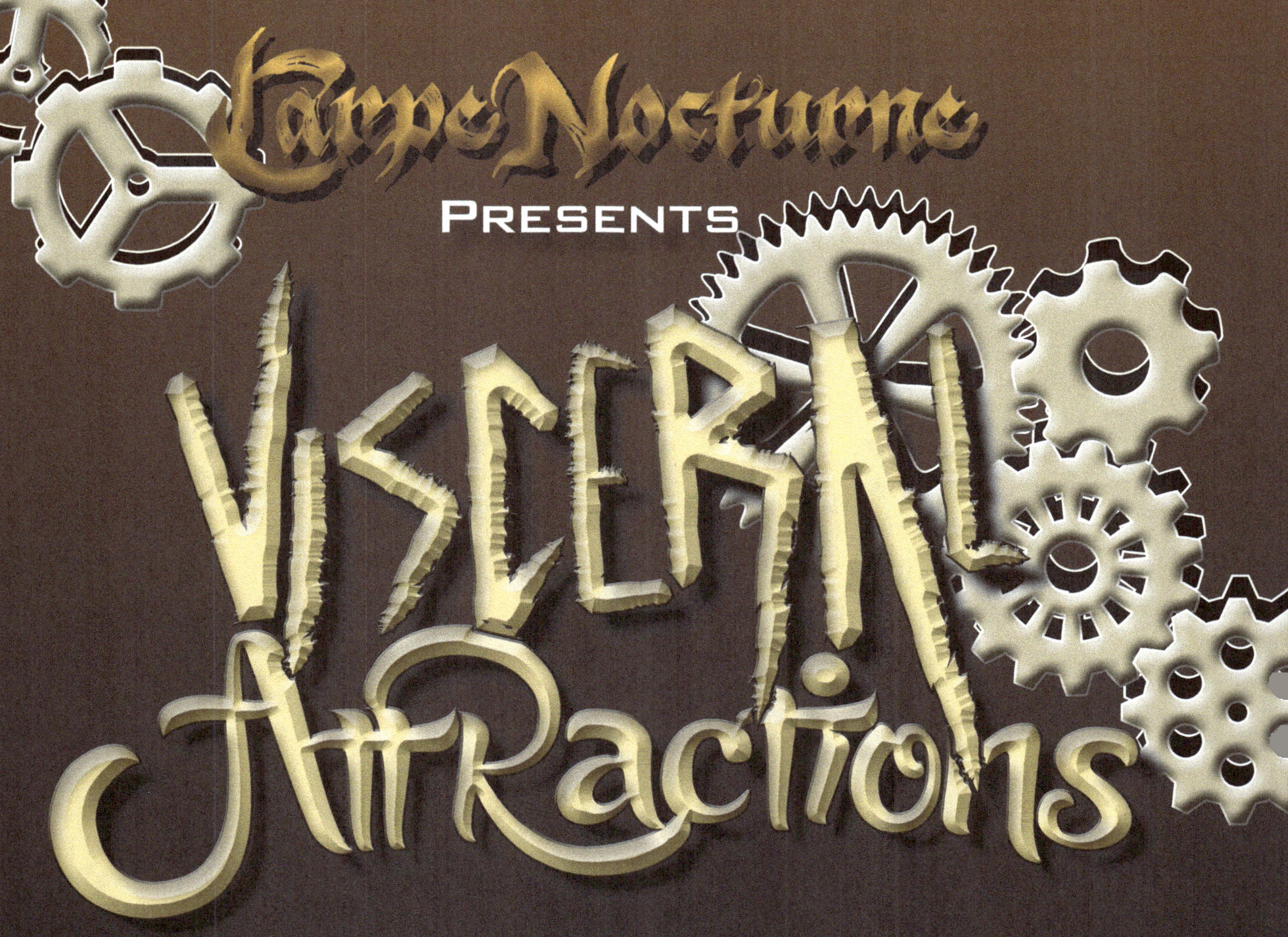

/VIS(ə)RəL/ -

coming from strong emotions; not pertaining to logic or reason

Visceral Attractions is Carpe Nocturne's official Fashion insert, spotlighting the most unique and decadent counter-culture fashion designs out there. Every quarterly issue features full page spreads of fashion, fetish and cosplay photographs to the theme of Goth, Fantasy, Sci-Fi and Steampunk.

THEMES:

Summer - Steampunk
Fall - Goth
Winter - Fantasy
Spring - Sci-Fi

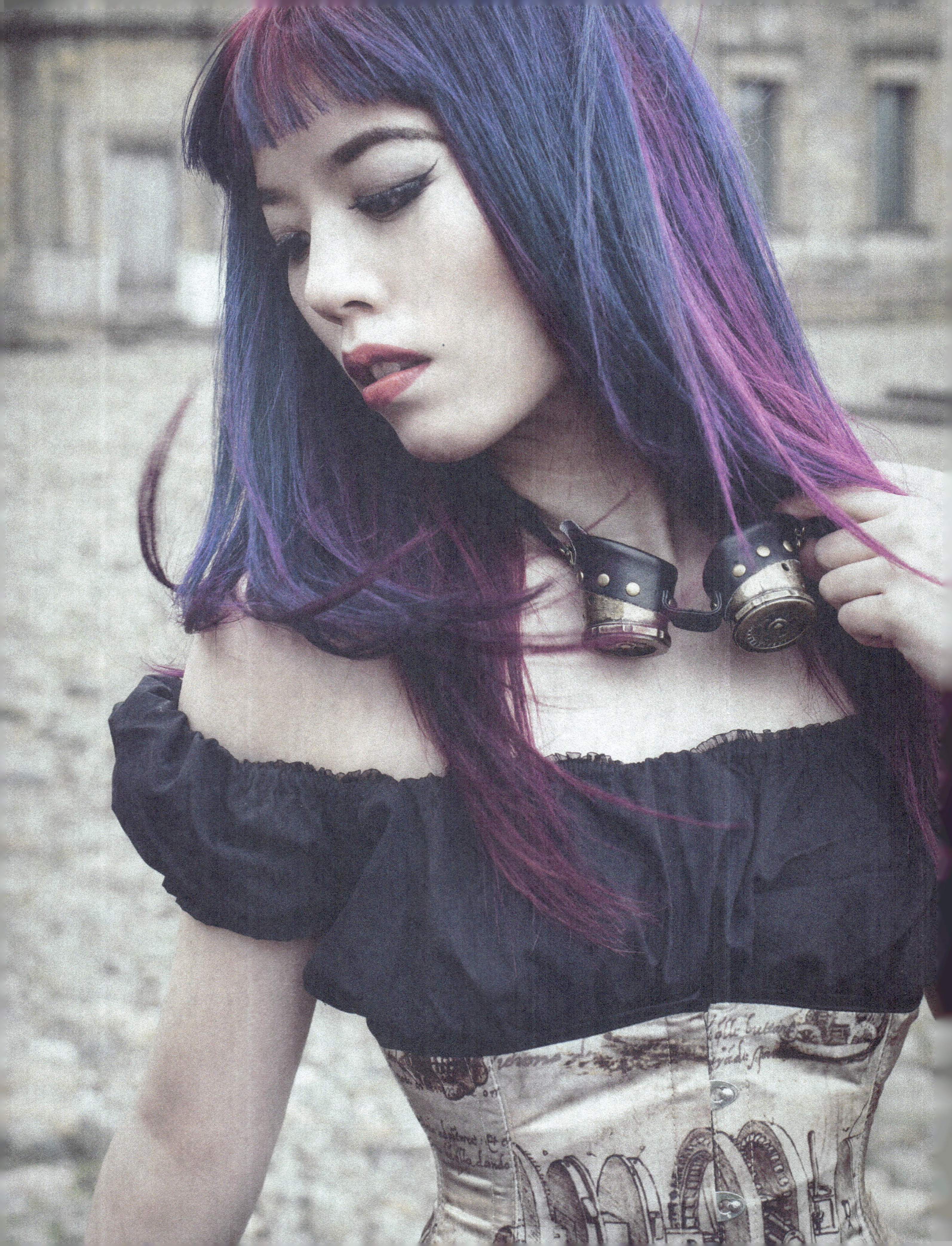

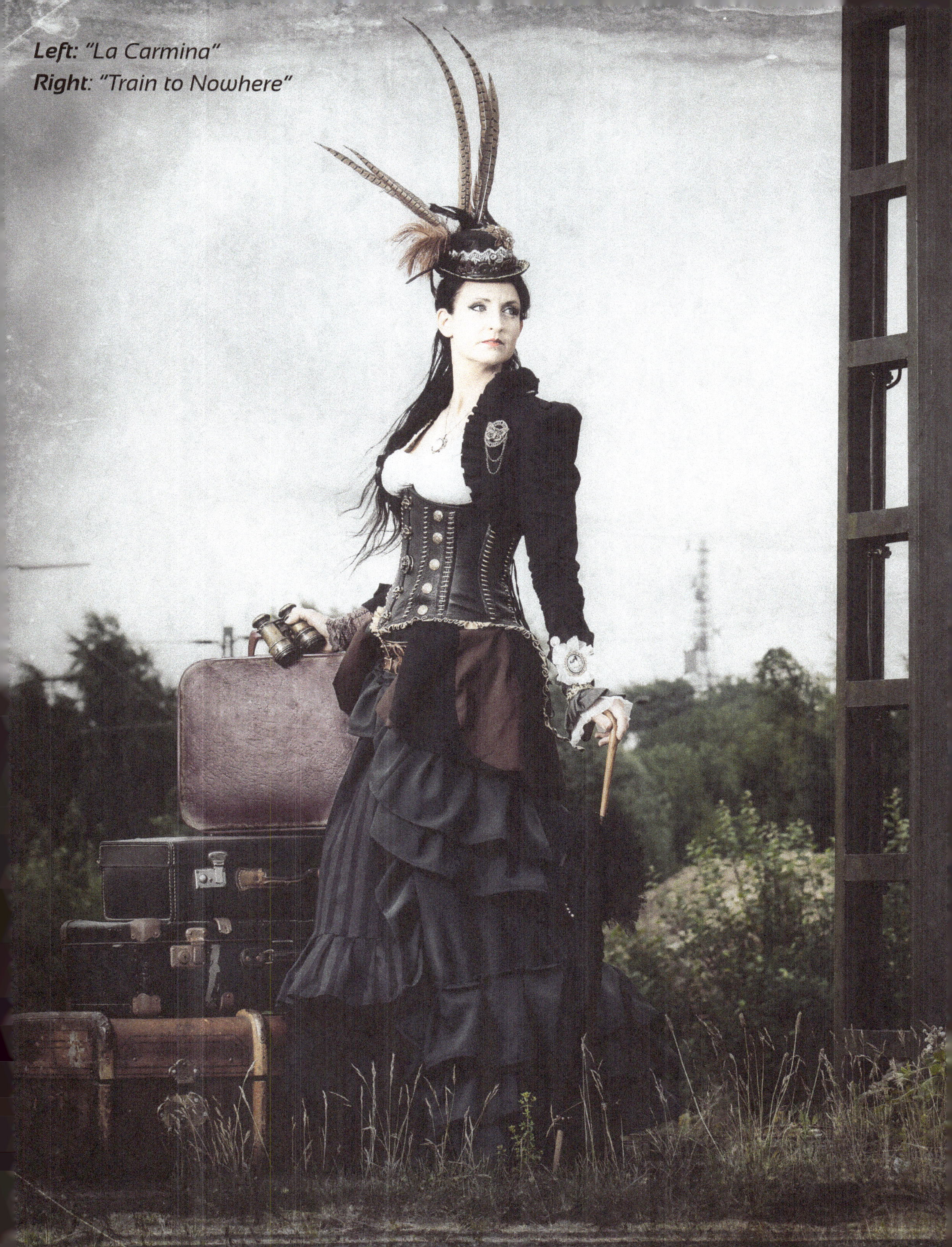

Left: "La Carmina"
Right: "Train to Nowhere"

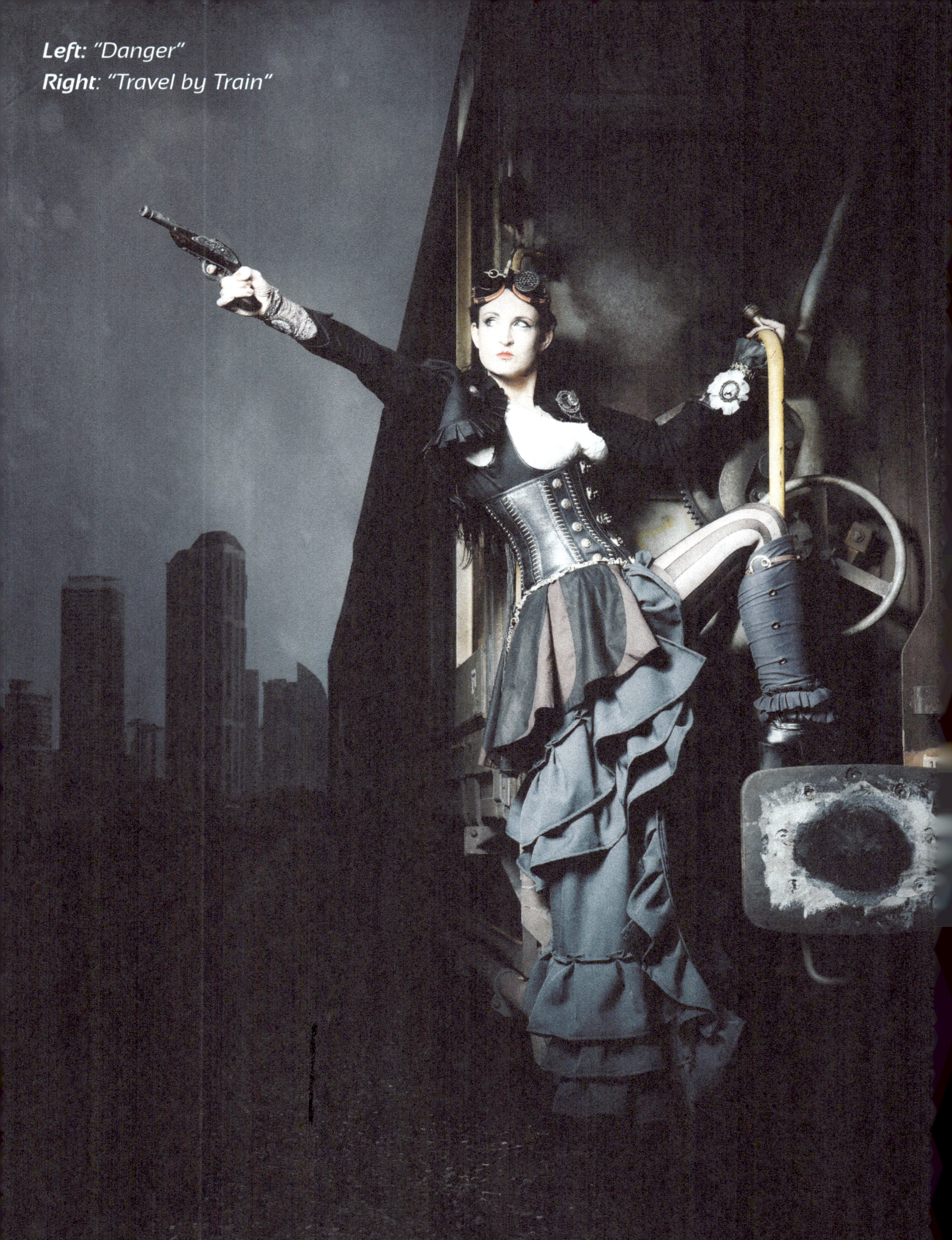

Left: "Danger"
Right: "Travel by Train"

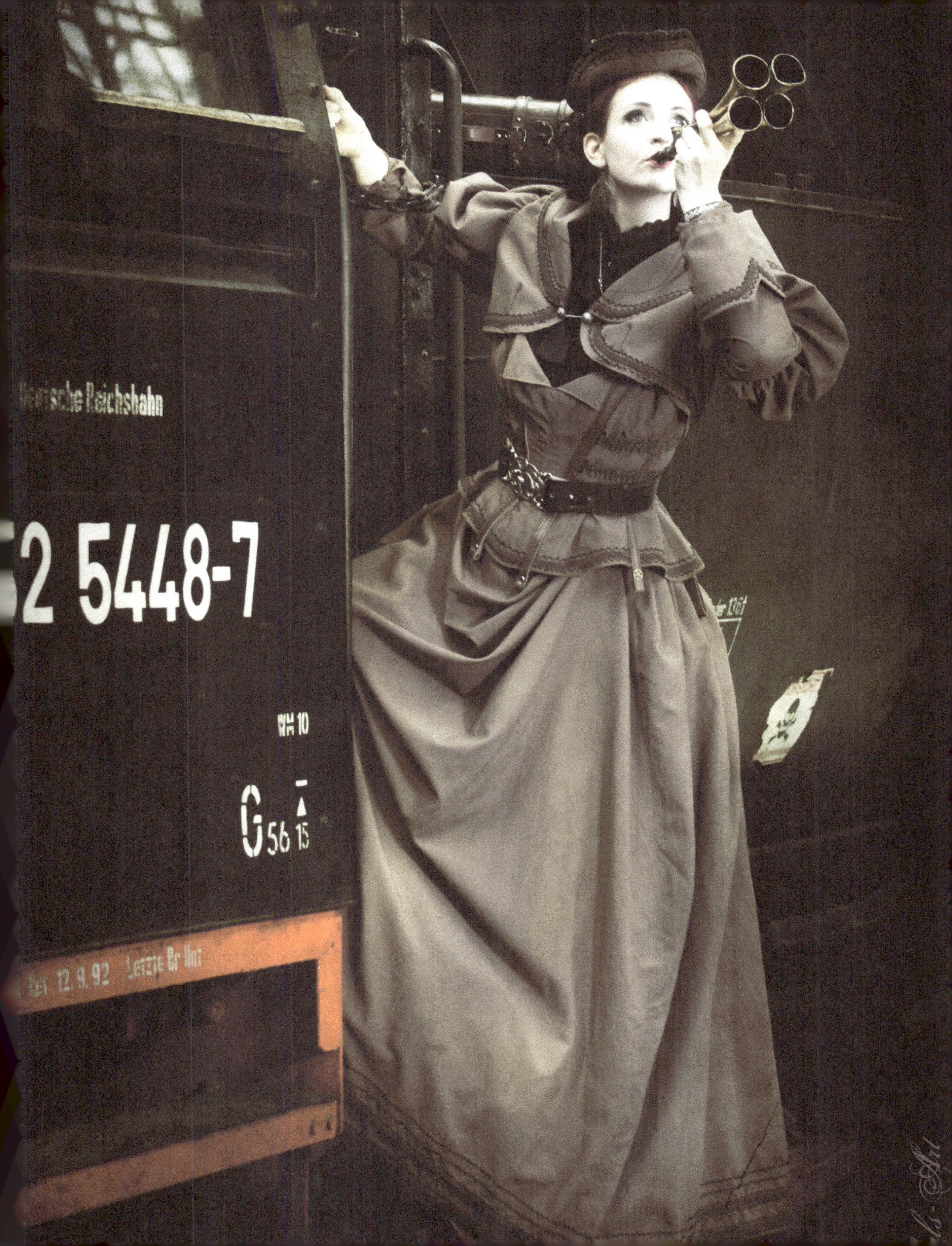

Harische Reichsbahn

2 5448-7

WH 10

G 56 15

Rev. 12. 9. 92   Letzte Br Unt

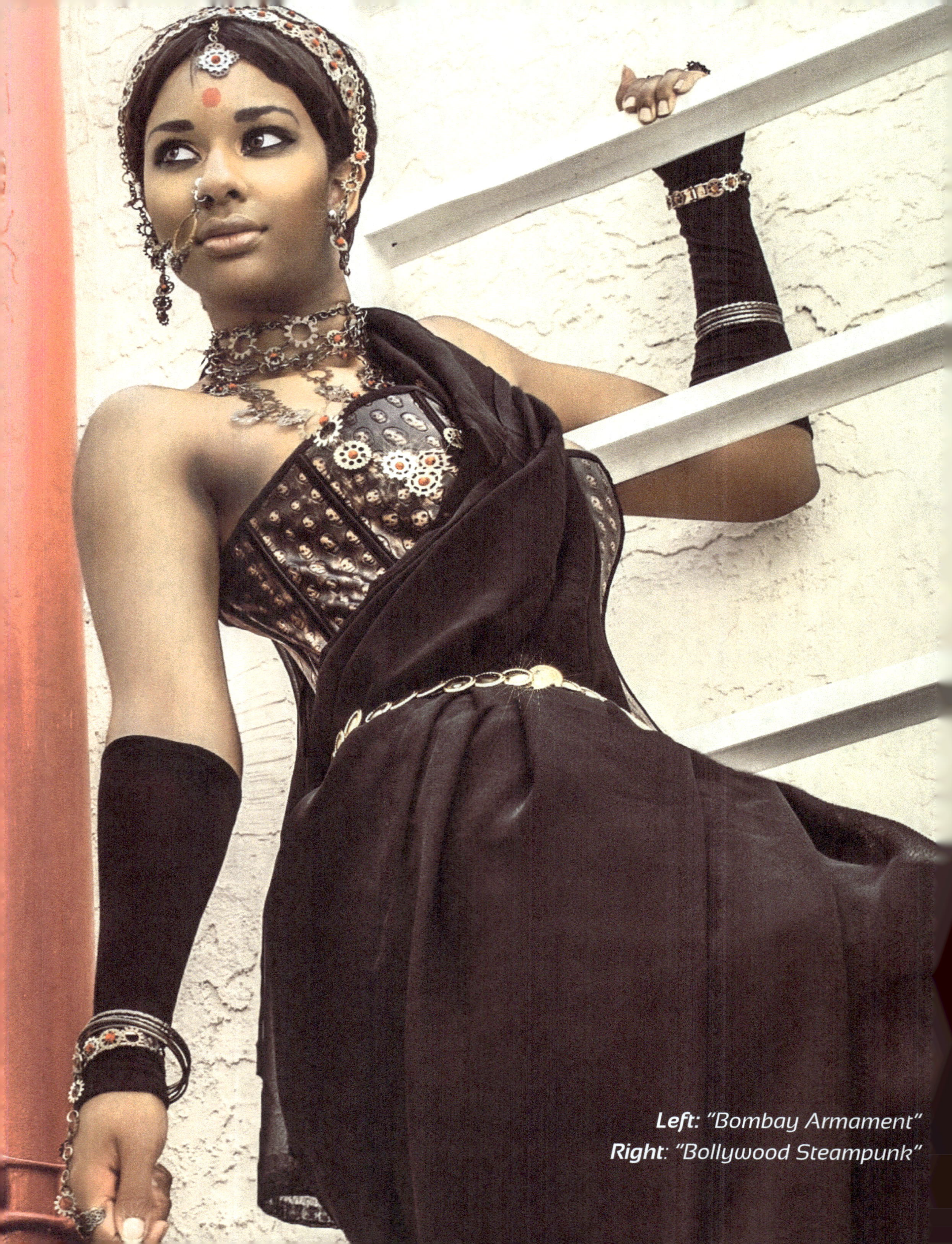

Left: "Bombay Armament"
Right: "Bollywood Steampunk"

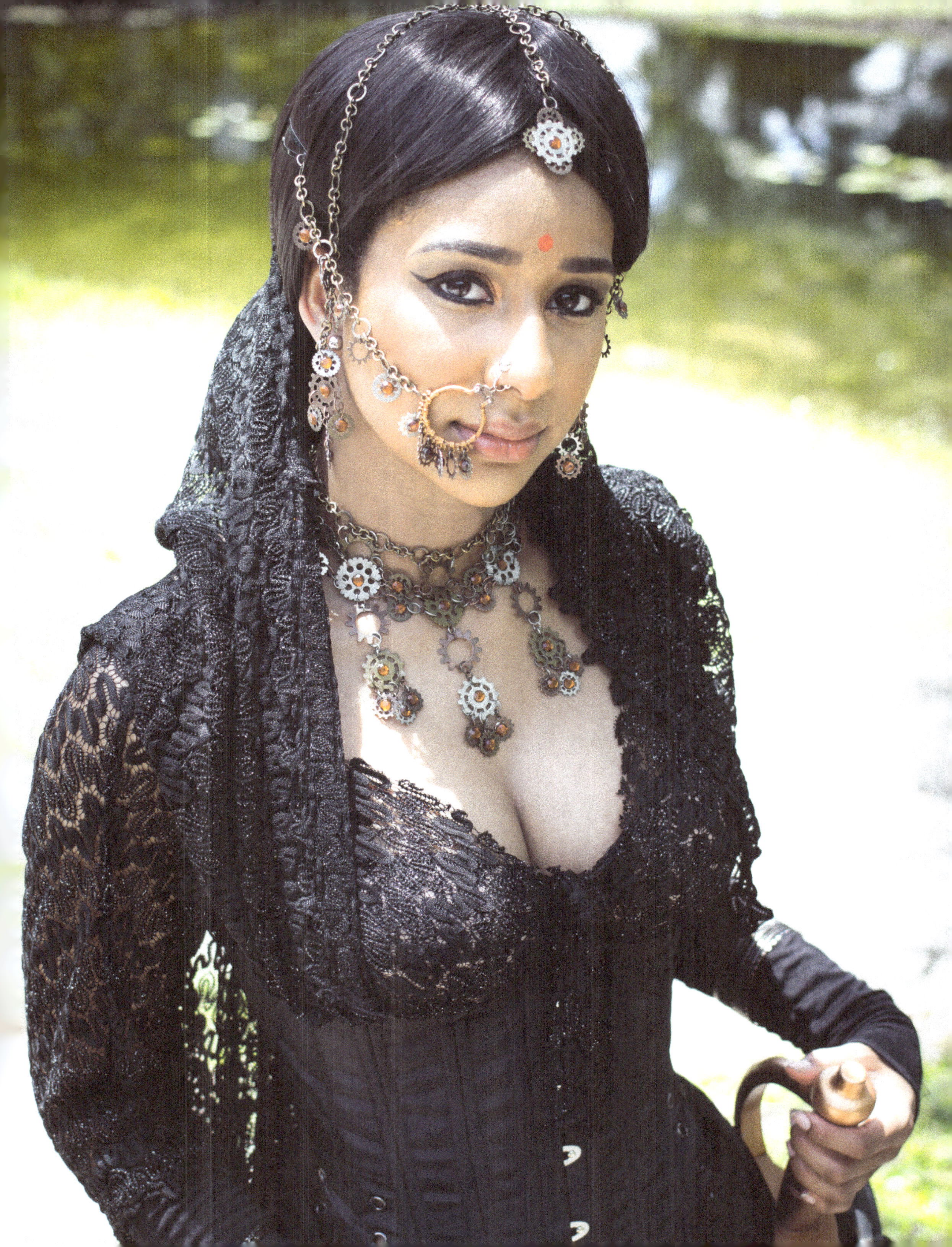

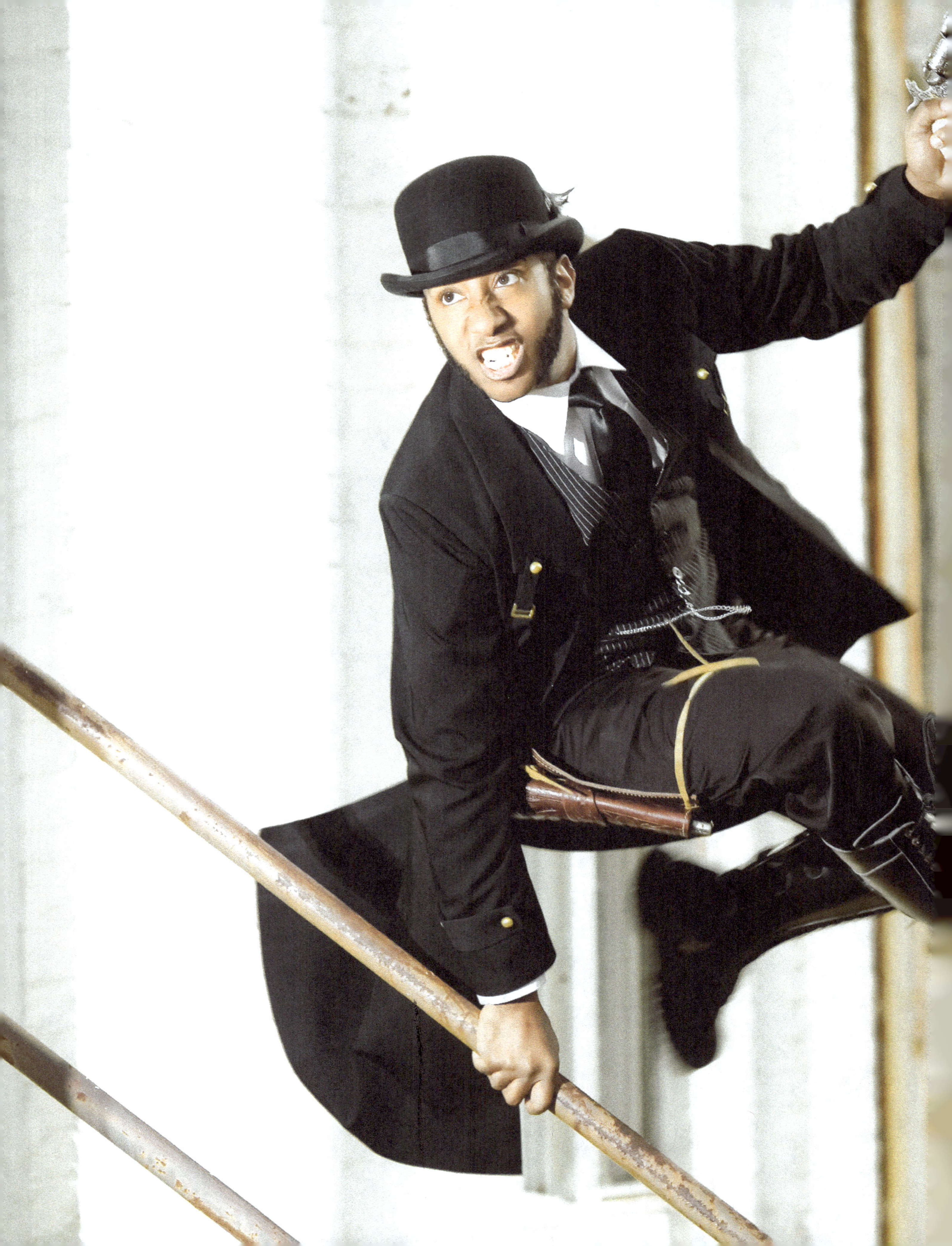

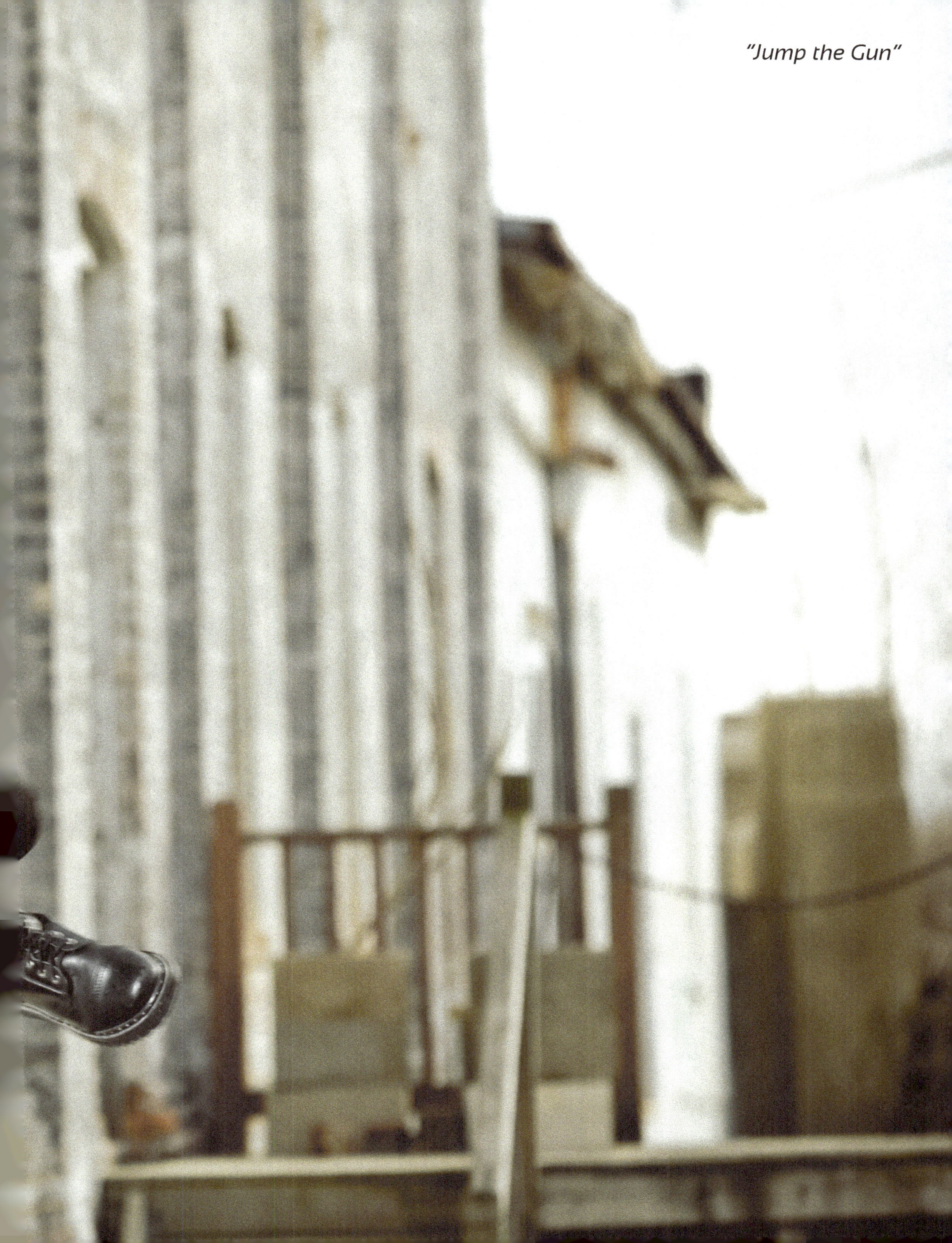
"Jump the Gun"

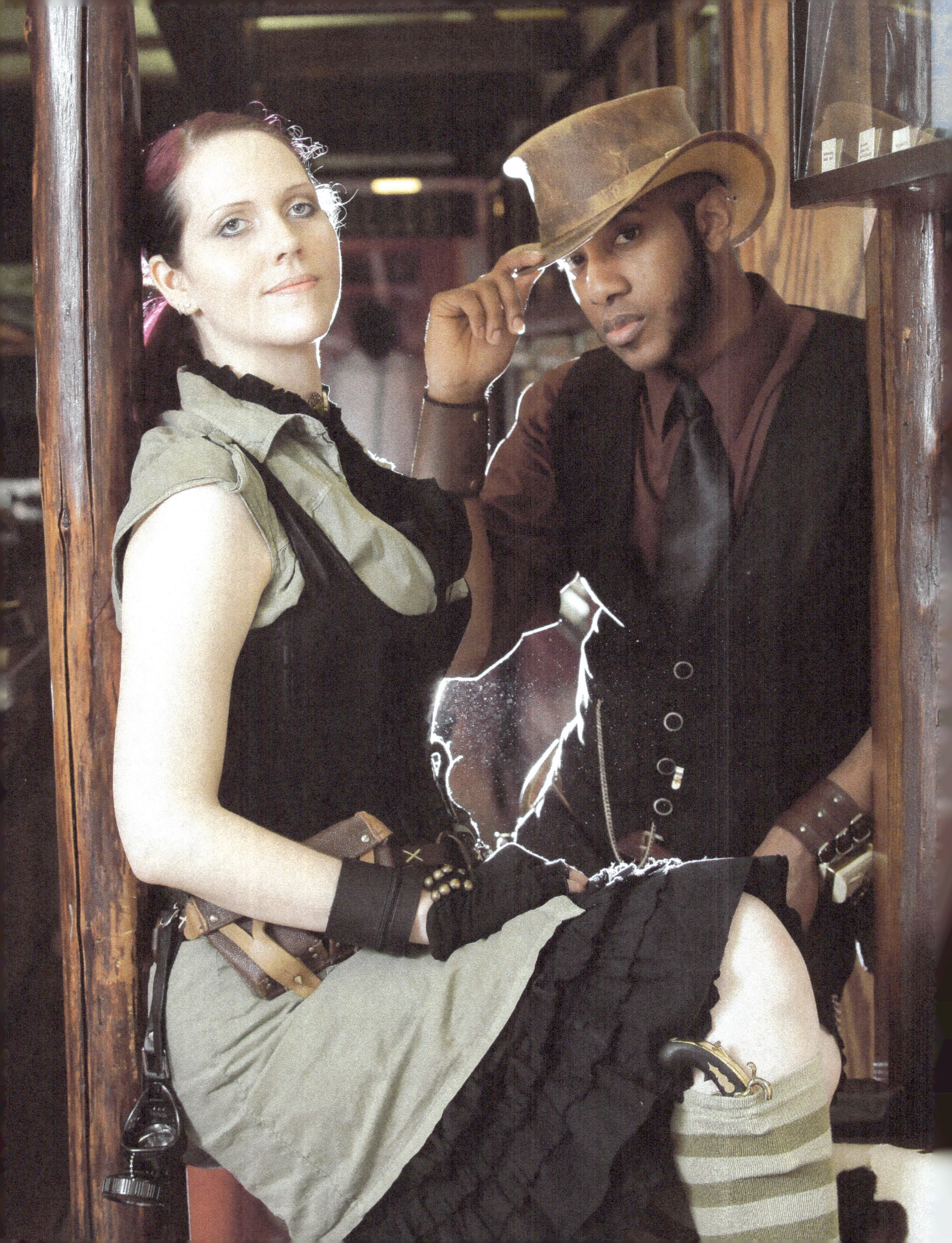

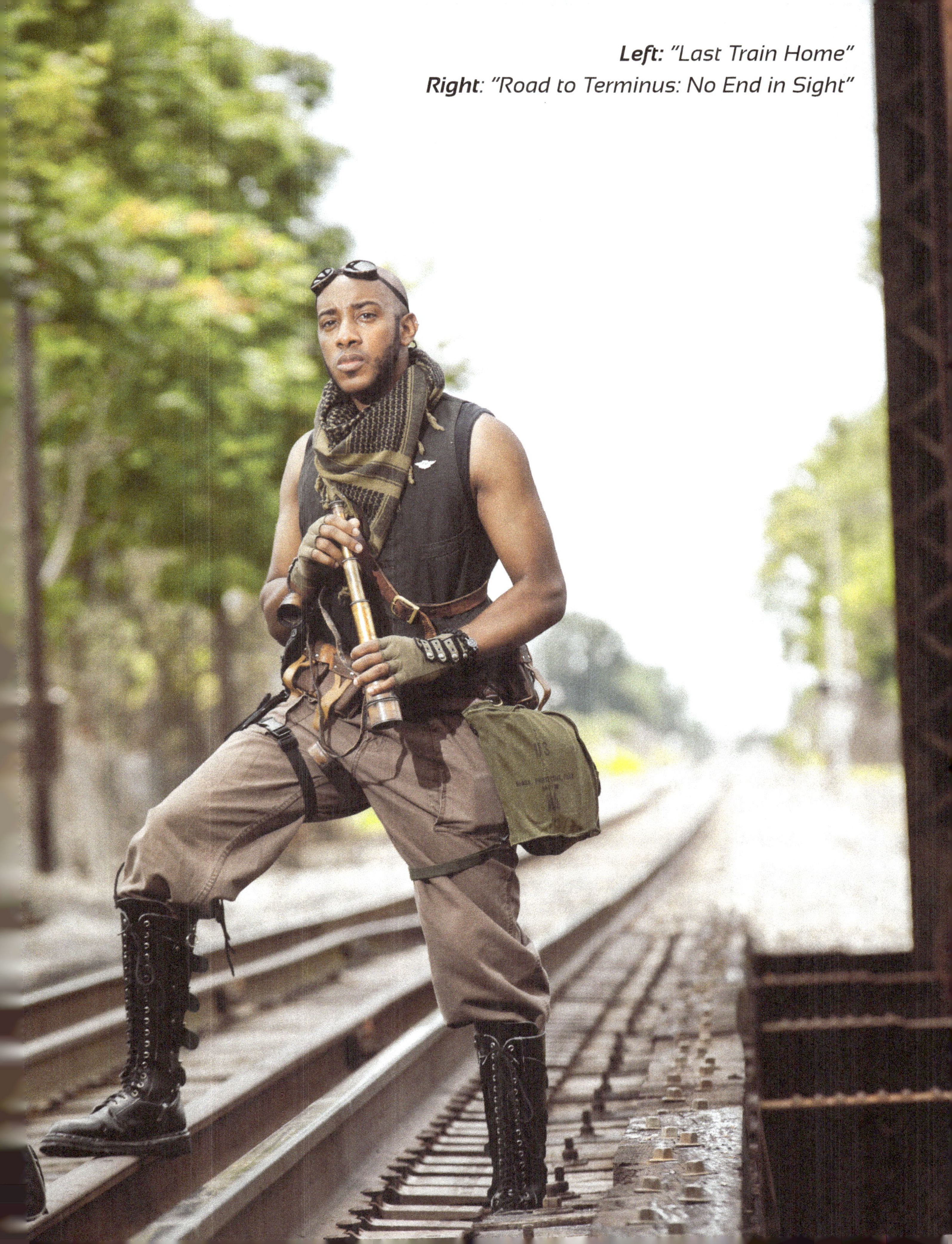

Left: "Last Train Home"
Right: "Road to Terminus: No End in Sight"

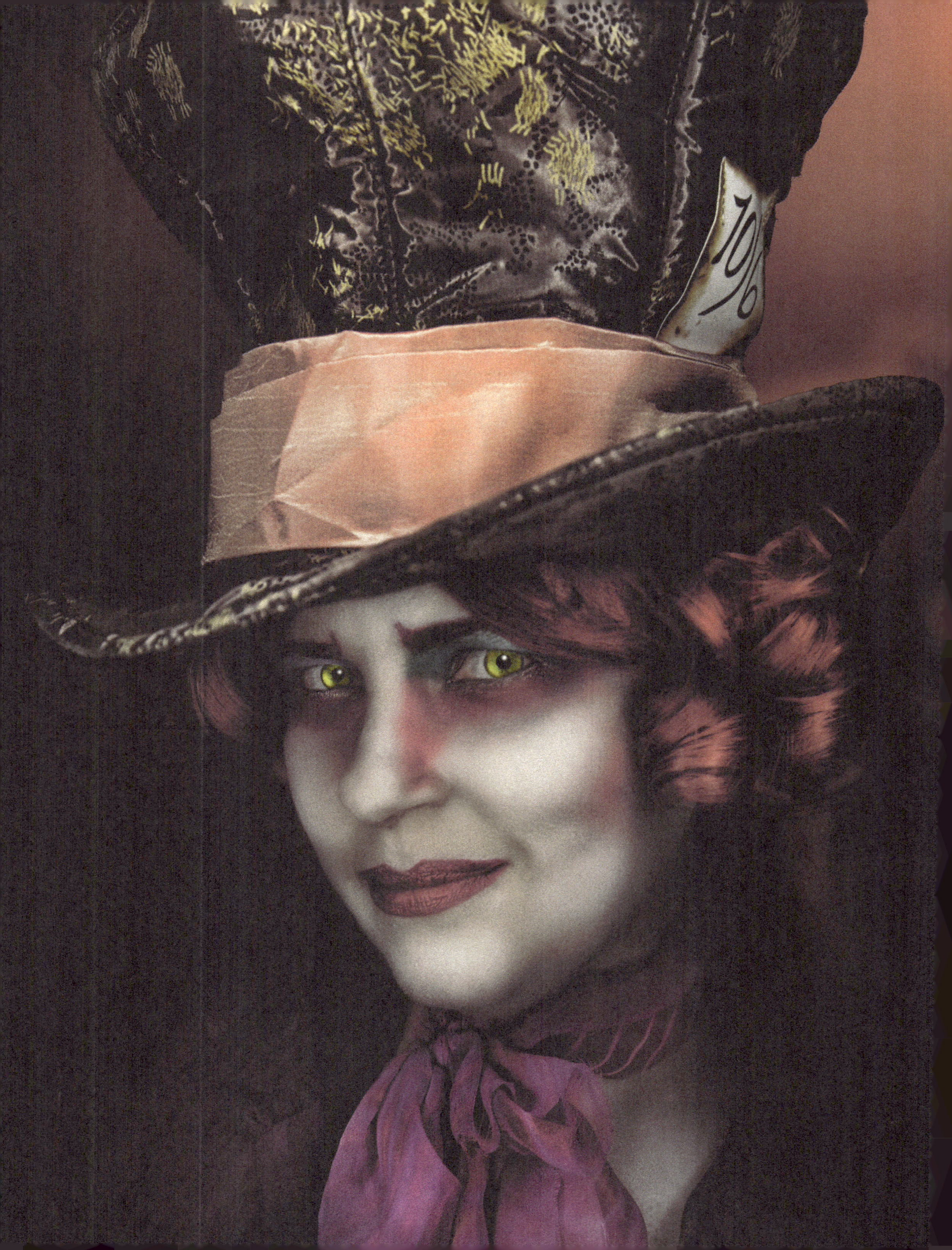

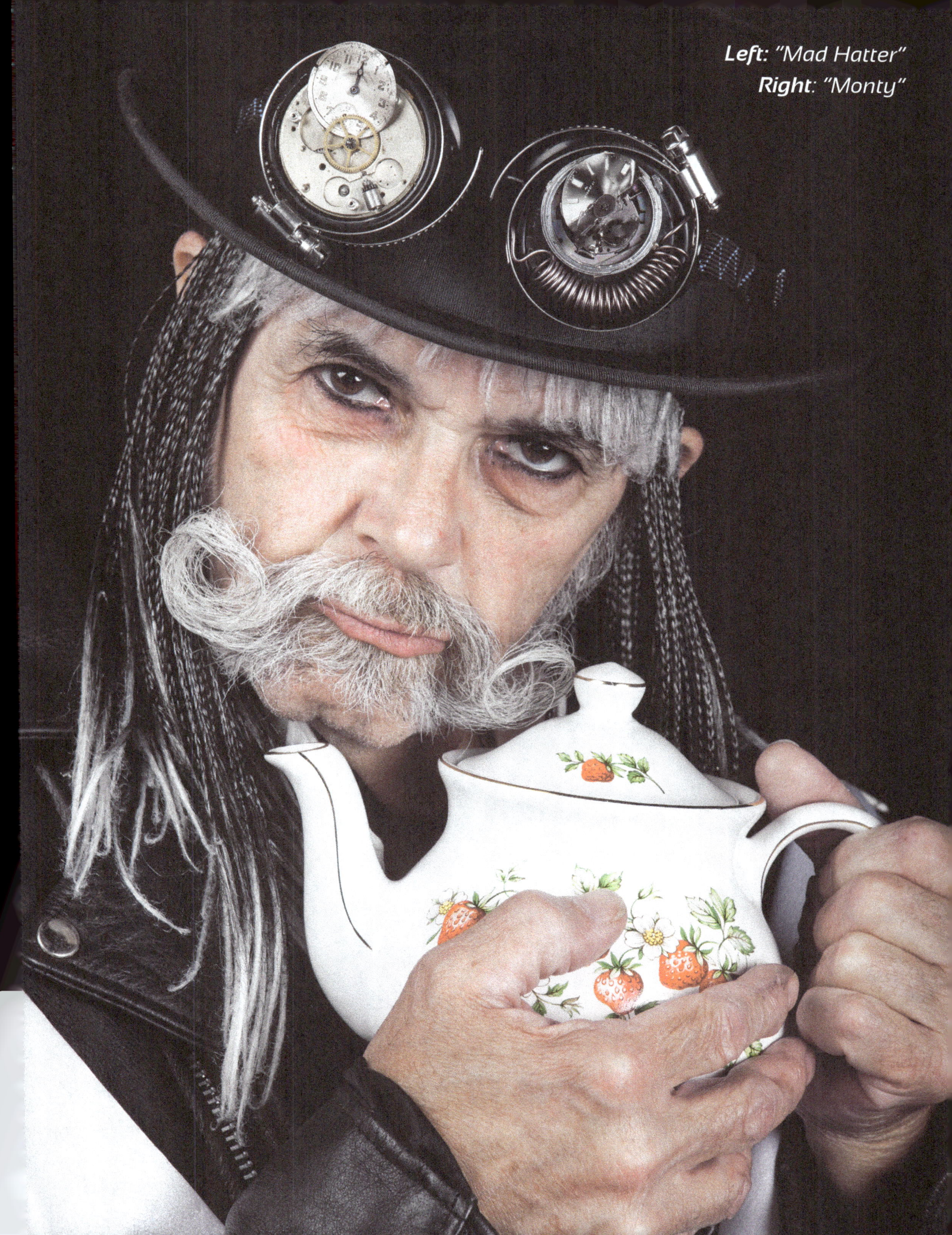

Left: "Mad Hatter"
Right: "Monty"

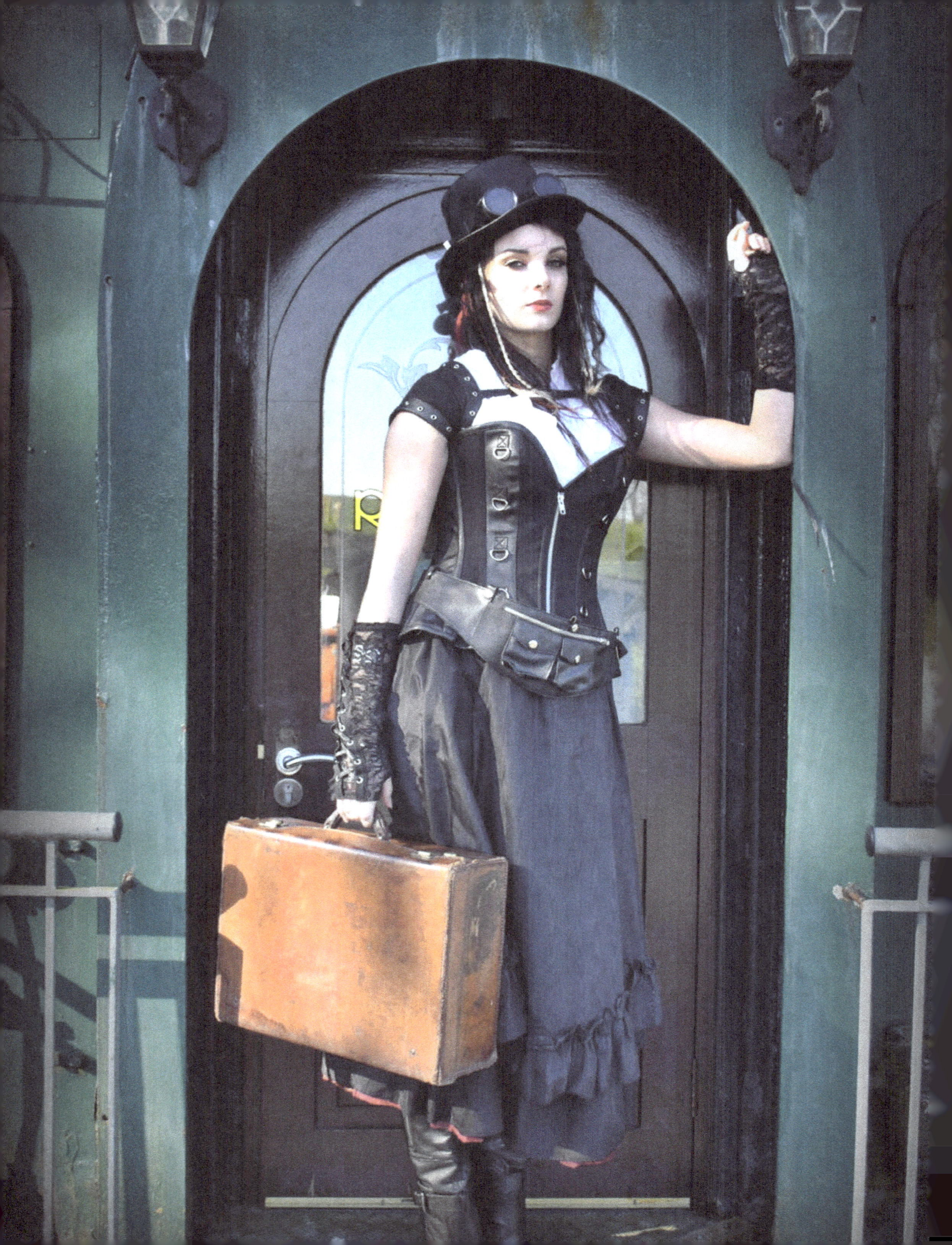

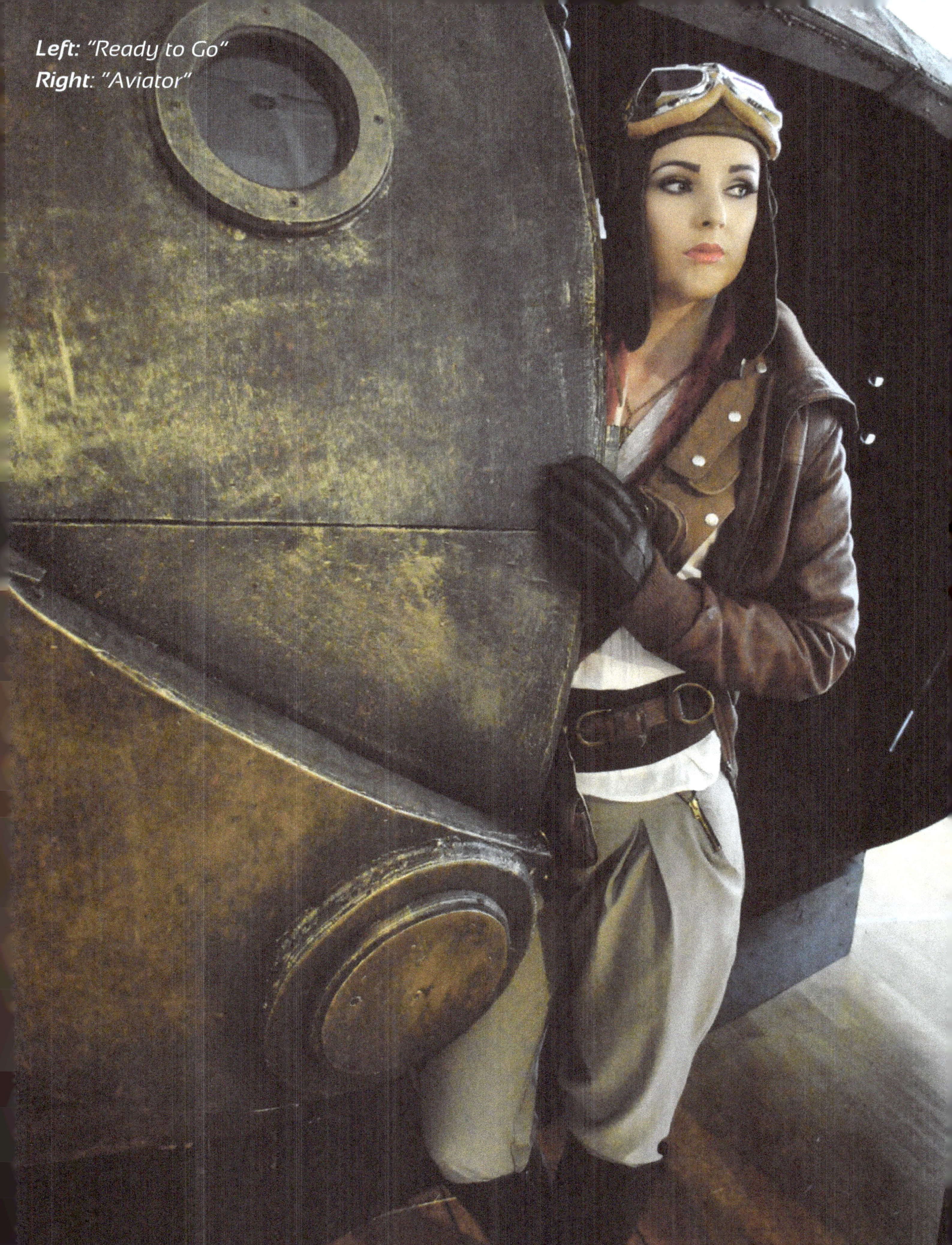
Left: "Ready to Go"
Right: "Aviator"

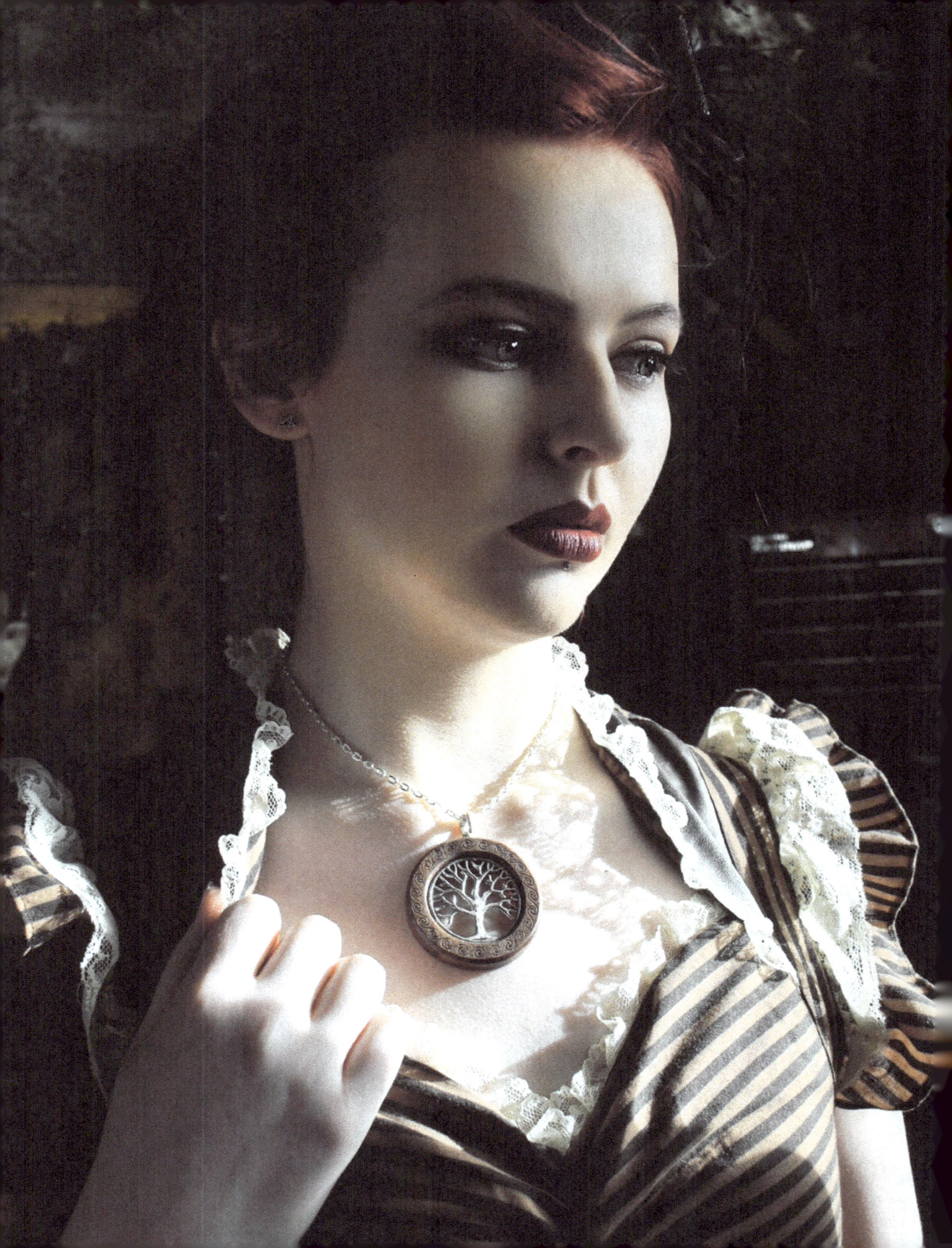

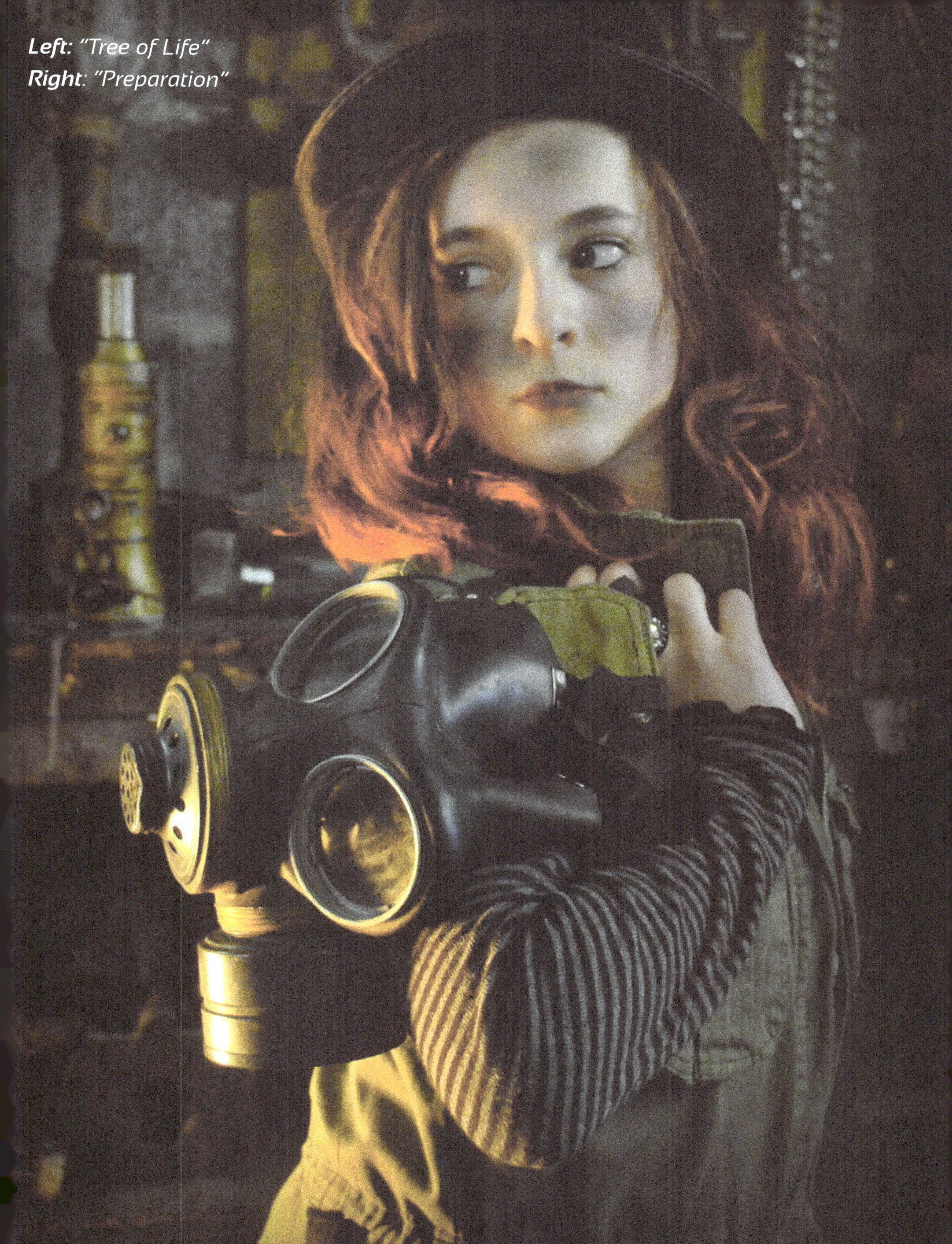

Left: "Tree of Life"
Right: "Preparation"

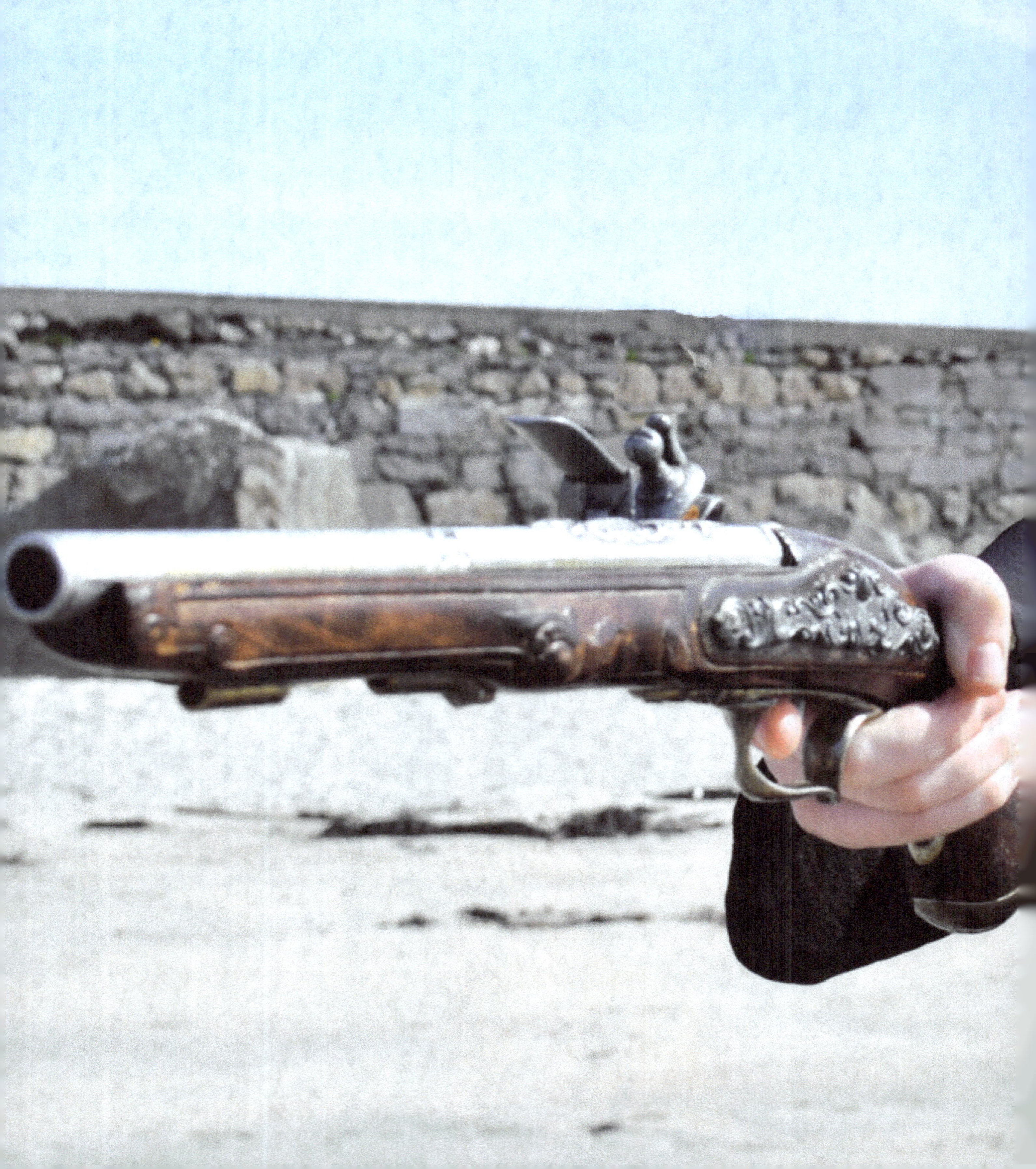

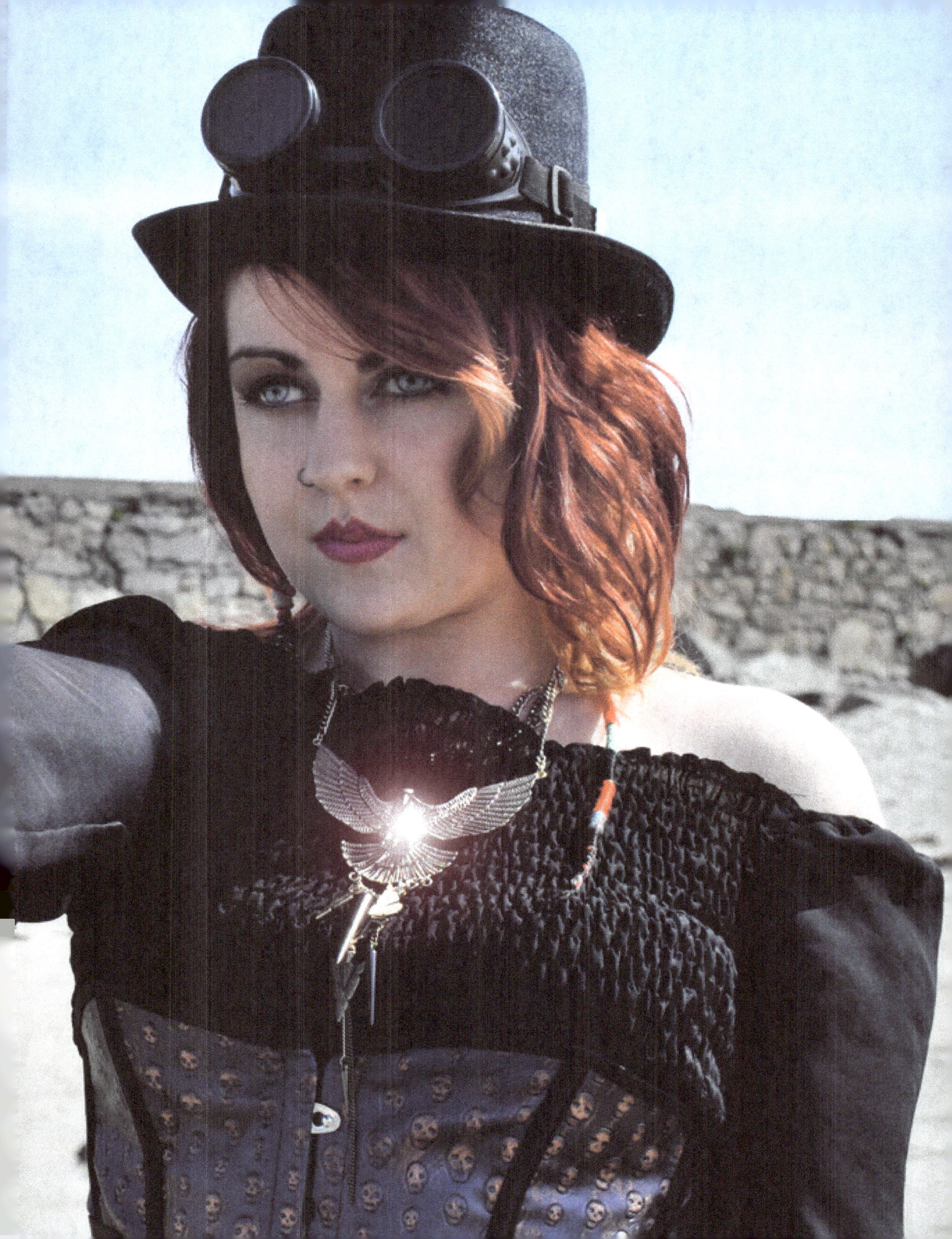

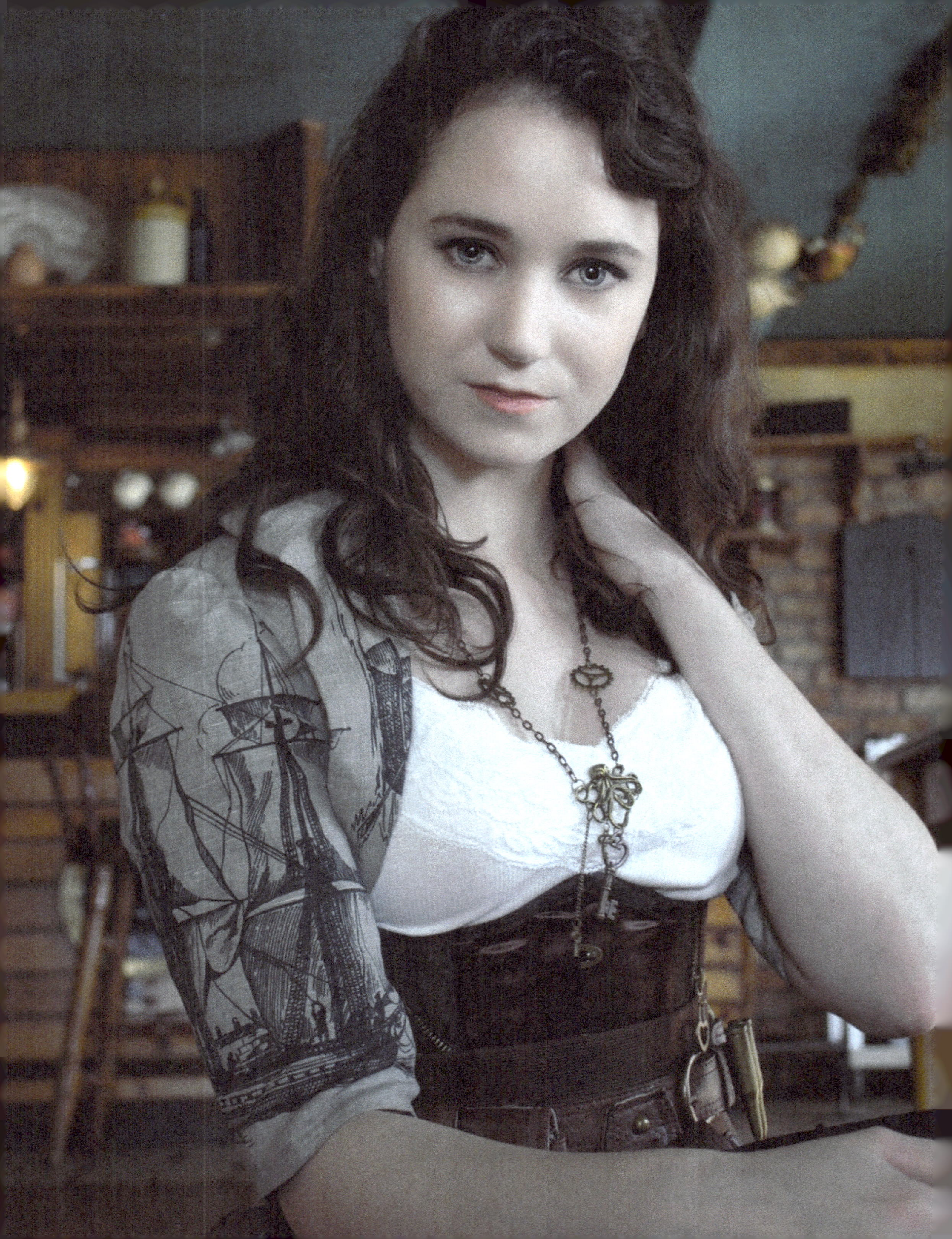

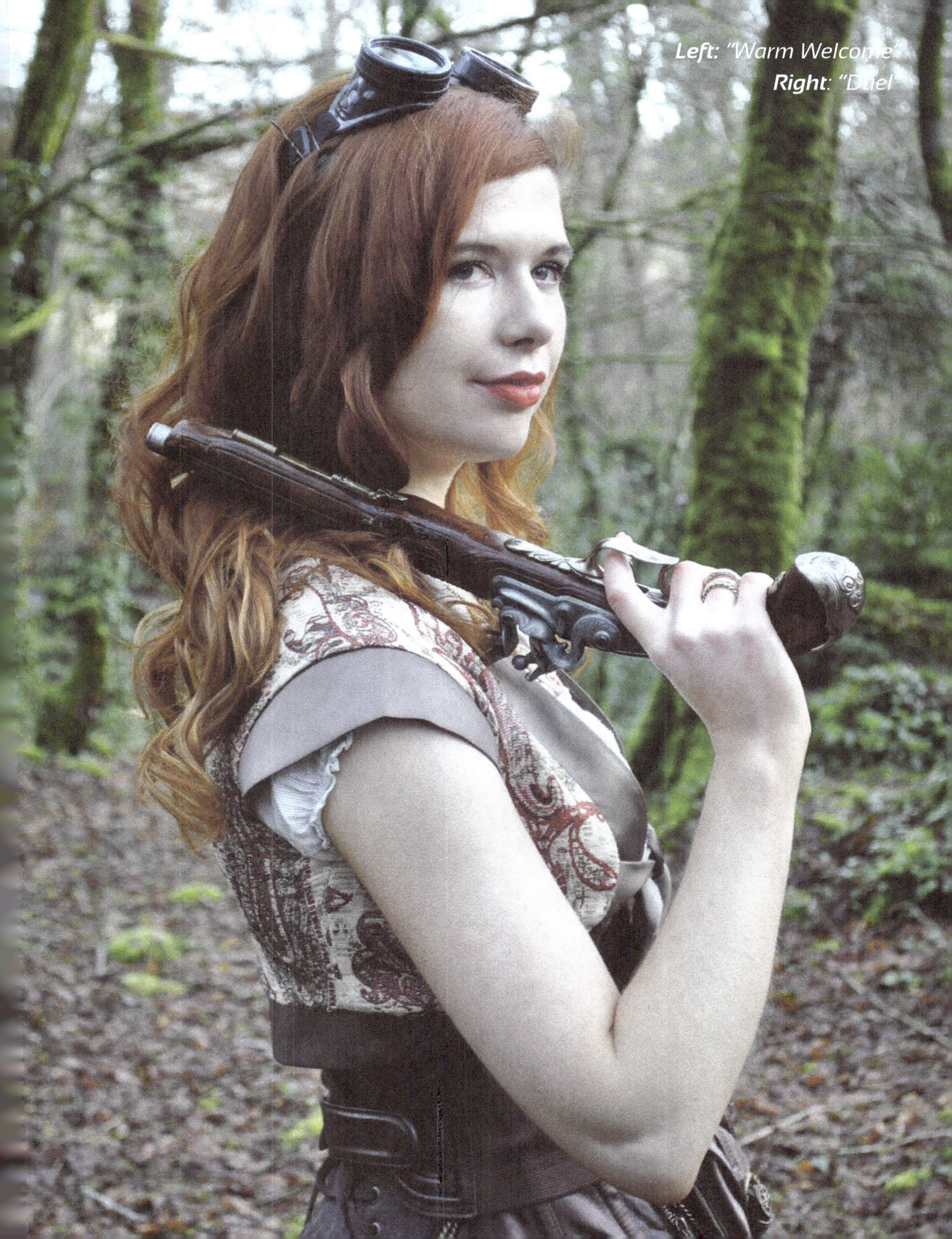

Left: "Warm Welcome"
Right: "Duel"

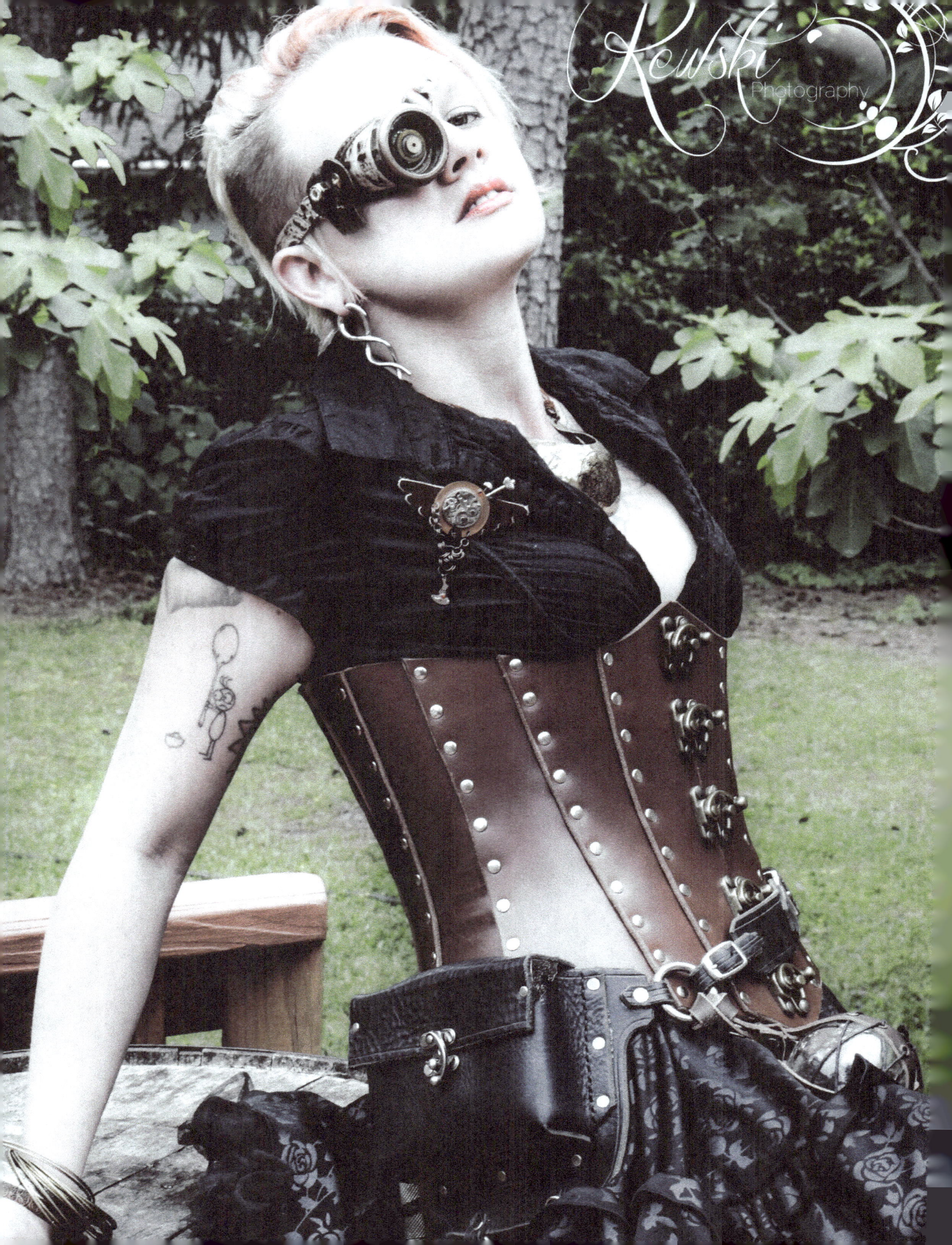
Kewski
Photography

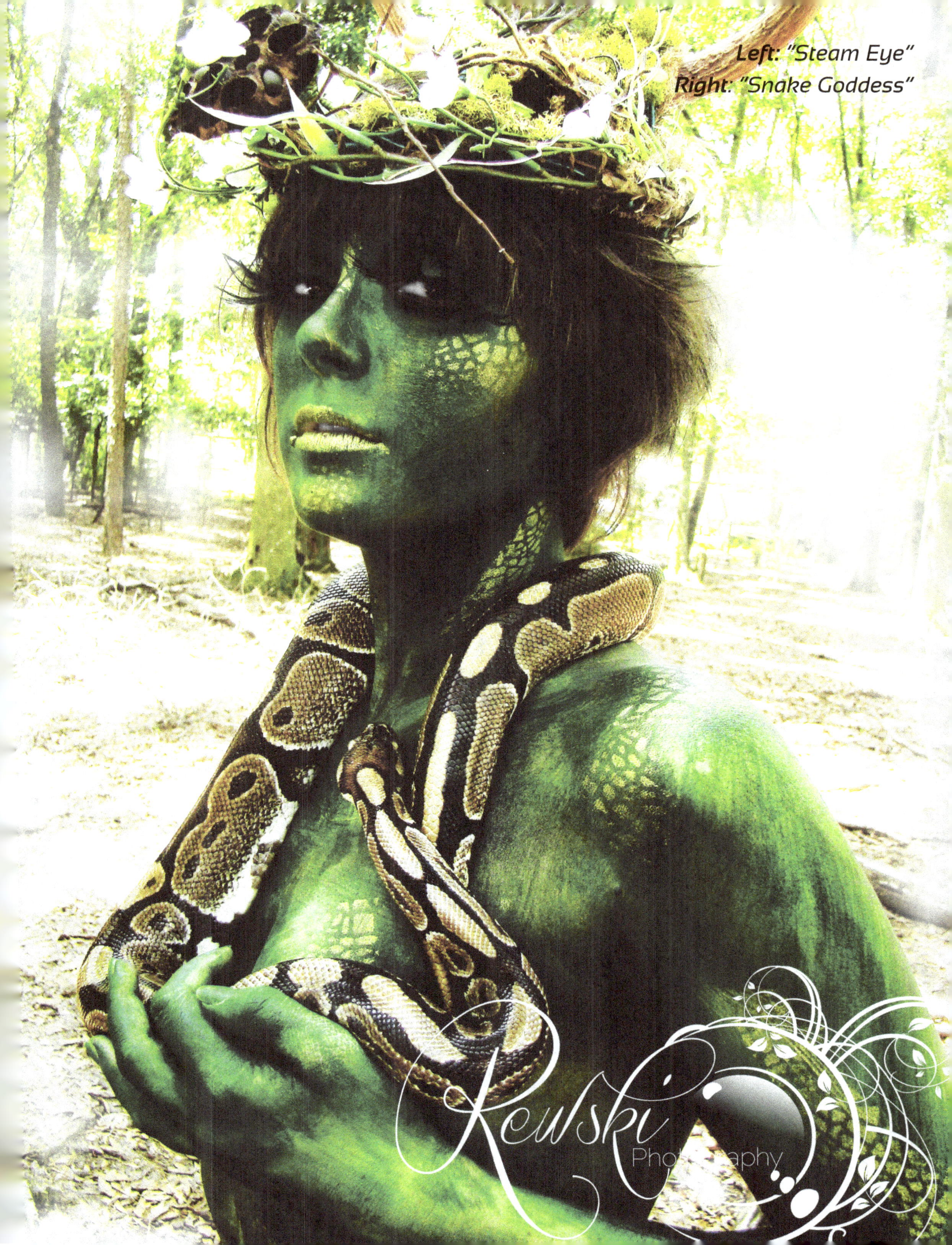
Left: "Steam Eye"
Right: "Snake Goddess"

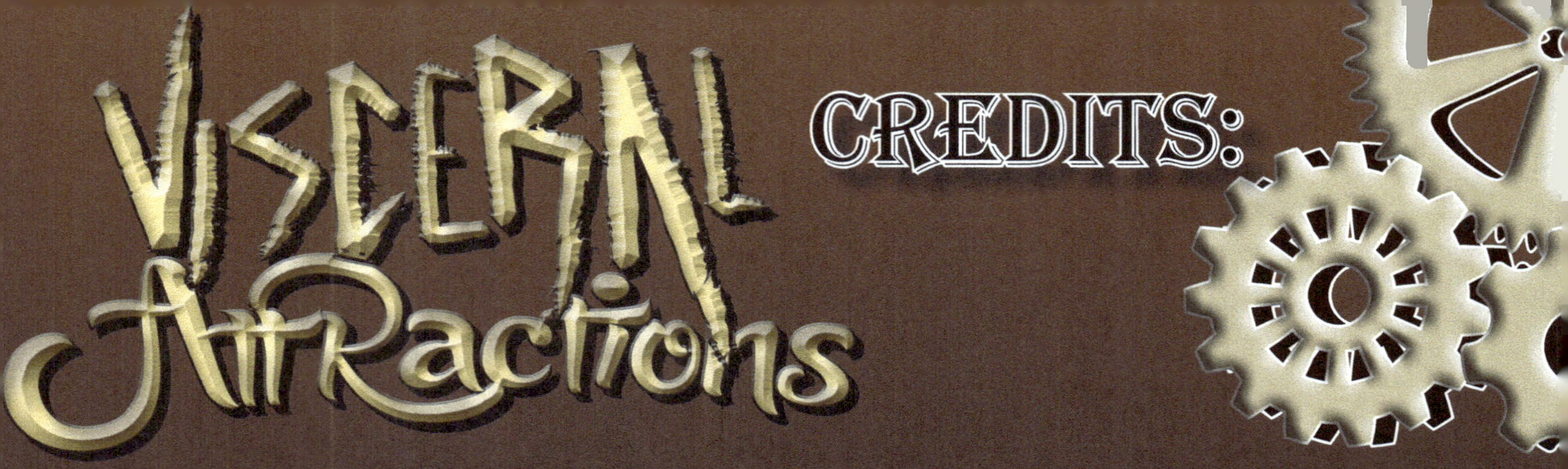

If you are a model or a designer who would like to have your photographs featured in Visceral Attractions, please contact the editor at fashion@carpenocturne.net.

"La Carmina"	Model: La Carmina - www.lacarmina.com Photographer: Joey Wong Hair: Stephanie Hoy - Stratosphere Salon, Vancouver
"Train to Nowhere" "Danger" "Travel by Train"	Model: S-T-A-R Gazer Photographer: Ernst Weerts - www.ernstweerts.de Photographer: Wuschels Art -www.wuschels-art.de
"Bombay Armament" "Bollywood Steampunk"	Model, Hair and Makeup: Ariel Dixon Photographer: Fernando Sedano - fdsedanoarts@gmail.com
"Jump the Gun" "Last Train Home" "Road to Terminus: No End in Sight"	Model: Capt. Anthony LaGrange Model: Sally Van Eycke Photographer: Rob Manko
"Mad Hatter"	Model: Jezzabell Photographer: Lawrence Munne
"Monty"	Model: Montague Jacques Fromage
"Ready to Go"	Model: Cath, Makeup: Flora Photographer and Styling: Caroline Walsh
"Aviator"	Model and Makeup: Katie O'Brien, Jewelry: Debbie Louise Finch Photographer and Styling: Caroline Walsh
"Tree of life"	Model: Larissa McCormick, Makeup: Lash and Brow Studio Jewelry: Curra Celtic Jewelry, Photographer and Styling: Caroline Walsh
"Preparation"	Lucy, Photographer and Styling: Caroline Walsh
"Draw"	Model: Muireann Kenny, Makeup: Zoe Ryan Lammers Photographer and Styling: Caroline Walsh
"Warm Welcome"	Model: Sarah Maher, Makeup: Glo Carmel Ryan Jewelry: Debbie Louise Finch, Photographer and Styling: Caroline Walsh
"Duel"	Model: Teresa Casserly, Makeup: Zoe Ryan Lammers Jewelry: Curra Celtic Jewelry, Photographer and Styling: Caroline Walsh
"Steam Eye"	Photographer: Kayla King
"Snake Goddess"	Photographer: Kayla King

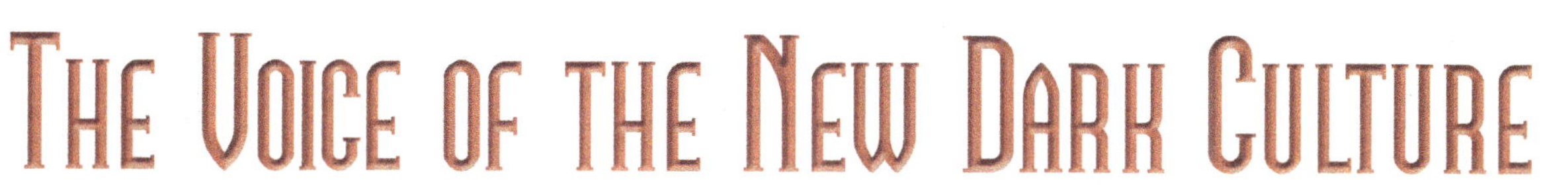

The Voice of the New Dark Culture

Dating 101- Goth style

By Chirality

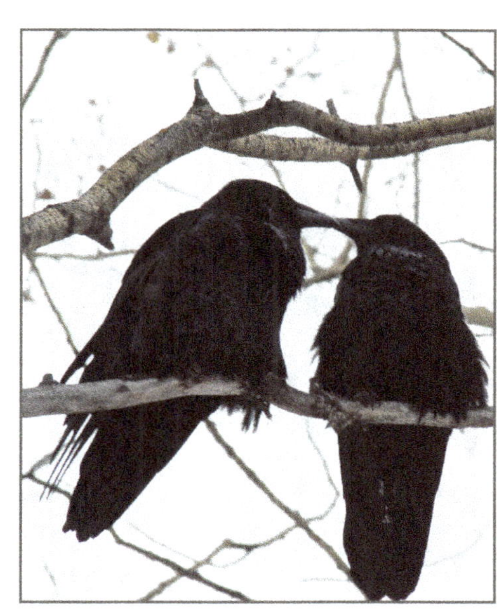

Dating is hard enough, but trying to date someone who understands us?! That is even tougher. I have dated all kinds. I have dated in the "scene," but let's face it, when we do this we are playing six degrees of Kevin Bacon. Don't get me wrong, if you are one of the lucky few to have met someone in the scene, then good for you! You may be ahead of the curve. Also, you could meet someone outside the scene who is open, open to you, and excited for the new experiences they will encounter.

I am about ** years old. Dating nowadays in any capacity is sort of like fishing in a septic tank. Am I bitter and jaded? Yes, so please take this as what you will. You may be reading this saying "Oh I am madly in love and you are just jelly." Perhaps, but I know and my friends know that if you are single and dating it is so tough, especially if you are a "goth girl."

Last year I had a break up from someone "in the scene". That was hard enough because you still see them at the club, at shows, and if they are interested in someone else, it becomes widely known and it's always in the forefront. I ducked out for a bit because I could not stand to see him with someone else. I decided to branch out and join Ok Cupid. The first responses I got were the same thing, "Wow, I love goth girls." Do you? I suppose I am a fetish. You love the idea of a girl in corsets and spiked heels. I get it. But when you see that sometimes we are painfully normal, the fetish wears. We go to CVS, the bank, etc and we are not always wearing our fishnets to go grocery shopping. I once had a man message me and ask "What do Goths do on a first date?" To which I replied, "We hang out at the cemetery, sacrifice babies, then sleep in our coffins… duh." Don't get me wrong, that actually doesn't sound like a bad night. This experience came after I hung out with someone where I asked myself… 'what am I doing?'. He had an alligator on his shirt. Sure enough he started to mention how I was gorgeous as a blonde (my natural color), asked me why I had so many tattoos, and why didn't I wear other colors. I was like HELLO?! Did you read my profile? Or did you read it and think…'I can change her'. You can't!

I have found two thing while being a Goth girl dating: 1. You meet and date someone in the scene but sometimes your drama can spill over. Also, there are those thirsty girls and guys out there in the clubs and it becomes taxing. 2. If you date outside the scene you run the risk of being a fetish or worse…meeting that someone who says they are "open" only to eventually really not get it.

I am dating someone now. He is not in the scene. It scares me a bit. While I like dating someone on the outside, it would be nice to have someone to sing along to Wolfsheim with. Does this make sense?

Maybe I don't even know what I want at this point and I KNOW I am not alone. Like I said, if you are one of the lucky few who met someone in the scene and are rocking it, then GOOD FOR YOU! Awesome and God Speed…. but for the rest of us just trying to muddle by and meet someone we connect with either outside or in…. good luck. We need it.

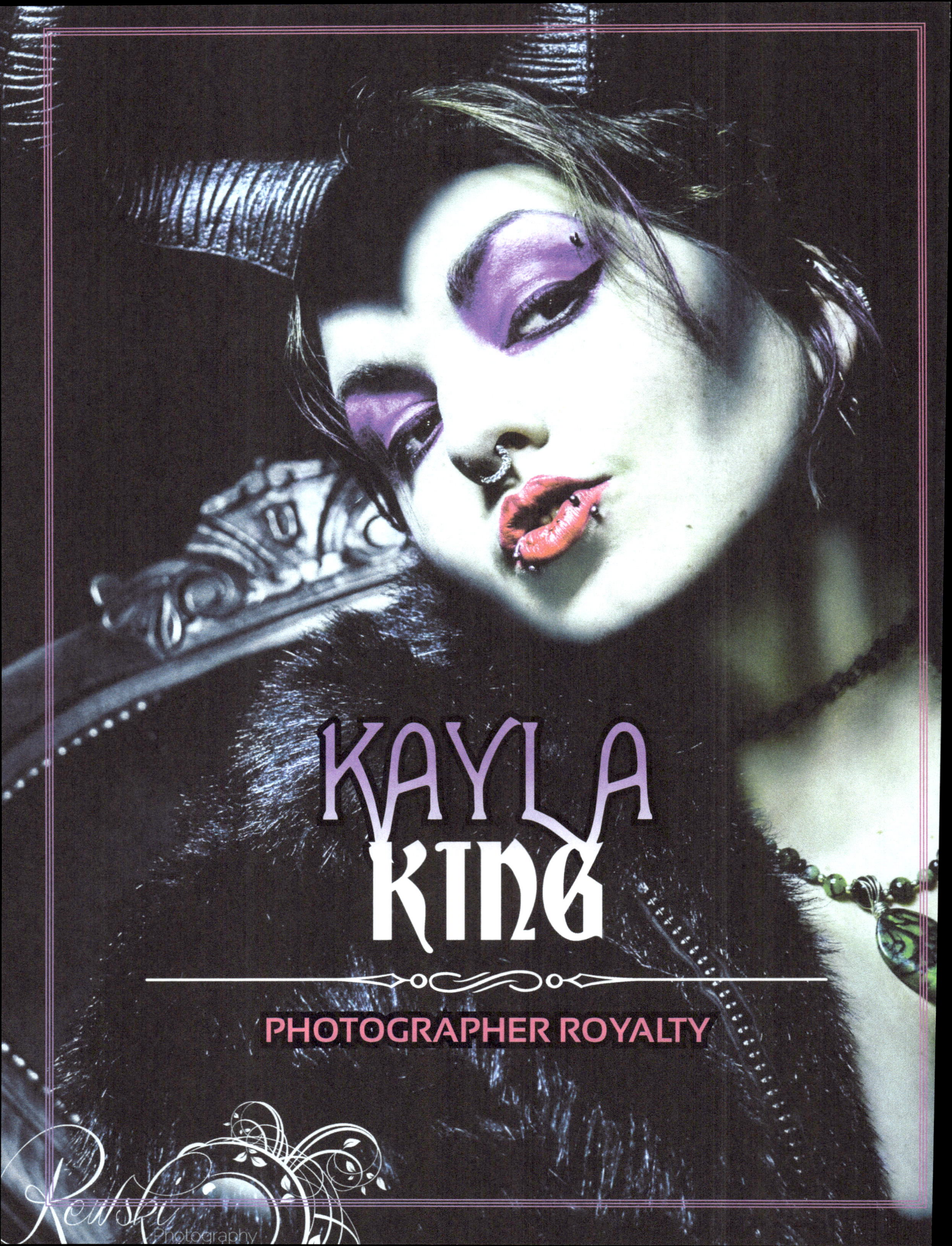

KAYLA KING

PHOTOGRAPHER ROYALTY

By XXX ZOMBIEBOY XXX

[XXX ZOMBIEBOY XXX] *Hello Kayla and thanks for taking the time to talk with us! Congratulations too on your recent marriage to Thor! Must be exciting for a comic inclined woman!*

[KAYLA KING] The pleasure is all mine! (pun intended!)

[ZB] *So the zombie apocalypse occurs! Do you grab your gun or your camera?*

[KK] Someone needs to document such a thing, right? I would indeed be the one riding on the back of my Viking husband with a go-pro and a machete. We are quite the team.

[ZB] *The inevitable question. What drew you into photography?*

[KK] Just a few years ago I was in a state of depression that was easy for me to succumb to. No matter how much I tried to change my outlook, there was always a lack of passion. I was vulnerable, weak, and feeble minded as any 21 year old would be. Well... I found an outlet. I developed a passion that was more than just taking photos. It was making people feel beautiful.

[ZB] *Give us a grocery list of weapons and tools of the trade.*

[KK] In my opinion, less can be more. What separates magazine-worthy photos from their less impressive counterparts isn't a fancy camera or expensive equipment. It's an understanding of what it takes to compose an appealing image and the confidence to execute your vision. Details like composition, lighting, and styling, which apply regardless of whether you're using a digital camera, a simple point-and-shoot, or an iPhone is what brings the photo to life. It begins with a concept. You build from there by choosing a location, a model, a makeup artist and hair stylist if you need one. Then you determine whether you need additional equipment besides your camera such as extra lighting, backdrops, props, etc. Taking a photo is way more than just clicking a button. Collaboration is key to success!

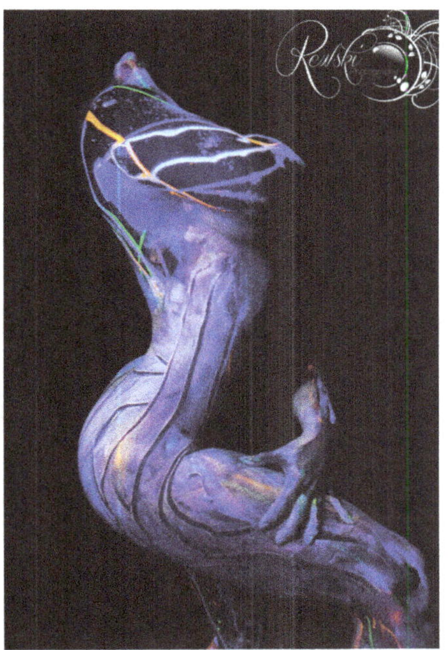

[ZB] *Your models come from all wakes of life. In all shapes, shades and sizes. What do you look for in a subject?*

[KK] Charisma, commitment, and reliability! Personality is more radiant than any trait of a human being. It really shows and completes the image when the model is true to him or her self. Good looks and a nice body is always a plus, but is never, ever mandatory. In fact, I love the challenge of boosting egos no matter how someone looks.

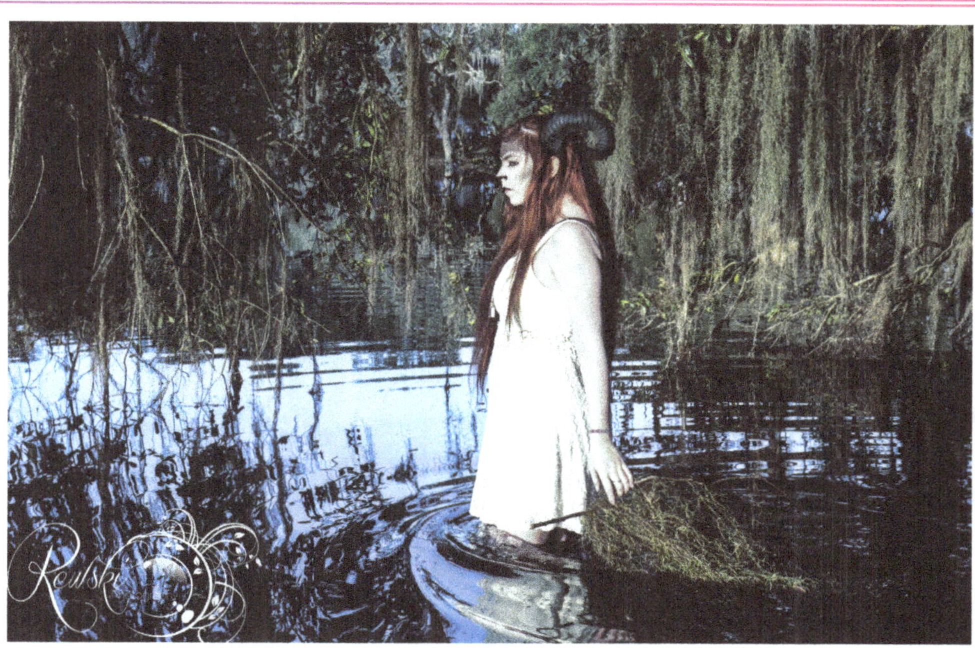

[ZB] *Is there anyone you particularly hope to shoot?*

[KK] I struggle for inspiration working with male models. I've reached a comfort zone and I hope to surpass these boundaries and expand my vision even more!

[ZB] *Do you collaborate with other photographers? If so whom?*

[KK] Sometimes! There are two types of photographers. One who collaborates and one who competes. Sometimes I prefer to work solo on a project that I come up with conceptually. In fact the fewer people I work with, the better. It allows the model to adapt faster to their surroundings without the struggle of becoming comfortable due to someone else's presence. When I do work with another photographer, I make sure that the model is aware. I love conspiring with other local talents whether they are photographers, makeup artists, or models. It's the best way to network and learn from each other!

[ZB] *Your subject matters vary in style and feel, which is awesome. Do you have a favorite?*

[KK] I definitely have particular models in mind when I think of particular concepts. Sometimes I'll even get inspired by the model's natural look and I'll think of a way to completely transform her and compliment her beauty even more. My favorite style would be the dark macabre feel with a little bit of sex appeal. The bloodier the better!

[ZB] *What steps do you take to produce that look and feel?*

[KK] I consider myself a creator of visual arts. Simply looking at a photo should narrate a story without words. First, a concept is thought up, which makes it easier to put the pieces together to tell that story. Then you need a model , a location , and a camera. What you use beyond that is purely from your imagination! Who knew zombies could be so sexy!?

[ZB] **Note: I waved frantically at this point.*

[KK] I have to commend my models when it comes to creating some of my work. Sometimes a particular model would come to mind whether it's because of how they look, how well they would adapt to a dangerous or disgusting location, or simply because they have to prep for 6 hours just to shoot for 30 minutes without complaining. In the

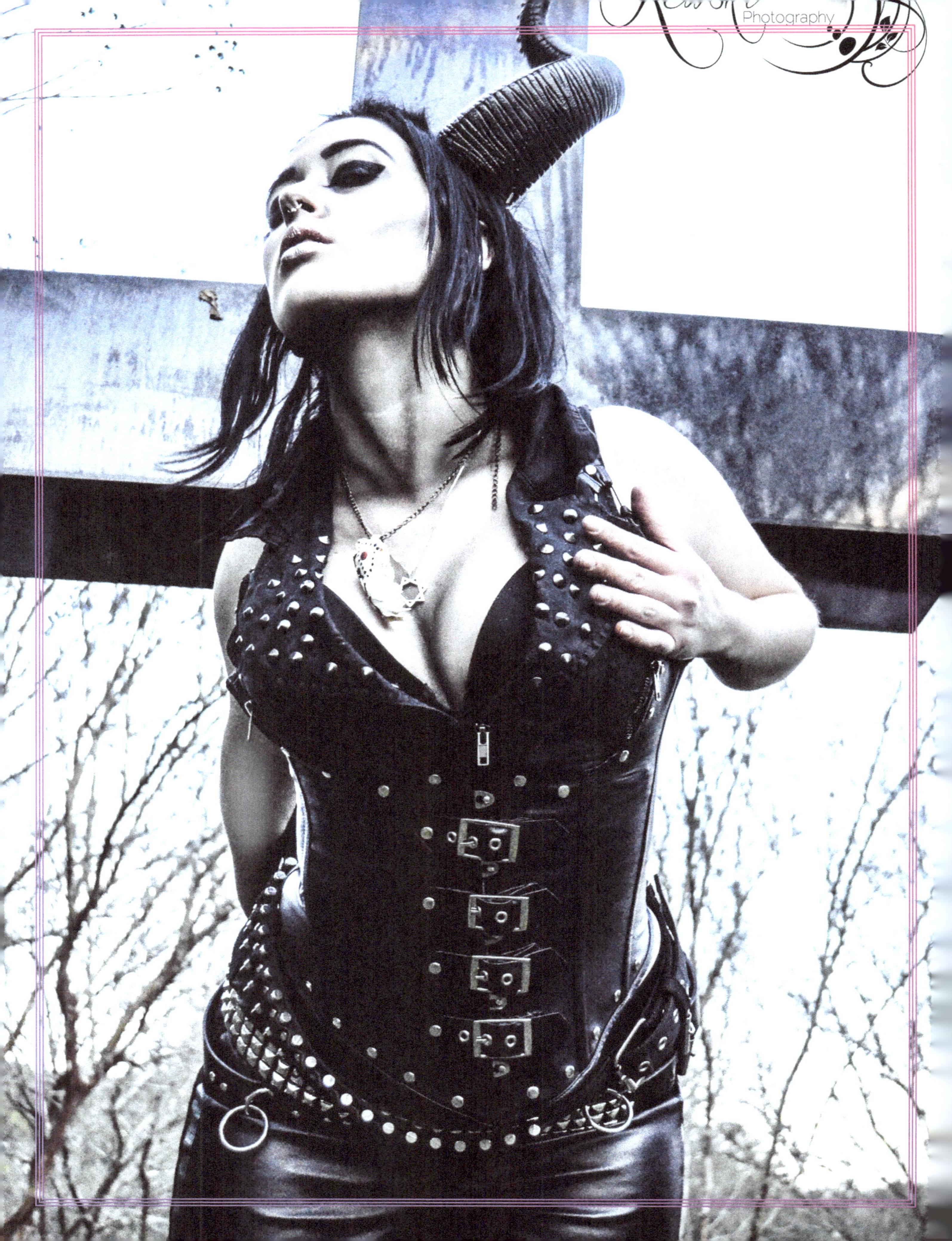
Photography

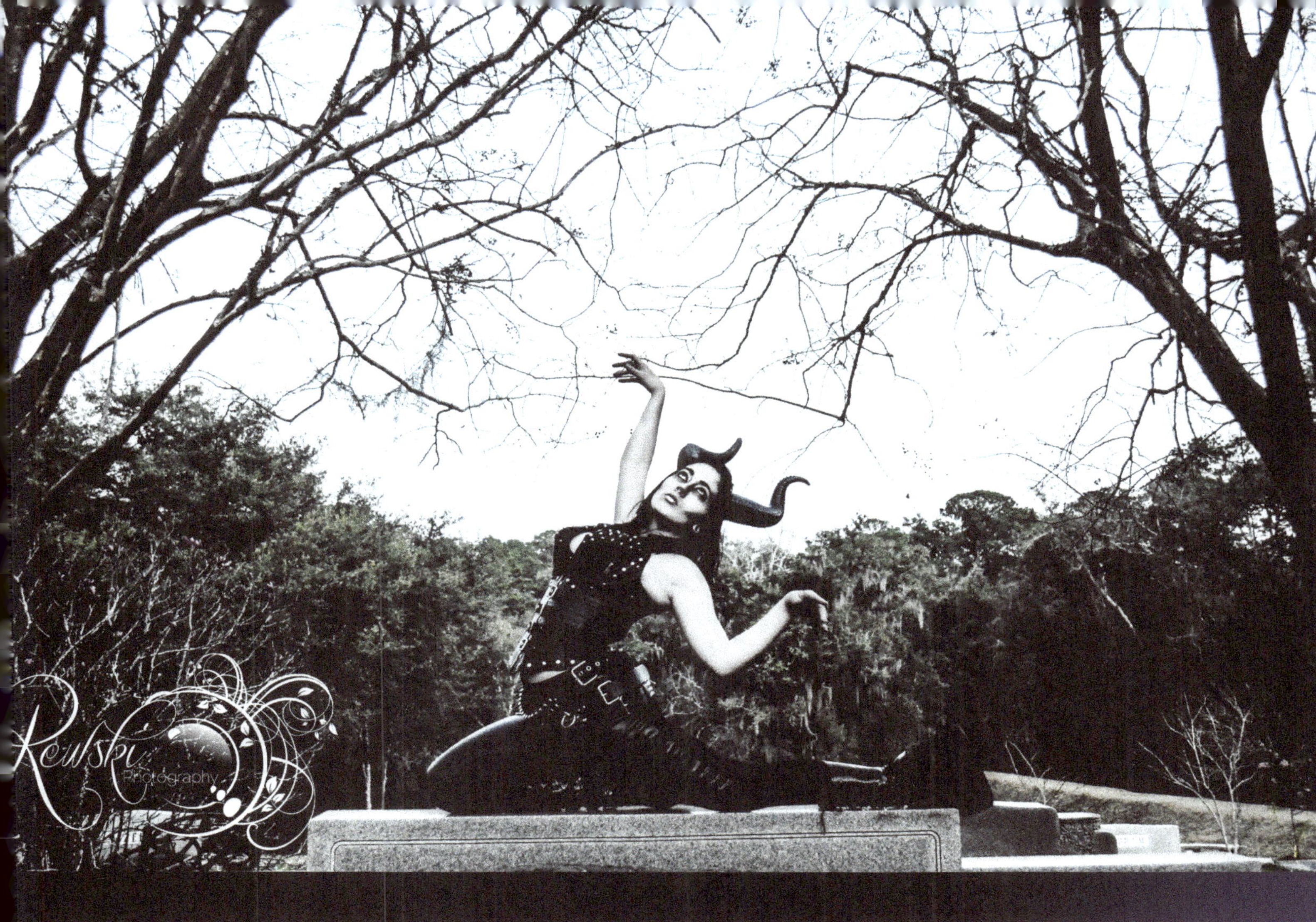

end, it's always worth the sunburn and bug bites! Post-production takes a big part as well. Whether it's lighting, contrast, or color adjustments, it's always convenient when you can cover a blemish and remove a fire hydrant to complete a look.

[ZB] *Florida is a state of ten-minute weather changes. How do you overcome this?*

[KK] To be honest, it is very difficult. The weather is only a single factor out of a hundred that you must account for when planning a photo shoot. When it's too hot, make up melts. When it rains, hair is ruined. When it's too cold, everyone in Florida hates it... so good luck finding a model! It's best to be understanding and open for rescheduling because you never know what can happen.

[ZB] *Any groups you belong to or models you would like to shout out? (Include websites if you like)*

[KK] There are too many to name! First of all, the local art community has SO much potential and I love every moment and opportunity working with all kinds of people. There is one person who really stands out, and so much of my work has been completed simply for the fact that this one person was involved. My left hand man would be my best Makeup Artist and such a great friend, Airen Sushereba of Airen's Oddities. She is the epitome of true genius and talent. Costuming, makeup, hair, accessories, She's the whole package! https://www.facebook.com/airens.oddities

[ZB] *Traditional film vs digital. Go!*

[KK] As much respect and love I have for film, the present makes it difficult to survive. I salute anyone who has the time and patience for such a skill. Digital is much more modern and easy that a simple upload to facebook can go viral and you can only hope that someone famous might have seen it! I think conceptually, digital is a great way to portray my wild imagination. It's just an edit away.

[ZB] *What aspirations do you have for the future?*

[KK] My goal is to never have to shoot weddings again! As much as I love celebrating happiness and love with strangers, I know I can do so much more. I never want to limit myself and hope that one day I can travel around the world with my Viking family and meet wonderful and interesting people. There is too much to see in this world. Not only do I want to see it for myself, but I would capture it for everyone else to see!

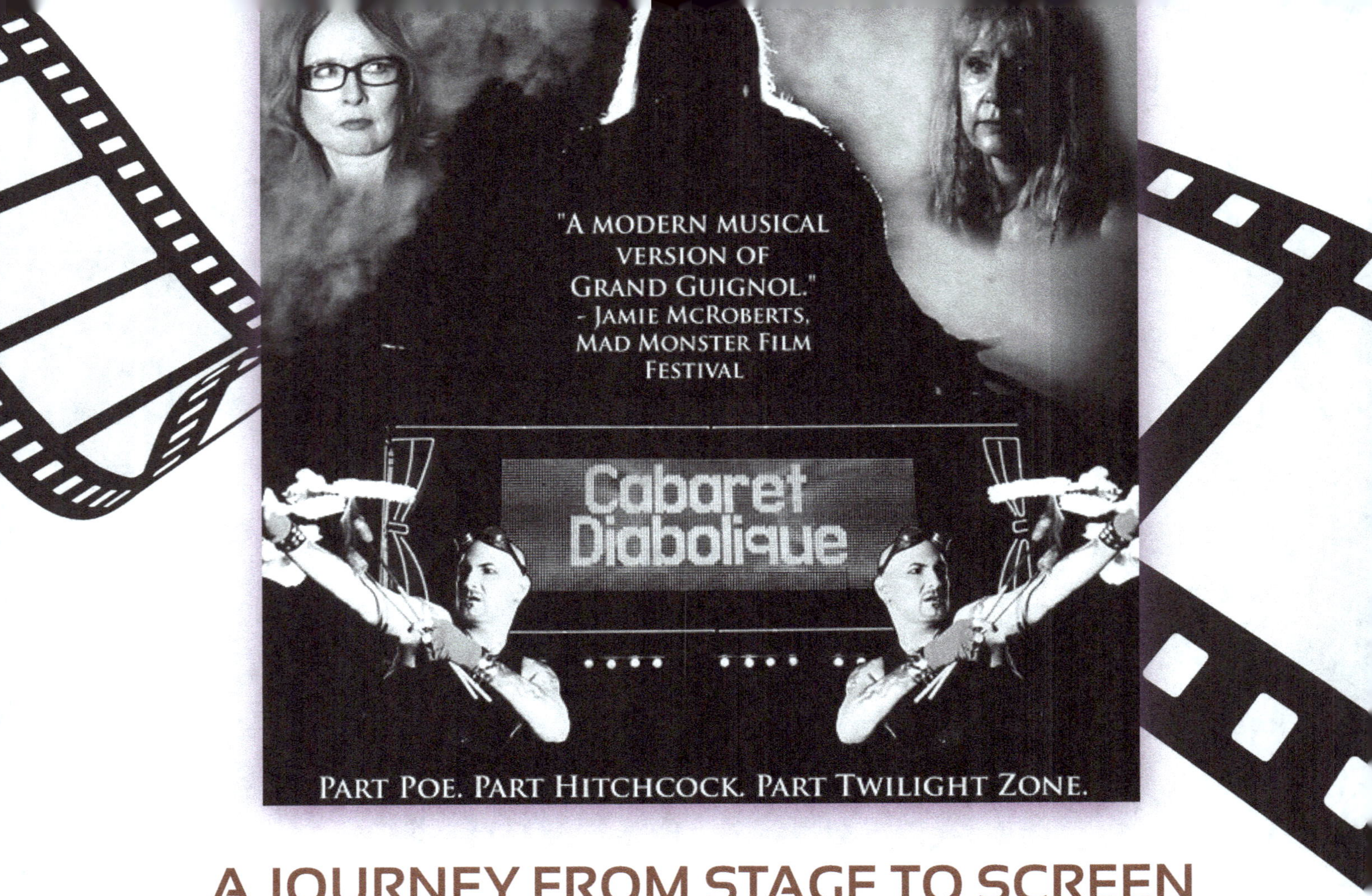

A JOURNEY FROM STAGE TO SCREEN

By Jezibell Anat

Cabaret Diabolique, a new horror/musical film, began as a stage show presented by Misfit Theatre Group in 2010 for a small audience at a gay nightspot in Augusta, Georgia. In 2015, this genre-bending film premiered at the Poison Peach Film Festival. The story, written by Jezibell Anat (the author of this piece) and Joseph Zuchowski, revolves around Charles and Yvette Mansfield, a brother and sister who headline Cabaret Diabolique, a glitzy, gory revue set amidst the decaying splendor of Atlantic City. The finale of this Gothic cabaret is an on-stage murder. The question is: is the murder real? Two detectives investigate the show and uncover a web of madness amidst the private lives of the performers.

The intricate plot revolves around Charles, who becomes involved with a new dancer named Jimmy. Unfortunately, their romance arouses the jealousy of Bruno Puglisi, the bitter manager of the casino, who is also attracted to Charles. Other members of Cabaret Diabolique include the Amazing Nikolai, a stage magician-hypnotist from Russia, his troubled young assistant Lucia, and Bashira, a sensual singer from New Orleans.

Dark, compelling songs by Christopher Forbes and Anat move the action through a stunning cabaret noir setting. The film was shot in Augusta, Georgia, and on location in Atlantic City, New Jersey.

Four members of the original cast reprised their stage roles in the movie - Jezibell Anat as Yvette, Robert Seawell as Charles, Joseph Zuchowski as Nikolai, and Steve Deitch as Bruno.   The film's cast also includes two actresses well-know to horror fans: Linnea Quigley and Camille Keaton.

Quigley is best known for her role as Trash in Return of the Living Dead, the cult classic that first verbalized the desire of zombies for brains. In Cabaret Diabolique, Quigley plays stage manager Amy, who does her best to keep the performers out of trouble. Keaton's claim to fame is her role as Jennifer in the controversial I Spit on Your Grave. Keaton

appears in CD as Marcia Wilson, an FBI agent who is supervising Nikolai.

Cabaret Diabolique also features a multitude of interesting methods for killing its characters. Special effects artist Roger Letizia created devices including a "Tenderizer" to grind up one victim, a "Stretch-O-matic" to pull one apart, and the "Toast-Her" to electrocute the film's female victim.

With all the music, dance, and gore, the focal point of Cabaret Diabolique is still the story. It's a thinking person's horror movie; rather than focusing on a haunted house or a slasher, it offers a mix of characters whose interactions become fatal. An audience member at one screening described Cabaret Diabolique as part Poe, part Hitchcock, and part Twilight Zone.

Cabaret Diabolique will be showing at several horror conventions this year, including Mad Monster, Spooky Empire's May-Hem, Scares That Cares, and the Martinsville Horrorfest.

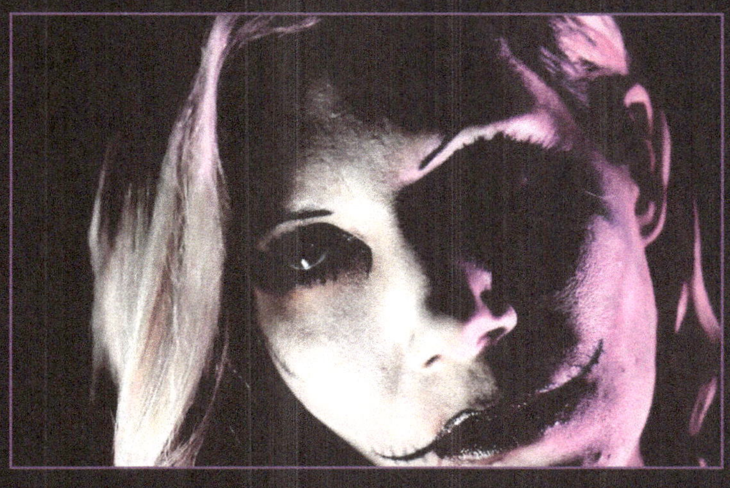
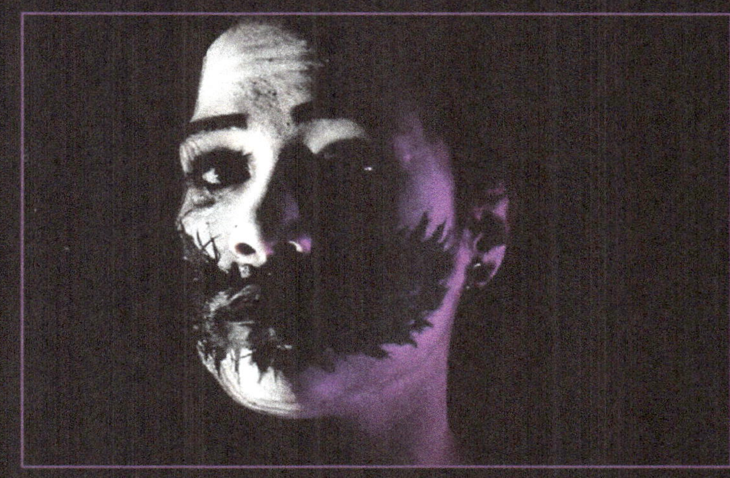
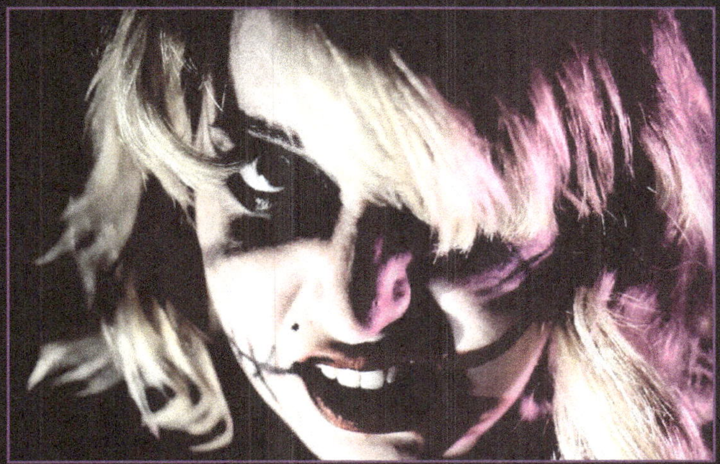
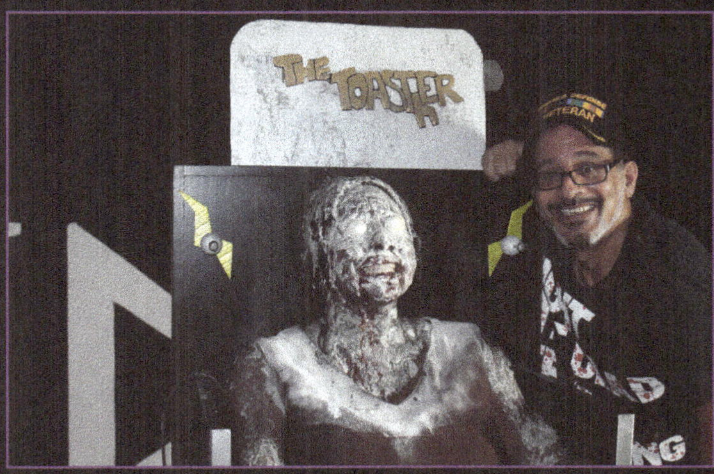

Nightmare Circus Creepers:
Minxy Monroe
Schuyler Hart
Tarynn Stineman

Cheryl Martin being electrocuted in
Roger Letitia's "Toast-Her"

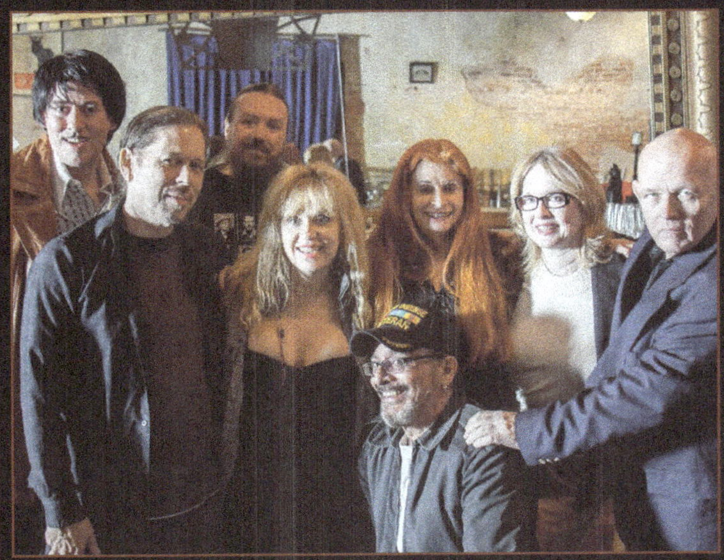

Cabaret Diabolique cast and crew - actor/camera operator Stephen Gilliam, director Christopher Forbes, actor/camera operator Dan Beck, Linnea Quigley, special effects artist Roger Letizia, Jezibell Anat, Camille Keaton, Joseph Zuchowski

Linnies Lost Favorites

By LinnieSarah

Don't Deliver Us from Evil (1971)

Not to be mistaken with Deliver Us from Evil, the 2014 possession film from Scott Derrickson, this lost classic is about a pair of girls who are more than content to be left in the company of Satan. Written and directed by Joël Séria, Don't Deliver Us from Evil was so controversial upon its release, it was banned in its own country. And when an intensely religious country is shown a film about two teenage girls who kill, seduce, and generally sin up a storm, all in the name of the Devil, it seems pretty clear the movie was going to ruffle some feathers. But France's loss is our gain, because Don't Deliver Us from Evil has gone on to garner well-deserved cult status and enter the annals of film as one of the most balls-out insane summer vacation films ever made.

Take THAT Griswold Family.

The Story: Anne and Lore are two young girlfriends who attend the same convent/boarding school. However, the girls discover that Jesus just isn't their bag, and they'd rather devote their free time to worshipping Satan and strangling parakeets. Inspired by the Parker/Hulme murders (which would later go on to inform the Peter Jackson film, Heavenly Creatures), Don't Deliver Us from Evil is less about religion and more about what can happen when two teenage girls are allowed to descend entirely into a world of their own making.

Despite all of the furor over the religious themes in Séria's movie, Anne and Lore's devotion to Satan is less relevant to the story than their devotion to one another. In fact, most of the Satanic worship in the film seems more like the girls trying to behave as they imagine "bad girls" would. At its core, Don't Deliver Us from Evil focuses more on what happens when the coming of age of two girls turns deadly, and their spoiled upbringing teaches them that their needs and desires are more important than anyone else's.

However, what makes Don't Deliver Us from Evil so deeply memorable is how shockingly violent it was given the story and timeframe. Played by Jeanne Goupil and Catherine Wagener, Anne and Lore only LOOK like children (thank Godzilla), but there is still something so unsettling about watching these two baby-faced women commit increasingly unspeakable acts. By the time we reach the final act, inevitable but still totally shocking, you find yourself both rooting for Anne and Lore to meet their maker, and still somehow feeling a tinge of sympathy for these twin devils. It's a testament to both actresses and the script that you will never fully get this movie out of your head.

After lingering in limbo for years, Mondo Macabro released an uncut special edition of Don't Deliver Us from Evil. So if you're feeling brave, bring Anna and Lore home…

Just make sure to hide your pets first.

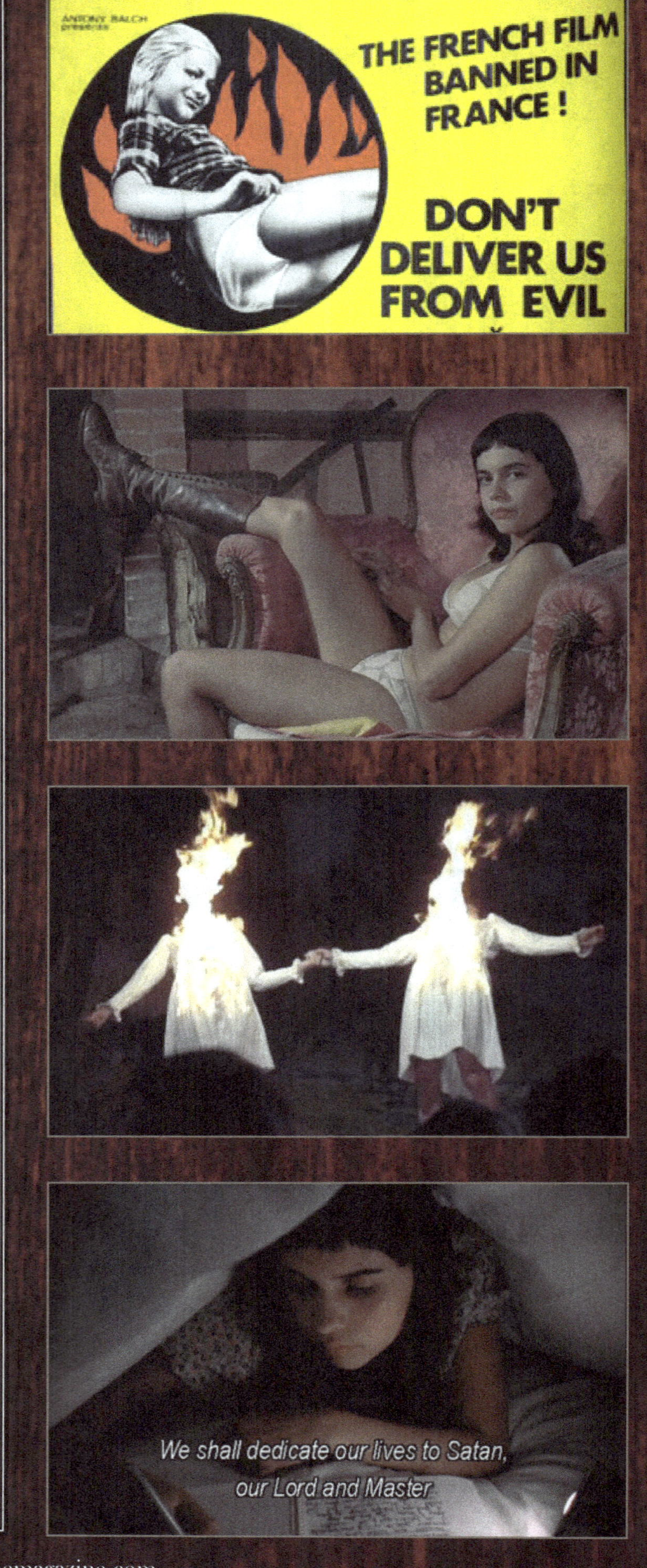

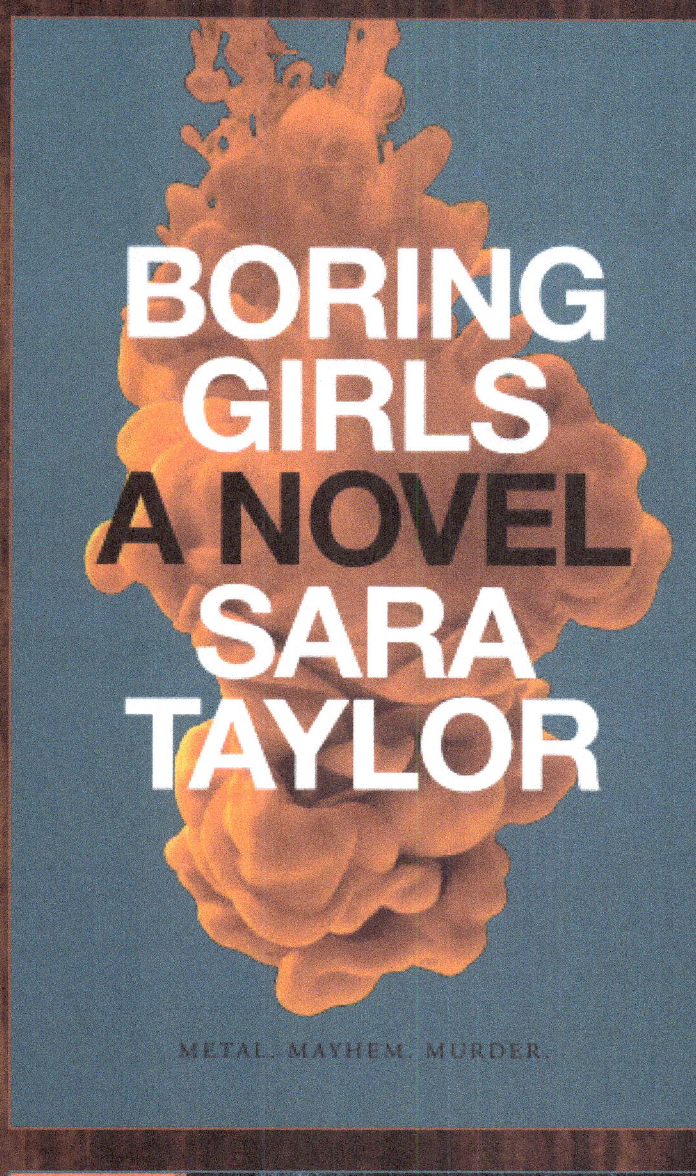

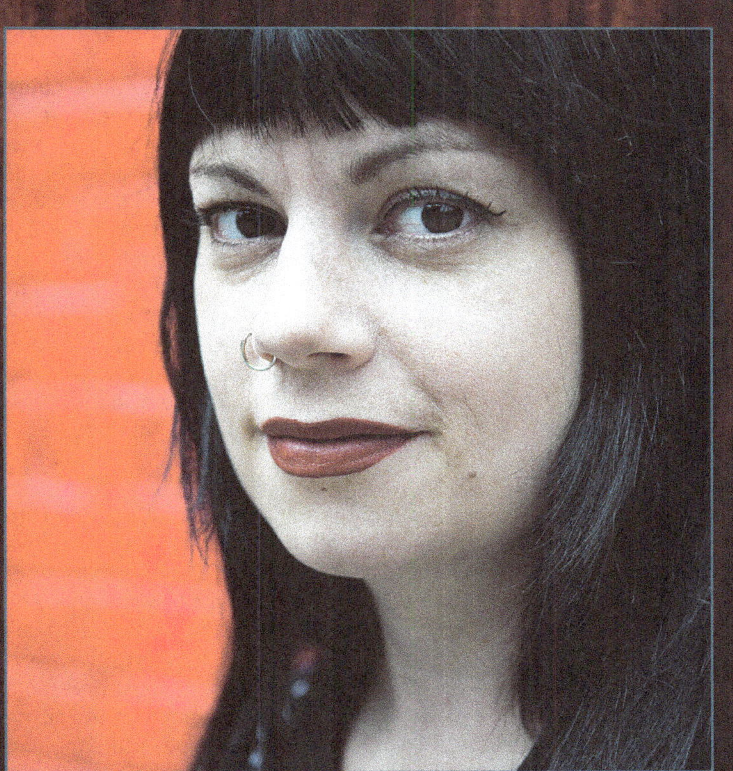

Boring Girls isn't Boring... But it isn't Fantastic Either

By LinnieSarah

In recent years, the world of young adult literature has become absolutely saturated with seemingly-strong female characters, often in positions of extreme peril, who then go on to save the world. It's gotten to a point where these leading girls are becoming interchangeably generic, and for the most part, aren't remotely as empowering as their authors believe them to be. Sara Taylor's debut YA novel Boring Girls introduces readers to a pair of entirely different teenage anti-heroes and while it was refreshing to read about two genuine outsiders, the book as a whole didn't live up to its promise.

The Story: Rachel feels like a total nobody at school, until she discovers the world of heavy metal music, and beautiful and likeminded new friend Fern. It isn't long before Fern and Rachel start a band, determined to become the new female face of the metal scene. But before that can happen, Rachel and Fern share a joint, horrible experience when they meet one of their favorite bands, and are left questioning just what their roles in metal truly mean. Armed with newfound purpose and a taste for bloody revenge, Rachel and Fern's band takes the metal world by storm, thundering forward to an inevitable and violent conclusion.

Everything about Boring Girls is just enough. It's well-written, but just enough to not be noticeably frustrating. There are multiple "first-time novelist" problems, from repetitive word use to simplistically styled dialogue. A young adult reader would be unlikely to nitpick issues like this, but Boring Girls isn't a YA novel that is going to cross genre lines and appeal to adults. There were multiple occasions where, despite ample self-control, I was left rolling my eyes at overly juvenile conversations that felt rehashed from so many other coming-of-age novels that have been done before.

However, Boring Girls was just interesting enough to keep me engaged through to the end. But this isn't to say I wasn't ever bored. The expositionary portion of the novel takes far too long, and too much time is spent on events and characters that don't actually end up being relevant in the end. We are rushed forward to a conclusion, and just when things get truly interesting, the book abruptly ends. I was deeply irritated that this ending I had spent so much time anticipating was rushed through in favor of dawdling over irrelevant details.

As the lead singer of The Birthday Massacre, Sara Taylor has a unique insider's knowledge of what the metal scene is like for young women, and this shines through Boring Girls without fail. The book has something important to say about misogyny and the culture of violence inherent in the industry, and for that reason I think it's an important read for young women who pink cloud the life of a musician. But for everyone else, I'm not sure Boring Girls will be a book they'll be excited to visit.

Rating: 2 ½ smelly tour busses out of 5

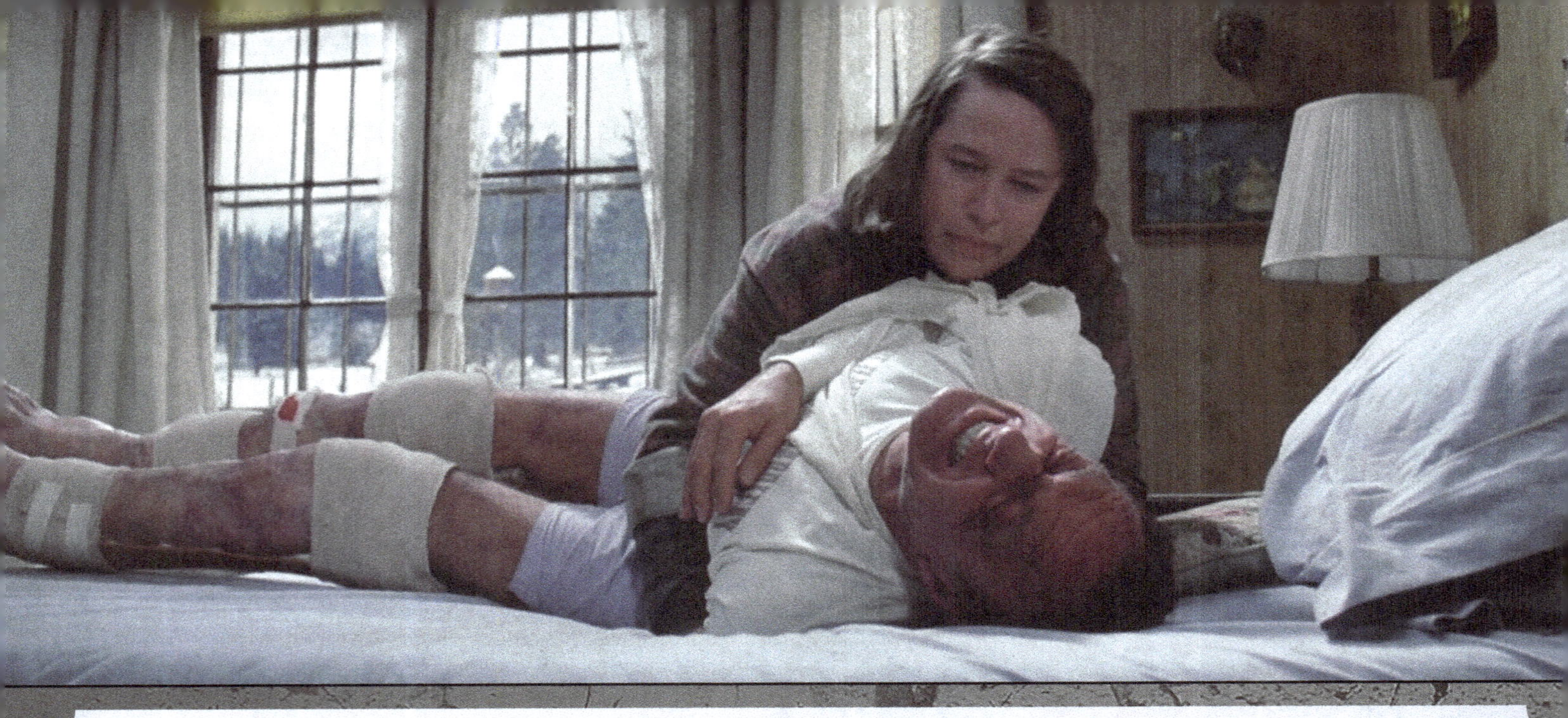

MISERY'S NUMBER-ONE FAN!

By Jesse Orr

Stephen King is not infallible. Nor is any writer, director, musician, or creator. However, in my opinion, his novel Misery and the subsequent feature film, are shining examples of a writer firing on at least nine of ten cylinders.

Misery is a story about amputation. It's about destruction. It's about confinement of one's own creation realized too late. It's about addiction. It's about hope, and redemption, gripped from the depths of the human psyche.

Romance novelist Paul Sheldon is best known for his series of books featuring a sweet but dim-witted woman named Misery Chastain. This series has culminated in his last book, in which Misery dies while giving birth to her child and is buried. The story follows Sheldon as he leaves a mountain resort following completion of his next book, an attempt to break out of the soap-opera rubbish he loathes writing, which, although vapid and stomach-turning, pays the bills. Driving into a snowstorm after drunkenly celebrating, Paul is unable to maintain his Camero's grip upon the road and ends up in distress. Fortunately for him, his number-one Misery fan just happens to be on hand to pop open the door and rescue him from being frozen alive. Upon awakening, Paul finds his body shattered, both his mind and body addicted to a codeine based painkiller, and that his number-one fan, Annie Wilkes, also his one and only nurse, is completely insane.

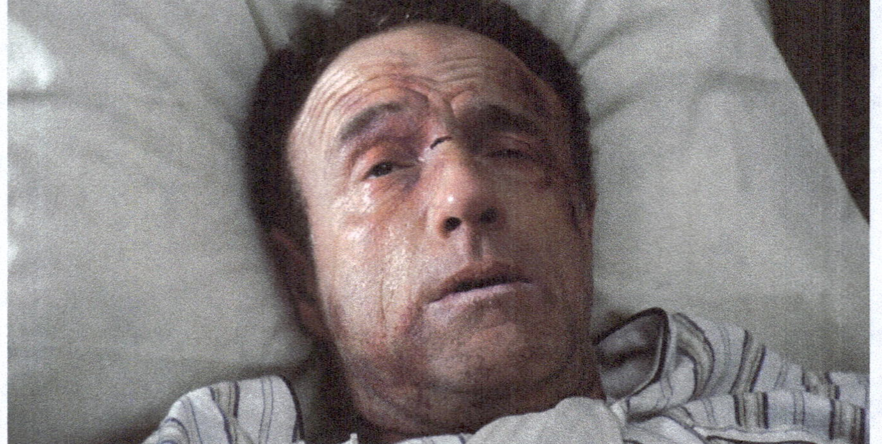

Insane can be a frightening word, and King has gone to great lengths to accurately portray Annie's psychosis, researching various psychiatric conditions to create a list of symptoms, only taken to the extreme. Indeed, Annie's disturbing nature comes not from her resemblance to any boogeyman, but her similarities to people we see every day, or rather, the public faces they choose to show us. Contrasting that with the helplessness of our protagonist, Paul seems doubly in danger, not only from an insane(ly) overzealous fan, but from a woman who is genuinely mentally ill, and who, it is revealed, has gotten away with murder. Not to mention the completely different yet similar hold Annie has over Paul by her control of his painkillers, a fictional drug known as Novril. As Paul notes, "you may spell relief R-O-L-A-I-D-S but you spelled Novril C-O-D-E-I-N-E." This dependance on prescription drugs by our protagonist is more than likely a not-so-sly nod to King's own issues with drugs and alcohol, for which he has stated the book and the character Annie Wilkes is a metaphor.

While the main focus of the story is initially on Paul's struggle to survive, and escape Annie's clutches, Misery slowly morphs into a focus on Annie's desires: a new book, written just for her, about her hero, Misery Chastain, alive and well again. When Paul balks, she convinces him in a number of unpleasant ways, that writing her book is his best option. As Paul writes, he is sucked back into the easy-to-write melodramatic world of Misery and pens the most gruesome novel in his series. The reader is treated to typewritten pages of the first draft of Misery's Return, complete with Paul's typewriter's missing

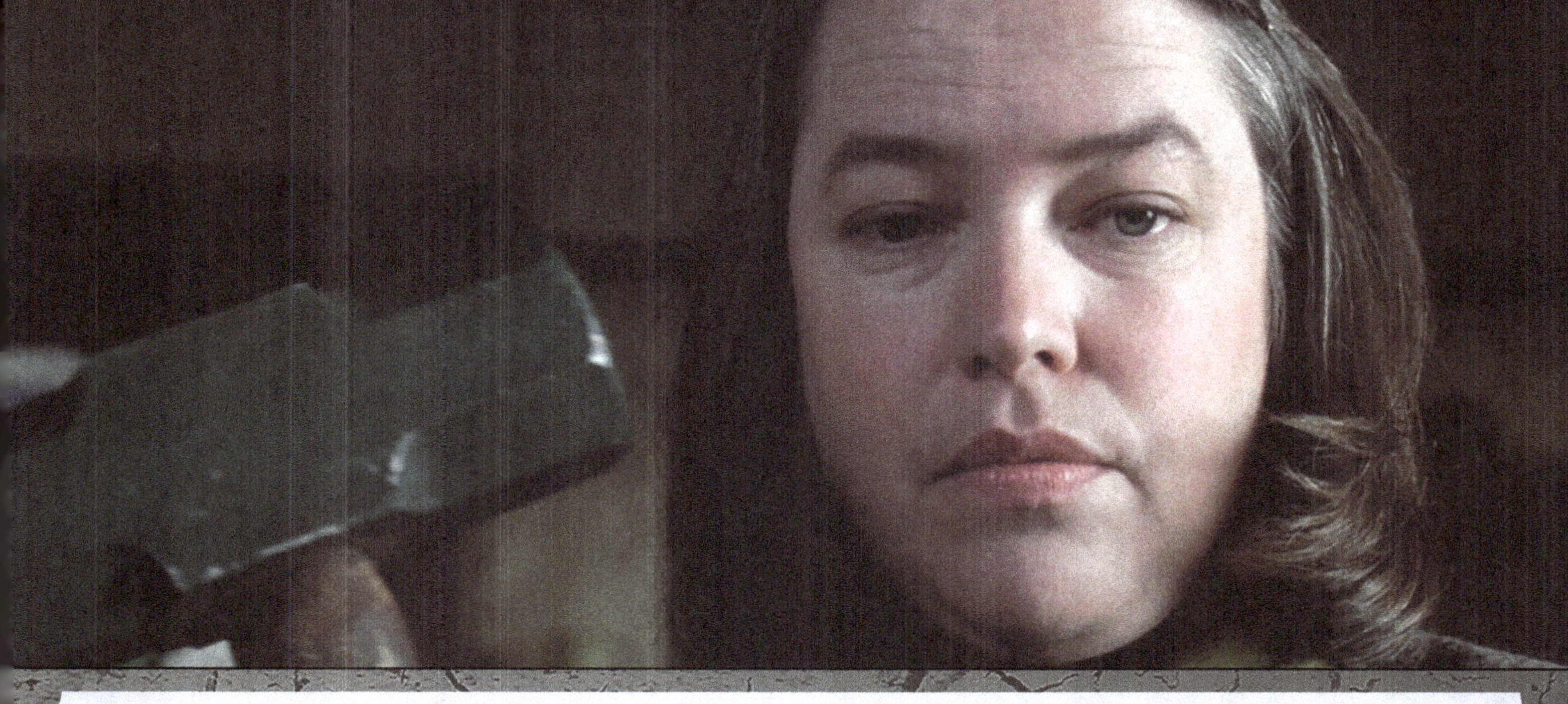

N key providing gaps for realism. The first chapter concludes with the twist that Misery was buried alive and has dug herself out of her grave only to fall unconscious with her fingers worn down to the bone.

This, for me, was not an appreciated diversion from the main storyline. Only when I had read the novel several times was I able to focus on the story-within-the-story and focus on Paul Sheldon's created character. I must confess that for the first few times through the novel, I skipped all of Misery's excerpts. As the novel continues, Paul's physical and mental states deteriorate as the typewriter continues losing keys (perhaps a correlation?), and eventually he begins writing by hand. Those pages of the book are fortunately few, but nearly illegible, and do much for breaking up the flow of the reader, until they are able to overcome their concern for Paul enough to focus on his writings.

Many books are better than movies, and many movies are far worse than books. In this case, the book is better than the movie, but the movie is not significantly less entertaining than the book. In both, there are elements of horror, suspense, humor, shock, and humanity. Even Annie Wilkes, the demented psycho that she is, is impossible not to pity, and indeed, even to empathize with. Who among us has not been so passionately caught up with the object of a writer's imagination, that when the subject takes a turn with which we are displeased, we object? Even Sir Arthur Conan Doyle, upon informing his mother he intended to kill off Sherlock Holmes in an upcoming publication, was admonished "Kill that nice Mr. Holmes? Foolishness! Don't you dare!"

Annie Wilkes just takes it to a new level.

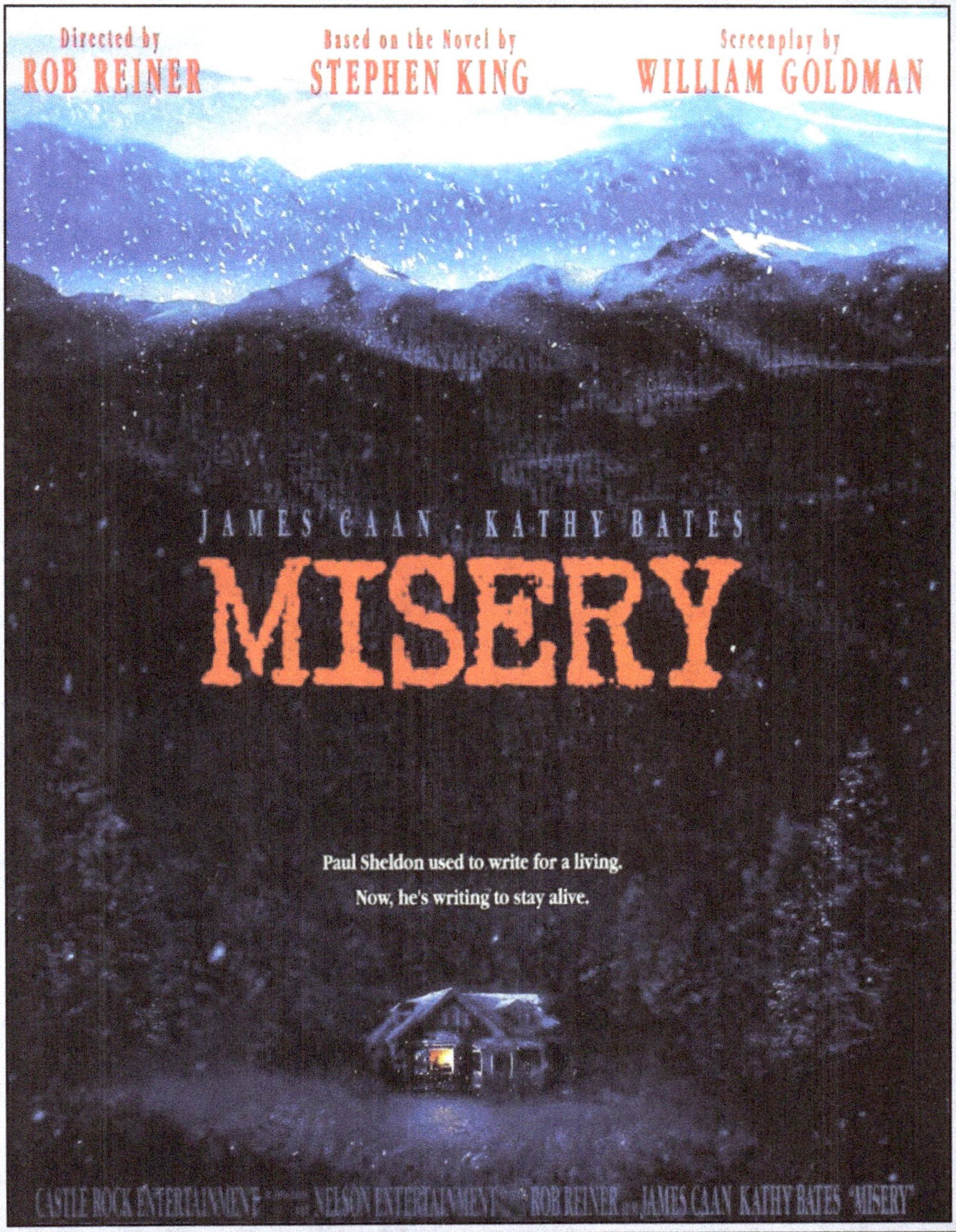

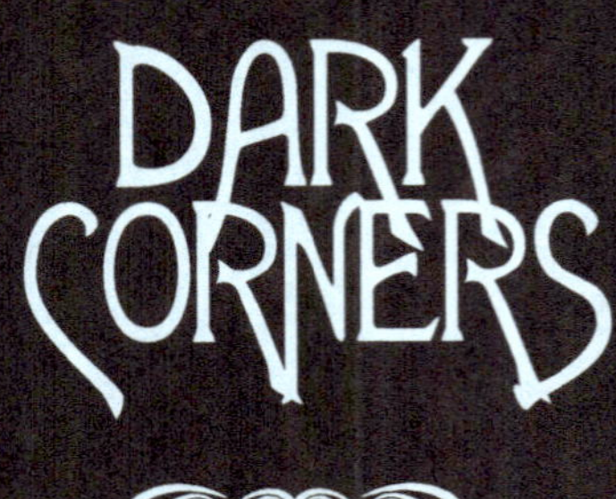

DARK CORNERS

From the darkest corners of our imaginations, soar the most beautiful creations

"BASOREXIA"

By Zombieboy

from the novel "Kouzins"

Inside I feel it calling me

The Carnal desperate beckoning

Deep red copper essence vice of pain

Into deep wounded wanting

Venom flowing into every chalice

Warm wishful needed tasting

Wrapped around me like a vice

Her love in my mouth I am holding

Biting into salted warm

Given into hungry wanting

Pain from pleasure and reverse

Feel her overflowing

Taste as sweet as summer wine

Love made flesh for the holding

"BENEATH"

By Zahara

Slumbering 'neath the sands of time,

swaddled in layers that gently bind,

Arise for me, my shrouded love,

with all the coo's of a dusty dove.

Unwrap for me, your skin... your soul,

and bring your heart in its sacred bowl.

Sigh for me through muzzled lips...

reach for me with death's fingertips.

Bound to sand, this tomb's your fate...

Left alone to disintegrate.

I've come for you, slip from your sheath

and bare to me what lies beneath.

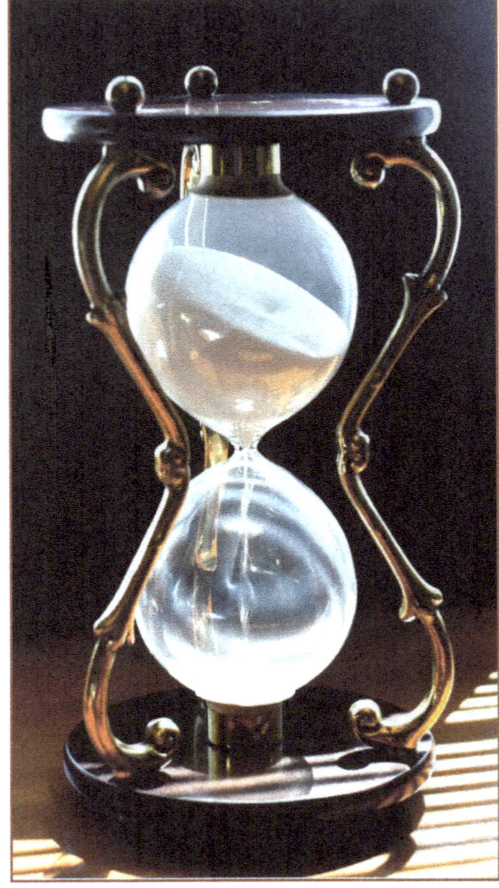

"BLOOD CROW"

By Dannette Tillery

Red dripping fangs can be felt from the one who is blood stained...

his touch is death, yet you lust upon it, the heart beat

and vain's is his pain, a feathers touch like a haunting melody.

It's to late to back away yet if you only knew would you stay?

Giving in is the only way to be free, though a prisoner you shall be.

A simple touch will give away, to the only sound that will never be found.

Sight is born a new by his feathery kisses...that sing to you,

"will you love me forever?" he whispers as those fangs

began to dip. I believe I heard a "yes" on the wind of pain

and ecstasy given to bliss of his bloody crows kiss.

"TEATIME"

By Asylum Attendant

Chatter echoed throughout the garden

As afternoon tea prompted women

To spill their innermost thoughts and dreams,

Which husbands could never hear, it seemed.

Clothed in tightly laced corsets that pinched,

Since a woman's waist looked best when cinched,

These women knew they must look decent

And that breathing was unimportant.

Along with the tea were served muffins

And cherry scones placed in fancy tins,

Which were clearly only there for show

'For no lady wants a healthy glow.

To protect the women from the sun

Were quaint parasols for everyone.

Because Victorian ladies know

A tan is a definite no-no.

Placed throughout the garden were wickets

For the dames to play croquet in sets,

Since it was unlikely to tire

Whilst knocking balls through small, arched wires.

Little girls pretended to drink tea

Nearby their mothers, smiling with glee.

Little did the ignorant girls know,

Poison-spiked tea is hard to swallow.

The pleasant aroma of roses

Wafted into many pale noses,

Much unlike the stench of master's breath

When his rapes his lady 'til her death.

Two of the women sat together

And had been best friends for forever.

If their hidden romance was revealed,

Then love from doctor could make them healed.

The hostess refilled dainty teacups

As one dame tried to stop her hiccups.

And once the party had reached its end

The ladies feared their frail hearts would rend.

Alas, the women said their goodbyes

And a few even began to cry.

Because they all knew their fun was over

Until they fucked their secret lovers.

Think your poetry is good enough to be published in Carpe Nocturne? Send submissions to mj@carpenocturne.net, subject line "Poetry."

All submissions must be under 250 words, and will be judged by Managing Editor Michael Jack and Art Editor Zahara.

The best entries will be featured in our next issue along with our very talented staff.

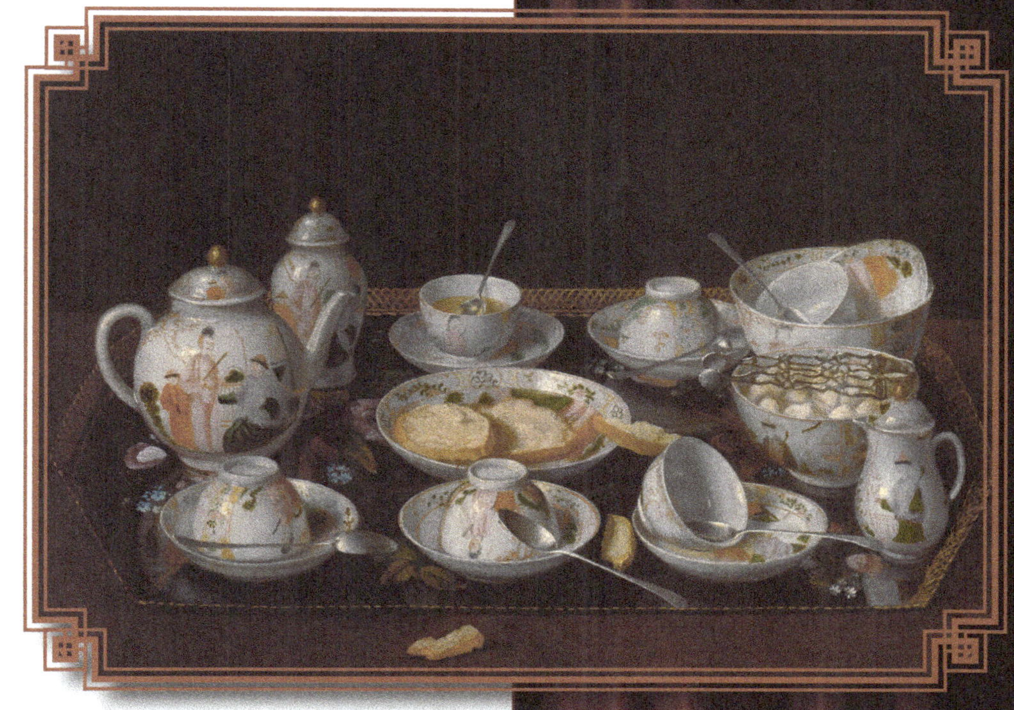

A GATHERING OF THINGS IN NOIR STYLE

Dark Horses
Black Music

Produced by Richard Fearless (Death in Vegas) Dark Horses represent a gloomy B-side of British neo-psychedelic sound, something like a photo turned into a negative. This Brighton-based group appears a lethal amalgam of illustrious influences, including The Doors, Opal, Mazzy Star, Sonic Boom, among others, recognizables here, there and everywhere inside these compositions. An album that is a tapestry of vaguely noirish-goth moods, marked by the bewitching voice of Lisa Elle, confortably absorbed within the clangor of guitars, Vox organ and drums. A whirling kaleidoscope of dark emotions on the razor's edge of a psychedelia deprived of its usual colors.

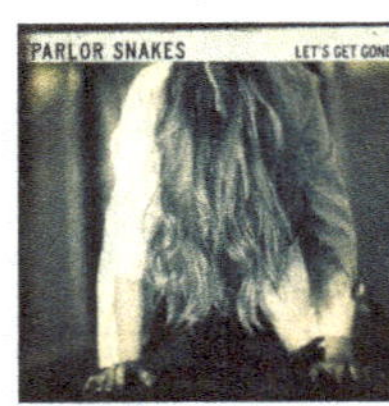

Parlor Snakes
Let's Get Gone
Tomorrow Never Comes

For those who loved the voodoo-rock of Cramps and Gun Club may be a little surprise to discover the swampy and crawling sound of Parlor Snakes. This Paris-based French-American quartet, is much less "depraved" (especially outwardly) of its inspiring fathers, but anyway also more than a tasty but mere revisitation of that unforgettable season called psycho-billly. Eugenie Alquezar, the talented "femme fatale" vocalist of the band, is in her full element here, amongst this dangling and distorted handfull of songs, from "Light Up The House" to "Unsatisfied", similar to a burning pinwheel in the hands.

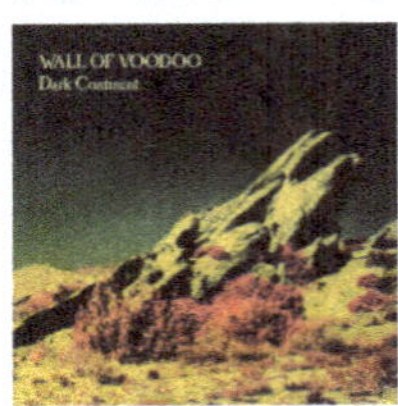

Wall of Voodoo
Dark Continent
Call of the West

With a brilliant one-two punch combination, the first couple of albums made by Wall of Voodoo burst onto the new wave scene, in the early eighties, deconstructing the myth of the frontier thanks to a unique blend of Morricone, Johnny Cash, Suicide and Devo. Amazingly, the eclectic mind of Stan Ridgway was able to cook a spicy tex-mex dish, immersed in some sort of goth-sci-fi sauce, obtained by adding a large amount of deviated electronic sounds and minimalistic stories of losers and misfits. Many of these characters, seem to have sprung from the pen of Raymond Chandler, David Goodis or Jim Thompson and we will find them again in The Big Heat, the totally noir first solo album released by by Stan a few years later.

"Call Box", "Animal Day", "Mexican Radio", "Lost Weekend", track after track, a memorable sequence of hallucinated tunes flows away, drawing an imaginary soundtrack for some classic noir-western – perfect for Bad Day at Black Rock, for esample - and making it clear what actually Troy Paiva, photographer and one of Stan's best friends, was listening when he took shots of carcasses of abandoned cars rusting in the desert.

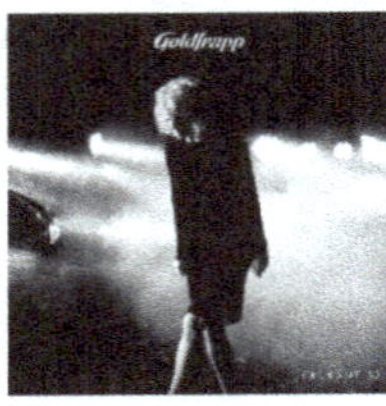

Goldfrapp
Tales of Us

A person's name for each song (with the exception of "Stranger") and a story behind every name, Laurel, Annabel, Drew, Jo.. Alison Goldfrapp and Will Gregory are back on their feet, those of Felt Mountain, enhanced by the rarefied atmospheres of "Lovely Head" that made them famous, but now drawing inspirations from Patricia Highsmith and Dorothy B. Hughes among others.

Tales of Us surfs that same wavelenght again. For at least five songs, music and images are here almost inseparable. Alison walks slowy, opening the blazing short movie of "Jo" with charming steps along a dark and desert street, almost a film-within-a-film itself . Her voice is sensuous, dramatic, impalpable, a dreamlike sequence, cadenced by the beat of a piano. This is the true noirish gem of the bunch, followed by the astonishing and fading "Laurel", a plot that blends together Hollywood, stalkers and serial killers and characterized by a languid, melancholic, orchestral arrangement, between David Lynch and Alfred Hitchcock.

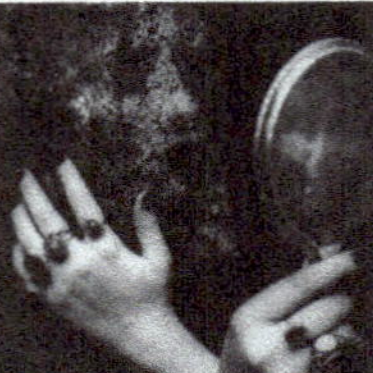

Tropic of Cancer
The Sorrow of Two Blooms
Permission of Love
Restless Idylls

In the eighties, Exene Cervenka and X scraped the bottom of the barrel of alienation, with a dirty and wicked country-punk, becoming the iconic image of a sunless California. Today - and wearing (often) very different dresses - another woman, the elegant and severe looking Camella Lobo, seems to reinterpret the same vision, even if using another music lexicon.

Tropic of Cancer is substiantially her solo project, fascinated, intrigued by the dark side of the city - and Los Angeles in particular - kneaded of crime, passion, sorrow, desolation. Synth, drum-machine and guitars plot a cold-dark-wave texture, incantatory and obsessive, ideal background for the icy and profane litanies sung by Camella, almost an attempt to investigate the subconscious and its dephts. As for Portished, Lana Del Rey or Goldfrapp, both - images and B&W videos - are connected in parallel with music and frequently in pure noir-style.

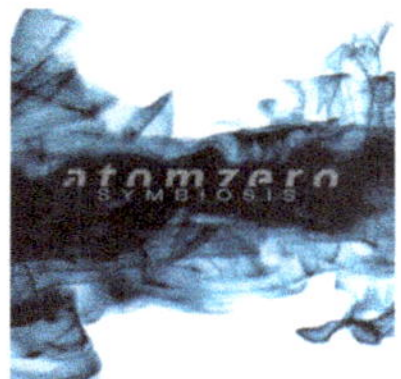

Atomzero
Symbiosis

A little bit VNV Nation, a little bit Nine Inch Nails and a whole lot to say. That's Canadian EBM group Atomzero. Their debut special edition album Symbiosis was released through AnalogueTrash Records in the UK and Europe this past December. Symbiosis is filled with apocalyptic future-pop that would entice any Cybergoth to swing their synthetic dreads right off their head.

Atomzero's melodic first single "MisDirection" is a heavy dose of synth-pop about a volatile relationship. "Nature Without Sound" is probably one of the most industrial tracks on Symbiosis. The synthesizers are very foreboding as the lyrics tell the tale of a planet destroyed. Those looking for something spunkier would savor the pounding "Build Decay". The normally tenacious vocals are amped up to compete with the nonstop syncopation. The completely instrumental track "Divisions" displays the mellower side of this dance club ready group.

The power technology has over humanity is discussed on "Dissent". You can hear the struggle between beeping synths having an argument during the electronic solo in the middle. These instruments have minds and opinions of their own. Melancholic guitars and shadowy vocals compose "Ghost Inside", a song about the loss of identity. A lack of control over oneself and a person's environment is a reoccurring theme on Symbiosis.

Symbiosis is definitely a balance between organic and electronic soundscapes, dark and light lyrics, and hard and soft rhythms. Atomzero meanders through genres with such delicacy and impressive precision. Their melodies work together to exist in harmony. With a recent lineup change on vocals, the future of Atomzero is sure to be ever-evolving. - **ASYLUM ATTENDANT**

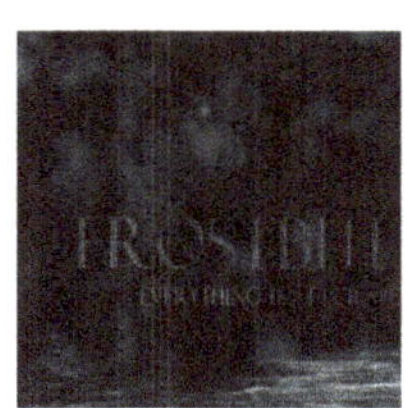

Frostbite
Everything I Crave

If I could explain this CD simply, I would say if you took one part Metallica, one part Alice in Chains, sprinkled in some industrial sounds, and added a pinch of operatic metal, you would have "Everything I Crave" by Frostbite. This album is dark, building a slow grinding momentum, like an army marching across the field to their inevitable death. That's the feeling...nervous helpless despair. If I can take the liberty of comparing this album to one more band, I would say "Everything I Crave" builds the a similar emotional atmosphere to Tool.

Beginning with the opening instrumental track "Nightmare," one-man wrecking machine Christopher Lee Compton lures you in with symphonic melodies. The mood turns black as the choir gives way to a wailing guitar. Eventually both come together, and opens the door to the next nine tracks that will follow. The second track is an introduction to the more Gothic-Industrial sound Compton can deliver. Overall, I would consider "Everything I Crave" more of a doom metal album, but it definitely contains strong elements of various genres. Compton does a masterful job of blending them all together to create a sound uniquely his own. Without a doubt, the composition on this CD is tight, and the arrangement flawless.

If I had to pick a favorite song on this CD, I would have to say "Afterlife Mine." I'm always a sucker for the slower tracks, and this one delivers. Compton's voice really shines in this song as he displays the amazing depth of his range. "Afterlife Mine" is a driving metal ballad mixed with a heavy dose of Gothic forlorn. I want to listen to this song over and over again. It's brilliant. Excluding the bonus track, "Everything I Crave" ends with the ethereal dirge, "Death of a Friend." At this moment, you truly feel your journey is complete. The soldiers are at rest, lining the battlefield with their war torn bodies. The angels arrive to carry them home. "Everything I Crave" delivers this kind of imagery. I strongly recommend experiencing it. - **MICHAEL JACK**

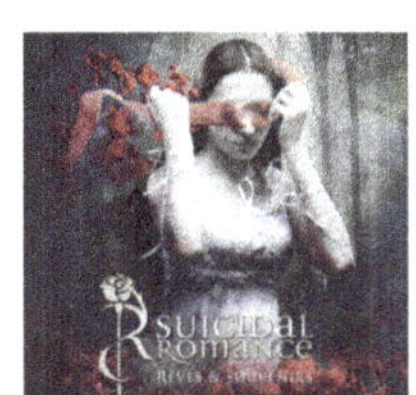

Suicidal Romance
Rêves & Souvenirs

Suicidal Romance really is the perfect name for this fiendish, yet angelic electronic duo from Estonia, the land of forests. Their compilation album, Rêves & Souvenirs, features songs from past albums such as Love Beyond Reach and Shattered Heart Reflections. The album also includes new collaborations with artists such as dark wave singer Felix Marc and the Estonian progressive metal band Emphasis. Rêves & Souvenirs is a must listen for audiences who are unfamiliar with the work of members D. Darling (who's also the lead singer of industrial rock band Freakangel) and Viktoria Seimar.

My favorite track would have to be "Dreamers", the inspiring synth-pop song featuring Viktoria's soaring tone and signature note-floating laments. The buzzing synths and numerous melodic change-ups throughout the song keep the listener focused on the message of perseverance. "Whisper Goodbye" contains the harsh, growly vocal stylings of D. Darling and industrial drill sounds. Many of the songs on Rêves & Souvenirs have similar haunting melodies, yet each one is so different instrumentally that the melody sounds fresh each time.

The male and female vocals interlace seamlessly on "Remember Me". Darling uses a softer tone and the dreamy synths throughout transform the song into a pleasant memory. Emphasis' rock cover of the song gives it some grit with prominent guitar riffs and a more aggressive female vocal. This version brings the lyrics out of the dream state and into reality. "Ecstatic" featuring Felix Marc is a nice change-up from the original song and his vocal back-and-forth with Viktoria among the driving beats is eerie. The desire and keyboards are strong on "Touch", forming a lovers' duet.

The alternative electro sounds and pensive lyrics on Rêves & Souvenirs foreshadow the spellbinding songs to come from Suicidal Romance. - **ASYLUM ATTENDANT**

More Reviews - - - - - - ->

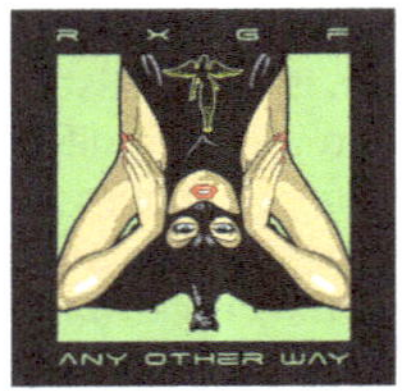

RxGF
Any Other Way

I get a lot of CDs that come across my desk, but there are very few I have enjoyed as much as RxGF's fourth release, "Any Other Way." I'll be honest, I have never listened to them before, but everyone needs a starting a point. If this CD is any indication of what their past worse seven tracks. The song "Antidote" I can hear coming right out of the mind and mouth of Shikhee from Android Lust. I hate to keep comparing, but these are great artists to be compared to, in my opinion.

Starting with track eight, "The Dying Grace of Machines," this CD takes a decisive turn. Suddenly, Schaaf almost completely disappears, and is used sparingly as backing vocals. "Any Other Way" becomes almost straight Electronic-Industrial, complete with sound bites and crunchy heavy guitars. To be fair, the CD has been building towards this, but the turn still seems abrupt. "The Hit" is an excellent song, and strays from that straight industrial format, but then it is followed by "10 Things that Go Bang," and leaves me confused to what this CD is supposed to be. Maybe that's the point, but I'm not feeling it.

Overall, I would highly recommend "Any Other Way." The songs "Tombstone Soire," "How to Make It," and "Antidote" are completely amazing. In fact, all seven of the first tracks are, but those three are my personal favorites. I'm sure you will have your own. I think RxGF will explode into the underground scene as long as they build upon the first half of "Any Other Way." They have a unique and infectious sound which is among the best I have heard in a long time. - **MICHAEL JACK**

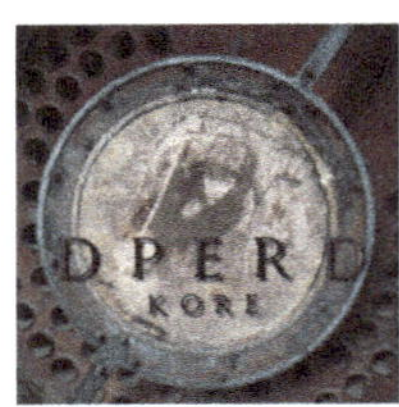

DPERD
Kore

Carlo Disimone and Valeria Buono are the couple of musicians based in Enna, Sicily, behind the project called Dperd. Kore is their third album that fills the fields still empty of a broader design begun many years ago and arrived now at his most accomplished work. The aesthetic background of the legendary British label 4AD encounters here the great tradition of the "canzone" (song) and the legacy of those Italian Prog-Rock bands who had their peak in the seventies. All the songs are in Italian – of course – and contain a strong dose of nostalgic-melancholic mood often sunk among the perilous reefs of an unending beat of drums.

"Non è il cielo " opens with delicate piano circles and reminds me of Mina, the Italian pop icon. "Fa male" and "You'll be watching me" follow silky melodic lines, preluding to the absolute beauty of "Io sono un errore." This song is characterized by a gently-abrasive guitar, slightly in a Robert Fripp style.

"Catena cieca" and "Risalgo il buio" raise the rhythm and the general tension of the disc with their catchy constructions, preluding to "Sono qui," a little masterpiece of bright melody and superb vocal performance inside a gorgeous arrangement enriched by precious nuances. The intro of "Train song" takes us back in time to a never forgotten British darkwave that dissolves quickly into a (perhaps) unconscious recall to certain neoclassical Prog groups such as Saint Just and Opus Avantra.

This albums looks like returning to a place left in a distant past, with its dusty shadows inhabited by memories, scattered objects under the window and an old ruined mirror on the wall. - **SERGIO MANGHINA**

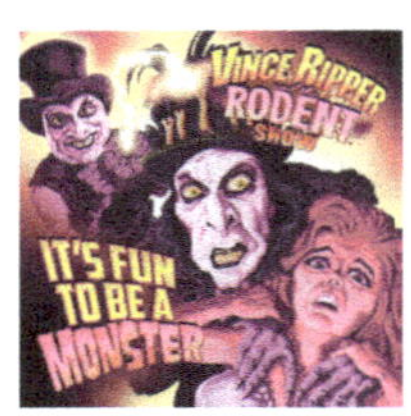

Vincent Ripper & the Rodent Show
It's Fun to be a Monster

Horror themed gothic punk is alive and well in the UK. Vince Ripper and the Rodent Show are back with a new CD and frightful stage show. IT'S FUN TO BE A MONSTER features veteran musician/DJ, Vince Ripper and (ex-Alien Sex Fiend) multi-talented Master of Ceremonies, Ratfink. This diabolically twisted duo incorporates the best of groovy garage punk'n roll with a psychobilly twang. Paying tribute to the dearly departed original founder of the Cramps, Lux Interior, you will find the reincarnation of a very early Cramps single, 'Sunglasses After Dark' as well as a cleverly fiendish version of 'New Kind of Kick'.

Other notable tracks include Suicide's 'Ghostrider' and an offensively salacious 'Smells Like'. The cool 'Jukebox Baby' compels you to kick up your heels and sway your hips. Many of the tracks are preceded by amusing verbal excerpts, reminiscent of black & white creature-feature matinée movie trailers and some intricately layered with crazy loops and sound effects. Overall, IT'S FUN TO BE A MONSTER is….well, FUN!

While the new CD proves to be an entertaining listen with fresh outtakes of classic covers and trippy tracks, it is the show's blitzkrieg of spooky kooky visual aesthetics accompanying their live performances which make them all the more extraordinary. In addition to great stage props and lighting, projectors spew a mash-up of 50's & 60's classic B-Movie horror phantasmagorias throughout; this includes a surprise interlude where The Rodent hands out 3D glasses and instigates the crowd to participate. The live show also includes other feral performances of classic Cramps and Alien Sex Fiend tracks complimented by Vince Ripper and the Rodent Show's own unique spellbinding flair. Both still hold that certain ghoulish exuberance from their earlier days on the scene which is what makes this release all the more appreciated. A throwback to a Golden era, it is the nostalgic aura and the static feeling of holding on to our own fountain of youth which gives bands like Vince Ripper and the Rodent Show a sense of continuity.

For the past couple of years, these gentlemen [respectively, Vincent Cornwall and Andrew Wilson] have been working very hard assaulting many stages across the United Kingdom performing at: Whitby Gothic Weekend, Midlands Goth Festival, DV8 York, assorted clubs such Club Antichrist and more recently Reptile. I was fortunate enough to attend the latter and picked up my copy of IT'S FUN

TO BE A MONSTER. And judging by their energetic full live set, I believe them. - **TRIXXI DIVINE**

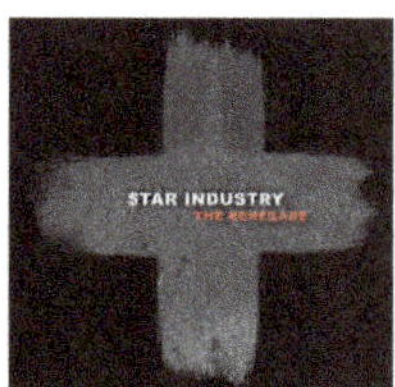

Star Industry
The Renegade

As the new season advents upon us, the much anticipated LP by Star Industry bestows upon us their newest release THE RENEGADE. These highly revered Belgian musicians and veteran performers of many European festivals have put forth their best recording to date. Layered with rich vocals, contagious melodies and atmospheric samples and synths, THE RENEGADE has expanded upon a deeper exploration of their proven talent and refined it with a seductive yet sublime edge. I cannot stop listening; definitely worth the long wait!

Members: Kurt Lantin (drums); Peter Beckers (guitar/vocals), Stijn Kuijpers (bass) and Xavier Vranken (guitar/backing vocals) [and hopefully Utz (synthesisers)] opted to work with the young talented producer, Tom Proost, capturing a highly evolved yet much recognized sound. Many tracks, such as the title track 'Renegade' and 'Selling Icons', portray a reflective ethereal mood enhanced by Annelies Van Dinter's familiar studio-recorded vocals; they are used judiciously throughout this LP. It is Peter Becker's exploratory vox on songs 'For the Lost' and 'Shiver' that shine brilliantly. I really love the retro-industrial vibe Star Industry is known for on 'Revelation', a slow and sexy anthem. 'Driven' is a guitar driven track, as is 'For the Lost'

which is very reminiscent of a far-away traditional gothic era not lost to us, and uses strategic synth hooks to polish these gems. 'Eilyne' was the first track to be released promotionally, last autumn. It's a decidedly danceable teaser to this accomplished LP. Look for the remixes which are playing on eclectic dancefloors across Europe as well as a rediscovered B-side treasure, 'Seventeen'. A bonus 2nd disc is also available with the limited addition carton box set. All ten tracks are exceedingly remarkable and stream together fluidly to create a pleasing listening experience. Star Industry is back on the musical radar and will be sure to satisfy their long-standing fan base as well as newfound listeners.

THE RENEGADE will be one of 2015's exceptional musical releases; it succeeds in capturing the true essence of Star Industry. There are hints of future tours to new localities across the globe; however Star Industry will be performing, for their 5th EUROROCK Festival in Belgium this season. THE RENEGADE is released by the Alfa Matrix label in limited edition. Welcome back, Star Industry! - **TRIXXI DIVINE**

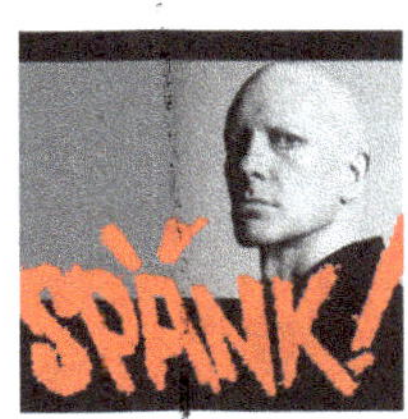

En Esch
Spank

Are you ready to be amazed? If you are, then Spank is the Album for you. As the third track on this album says, "Give the people what they want, give the people what they need." This CD does just that.

With a sound mixed with Punk, metal, and gothic under tones, En Esch has hit the nail right on the head. Being he is no newbie to the scene of music, I was not surprised, yet completely amazed at the same time.

This Album is a treat, and a very early Christmas present to say the least, making me recall the 90's when metal, punk, etc. was at its best. This CD just made it all come back to life for me. Just when I thought that everyone was turning dub step, En Esch has given me hope again. He has a sound like Depesh mode, but darker. The Gothic atmosphere is created by sinister spaced drum beats, En Esch's smooth and striking voice, layered with mid tones of echo and dragged out melodies.

"Spank," and what a name to behold. I have been spanked, and I love it. I'm not getting kinky here, I'm speaking musically. I'm getting into this album the more I listen to it. When you get to track # 4 "Soul to Steal," you will understand what I mean. This track will bring you to that Gothic undertone element I spoke of, bringing to life that yummy dark voice of En Esch, and in this track he is joined by vocalist Trixie Reiss which brings the feel of this song to life. You must hear it for yourself to get the full effect. When you listen you feel as if the two singers are telling a story of a spiritual fight between worlds. I am very impressed with En Esch as an artist, and very pleased with this new Album.

As you may or may not know, En Esch has worked with some great names in the industry, such as RAMMSTEIN and KORN. I can see why. Talent like this always has greatness around them. I mean, how could they not? I was honored to be able to do this

review, and it was a treat for my heart and ears. I can't wait to hear more. - **YASAMAN VRD'DHI**

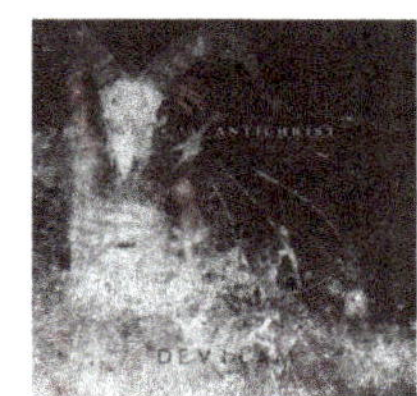

Devil-M
Revenge of the Antichrist

Get ready for some heavy food for your metal ears with a classical instrumental touch that will leave you begging for more. Revenge of the Antichrist has a very unique sound. Each track on the album is interesting and enticing. Some bands in this Genre of music can get repetitive after the 5th track, yet this is not the case with Devil-M. Even with the remix tracks being a song that's on the CD, you still get something different for your ears.

Once I played the first song on Revenge of the Antichrist, I immediately fell for the beats and the musical layout. The lead singer's voice (Max Meyer) just fell into place with the tones and effects. You will get your head banging going, then feel like you are swimming free in an ocean of a classical heaven. This is a very new and different style to this type of music, and very welcomed. Track 16 is very well composed, and the beat will have you closing your eyes and bouncing with it's rhythm's before long. Listening to the piano undertones that lead into a solo creates this classical ending that will scream "Gothic," which I loved!

Apokrypha is one of my favorite tracks because it brings back memories of my teen years of head banging. You can understand every word, then before you know it, you sink into the atmospheric tones that follow. The sounds in this track give you a mind melt effect. Because of the varying instruments used to compliment the drums, you find this Album is full of surprises. I cannot wait to hear more from Devil-M. They have a very strong unique sound that I loved and cannot get enough of. If you like German based metal bands, then you will love Devil-M. If you have never once heard a German metal band, then you are in for a real treat. Keep your eyes and ears open for the next album from Devil-M. I know I will be. - **YASAMAN VRD'DHI**

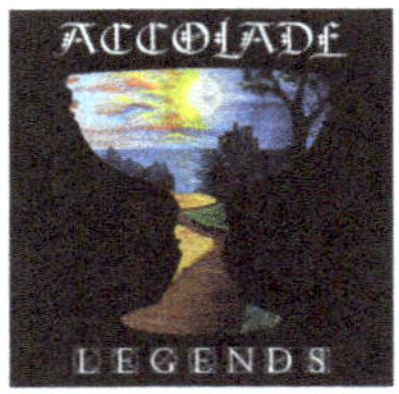

Accolade - Legends • By Yasaman Vrd'dhi

Legends are born and legends are told. Today, legends were played. Accolade will take your mind back to a time and place you may have never been, or a place you have always wished to visit, but you won't need to leave your bedroom or house to make that visit.

The Album "Legends" has an old world feel and sound, with flutes, lutes, drums and more. If you have a like or love for folkloric sounds that tell a story, then you will be spinning and twirling as soon as you put this CD in the player. Although Accolade is billed as Rock, or Progressive Rock, I would have to disagree. The music is very high pitched at times, which may distract from its soothing tones. The lead singer has a very nice voice when she is singing in the lower tones, yet, when she takes on the faster sounds of the instruments, her pitch becomes a type of screeching.

I can feel the point of this Album and the setting, yet the Lead singer Stefanie Renee tends to take you out of the mood once she gets going with the high pitch singing. I understand that is the style which she is trying to pull off, but she tends to start singing off key, making it hard to really enjoy the rest of the song she is "singing". The album's best track is the Elf King. It is well done, and the music comes together with the Stefanie Renee's voice more than any other track.

I hope to see more music from ACCOLADE in the future with lower toned soothing elements. More songs like the "Elf King" will be very welcoming. I would say that Accolade should be labeled under New World folk, not Rock of any kind. Faster pace and faster tones do not classify music as rock.

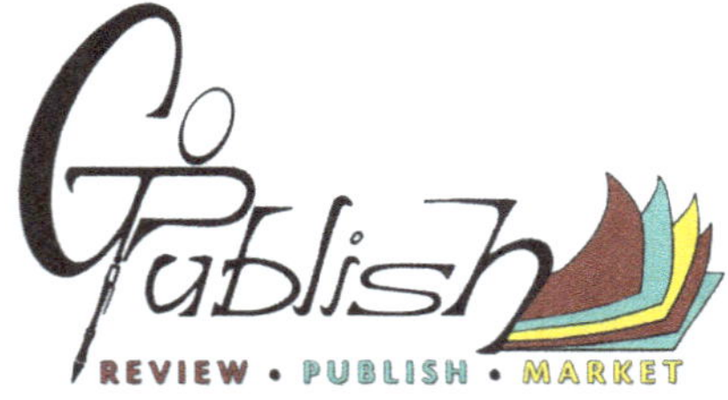

YOU HAVE A STORY, NOW WHAT? TAKE YOUR BOOK TO THE NEXT LEVEL!

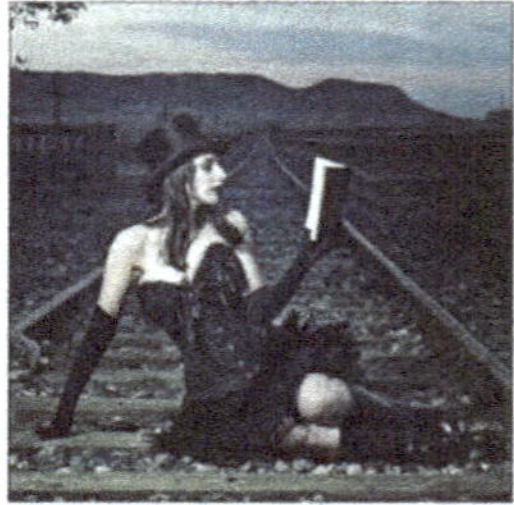

IF YOU'RE WAITING FOR THE RIGHT TIME TO PUBLISH YOU BOOK, NOW IS THE TIME. SEE YOUR BOOK IN PRINT.

JUST REMEMBER, IT'S YOURS . . . SO GOPUBLISHYOURBOOK.COM

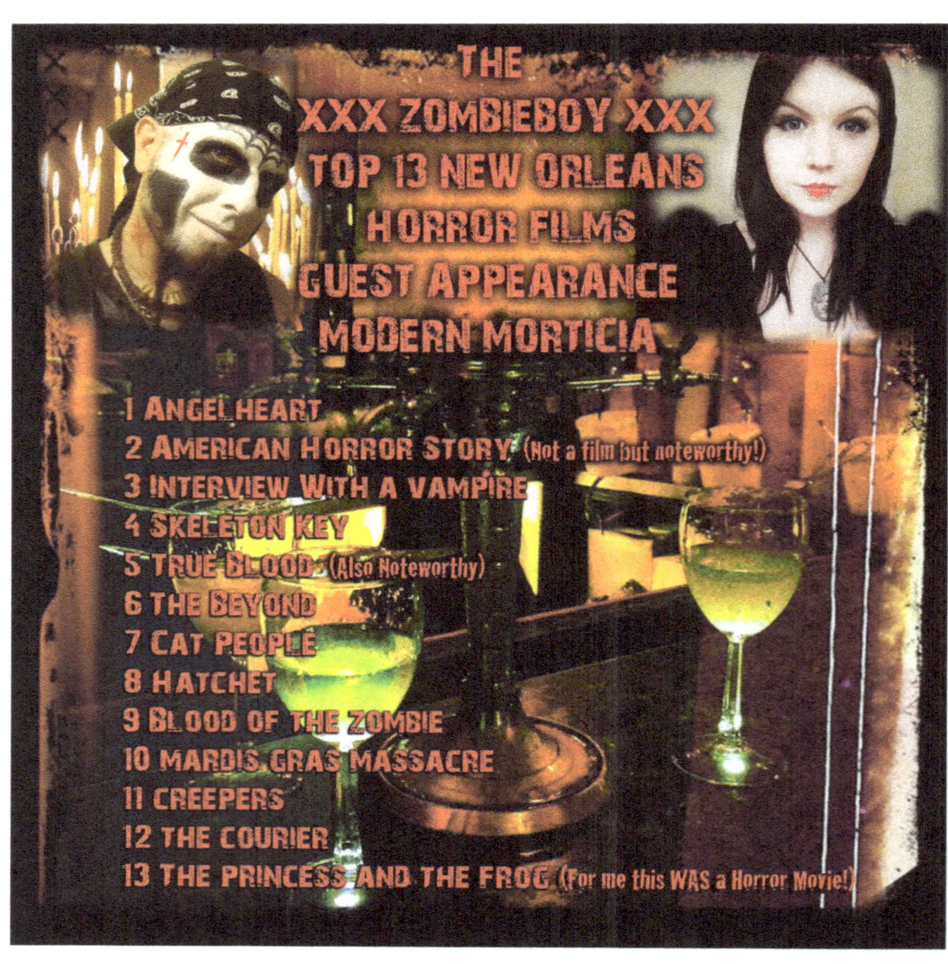

By Chirality

Rozz Williams 1963-1998

It wasn't until I was older that I discovered Rozz Williams. I saw his image a lot, but sadly, I was indeed a late bloomer in regards to Christian Death. I do, however, know the impact he had on many others including many musicians. Rozz was only 34 when he passed away. Who knows what could have been and what strides he would have made in the scene?

It is interesting to note that he was raised a Southern Baptist but his taste was Bowie, Roxy Music, Alice Cooper and so on. He started to perform at age 16, playing in random bands before Christian Death in 1979. Rozz Williams was also a painter and had many works on display in various shows. His artwork was the cover of their Theater of Pain release in 1982. The album was critically acclaimed, but stirred some controversy. The album was even broken on a religious show on air, stating satanic influences. The performances were elaborate and unique with Rozz in a wedding dress, or being hung from a cross. This led to album burnings and them being banned from places around the country.

Rozz left Christian Death in 1985 and tried to revive a past project called Premature Ejaculation. They performed some shows around the area, but eventually Rozz married and moved to San Francisco where he started the Shadow Project. Rozz then agreed to a reunion tour with Christian Death in 1989 and 1990. After the reunion tour, Rozz and his wife moved back to LA to work with other musicians on Shadow Project. Sadly, by about 1992, Rozz was divorced but decided to tour America with Shadow Project. Throughout the 1990's Rozz toured US and Europe and recorded not only music, but spoken word albums as well.

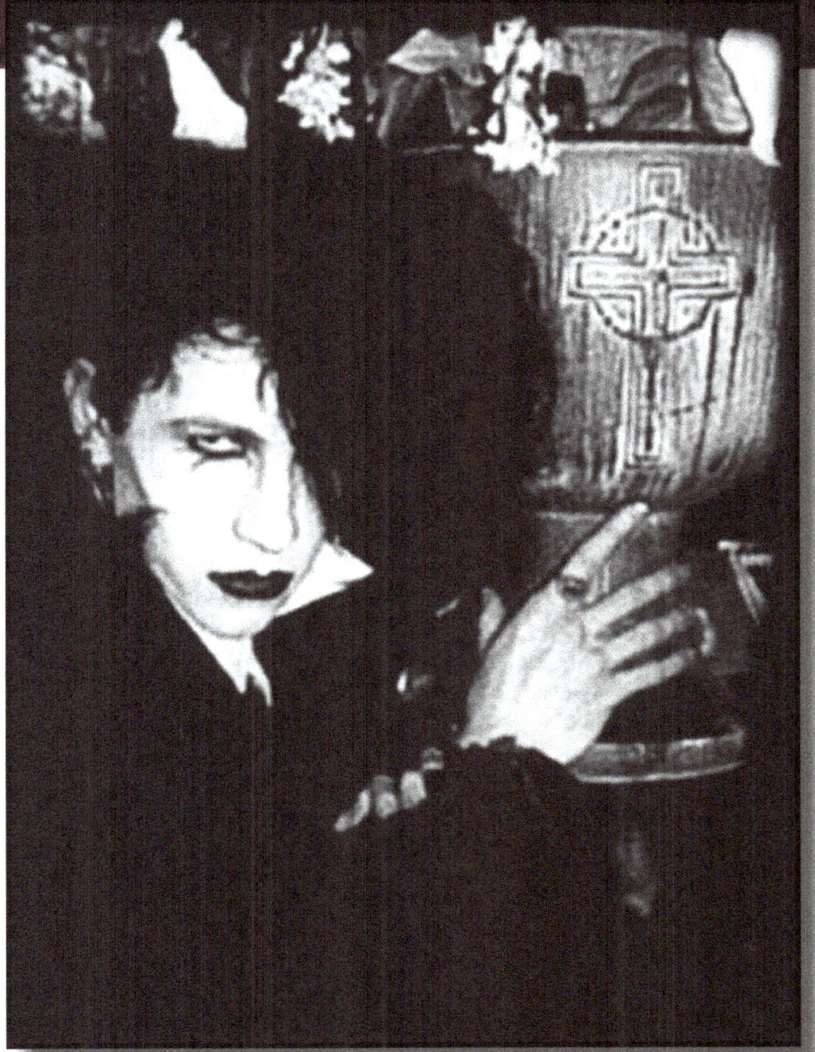

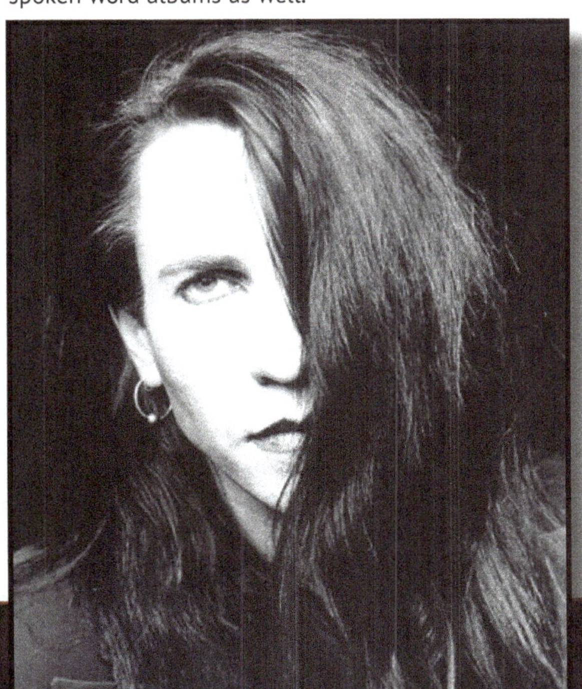

Rozz Williams hung himself on April 1, 1998. There was no suicide note, so no one really knows why he took his own life. It is said he had a problem with drugs and alcohol. Before his death he was working on a movie called PIG which was released in 1999. In 2000, a book with his art was released to the public. The cabinet from which he hung himself and his artworks are on display at the LA Museum of Death.

I find it ironic that a lot of musicians passed in April. For me, Rozz was the epitome of Goth. From his look to his sound to his music, the darkness resonates. You can hear his influence in so many things today. I have heard Faith and the Muse cover a few songs from Rozz. No one knows why people do the things they do. All I know is there is a hole that remains to be unfilled, and it's too bad Rozz is not here to fill it. Who knows what could have been, but then again, no one knows what someone else is feeling.

RIP Rozz Williams 1963-1998

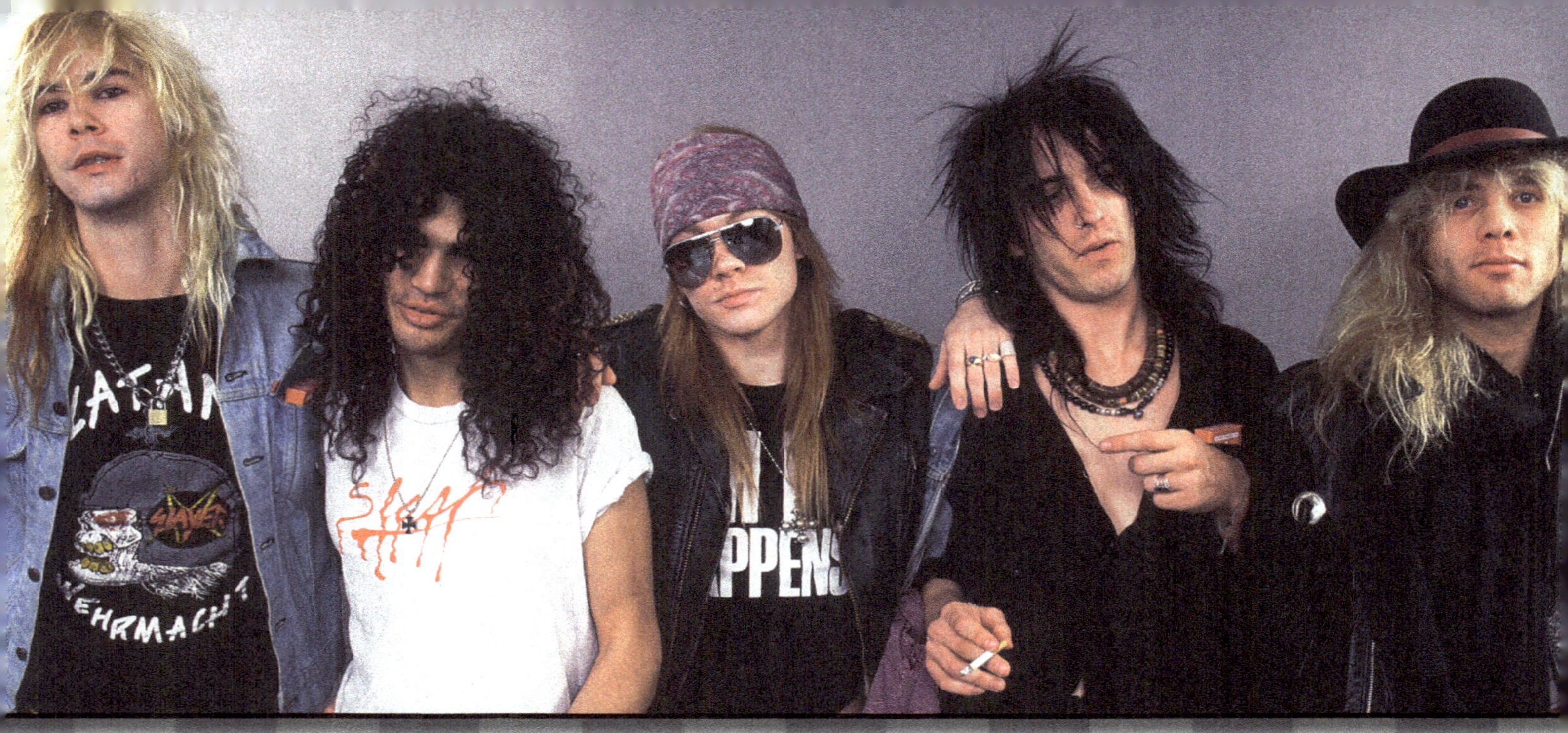

Guns and Roses
DIRTY, GRITTY AND A BAND EVERYONE LIKED!

By Chirality

Do we really need to go into the depth of Axl's childhood? Or who Slash is? We all know GnR, and if you don't, then you need to be schooled. Goth or not, we all know Goth is relative and there are people who listen to things other than VNV. If you don't, then I pity you. "Goth" is all about expansion and experience. You cannot deny that everyone once sang Sweet Child O Mine loudly and badly.

I am not going to make this a boring history of GnR article. I am going to say that GnR is probably the band that shaped myself. When kids were listening to NKOTB, I got my hands on Appetite for Destruction. I remember listening to It's So Easy and thinking this it is. This is revolutionizing rock and roll. You may not agree, but in an industry that was filled with glam metal (which I love) and Pop, GnR came out and were themselves. Axl was the perfect frontman. He was wild and uncaring with the middle finger to the world.

Guns and Roses came straight out of LA with Axl, Slash, Duff, Steve and Izzy. They were formed in 1985, and signed to Geffen in 1986. Appetite for Destruction was released in 1987 and shot to number one on the Billboard charts. Soon followed was Lies and then the Use Your Illusions 1 and 2. The Spaghetti Incident was released in 1993, and pretty much flopped. The long anticipated Chinese Democracy was released in 2008 and soared to number 3, but overall failed expectations.

GnR's lineup has changed many times over the years. Axl has proven he is his own worst enemy with stories of a diva attitude, drinking and a ton of heroine. Rumors have gone around about a GnR reunion with the original line up. In a 2009 interview Axl said: "What's clear is that one of the two of us will die before a reunion and however sad, ugly or unfortunate anyone views it, it is how it is. Those decisions were made a long time ago and reiterated year after year by one man. I could see doing a song or so on the side with Izzy or having him out [on tour] again. I'm not so comfortable with doing anything having more than one of the alumni. Maybe something with Duff, but that's it, and not something I'd have to really get down into, as I'd get left with sorting it out and then blamed on top of it. So, no, not me."
I suppose this all has yet to be seen because it seems all they have encountered is lawsuits and bad blood.

In July of 2014 Dizzy Reed, current member of GnR, has said a new album is almost finished. They just need to figure out what songs will go onto it. He even mentioned there were enough songs to make two records. No confirmed tour as of yet, but record production seems to start and stop.

I for one would love to see them bury the hatchet and reunite with the old members, but am glad to see Axl still going, albeit badly. GnR will always have an influence in music. They were grimy, gritty and raw, and that is what made them awesome. They have seemed to surpass time and fashions. I just hope they do not turn into elevator music anytime soon.

Goth or not, everyone likes at least one GnR song.

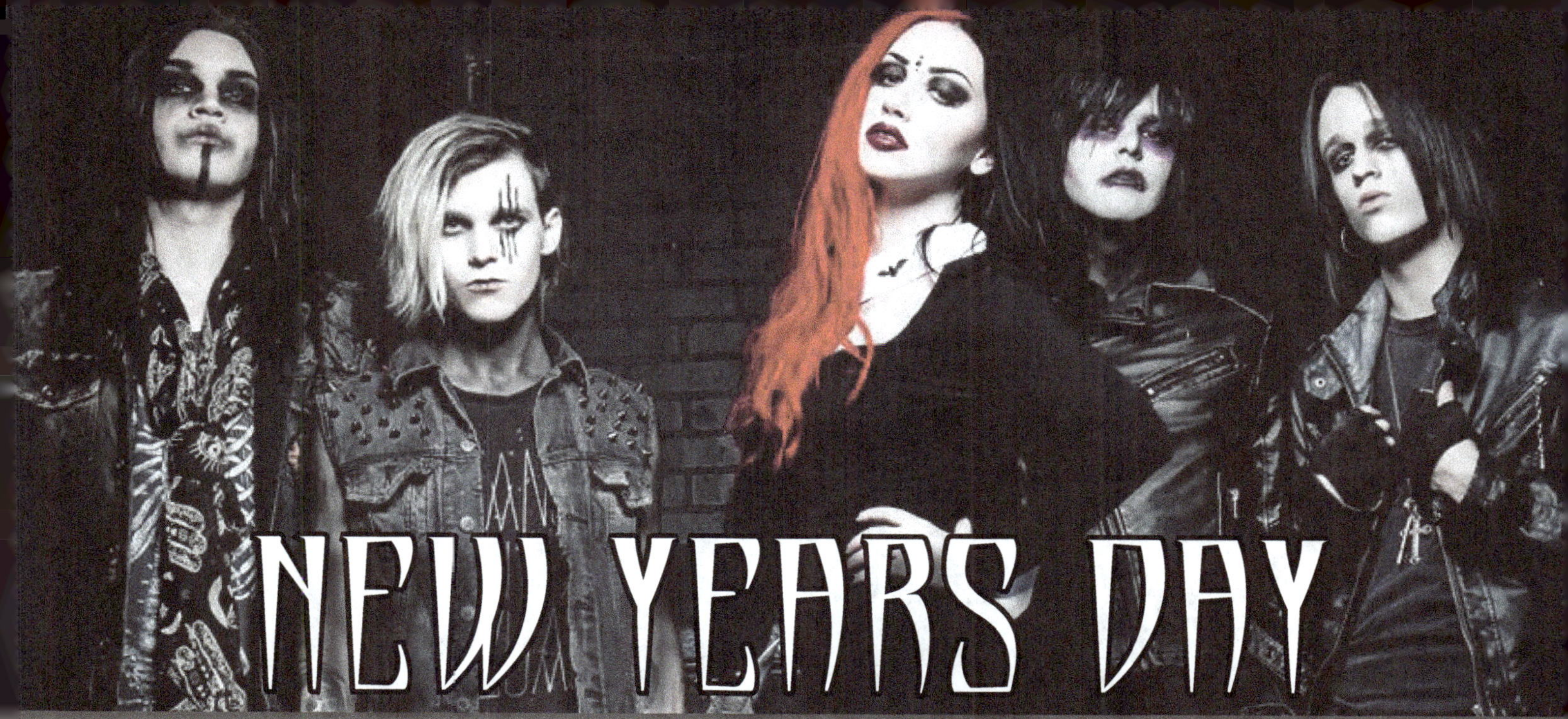

NEW YEARS DAY

By Dawn Wood

I had the pleasure of opening for New Years Day and the Birthday Massacre with my band Murder Weapons in Seattle at the end of 2014. I was pleasantly surprised at the charisma and talent of New Year's Day. Their music appealed to Metal/Gothic and Industrial fans and their humility in relating to the audience/fans was refreshing.

Their new 5 song EP entitled: "Epidemic' is brilliant, with the title track "Epidemic" being a huge fan fave.

New Year's Day formed in 2005 and began an aggressive DIY promotion of their music on Myspace. They were featured on "Myspace Record 1 Compilation". Since that time, they have toured with the likes of: The Birthday Massacre, Motionless in White, Blood on the Dancefloor just to name a few.

They describe their music as:

"Imagine if Dexter Morgan with side kick Eric Northman, hosted a late late late night talk show in a haunted mansion deep within the enchanted cemetery, then NEW YEARS DAY would most assuredly be their house band with warm blood-spattered bottles of True Blood offered in the red room for the visiting undead."

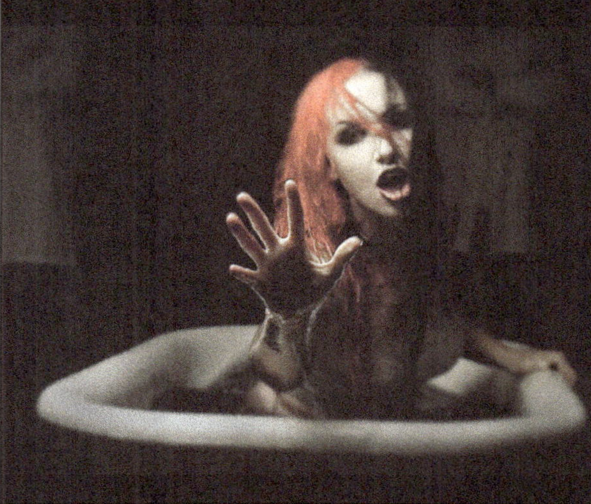

Members include:
Ash on vox
Tyler & Jeremy on guitars
Nick on drums
Anthony on bass

Check out these links to New Years Day:

Facebook: https://www.facebook.com/nydrock
Twitter: NYDROCK
Lastfm: http://www.last.fm/music/New+Years+Day

NEW EP: http://www.nydpreorder.com/

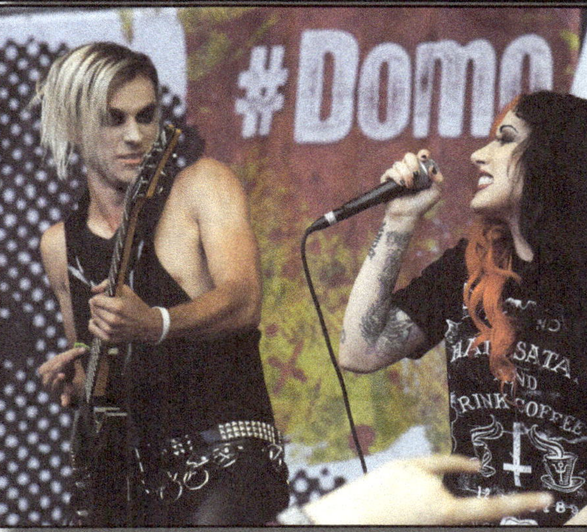

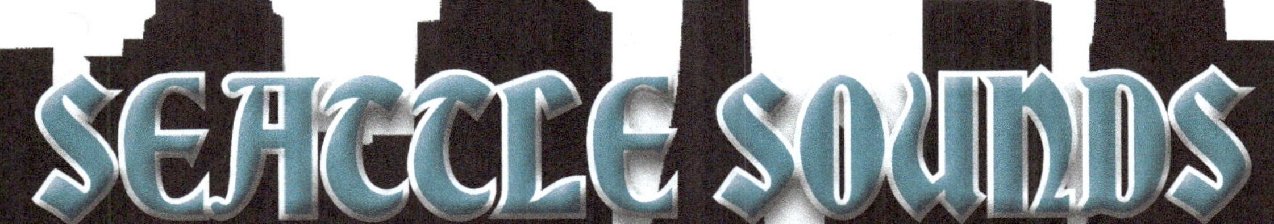

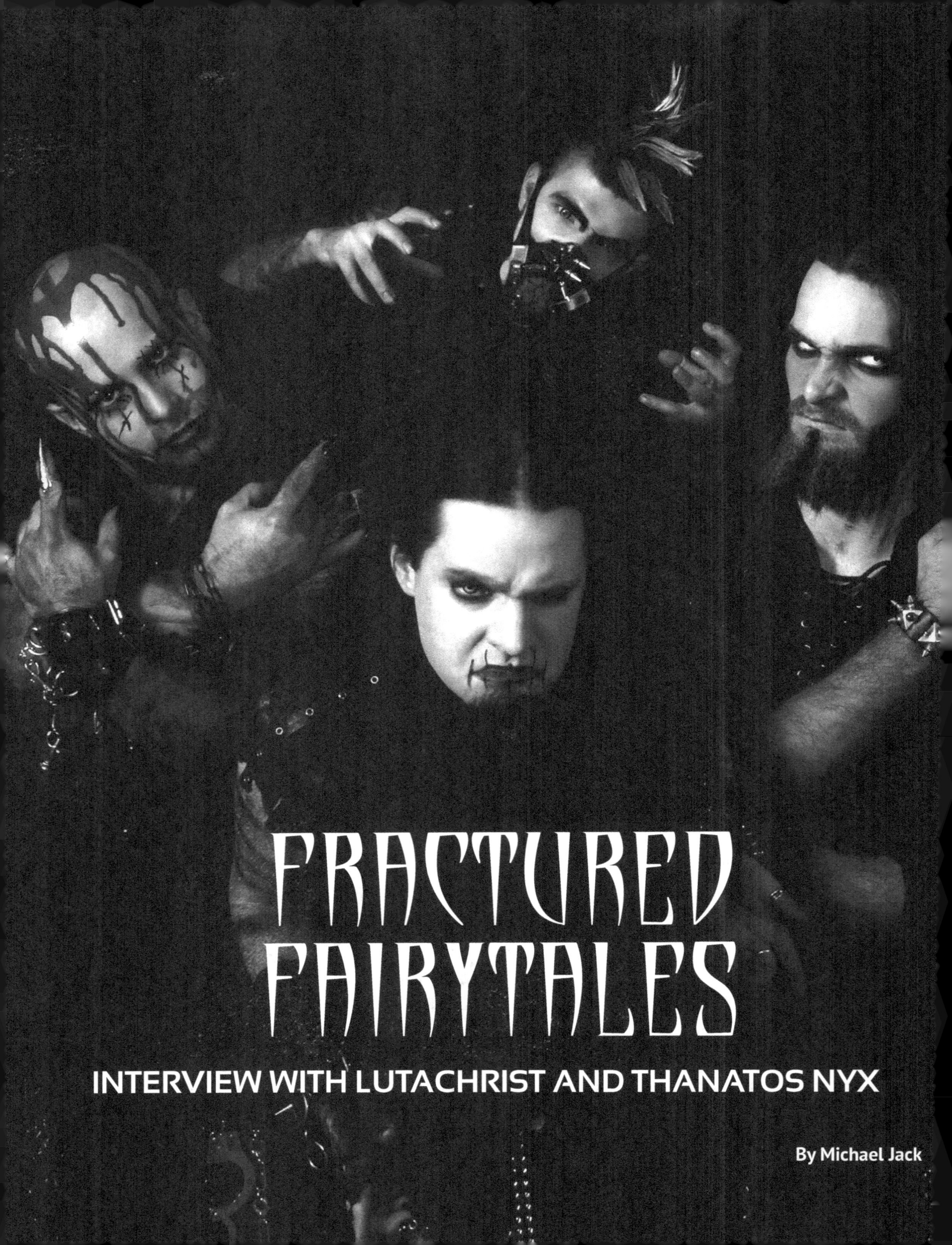

FRACTURED FAIRYTALES

INTERVIEW WITH LUTACHRIST AND THANATOS NYX

By Michael Jack

[Michael Jack] *Currently you are on tour promoting your new release "Egregore," with the amazing supporting bands Abbey Death and Knuckles and Guns. How is the tour going, and were there any special highlights for you so far?*

[Lutachrist] The tour is going great. It's always a nice change of pace when we get to the touring part of promoting an album after being barred in the studio for months and months. I come out like a mad man that has to be reintroduced into society. It has been one hell of a run so far indeed. I have seen everything from Orpheus swinging from the Dobbs sign on the roof of the building in down town Philly in front of hundreds of on lookers to having to break up late night parking lot brawls. Shit loads of driving, dank hotels, gas station "food", all night parties, stage injuries, lost gear, psycho stalking weirdoes following us around, good friends, old fans, new fans, new friends, awesome local talent and Taco Bus (Abbey and Valerie knows what I'm talking about) , the works.

[MJ] *After listening to "Egregore," I have to say...damn dude, that's dark. I mean, "Unvale" was disturbing, but "Egregore" takes it to a new level. Where do you go from here?*

[Lutachrist] If you look at each Fractured Fairytales album there is a black hole found in the artwork. Each one has a different meaning but I like to leave it open to interpretation. On Murmur the hole was in the heart, on Unvale the hole was the third eye and on Egregore the hole is the pyramid eye torn from its socket, found the inside of the cover. The pit is bottomless, the pit is in the human soul. We will just keep exploring these dark Nether regions going further and further in. Do not confuse darkness with heaviness though some people tend to do that...there is Christian black metal. I write solely on feeling and go with the flow inspiration. I don't want say that the next album will be heavier or darker or what have you but thus far the trinity we have out now follows that order. The world just keeps getting worse and worse, life is more and more fucked up and it just seems to be the natural flow of things. Fractured Fairytales is a reflection.

[MJ] *To build upon the landscape that is "Egregore," the video for "Null and Void" is extremely intense. I have to ask where did the idea for the video come from?*

[Lutachrist] Null and Void is an intense and uneasy song. It gives off an urgent anxiety. I really enjoy horror like imagery with sporadic editing. Putting a girl on the FF cross was something I have wanted to do since we burned the one at the end of the Return To Dirt video. Other than there was some scenes of an alter, some flashes of some low dwelling spirits and us in a bloodied room performing the song. An incantation is occurring. More on that will slowly be revealed in videos to come.

[MJ] *Ever think of throwing your hat into the film arena? I would love to see what kind of horror flick you could make.*

[Lutachrist] Maybe one day when the time is right. As of right now we are focused on bringing the world Fractured Fairytales content. If the inspiration ever subsides in that realm I may branch over to film. We do have plans to release a DVD that may include some extensive intros for music videos but that's as close to that area as we are going to get for a while.

[MJ] *I know you draw inspiration from the world around you. Can you give me one example of something that happened and how you used it to compose a song for "Egregore?"*

[Lutachrist] Yes, Let's look at the song Fall Forever. It could easily be the title track for the album. Looking at the artwork for Egregore you will find a four armed nullified creature nailed to a FF cross with the Eye of Providence sewn shut for a head. A lot of symbolism going on there. Let's pretend for a second that there is a higher governing class of humans that no one knows that name of and no one ever sees. Let's say that they govern the worlds recourses, technology, wars, large corporations and so on. They introduce sickness to keep us weak, they feed us poisons to destroy our very DNA, indoctrinate us with bullshit thinking skills and lies so that they can evolve while the masses de-evolve into an actual lower form of human. They feed off of our spirit like a giant physic vampire. The only thing that can set us free is a mass awakening which is what they are hell-bent on preventing from happening. Even though we have been in the technological dark ages, through various means on the internet people have began sharing to the masses forbidden knowledge. Even some of it is tarnished and even purposely misguiding as a deterrent, it still opens people's minds to seek truths and breaks down the set in place thinking barriers we are all instilled with. The song Fall Forever shows that hope can be seen in the distance, touches on the symbiotic relationship between the two, a lot of people enjoy the fake world and dreams, and also reminds us that they will turn the transition, if is ever occurs.... into a war.

[MJ] *You are very outspoken, and as a result, there is a lot of backlash... especially in your home town of Fayetteville. How does this affect you personally? Does it just add more fuel to the fire?*

[Thanatos Nyx] We have always gotten heat from our home town. There is nothing like us here, and people tend to shun or hate what looks and sounds different from everything else in the area. We have always strove to turn heads and make sure we stand out of the norm to people. So yes, we have had backlash in our home town but to us it just means we are doing something right. People want to come out and see what all the hype is about. To answer your last question, yes, in the end it does fuel the fire.

[MJ] *Fractured Fairytales is a band that truly believes in doing everything themselves. I mean everything. What is the hardest part of what you do...the music, marketing, videos?*

[Lutachrist] Marketing by far is the most expensive, soulless and tedious part of being completely independent. There is no such thing as too much marketing and there is no such thing as spending too

"We live in a world of Trickery..."

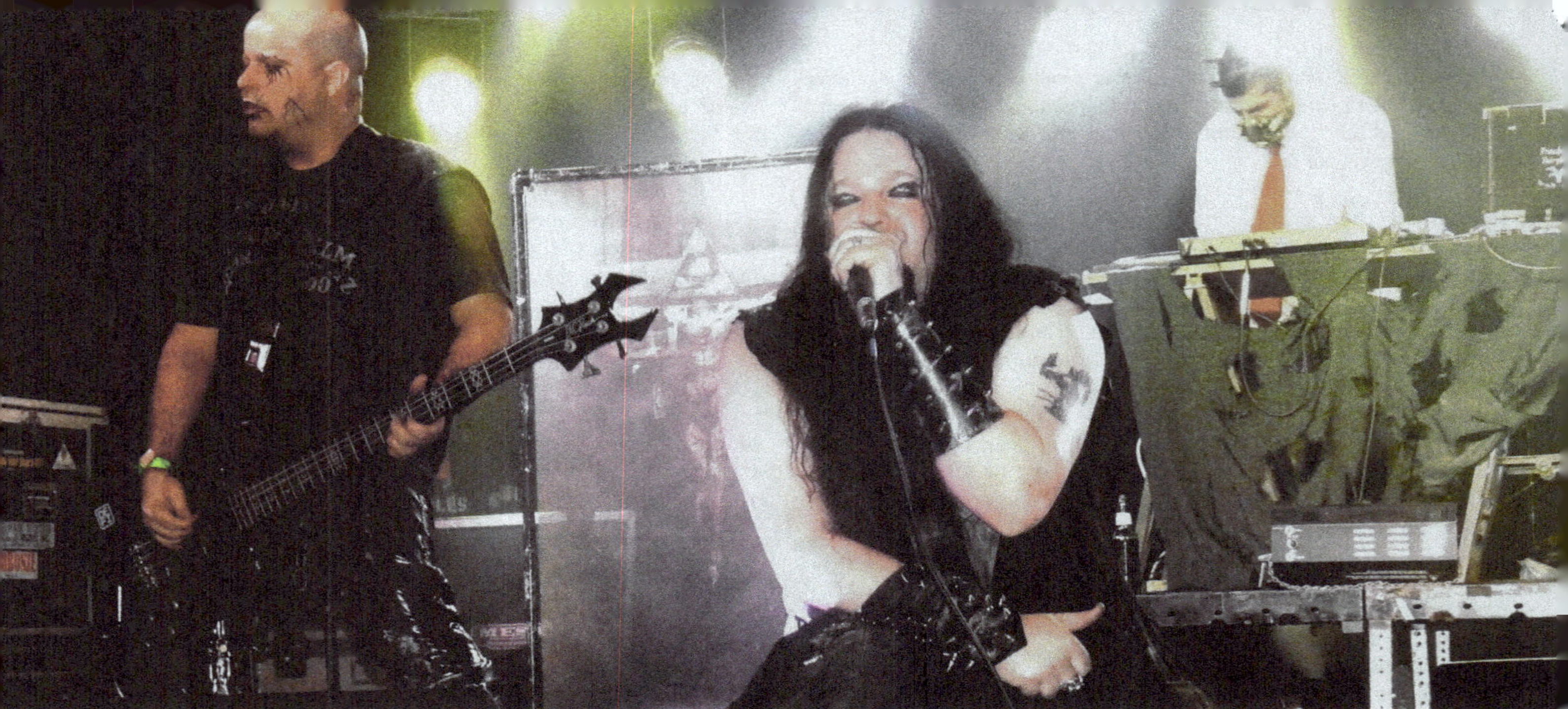

much money on marketing in our little perceivable universe. A lot of people say it is easier now to reach an audience online than it ever was but in fact the big websites still choose what they show to you. Also there is a major saturation of artist since anyone with a computer can "produce' an album now. It is very hard to rise in the ranks and not drowned in obscurity.

[MJ] *A couple of things I love about your music is the complexity and layers of sound, and the abrupt changes within the songs themselves. I want to know how much of this naturally comes out, and how much of it is done after the basic track is recorded?*

[Lutachrist] The songs are built and arraigned piece by piece. I have an extensive death metal background and I grew up listening to a lot of metal which explains heavy aspect or our music. I also like shit that is all over the place like Mr. Bungle and Dog Fashion Disco. I like extreme changes in a song. Going from slow and grimy to some intense machine gun fire kicks layered with chunky guitar and synth madness. I listened to a lot of Nine Inch Nails and Marilyn Manson back in the mid 90s to 2000s when I was still a spud. Just like any artist I took inspiration from my heroes, had a dream and created my own thing. I would imagine that some aspiring artist may listen to some Fractured Fairytales one and draw inspiration from us. Then when they create, they will sound differently than they would had they never heard FF. It's about the evolution and continuing the thing you love for the next generation.

We have lost all sense of self. It is my belief that we (humans) have a purpose that is being hidden from us, or has been hidden. It is that thing that everyone searches for. People are lonely with love. People are in tombs with their riches. No matter how much we have, we seek more, we seek something else. It is not more that we seek. It is the truth of what we are supposed to be. The spirit has a hole in its essence, the missing piece is hidden. We live in a realm of Trickery.

[MJ] *Ever think about doing a remake? I would love to see what you could do with "All Murder, All Guts, All Fun," by Samhain, or some other classic horror-punk song like that.*

[Thanatos Nyx] We have experimented in the past with a few cover songs, but at the end of the day we have never been satisfied enough to release any of them. We are toying around with some songs at the current time and will know the right one when we hear it.

[MJ] *You sing about many apocalyptic themes. Therefore, in your opinion, how will the world end?*

[Lutachrist] We will without a doubt fabricate our own demise. The Nuke carrying super powers in the world have literally almost launched nukes at each other several times over and the threat of that occurring grows daily. Intelligent enough to destroy the world and not smart enough to save it.

"There is nothing like us here, and people tend to shun or hate what looks and sounds different…"

[MJ] *Going back to "Egregore," I always like to ask one gratuitous question about my favorite track. I love "Trickery." What can you tell me about the meaning of this song?*

[Lutachrist] Trickery is about everyone predominantly being lost whether they are aware of it or not. I think everyone deep inside feels that they are living with some sort of amnesia. We are instilled with false doctrines widely propagated for generations and generations.

[MJ] *It is very easy to sit here and talk about dark themes and horror when talking about Fractured Fairytales. It can't be all doom and gloom all of the time. What is something more lighthearted that may surprise your fans? Maybe you knit little ghoulish doilies on the tourbus or are die-hard ping pong enthusiasts.*

[Lutachrist] Well actually, it is pretty much gloom and doom for us. When I'm not doing band stuff I'm doing band shit. I would say the most "lighthearted" thing that we do, the thing that may be perceived

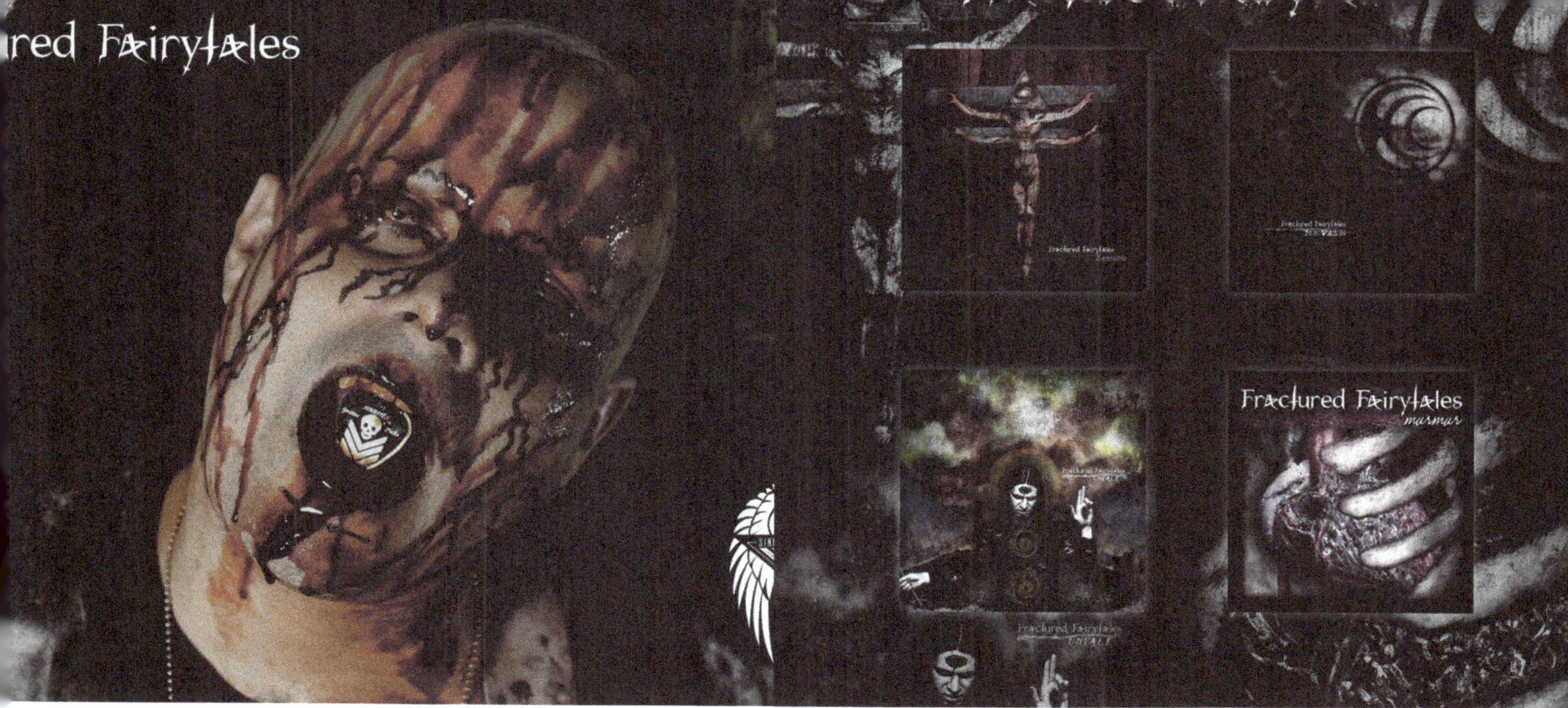

as the most lame is that we all play Clash of Clans. We are all in a clan together called Kult Fractured. It is something we do on those ten and a half hour rides. It keeps us from harassing the driver and other vehicles for a little while. After writing songs, filming videos, editing songs, editing videos, booking shows, practicing, maintaining gear, promoting shows, updating websites, mailing items off at the post office, driving to shows, renting vehicles, doing interviews, partying, networking with bands and maintaining the health to do all that efficiently it is time for sleep.

[MJ] *Any last words for your fans?*

[Lutachrist] Thank you all for the years of support!!! Stay dark, keep the fire burning, question everything and don't let the abyssal downdraft restrain you while you are strong enough to withstand it. Hailz!

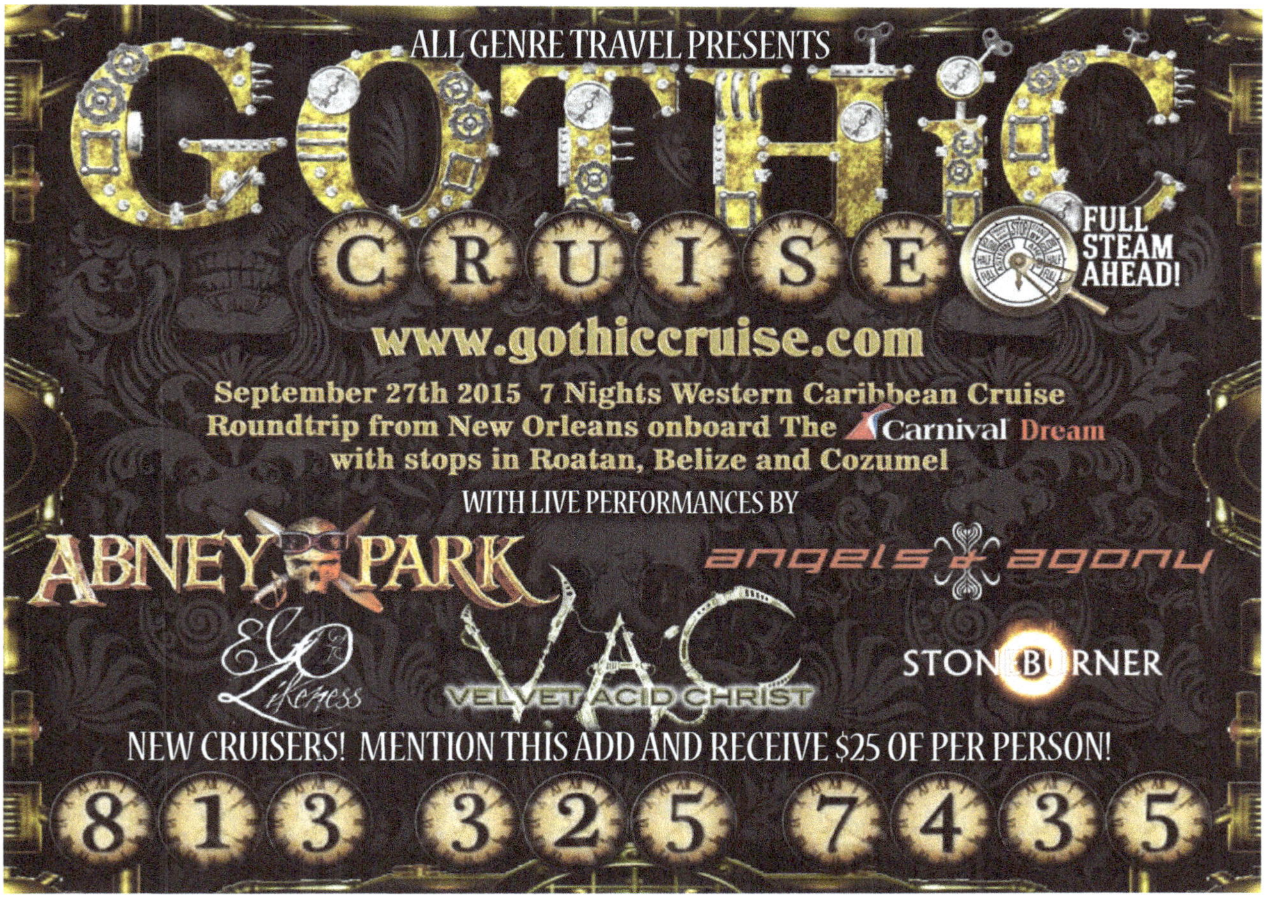

die kur

By trixxi divine

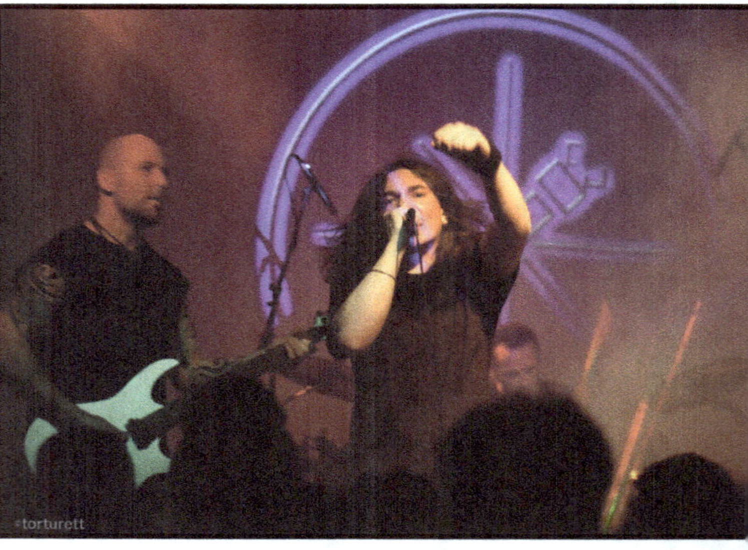

NMTCG is has finally released the anticipated fourth official album of London's hybrid industrial metal band Die Kur. The MANIFESTO launch party was held in March, presenting us with a variable collection of tracks recorded as a two CD set, Part 1: "Modern Society Manifesto" and Part 2: "Songs of Freedom". The overall statement of this prodigious recording imparts a vision for a richer life without all of the trappings of the volatile, superficial or adverse political influences affecting human society. Die Kur achieves a highly conceptualised missive without an evangelistic resonance. Expect the hard-edged Industrial Metal caressed by Electronica and pensive instrumentals in which Die Kur is renowned for. With a keen attention to detail and valuing quality more than quantity, mastermind Ays Kura has reached his stride in what he reflects as a significant achievement.

Ays, the voice of Die Kur, also produced, engineered and plays various instruments in the studio as well as live. Now based in the UK, he was born and educated in Italy and is a professional Sound Engineer by trade. Back in the later 1990's, just as Trent Reznor had done before him, Ays began working in a recording studio with the arrangement that he could use the studio in the "after work hours" to record his own material. The first recordings were experimental in using new studio equipment whilst trying to adjust composition skills to his high calibre standard. Over time and with patience, the band's current members [from a collective pool of talent whom which Ays had previously worked] enthusiastically united for MANIFESTO, Die Kur's strongest incarnation thus far.

Tracks which stand out on this collection are the instant hit singles: 'The Order of Things to BE' and 'The Leader of Zeros'. 'Memories of a Fallen Empire' is a gorgeous intro-instrumental leading into the powerful 'Another Battle Ahead.' 'Manifesto of My Generation' is an endearing homage to the alternative nation and the notorious dwellings where we come together to escape a world which is not our own. 'We are the Aliens' is a

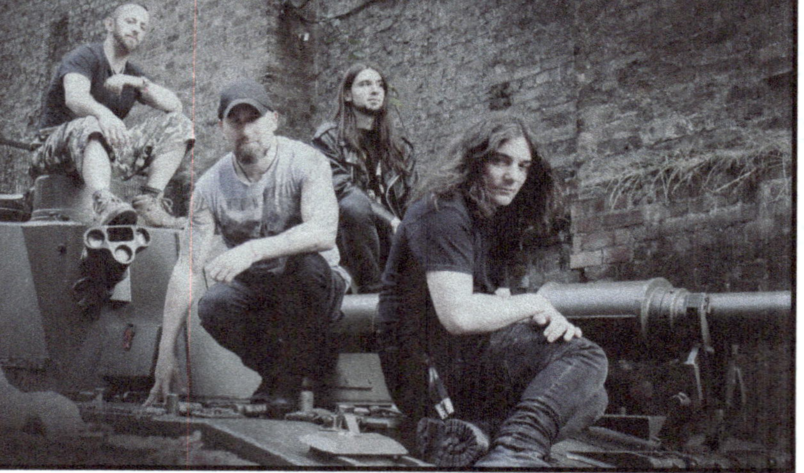

commemorative piece to a fallen comrade, a track that shines with a uniquely progressive appeal. Each member is equal to the sum of their whole and there are no holds barred here. The guitar work by Barry Carrera is complex and extensively calculated. It is apparent that he possesses a comprehensive range of style and influence. Drake Bocci really throws down some serious drumming on the heavier material; a consummate professional as well as teacher, Drake owns the DrumPod recording studio and has contributed to myriad other projects over the years while working on an advanced degree in Music at the Tech Music School. Amadeus remains a bit of an intrigue yet his basslines are consistent and deliberate, cementing the band assertively into its rightful place. Ays includes some special guests in the studio, too many to name [purchase the CD for the liner notes and keep our music alive].

During their long reign on the London's underground music scene, Die Kur has supported bands: Young Gods, Die Krupps, Aesthetic Perfection, AngelSpit and Bloody Mary as well as headlining their own shows. Last autumn, Ays organised the Renaissance Alternative Music Festival which brought together twenty-one recognized underground bands throughout the UK and Europe. Die Kur closed the event with a fantastic set of their own, always bearing their indelible impression as a great live band. Known on the scene as a selfless and giving individual, this humble musician works hard to assist in production as well as performing on projects with currently active bands in the music scene. He is supportive and considerate of other's talent, always elevating peers within his industry. MANIFESTO presents the voice of a gracious yet confident human being, backed by a solid and immensely talented band. Ays, himself is a very self-aware and relaxed individual which made interviewing him a pleasure. Here's what he had to say about Die Kur's new CD and his bandmates who worked tirelessly to create their inspiring new release and continue to draw a consistent following at their live events and festivals:

[Carpe Nocturne]
Congratulations on your new CD; I'm really enjoying my copy. Share with us what musical influences you have had and what motivates you to compose and perform music.

[Ays Kura] To be honest, I've never really thought about it. It's always been about making music and evolving it through the times, arriving to the form in which it is now but more refined. In the beginning I was more interested in making sounds and arranging melodies.
There's never really been an inspiration or the sense "Oh! I want to be like this particular band [sic]" because I like different styles of music, all of the classic metal bands. I've not had a singular inspiration. I like to make the music I want, really.

[CN] *Your lyrics are never contrived and that has always been consistent throughout Die Kur's other work, as well. For MANIFESTO, I have noticed the overtone or a message; if you will….Can you share your personal thoughts?*

[AK] Overall, the direction was to raise consciousness towards people or to describe the world as I see it. I didn't want to push a message, of course. With most music, it is like a conversation or a form of communication in one way or another. The lyrics on MANIFESTO are not based on my own personal opinion. For me, it is about observing human nature or observing the propaganda around us in the modern world. It is about the changing way of how people are communicating and how we are we are changing; even if it is just hidden. Also, the way people are controlled by the media. Technology, the current digital tools and the internet, is on a much higher level now and everything is much more intrusive; just a click away from something else popping up to distract us or manipulate us. Not necessarily advertisements, but the misleading things people don't see without their being conscious. It is something for people to think about. I wanted to create awareness.

[CN] *You are a professional Sound Engineer and you also play several instruments with Die Kur; notably, keyboards. You chose to use a Harpsichord on MANIFESTO.*

[AK] Yes, I wanted to experiment with different sounds and this was an interesting fit for what I wanted to accomplish. A special thanks goes to Mark Ransom, of the Harpsicord Workshop, for providing his expertise and wares so we could create MANIFESTO. He played on the instrumental 'Antiphon'.

[CN] *What is your favourite instrument to play or an essential composition tool you must have for recording?*

[AK] That's an easy one. Anything that makes noise!

[CN] *Die Kur has evolved over the years; mainly in terms of finding solid personnel to compliment your vision. Tell me a bit about how your current line-up.*

[AK] I've known these guys for a while now, a couple from working with them previously. I worked with Drake when producing with Drilling Spree and have previously shared Barry (Motion Static, Cybercide) who had contributed on The FALL of an EMPIRE LPs. Amadeus Rx is another musician I have known and worked with on the scene for quite some time, as well. He's a guitarist but I had asked if he wanted to contribute bass on Manifesto and he jumped right in. Overall, I am pleased with the direction of Die Kur and enjoying performing with these talented guys.

[CN] *'A Manifesto For My Generation' is really touching, especially for those who live or perform musically in London.*

[AK] Yes, this is my way to say thank you to everyone who has been with us through our journey. Those behind the scenes; they do all of the hard work and never get the recognition and it is a lot of work to organise a night. They do a good job.

[CN] *What about the good job you do?! Last winter you put on an enormous event, Renaissance Alternative Music Festival, which featured so many different bands, an*

art exhibition and a book release. *You always appear busy and I often see you out supporting or working with others in the scene. You should give yourself some credit, as well. Will you be doing the festival again, this year?*

[AK] Thank you. Definitely would like to do another Renaissance Alternative Music Festival. There are a lot of good bands out there that are not playing a lot of shows. Some have been established for a long time; I have played beside many of them or recorded with them. I wanted to do something for everybody and give back to those who also support us.

[CN] *The music industry is declining in on so many levels today. Business perspectives have changed, mainstream music and media has drastically changed and technology, as well. Digital media and marketing is taking over. It is harder to get onto a record label or sell hardcopy CD's, tour in different overseas and make a living from writing and performing music. How do you feel about that? Do you see the method in how music is distributed as an obstacle?*

[AK] In a way, I think it is easier. Self-producing is better to take control of your own music but at the same there is also less opportunities for new bands to get recognised. When you trade your artistic freedom, it is true that you find a compromise; you trade that for being on a label with proper promotion. I think digital is an easier medium to release music, more efficient, as well. There is no pressure with someone telling us what we have to do. I like having more options to choose in distributing music.

[CN] *Overall, is there anything else you wish to share about the direction of Die Kur or life in general?*

[AK] Quite simply, we are all human beings who are a part of life and we should all be thankful for all the things which we take for granted. People should relax and close their minds sometimes and not think of their jobs and the outside world. Sometimes you go out into the world and you see a lot of people are so stressed; they should try to just make things simple and enjoy themselves more. Life is a gift, appreciate it.

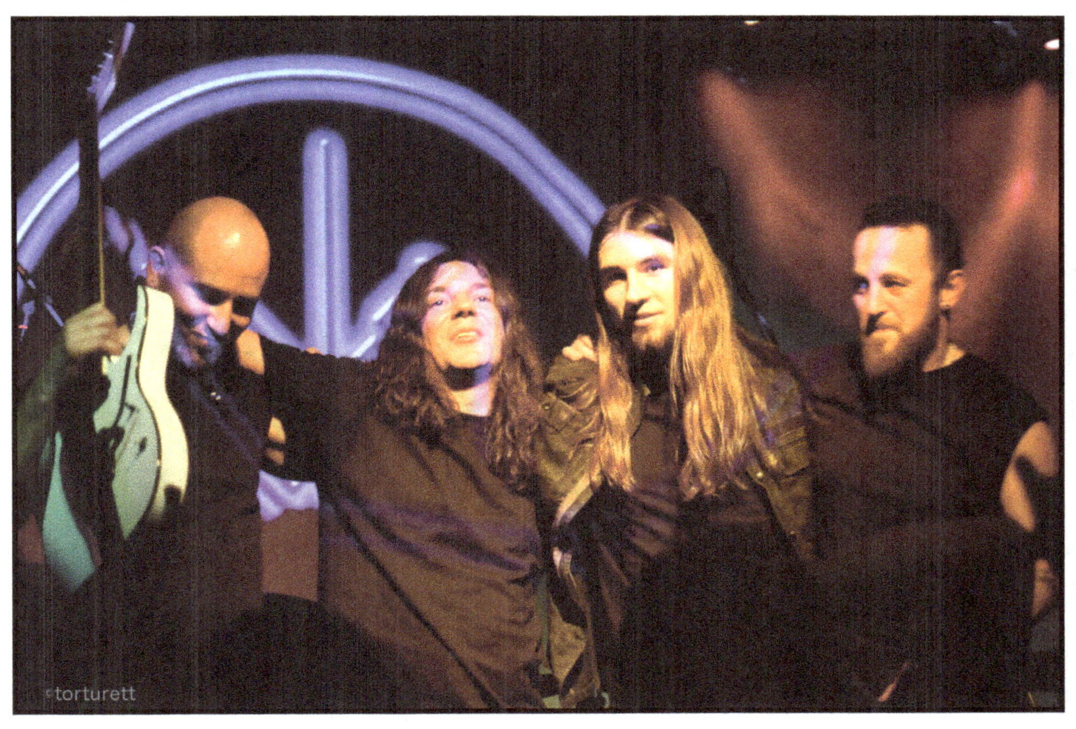

NATASHA COX

INTERNATIONAL AND UNPREDICTABLE

By Michael Jack

I have been writing for Carpe Nocturne for a fairly long time now, and I have had the privilege of meeting some amazing artists. When I decided to reach out to Natasha Cox for an interview, I did so as a fan as much as I did a writer. When she agreed, I was beyond elated. I am a huge Mankind is Obsolete fan, and am continually astonished by the talent of frontwoman Tash Cox. I speak often about bands and artists who are diverse, but very few take it to the level she has. Natasha Cox performs in many, and completely different, genres of music. She is brilliant in each. It is my absolute pleasure to present my interview with the amazingly multi-talented Natasha Cox.

[Michael Jack] *Congratulations on Mobius Loop! It's another great album, and like the rest, very eclectic. Where did you draw the inspiration from for this CD?*

[Natasha Cox] Thank you! I really appreciate the kind words. When you put out an album, it represents a chapter of your life, whether it is your own experiences, others around you, or inspiration that whispers in your ear. For this particular album, I had to go on a deep life journey to make it happen. The kind of journey that takes you to Mordor and back. My hope is to connect with other kindred spirits who can relate.

[MJ] *I know artists hate this question, but how would you describe MKIO's music? I know it's a challenge for me when dealing with bands as diverse as MKIO, so I want to hear it in your words.*

[NC] When Jon and I first started the band, we consciously made the decision that we never wanted to put a box or limitation on our music. We didn't want to be defined by a genre or to have a boundary in terms of what we created. We simply wanted to write songs that were honest and raw. At the time, we were listening to a lot of Godflesh, NIN, Skinny Puppy, Tool, and Neurosis. I know what we put out definitely reflects those influences. At the time, we were still learning how to play our instruments, write songs, make sounds, record, express. It's all such a process to figure this stuff out. Jon was playing with Hate Dept at the time, so we had the great fortune of being able to work under the guidance of the brilliant Steven Seibold, who mixed our first album. I have such great admiration for the fact that Seibold has such an amazing command of the studio and yet such a raw approach to music, which was completely in line with what we were going for. The consequent albums that have followed have been reflective of more influences and growth….learning more about our instruments, songwriting, ourselves. I don't know if I could give you a singularly descriptive phrase to describe our music, but I can say that we love to play with dichotomy…light and dark, abrasive and soft, electronic and organic….and that we really love to make music that has a lot of energy live.

[MJ] *I know you have been playing some shows recently, but any plans for a MKIO tour?*

[NC] We're playing the Darks Arts festival in Montana in the summer and are definitely looking to tour more for the rest of the year.

[MJ] *When is the red hair coming back?*

[NC] Haha! Well, splotches of it seem to be slowly appearing in my purple. So perhaps it's trying to make its comeback?

[MJ] *For your new video, you decided to crowd fund. What does it mean to you as an artist to get that kind of support from your fans?*

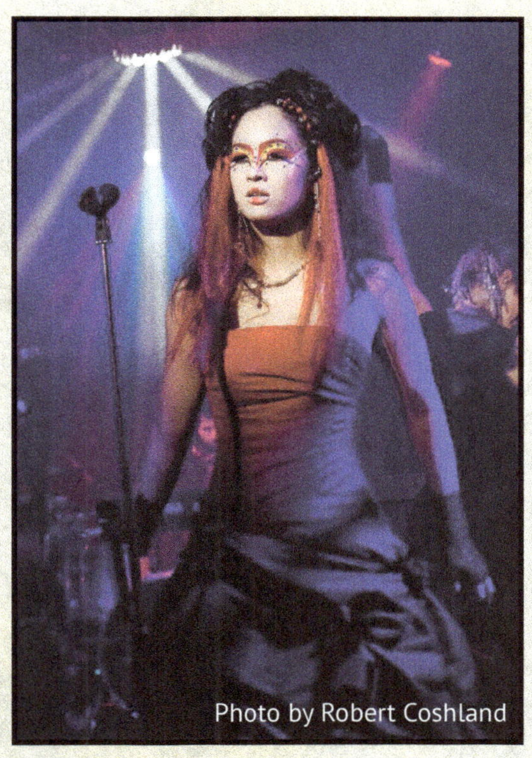

Photo by Robert Coshland

[NC] I like to think of our "fans" as friends with whom we share a long history. I feel incredibly grateful to be a part of a community of people who have supported our work from the very beginning. During our early tours, we made it from town to town because of the support of our friends, who bought our merch, housed us, and fed us. I'll never forget when our van was completely totaled in an accident, and so many people got together to help us out. Being a musician to me does not just mean playing music. It means getting to share moments and life with people who relate to you in some way. The crowd funding success is a testament to me in what an incredible group of friends we have. I'm really looking forward to sharing out the video when it's done. Clint Carney, our director, has been sending us clips of it as it's been developing, and I think that our supporters will be really happy to see what their support has created.

[MJ] *My favorite track off of Mobius Loop is "Lucifer's Song." In fact, it's one of my favorite MKIO songs to date. What was the concept behind this song?*

[NC] I was in the mind-frame of telling a story when I wrote the lyrics for this song. I thought of a story where Lucifer is the Morningstar and actually a woman. God has forgotten what love is and has turned his back on a dying earth. The world lies in ashes, and seeing a dying Lucifer in a dying world reminds him of what love is, after the fact, when it's too late. He holds Lucifer in his arms, and the song is Lucifer's dying song.

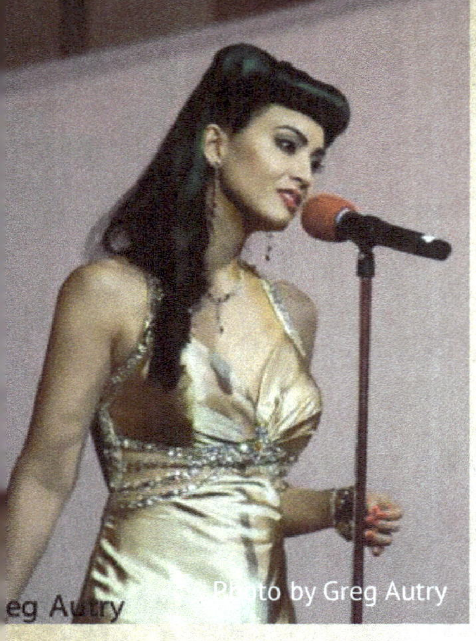

[MJ] *When I think of MKIO, I think of some amazing melancholy ballads....Prayer, Fading, More Than What I Am, and now, Empty. Where do these dark, desolate lyrics come from, and how much of this is Tash Cox?*

[NC] All the songs I write very much come from a very internal place...whether it's inside my own consciousness or inside a story I imagine. I have lived through many intense challenges in my lifetime, and writing these songs has been a way for me to cope with them. I truly believe that art and music are some of the most healing gifts that humanity has....it's the Hope in our Pandora's box. When people message me to tell me how much a song of ours has helped them with a particular situation in their life, it means the world to me to know that in some small way our music has helped them. Music has literally saved my life many times over, and I like to think that it can help others in the same way. I also love to encourage people to create art of their own, because the act of creating is such a transformative way to alchemize what originally can be the darkest of mud. Sometimes life doesn't make sense. We can't explain why things happen, but at least we can make beautiful things along the way.

[MJ] *In the period between Trapped Inside and Mobius Loop, yourself, Gordon, and Scott launched the indie project Alice, which combines music with performance art. How did the idea come about?*

[NC] After our year-long tour, we had a collection of songs that didn't fit MKIO. We played around with the songs as a three-piece before we started adding other members to the group and deciding that we were going to name this project Alice, an idea that stemmed from playing with surrealism and the concept of time. When we first started conceiving ideas for this project, we imagined it not as a singular band entity but a project in which music was just an element in a vast collective of artists who shared a vision in telling a story. We were asked by Joseph Corsentino, our long-time visual art collaborator, to play at his book release party for his project, Time of the Faeries. From here, we were introduced to the Sypher Art Studios and began a beautiful collaboration that we continue to cultivate.

[MJ] *Rumor has it you also sing opera. Are you still active in that medium?*

[NC] Yes, I am. I just finished a Puccini one-act opera called Suor Angelica, playing a nun named Sister Genovieffa. Definitely an interesting experience to switch gears in that realm. I love being able to explore these characters and stories with such beautifully written music. Plus my voice gets to explore ranges that it doesn't get to in other styles of music. Opera has helped me to unlock my voice in a way that I never thought was possible.

[MJ] *From Alice, to Alice Underground... a Jazz band (shaking my head). You are really unpredictable. The music is incredible, but why Jazz?*

"I truly believe that art and music are some of the most healing gifts that humanity has..."

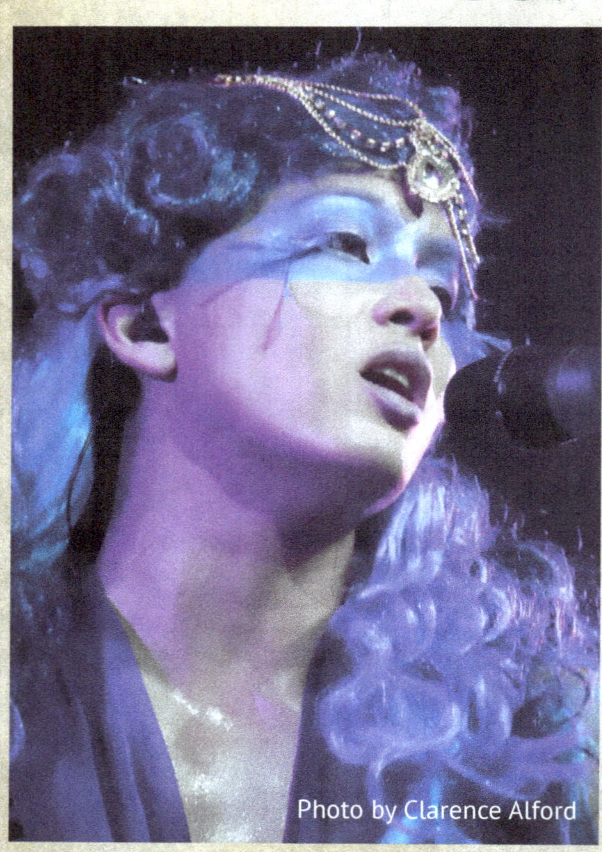

[NC] Alice has been performing at a masquerade ball called the Labyrinth of Jareth for the past four years. The event is put together by an amazing group of artists who go by Sypher Art Studios, headed by Shawn Strider. The Sypher group decided that they wanted to put a 1920s New Years Eve soiree one year, which became an annual event. Gordon is an incredible upright jazz bassist and was instrumental in helping us to traverse to the jazz world. I happened to have written a jazzy blues song years ago which just lay dormant, since I had no home for it. That particular song grew into a collection of songs that we started writing with Shawn and Sasha Travis. We wanted to explore a different era and yet make it in such a way that it was a time beyond time. After we finish up the next Alice album, we'll be putting out the Alice Underground album with all these jazz songs that we've been working on, with some videos that tell the story of the songs.

[MJ] *How is it working with the amazingly talented Sasha Travis?*

[NC] Amazing. Sasha is one of my dearest friends and collaborators. We're both from Texas and share similar senses of humor, ways of communicating (the accent comes out pretty thickly when the two of us are around each other), and creating. So needless to say, I have so much fun making music with her. We're also pretty intuitive when it comes to singing together and have found that we can say many things to each other without saying a word.

[MJ] *Do you find Alice Underground attracts a completely different crowd, or is the room still filled MKIO fans?*

[NC] There are some MKIO fans who traverse our worlds with us, but I've been finding that the crowds are vastly different from one another. This makes sense to me, because each style speaks to people in different ways. Some people need the energy of darker, heavier music, and some people resonate more with music that is more light. I love creating both....it's exciting to me to explore all the mediums that life has to offer, especially since as a human being we have so many layers of emotion and experience within us.

[MJ] *I have to ask, how much musical training have you had? Does all of these different styles come natural to you, or are there some that are harder for you than others?*

[NC] I have had a great deal of musical training. I started off with classical piano at two and have studied vocals with teachers from many styles, including blues, classical, Indian classical, jazz, and rock. I continue to train, with the hope of continual evolution. I find that studying different styles helps to expand my range and my inspiration. I find jazz to be the easiest to sing, followed by classical, with MKIO being the most difficult of all. Not easy to sing aggressively with the amount of energy it takes live, as well as being able to cut above a loud band in a live venue. Singing definitely does not come as easily to me as keyboards have. I enjoy the work that I put into it, though.

[MJ] *In 2012, Mankind is Obsolete was named Musical Ambassadors to Iran. How the heck did that come about, and how was the experience?*

[NC] One of our supporters introduced our music to a representative at the US State Department. The State Department has been trying to bridge relations with various countries with art and music. I really love this idea, because I do believe that music is truly a universal language. We were sent to Algeria to spend two weeks in three different cities, performing and teaching workshops for different bands in Algeria. We had the opportunity to meet incredible musicians while we were there and make friends with these wonderful artists. I was really blown away by how passionate and talented the people we met were. Singing is a normal part of their culture, as they have the call to prayer every day. The singing we heard while we were there felt like a natural extension of who they are. The experience as a whole was really amazing, as we had a chance to experience such a beautiful and rich culture.

[MJ] *You have performed with such great acts as Android Lust and Kidneythieves. Who is your dream band/artist to share the stage with?*

[NC] I feel like I'm already living the dream.

[MJ] *So what is next for Tash Cox? I'm gonna take a wild stab at this and guess Bluegrass.*

[NC] Hmmm. Bluegrass. Well, I've learned to never say never, but that may not happen for....a while. I'm actually really excited about a project that I've started singing for called The Beta Machine (www.thebetamachine.com). I've been friends with the bassist, Matt McJunkins, for a while, who actually used to occasionally play with MKIO. He started this project with a really gifted drummer, Jeff Friedl, and the two of them have created this incredibly beautiful, groove-oriented music. We're looking to put out an EP this year and to play shows regionally. Besides all the music, I've also been writing stories. I've been working on a children's book series, a screenplay, and a novel. I really love writing. Lots of stories and words that constantly swim around in this brain of mine. ;) And who knows where the tide will take me next? I feel like there are so many mediums to explore, so many people to create with, and so many experiences to be had. I'm just so grateful for the time I have and the people that surround me.

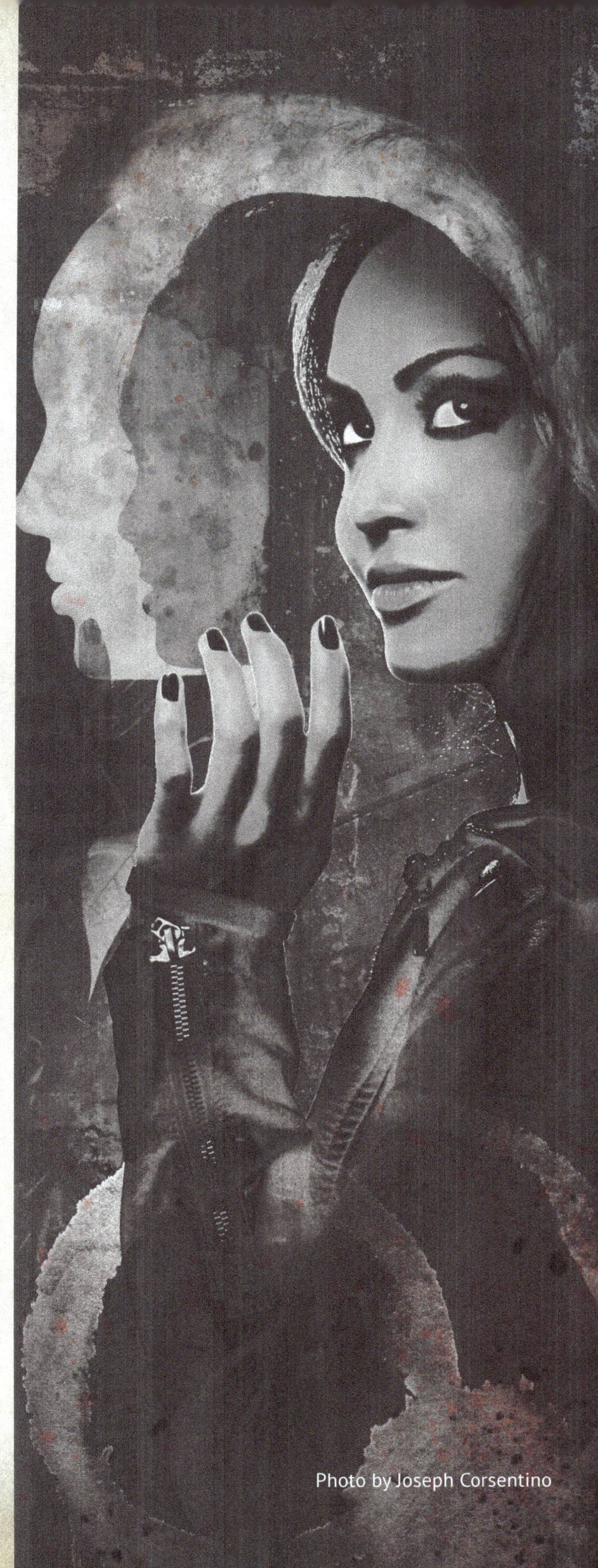

Photo by Joseph Corsentino

Imagine: Lights low, music on. A human marionette sits quietly on the lap of a buxom brunette, replete with carnival, side-show attire. Try as she might, the puppeteer cannot control her would-be wooden doll. The music swells, conflict begins, clothes are shed, and sight is lost regarding who is controlling who. The atmosphere settles. A partially undressed woman, with a freshly carved mouth, sits quietly on the lap of a human marionette...

Burlesque is defined as "a literary, dramatic or musical work intended to cause laughter by caricaturing the manner or spirit of serious works, or by ludicrous treatment of their subjects". These days most people define burlesque as some sort of glamorous strip tease with a limited reveal, usually including pastied boobs at the end. So, it's always refreshing to find a group of burlesquers that embrace and embody both of these definitions.

Athens, Georgia isn't a town you equate with burlesque - it's bars, music, bars, art, bars, UGA, and bars, sure - but not for a body-positive, all inclusive, vaudeville inspired, slap-strip, comedic burlesque troupe. But, lo and behold: Effie's Club Follies. Effie's has been an Athens staple for a decade; creating unique burlesque performances from the glamorous to the grotesque. Performers utilize their love of pop-culture and politics to put on a show that is, quite literally, titillating. I had the privilege of sitting down with Effie's Club Follies founder, performer, cheerleader, art director, recruiter, and MC Amanda Knisely-Medina (aka Miss Effie and Harry Dixxon) to learn more about this glittering, bedazzled spot in Athens, GA culture.

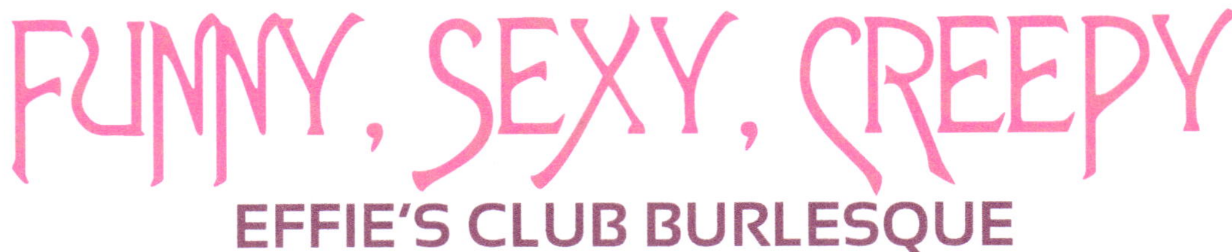

FUNNY, SEXY, CREEPY

EFFIE'S CLUB BURLESQUE

By Miss Bella Blitz

[Carpe Nocturne] *You've been going strong for 10 years. What/who inspired you to form Effie's Club Follies? And, how do you* keep *it going?*

[Miss Effie] I had been performing in drag for about a year, but found there were things I wanted to do as a female - that wasn't happening in the drag scene at the time. I happened to go to see the Suicide Girls at the 40 Watt, and found myself rewriting their sketches in my mind. I put up flyers to see if anyone was interested in starting a burlesque troupe with me and about 24 people showed up to the first meeting! In the last ten years there have been numerous times I've wanted to throw in the towel. Constantly bringing in new girls helps, their enthusiasm is infectious and keeps me going. Seeing the excitement through them makes it new.

[CN] *Why "Effie's Club Follies"?*

[Ms. E] We chose the name Effie's Club Follies to honor the whorehouse that was part of Athens for many decades. The original Effie's was a collection of houses of ill repute that operated from the early 1910's until 1972. When the first house was burned in 1977 as a firefighter exercise, an entrepreneur sold numbered bricks with a plaque that read, "a piece of Athens history." Our town had a lot of affection for something they publicly condemned. Over the last 10 years I've been honored to be told stories from people who remember the original Effie's. Hopefully, years from now we'll be remembered as part of that legacy.

[CN] *ECF is described as comedic-burlesque, but would you consider what you do to be more vaudeville?*

[Ms. E] It is closer to vaudeville than some other troupes I've seen, but it isn't exactly vaudeville. We do have spoken word, humor, and some occasional live singing, but so far no juggling since the first show, and no magic tricks. I'm working on it...

[CN] *What changes have you seen in the troupe's tone/style since it's inception?*

[Ms. E] The tone changes based on the members involved in any given show. We can have as few as 9 and as many as 24 in the troupe at any time. Each performer has their own strengths that shape the tone of the show. Some shows are dark and raunchy, while others are pretty and lyrical and a bit silly.

[CN] *You're an avid recruiter to ECF, what do you look for in potential performers? What is your "sales" pitch?*

[Ms. E] It always starts innocently enough, either after a show or while buying supplies for a show, I will see someone's face light up when we talk about burlesque. Most people I talk to have flirted with the idea, but are convinced they could never do it. I explain that no experience is necessary, it's more about desire and practice. We always create a character with a stage name, wig, and eyelashes. It isn't them that would get up on stage, it's their character. Maybe they should just come by and see a practice...

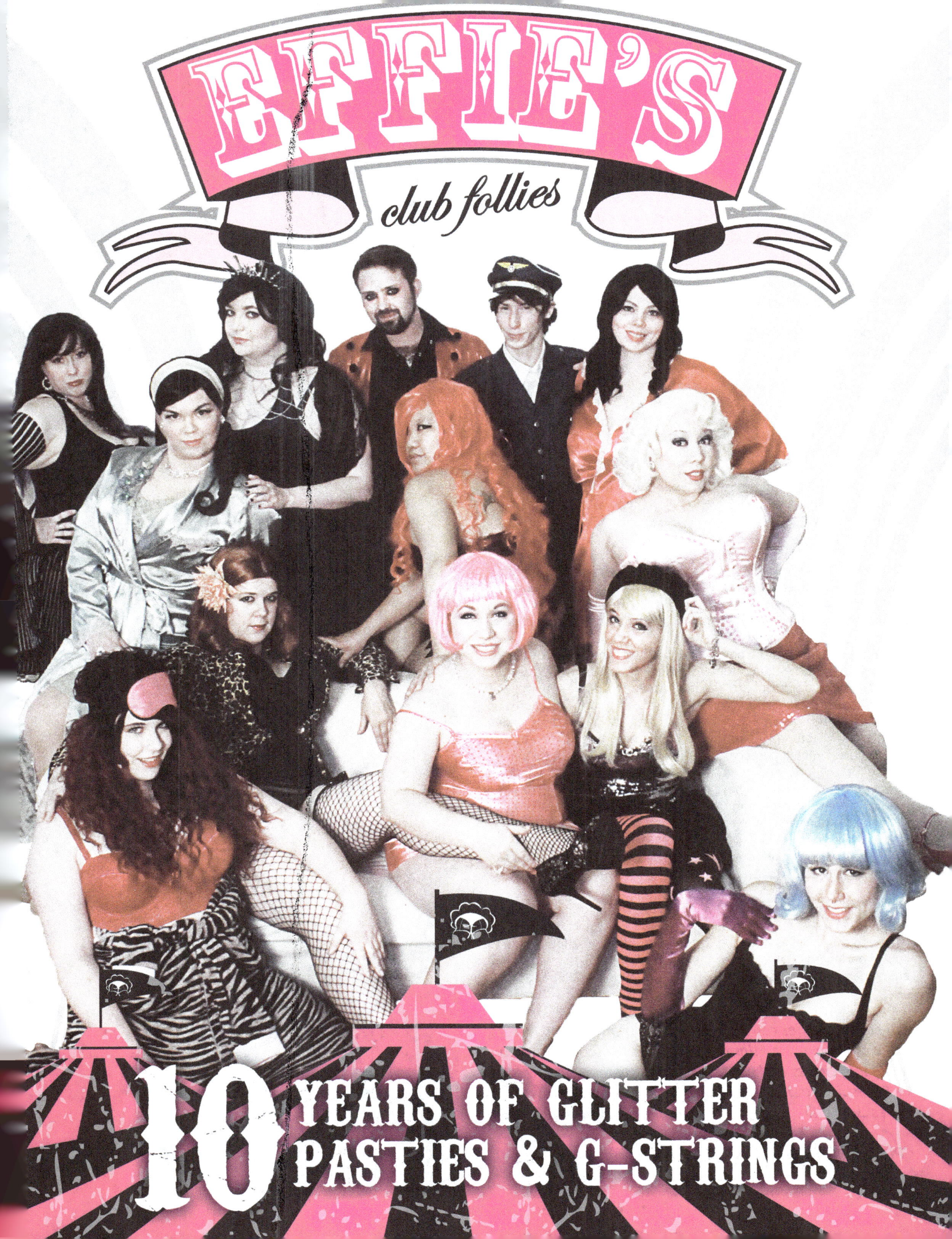

EFFIE'S
club follies
10 YEARS OF GLITTER
PASTIES & G-STRINGS

[CN] *Burlesque seems to embrace things/people/ideas that are outside the norm, what is your favorite aspect of this?*

[Ms. E] I love being able to watch people realize how sexy they are. When you don't see yourself represented in mainstream media you start to get the message that you aren't attractive. To see people gather the courage and take the risk to go on stage and to see the audience go on the journey with them and cheer them on, it is all amazing to be a part of.

[CN] *Do you find that burlesque audiences have a darker, more twisted sense of humor than most?*

[Ms. E] I think everyone has a dark and twisted sense of humor, but if you are paying money to see ladies take their clothes off in public, you're probably quicker to admit it.

[CN] *Do you find that you have a darker, more twisted sense of humor than most?*

[Ms. E] I think I have a cornier sense of humor than most. I'm the girl most likely to make a "dad joke."

[CN] *Do you/how do you encourage your performers to add more of their twisted selves into a number or persona?*

[Ms. E] Most people just want permission to show different sides of themselves. I just try to foster an environment without judgement. There are very few places that I draw line of something being unacceptable.

[CN] *What is your recipe for burlesque (boobs, costume, choreography, personality, humor, etc...) What is absolutely necessary for a successful number (ie - the choreography sucks, but the costume is perfect - does that balance it out? I feel like the total is more than the sum of its parts.*

[Ms. E] A number - in my opinion - should be funny, sexy, or creepy. If one of the elements (costume, choreo, etc.) takes away from the overall tone or atmosphere the performer is creating then I try to give notes on it. Boobs aren't necessary, they are the cherry on top. A performer doesn't have to be a great dancer, or an amazing seamstress as long as all of the elements help to tell the story of the number. Simple choreography is fine if well executed, costuming should fit properly and remove the way the performer wants, it doesn't necessarily have to have fringe and rhinestones. The story, the journey of the character from the beginning to the end of the number is the most important thing to me.

[CN] *Do you have any advice for newbie burlesquers - performers or audience members?*

[Ms. E] For performers my advice is to stop thinking about doing it and get your ass onstage. Watch as many shows as you can and decide what you think makes a number "good." Then you will know where to apply your energy. For audience member my advice is to strap in and enjoy the ride! Be loud, be rowdy, but above all BE RESPECTFUL.

Effie's Club Follies can be found galavanting around Athens, GA and the greater Atlanta, GA area. For more information, upcoming events, and photos, you can find them on facebook as EffiesClubFollies, twitter @EffiesBurlesque, their website EffiesClubFollies.com, and on youtube MissEffiesBurlesque.

"PRAISE TITTIES!" - Miss Effie.

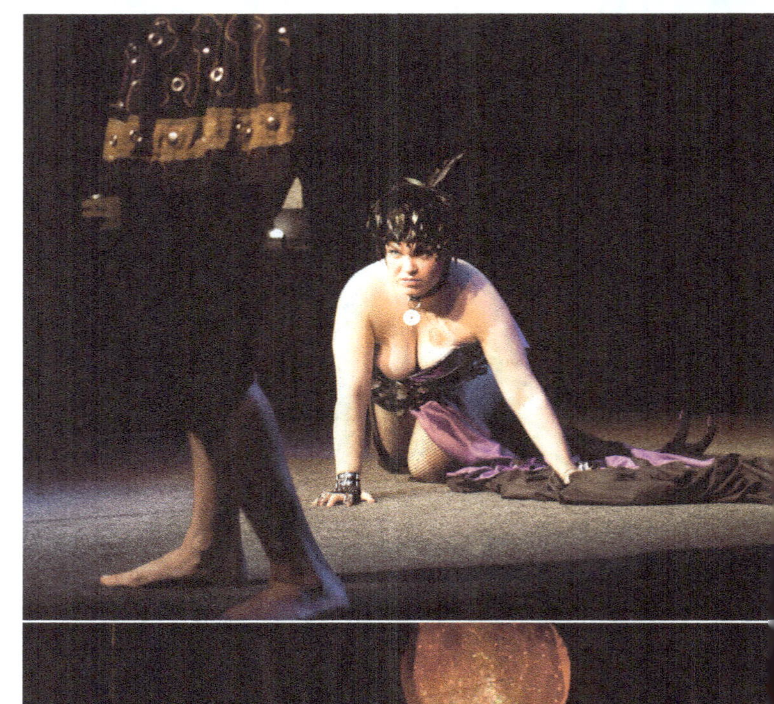

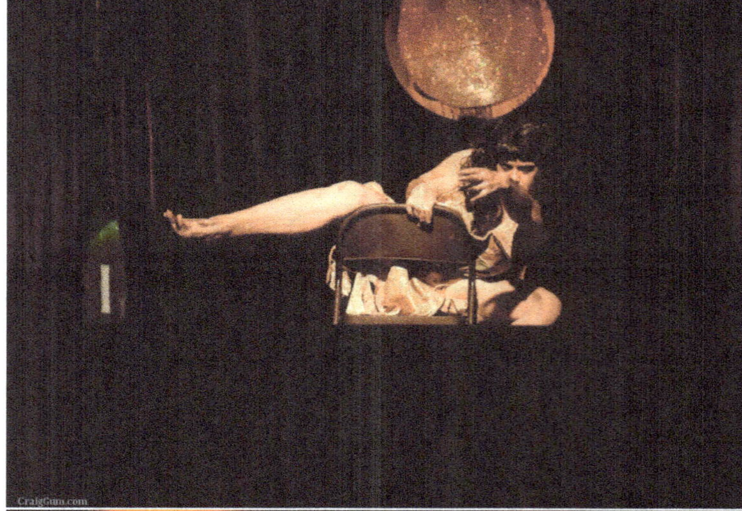

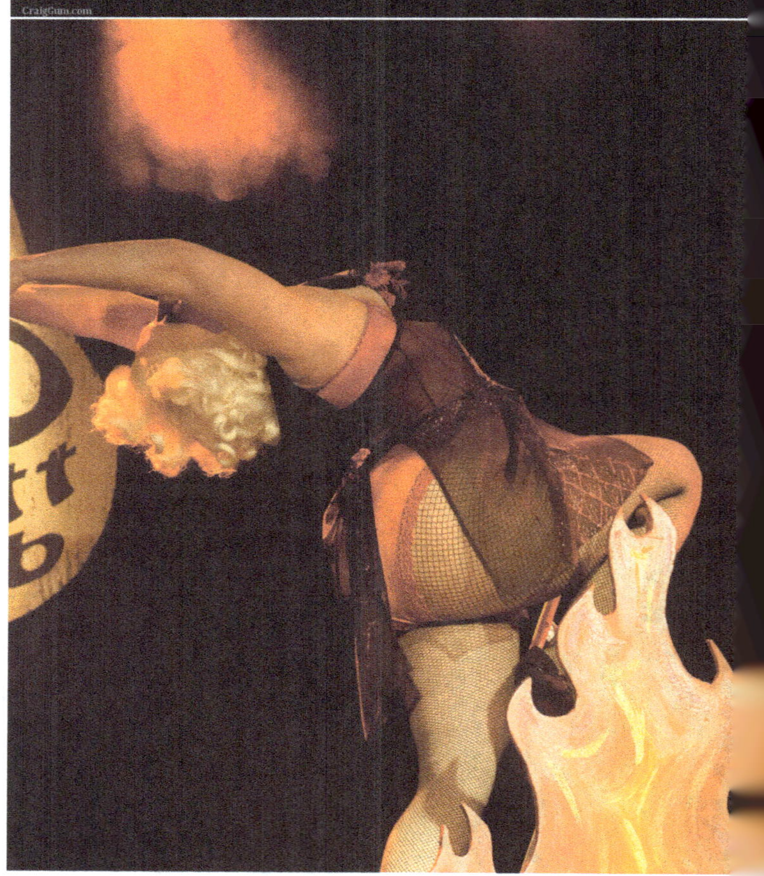

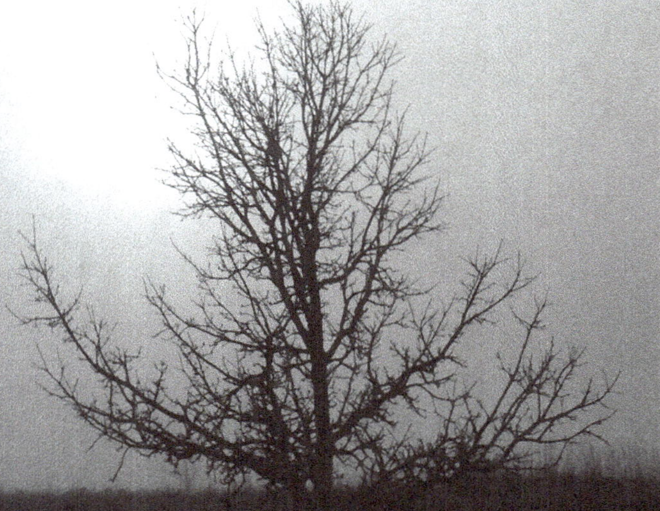

SANCTUARY OF THE STRANGE

WHERE DIVERSITY IS THE NORM

By Asylum Attendant

Sexual orientation, gender identity, gender norms…most people never even have to question these parts of themselves. They are innate and readily accepted by society. Those who cannot fit into the socially constructed box and are brave enough to share their differences with the world face discrimination, violence and fear. Of course I'm talking about the LGBTQ community.

This column, Sanctuary of the Strange, is meant to be a safe haven for anyone who's ever felt shame or sadness for being different. Whether you are asexual or transgender or androgynous or a supporter of the community, I want everyone to feel welcome here. I'll discuss all aspects of diversity and how this develops in the dark cultures. An asylum was always meant to be a refuge for the vulnerable and as the Asylum Attendant, it's my duty to support those who are often misunderstood by society. The gates are open, so do come in…

Masculinity/Femininity ≠ Sexual Orientation

How many male Goth friends do you have that wear makeup? The majority are probably heterosexual. However, those outside our culture would be quick to say these men are gay. This stereotype has always fascinated and frustrated me. An androgynous appearance or gender non-conforming behavior should not be a signifier of one's sexual orientation. So why is our society so quick to assign sexual orientations to people?

Some people pride themselves on their ability to determine someone else's sexual orientation based solely on their appearance or one simple interaction. That sort of mentality is seriously disturbing. Firstly, a person's sexual orientation is not up for discussion unless they bring it up and want to talk about it. Sexuality is a very personal part of a human's life. They definitely don't need a stranger passing judgments on something they haven't even disclosed. Gaydar shouldn't exist in my opinion. Find something more constructive to do with your time.

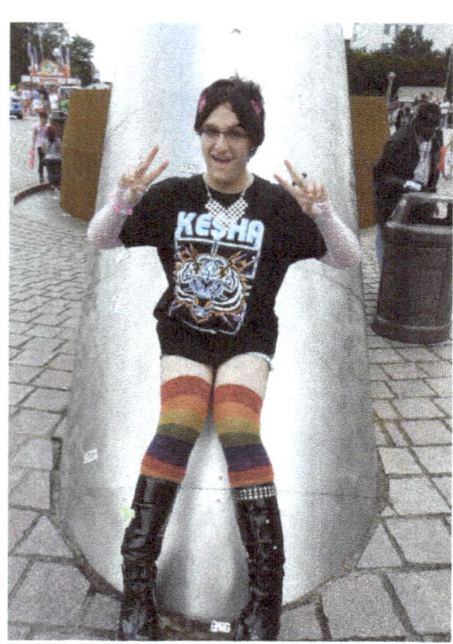

Our world exists on classification and labels. We like things to make perfect sense and maintain order. Gender roles are quite rigid and don't allow for much ambiguity. Androgyny messes everything up. A woman with short hair who hates makeup and likes to hunt defies the system. So, she's labeled a lesbian, even though the labelers don't know she's married with three children. People ask her all the time if she's a lesbian, much to her exasperation. They just cannot comprehend her androgynous identity and it

confuses them. Meanwhile, the woman is left wondering why society is so black and white.

Sexual orientation assumptions are based on a confirmation bias. A person meets one openly gay man who is super feminine and loves to shop. So, all gay men must be this way and this person only pays attention to these types of gay men to fulfill their bias. They disregard masculine gay men they meet as anomalies and keep their flawed beliefs at the forefront. The media perpetuates LGBTQ stereotypes and the cycle goes on and on.

I've always been a very feminine man. I wear my hair long, love fashion and the majority of my friends are women. Because of stereotypes, people always think I'm gay and some outright ask me. I never really know how to answer that since it's an annoying question and rather invasive. Who asks a masculine guy if he's straight?! Usually, I just change the topic to evade an answer. But, I shouldn't have to give any response at all. My likes and interests do not determine who I sleep with.

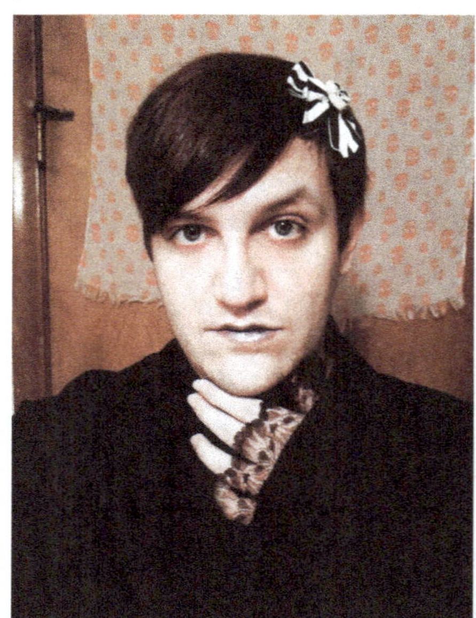

I don't mind people thinking I'm gay. That doesn't change who I am or what I think about myself. However, I wish society would validate so much more than sexual orientation. Instead of saying she's bisexual, talk about her amazing work as a journalist. Oh, and for the love of Lucifer, please stop referring to people you know/don't know as your asexual friend or the gay florist. These people are simply your friend and your florist. Why is their alleged sexuality getting dragged into the mix? Labels, labels, labels.

So, next time you meet an androgynous person, take them for what they are: a regular person with a unique style or interests. They're most likely a really fascinating person to get to know.

Visiting hours are over for today.

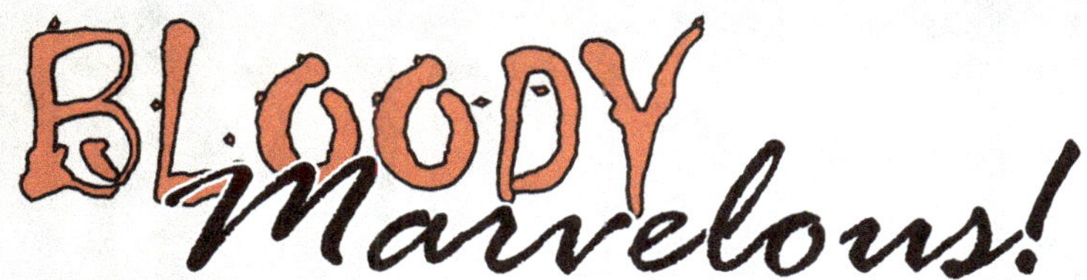

BLOODY MARY'S AND FOOD ODDITIES

By XXX ZOMBIEBOY XXX

Greetings and Salutations! This season, our explorations into strange and exotic foods brings us to the land that made Anne Rice and Poppy Z Brite famous for writing about. A land I will myself soon be moving to. And it is a perfect thing to write about for the summer. The New Orleans tradition of the Crawfish Boil!

"Mudbugs" as they are sometimes referred to, were not often prized as fine dining per say. In fact they were once considered refuse and only eaten by the poor people of the bayous, scorned by the "better class of people" *Rolls eyes*.

One popular legend is that the Acadians of Nova Scotia brought their beloved lobsters with them when they moved south. The lobsters however, either disgruntled with the change or just facing too far a move, lost their appetite along the way and shrunk. Therefore necessitating the cooking of several at once rather than one.

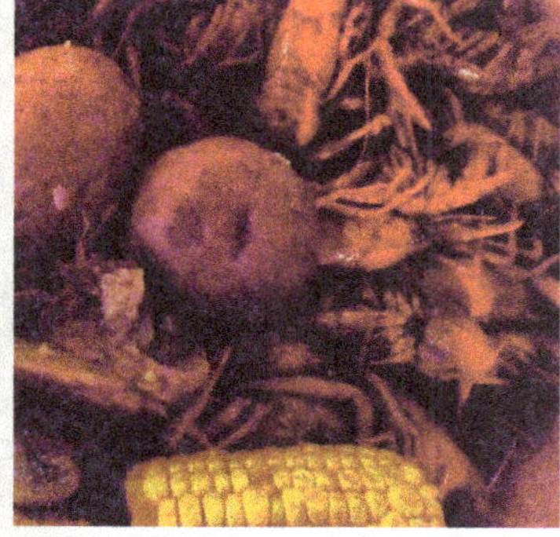

Of course our beloved little fresh water beasties have been right where they are now for countless centuries. And the scorn over their sweet meat was slowly but steadily overcome by the increase in technology of cold storage and transportation. After the Great Depression, crawfish found its way to the major cities and the economy surrounding the crawfish industry has only continued to climb.

The crawfish boil is a very social event and a tradition during festivals, picnics, gatherings and holidays. A picnic table covered with crawfish, corn and potatoes, surrounded by friends and family is a mighty good time indeed. There are many recipes and procedures for preparing a boil, but this is one of my favorites (with a few of my own touches).

Invite all your friends, family and tribe of like-minded trouble makers together with music, cold beer and a long picnic table. Yes this is part of the recipe. You also need all the necessary gear and ingredients. As preferences over brands, and quantities vary based on the amount of people, the quantities vary.

Rinse the crawfish. And rinse them good! Continue to do so until the draining water is clean looking. Don't worry, they will get spicy later. I have heard some say to do this in brine or salt water but I think it unnecessary. Get em' good and clean.

Fill your pot with water and begin to boil. This would be an excellent time to grab a cold Dixie or Blackened Voodoo. Basically the beer of your choice. And play some Zydeco.

Add your chosen seasoning to the boil. About a pound and a quarter or more. Everyone gives a different opinion on this. It should have oregano and cayenne pepper in it. Beer spillage into the pot is acceptable! Just not too much.

Some say this is when to add the garlic, onions and potatoes. Some say wait on the potatoes till later. I say get them good and

saturated in the spice. So add all of these. Be sure not to overcook the potatoes! Once the potatoes are close but still undercooked add in the mushrooms, celery and the corn. Corn should be on the cob. You can also include asparagus.

Remove the vegetables and put into the coolers. Add more spice to the water per taste and squeeze most if not all of the lemons into the pot. Drop the mudbugs in! Toss a few of the lemons in too.

Have another beer! Let them boil for 2-3 minutes. Kill the heat then let them soak for five minutes. Pour all the veggies back into the pot along with the rest of your seasoning. Stir for a minute. Down the rest of the beer.

Remove the basket and pour the whole steaming beautiful mess out onto the picnic table covered in newspaper. I recommend the Times Picayune for authenticity.

DIG IN! Play music, converse and enjoy the beautiful day! Oh and try my Bloody Mary recipe from the last issue, with the crawfish for a more eye watering experience!

Finally this brings us to the old question. How do you eat the crawfish?

You can eat or such on the claws. There isn't much meat but some love this so try it. Twist the head off. And (get ready for it) suck the head. No pun intended. Yes you do this! It is part of it. And don't worry, it isn't as gross as you may think. Most of not all of the "gross" will be boiled away. The juices gather here and are delicious.

Pull off the tail. Peel it. Pull out the vein if there is one. And eat that sucker.

Do not rub your eyes!! REPEAT!

The Alchemist's Closet

STIMULANTS AND SEDITIVES: PART ONE

By Michael Jack and XXX ZOMBIEBOY XXX

Navigating the world of stimulants and sedatives is no easy task. There really are not many choices found in your local pharmacy. You want to stay within the realms of the law, correct? Joe at the corner is offering something that might not only land you in jail, but also make you dependent on what he's selling. Avoid Joe. Instead, come to see me, or one of the many local pharmacists who have spent six years of their life studying these chemicals and medications. We will not only help you, but also keep you away from the life style Joe is offering.

Let's say you have spent all night at an Industrial rave, or just couldn't put down "The Tell Tale Heart" for your twelfth read. Now you have to go to work. You are exhausted and kicking yourself for not getting at least a few hours of sleep. What do you do? You can't call out of work, so you need something else to get you through your shift. You turn to me to recommend a safe and effective product to help you. My response is extremely easy, because there is only one active ingredient available over the counter to keep you awake…caffeine. Pick one. All of the products found on your pharmacy's shelf are practically the same. One pill is roughly equivalent to one cup of coffee, and the max strength formulations are roughly equivalent to two. Me personally, I drink coffee all day long; so I'd much rather reach for another cup.

There is hope, however. The makers of Red Bull have put together a product that not only gives you that initial boost of caffeine, but combines ingredients to keep you awake naturally. Packed with sugar, B vitamins, and amino acids, Red Bull supplies your body with the necessary natural components your body needs to stay awake and alert. Red Bull also contains less caffeine than the available over the counter "stay awake" pills, so there is less of a chance of unwanted side effects, like sending your heart racing. Because Red Bull contains B vitamins which alcohol rapidly depletes, drinking one or two of these during a night out will also greatly reduce the likelihood of a hangover. It is just one more reason to recommend Red Bull.

If you are diabetic, or don't particularly like the taste of Red Bull, there is another option for you. 5 Hour Energy delivers a similar combination of ingredients. Available in shots, it's quick, easy, and effective. 5 Hour Energy packs a bigger punch up front, because it is loaded with caffeine, but it'll give you that boost when you need it fast. Because it contains aspartame instead of sugar, 5 Hour Energy is also an excellent choice when you are trying to watch your weight. 5 Hour Energy also contains a blend of B vitamins and aminos, so it will keep you going after the caffeine has worn off.

Now you are finally home, but find you have overdone it with the Red Bull and 5 Hour Energy. Your body is exhausted, but somehow you cannot drift off to that much needed slumber land. Don't reach for that bottle. Alcohol actually disrupts REM sleep. Instead, get back out of bed, and trudge back down to the pharmacy to see me. I can help.

Like stimulants, over the counter sleep aids are all very similar. They all either contain the antihistamines diphenhydramine or doxylamine. So what do you choose? I'm probably near the end of a grueling twelve-hour shift, but with a helpful smile, I lead you to the sleep aid aisle. I point to Zzzquil. Vick's has a long history of making great products. Nyquil and Dayquil are my most commonly recommended cold and flu products.

Why should I turn anywhere else for a sleep aid? I shouldn't. Zzzquil contains the active ingredient diphenhydramine, and is roughly equivalent 2 capsules of Benadryl. It'll make you drowsy. Zzzquil also contains alcohol, but not enough to disturb that much needed REM sleep. The alcohol is just there to enhance the sedative effect. Available in liquid, Zzzquil hits the blood stream faster than any other over the counter sleep aid, and decreases the time between dosing and slumber. Zzzquil is very safe, carries little side effects, but should not be taken if you are currently on prescription or over the counter allergy meds. Check with your pharmacist first.

If it's chronic insomnia you are battling, the choices become a lot more complex, and generally involve a visit to your doctor. Before you take that step, however, I recommend trying Melatonin. This chemical is your body's natural hormone produced to regulate sleep. Melatonin is available in any drug store's vitamin and herbal section, and is often inexpensive. The general usual starting dose is 3mg, and can be adjusted upward if need be. Give this product at least a month before giving up on it.

If Melatonin is not enough for you, and for many it is not, then you need to see your doctor for a prescription. The biggest advice I can give here is…remember YOU are the one taking the medication. Therefore, YOU have a say in what is prescribed. Don't just let your doctor write out a script for a popular sleep med because that is what he is used to writing. Speak up, and voice your concerns. Communication is key here.

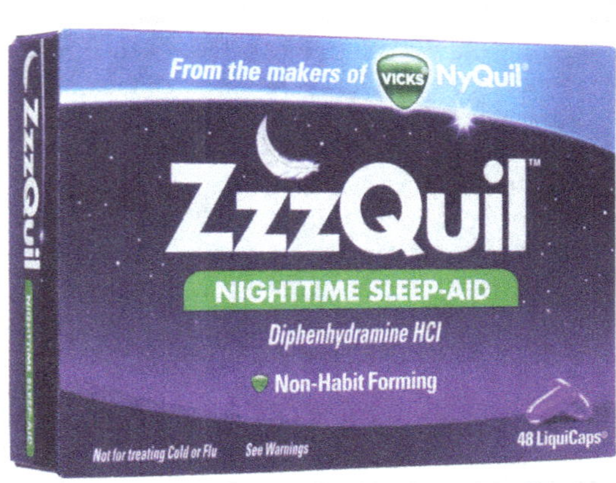

The drugs prescribed to treat in insomnia generally fall into one of two class of drugs…anti-depressants or benzodiazepines. There is also a third class, Ambien being the most popular one, but they act on the same receptors in the body as the benzos. Therefore, I will lump them together. The anti-depressant meds, like Trazodone, are effective and non-addicting, but they wouldn't be my first choice. These medications affect more processes in the brain than just regulating sleep. The benzos, like temazepam, Xanax, or the aforementioned related Ambien, ARE addicting. They also carry a lot more side effects than your other choices. I would only turn to these products if you absolutely have to.

Luckily, there is a third choice… Rozerem. This prescription medication is a Melatonin receptor agonist, which means, it binds to the melatonin receptors in the brain, and causes you to fall asleep the natural way. This medication is not only safe, but it is non-habit forming, and has a lot less side effects than your other prescription choices. The one draw back to Rozerem is it's only available in brand name. This means the costs will be higher. If you have insurance, Rozerem will likely be a tier 3 co-pay. If you don't have insurance, you really need to weigh benefits versus costs. My opinion is Rozerem is still worth the money. You should avoid taking this medication if you are currently on Luvox (fluvoxamine).

By XXX ZOMBIEBOY XXX

PART 2: FOOD

More important than simply not getting eaten is to determine how to keep eating your self. There is a lot of material out there on survival food, hunting, fishing, and to be perfectly honest, one could write a book on the subject. And with every climate on Earth, the game changes. There is no way that I could cover such a subject in one article. What I will do instead is give a few pointers to get you going. I may eventually do one for several different climates.

First, consider the environment you find yourself in. Learn ahead of time what plants can offer nutrition in that region as well as any region you may decide to head for. What game is out there to hunt or fish in? Are there stores of food that can be obtained? A place selling MRI's before it all comes down? These are things worth thinking about. Plans fall apart. Ideas stick and grow.

Next, be ready with a "bug out" bag. This I will write on later but a "bug out" bag is a pre-packed gear bag ready to just grab and go. Within this bag I recommend simple and re-usable fishing gear and light weight camping utensils for eating. I don't recommend any cooking stoves unless you have a vehicle because you need fuel for such. It may help at first but there will not be many convenient places to get fuel for them. Best to think in a more primitive mindset and learn what you can eat raw or cook in a fire.

It is important to maintain health and energy. For this reason I think it very important to mention one of my favorite camping delights and survival staples, Pine Needle Tea! Pine Needle Tea has 5 times the Vitamin C of orange juice, and is high in Vitamin A as well. Both are vital for health, immune system strength and also to prevent scurvy. Yes, even if you are not a pirate you can get that from vitamin deficiency. It is also an expectorant, decongestant, and can be used as an antiseptic. It also tastes better than you would think. Each type of pine has it's own flavor and mixing and matching can keep it fresh. All you have to do is collect a handful of needles. The younger the better. You then remove the brown ends and chop the needles into inch or so lengths. Boil water over a fire. I have often used soda cans for this use. Or a soup can. Drop the needles in and let them steep until most of them sink then drink! You can actually survive for a while on nothing but this. Well known by soldiers and aviators, and since conifers grow in many climates all over the world, this is a handy thing to know.

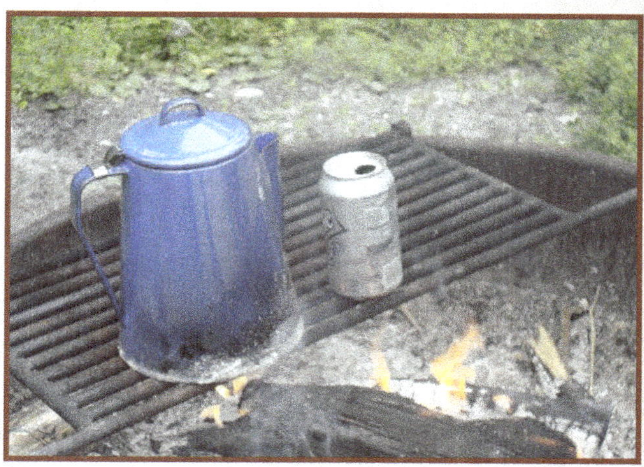

Next are BUGS! Start singing your Lion King songs because slimy yet satisfying is true! Once you get over the idea and the taste. They are plentiful all over the world, even in desert and winter climates and are highly nutritious. Many are rich in proteins, carbohydrates and fats. The best to eat are crickets (actually served in some bars in Mexico!), grasshoppers, ants (best if cooked but try eating the lower abdomen) butterflies, moths, scorpions, grubs and worms. The later two can be crushed into a paste along with leeches. This paste can be cooked until crunchy and actually does not taste that bad. Worms and grubs can be swallowed raw and whole without chewing. Remove heads, legs, hard shells and any stingers. Also cooking or roasting critters makes them more palatable. Be wary of slow moving, bright colored or fuzzy insects. These are indicators of poison and best to just avoid. Dig into that old stump and get dinner!

Learn to fish! You can survive indefinitely on fish if you have to. Learn to catch, learn to clean and learn to cook. Fishing can also be relaxing and reduce anxiety.

Nature is also full of natural greens all over the earth. A quick note on berries. Observe the animals and what they eat. This is a pretty good way to determine what may be safe to eat. If you are in a pinch try to taste test. If it is bitter spit it out. Or ingest a VERY small amount and wait. If you feel off then avoid! This method is best left when in a real pinch. Zombies don't like fast food. Being sick will slow you down a whole lot. There are also many edible mushrooms but I would avoid all unless you have a field guide and are 100% certain of the variety.

A small note on hunting for you carnivores out there. Pretty much anything that moves can be eaten. The Native American approach to hunting is a good one. Try to use everything you can on the animal. And it doesn't hurt to thank the spirit of the animal that you kill. Even bones can be used as tools, spear tips, fishhooks and weapons.

For those of you more intent on raiding and looting, remember two things. One, living humans are far more dangerous than zombies. And they will protect what is theirs. Don't risk theft. It is far better to be self-reliant. Two, if you do raid abandoned goodies, think about what spoils first and eat that first. And be sure it is not already spoiled. Getting sick is a bad idea in even the best circumstances. Remember too that if you can think of it, so can others. Don't try to take over a Wal Mart. Someone else may have already.

MRE's are great for a start but they can be bulky and don't last too long so unless you load up a carload of them, they won't help very much. Canned goods are heavy too. Check those expiration dates.

Water is to be thought of before food. You can go up to a month on almost nothing for food if you have too though you will be weakened. The record for going without water is something like a week. For most, the survival rate is about three days. Know how to collect and make safe. This will be discussed in a future article. In the meantime, Bon Appetite!!!

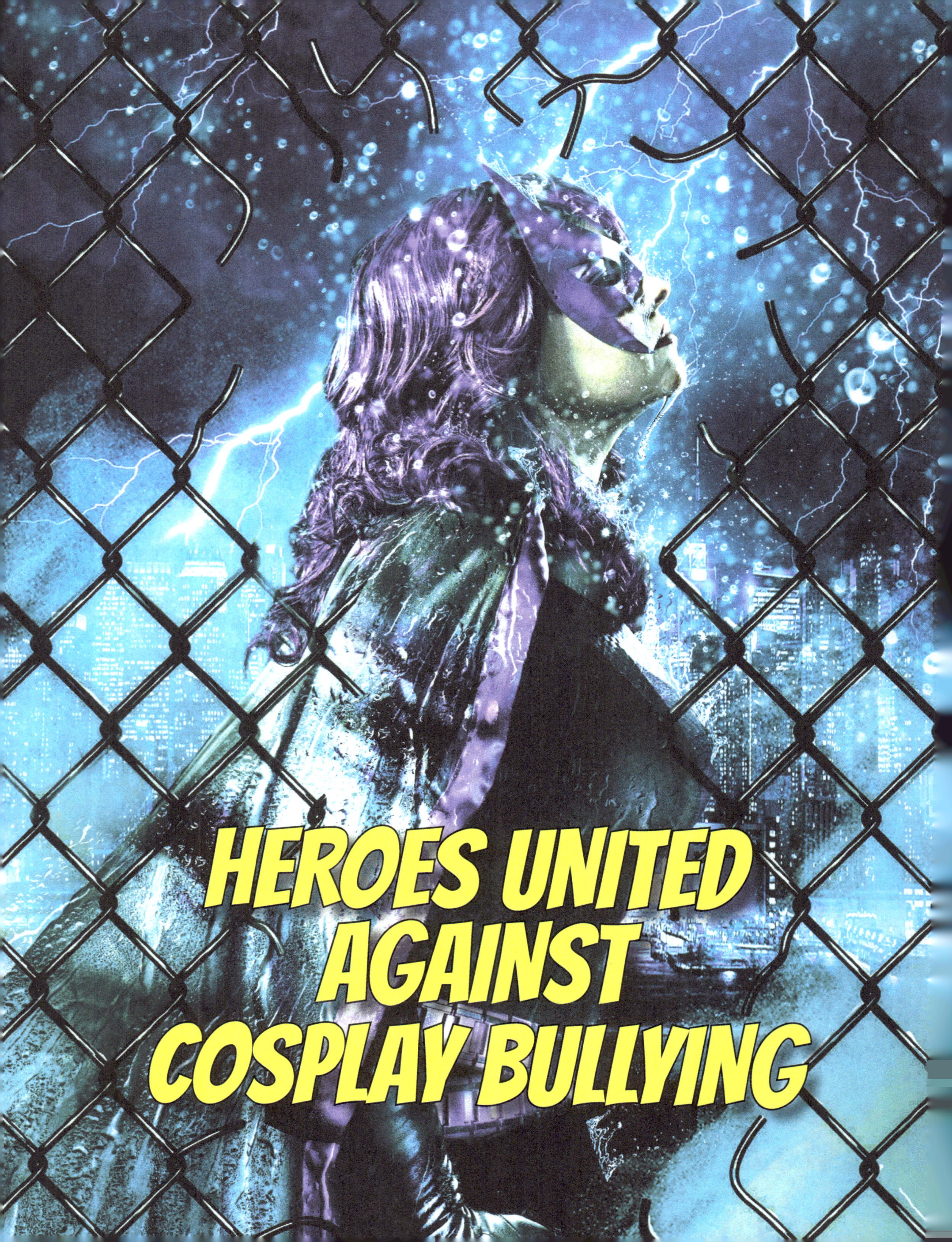

HEROES UNITED
AGAINST
COSPLAY BULLYING

Bullies love to target anyone who looks or acts different from the norm. As such, cosplayers are not immune to harassment and humiliation from outsiders and even fellow cosplayers with rigid standards on proper cosplay. Cosplayer and costume/prop maker JezzabellGem decided that she needed to do something about the negativity within the cosplay community. She founded the Facebook group Heroes United Against Cosplay Bullying to provide support and encouragement to cosplayers and erase hate from the cosplay world. Check out my interview with the gracious JezzabellGem below:

[Asylum Attendant] *What prompted the formation of Heroes United Against Cosplay Bullying?*

[JezzabellGem] Just over a year or so ago, I was looking into various social media sites trying to figure out which ones suited my business needs in the best ways. I created an account on Tumblr and I was searching for cosplay communities when I ran across a Tumblr page called "Shitty Cosplay". At first I didn't think much of it, because I'd never run across anything negative like that before, but what I found was awful. This site was collecting photos of what they considered bad cosplays, posting them and ripping everyone apart. The one that got to me the most was that of a girl who was clearly under 16 dressed as an anime character. Not everyone has access to loads of money to spend on expensive materials...her costume was home made and she did what she could with what she had out of love for that character. She looked adorable and happy. They called her fat, untalented, ugly, a horrible cosplayer and said she had no business ever wearing a costume or going to a convention. What was worse? I knew her. She was the niece of a friend of mine – a sweet and impressionable girl. My own daughter, also a cosplayer, was 14 at the time and as a mom I felt incredibly protective. I found several groups and communities that day that were/are dedicated to humiliating and publically shaming cosplayers who don't fit one standard or another. I helped get that site taken down, and the girl never knew her photo was up there. That's the day I formed Heroes United Against Cosplay Bullying.

[AA] *Describe the Heroes team.*

[Jezzabell] We are a team of five who run this initiative, and we all play very important roles:

I founded Heroes, and I'm the main admin. I'm probably the most central person most of the time, but Scarlett Rose Cosplay has been my admin partner since just a few months after Heroes was started, and we run the page together. Doozer La Fae is my table and panel partner, she helps me with content, set up, running the tables/booths and giving our panels. Commander Crazy is also present at panels here and there in representation of our LGBTQ+ fans, and she helps us make our videos and presentation slide shows. Loony Bin is my amazing offspring. She also helps with tables/booths, and she represents her age group as well as the LGBTQ+ community in our panels. Loony Bin came up with the idea for our new LGBTQ+ panel. I'm so honored to be teamed up with these amazing and supportive cosplayers. I couldn't do this without them.

[AA] *Why did your group choose Facebook as the safe space for your community?*

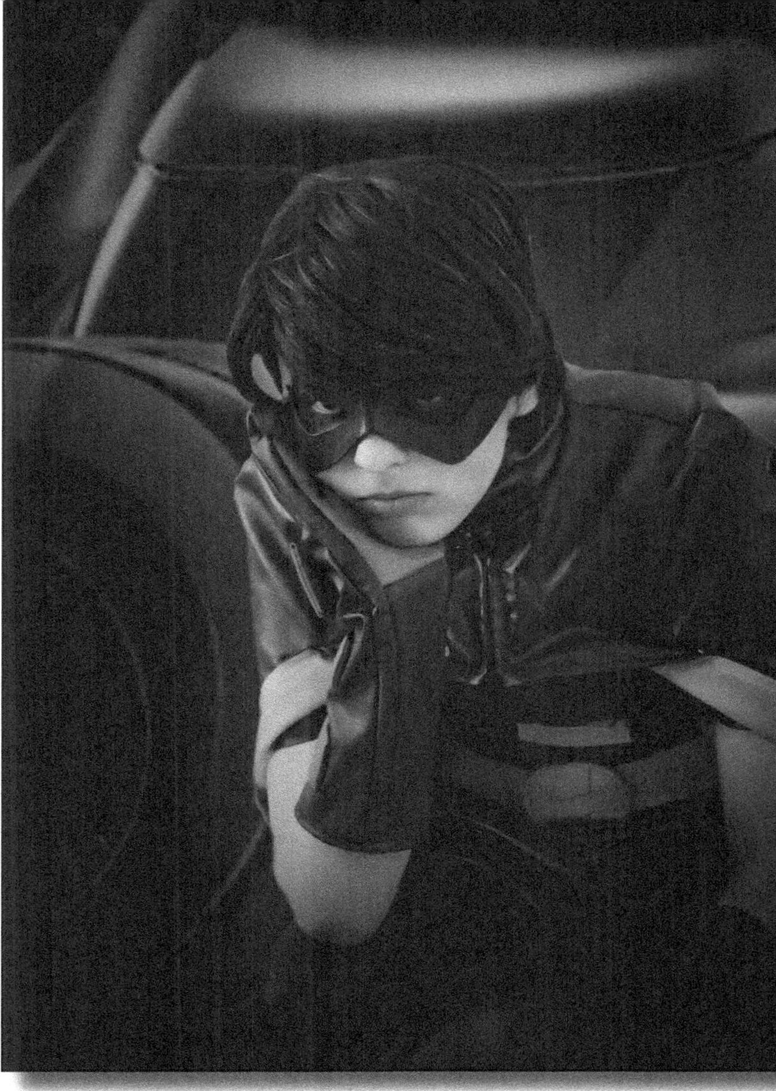

[Jezzabell] Facebook is the largest forum for the cosplay community next to Instagram and Twitter, so it made sense to start there. We do have an Instagram, and a YouTube channel that I plan to develop more with, but with the Facebook page being the most active, I have a hard time keeping up with more than that in addition to my own cosplay social media.

[AA] *What topics are discussed at the convention panels your group hosts?*

[Jezzabell] The main panel that we give is "Finding Empowerment Through Positive Cosplay". We share advice on how to deal with trolling, negativity and bullying both online and at conventions. We try and provide online resources for help and encouragement that are in addition to our own site, and we maintain that our page' and its fans are a safe place to share and ask for help. Once we've established those things, we open the panel up to the audience, because we're there for them. People are usually very active with asking questions, sharing stories, and giving advice.

We've also developed a new panel called "The Coast Is Queer: LGBTQ+ Support In Cosplay". We're hoping to start giving that one very soon.

[AA] *What is it like meeting some of the cosplayers you've helped in person?*

[Jezzabell] It's no less than amazing. I've met some very established and well known anti-bully cosplayers who've afforded me the opportunity to interview them on behalf of the page to help spread the "no tolerance" message through their own experiences. I've also met several fans of the page that have messaged us and shared their own struggles with us. We're always met with happy hugs and thank yous. I'm humbled and moved every single time I get to talk to someone who has felt supported by us.

[AA] *Why do you think bullies target cosplayers so frequently?*

[Jezzabell] Bullies target everyone for every ridiculous reason. I think cosplayers (young cosplayers in particular) are easily targeted for the simple fact of who we are and what we do. To the unfamiliar, we're those nerdy weirdoes who play dress up. What really gets me is the negativity and drama on social media that seems to occur within our own community toward each other out of jealousy and the quest for cosfame. That seems to be the hardest and most tricky form of bullying to deal with.

[AA] *What should a cosplayer do if they are being bullied?*

[Jezzabell] It really depends on the type of bullying you're dealing with. A good starting point is to think about the results you want, and be realistic about it. It's reasonable to expect that you can get the harasser to stop contacting you. It is reasonable to expect that you can increase your safety online. If it's an apology you're looking for or revenge, then you're most likely not approaching it in the most effective way. In most cases the smartest (and the hardest) thing to do is to completely disengage. They want your attention. They want you to feel hurt and helpless – that's how they feed themselves. Don't give it to them. Know that the real power lies within you. Reach out to groups like ours. Help is out there.

[AA] *The stories fellow cosplayers share on your Facebook page are very inspirational. How does everyone maintain positivity in spite of the trolls and haters?*

[Jezzabell] I think the sense of community that all of us have created with each other is what helps positivity the most. Knowing that you're not the only one going through it, and that you have people, fellow cosplayers, to look to for support.

[AA] *Cosplay is often misunderstood by the general public. What stereotypes would this group like to eliminate?*

[Jezzabell] The thing I notice the most is that people seem to think most of us have no social life and that we do this solely for attention. In most cases, that couldn't be further from the truth. We have magnificent and rich lives full of friends and "cosplay families". Most of us are very social and conventions serve as our chance to see all of our friends in one fan filled location.

[AA] *What are some of the most creative cosplays this group has seen/ created?*

[Jezzabell] The most inspiration and creativity we see are when people cosplay in groups, as a family or team up in any way. When we show our love for characters that we admire together – that's when it's the most impressive.

[AA] *What are the group's goals for the future? Where can people come and see your panel discussions?*

[Jezzabell] Our goal is to show support to our community by giving as many panels at as many conventions as we can, and to reach as many people as possible. We're really excited to have panels at Metro Con and Tampa Bay Comic Con this summer and we may even be giving a panel at Dragon Con!

Heroes United Against Cosplay Bullying
https://www.facebook.com/heroesunitedagainstcosplaybullying

JezzabellGem Cosplay, Props & Costuming
https://www.facebook.com/jezzabellgem

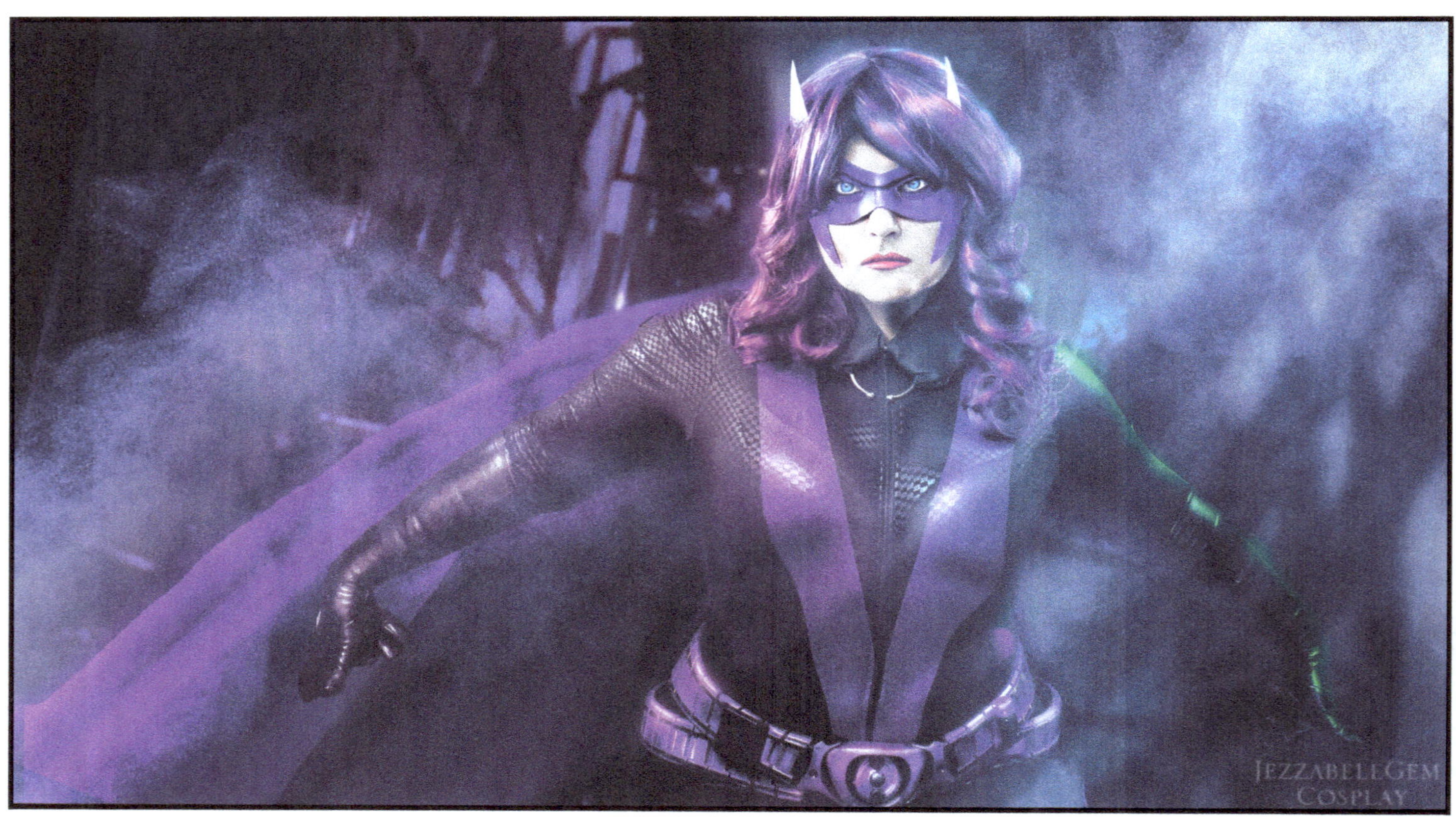

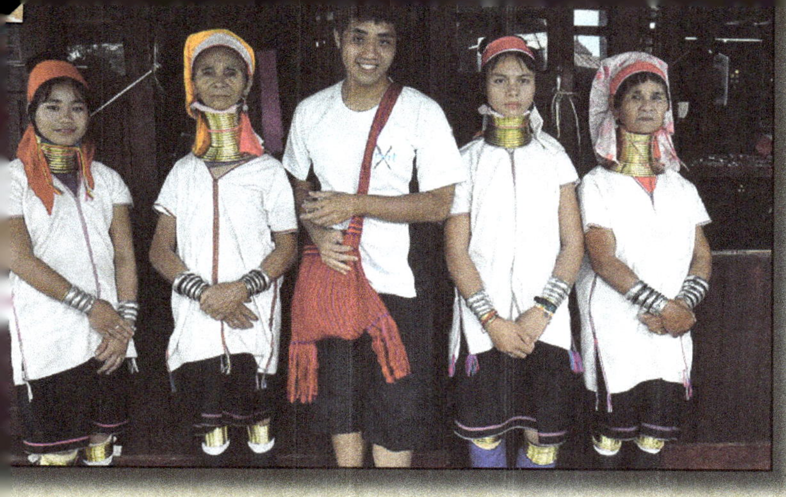

THE ART OF NECKBINDING

By Amunet Isfet

Body modification has many faces. They range from common alterations like the everyday belly button piercing to more extreme modifications such as corneal tattooing, tongue splitting, and subdermal implants. The majority of body modifications have roots in indigenous regions and tribes and many are still practiced today.

One such form of body modification is the practice of neck binding or neck rings. This form of body modification, while not seeming to be that extreme, has many fascinating aspects not only with the type of body modification, but also the importance it carries within certain cultures.

One tribe of indigenous people who still practice the art of neck binding hail from a small region in north Burma. The Kayan (Karen) people became refuges in 1969 when the military tried to wipe out all indigenous tribes. Sadly in modern times neck biding has little to do with traditional meaning, but it's more a tourist attraction in order for them to have a stable income.

Not much is known as far as the true origin of the wearing of neck rings, but there are many theories and legends as to how this body modification came into practice. The reasons range from protecting women's necks from Tiger bites to identifying the tribes' women. I personally like the legend that they are worn as a status symbol of being descendants of the "Mother Dragon".

Legend has is that a wise female dragon that lived long ago longed to see what humans looked like. One day she decided to find out. She set off and met a frog. She enlisted his help and after a time they came upon a cave. When the dragon entered the cave, she turned into a human. Someone had been living in the cave and she decided to clean it up and then wait for whoever it was to come back. A man came back, noticed the cave had been cleaned, but for some reason just decided to go to bed. This happened for a second time and he decided he'd better find out who had been doing this, so the next day he decided not to go so deep into the forest and catch the culprit. Well, he came back early and caught the dragon. In her human form she was the most beautiful thing the man had seen. He started asking her questions and fearing him finding out she was really a dragon, she lied. They fell in love, and had a baby. But, soon the man found out she was a dragon and left. After the man left and did not return, the dragon decided to retune to the sea, but before doing so left two eggs on the beach. A monk found the eggs and gave one to another monk. The first egg hatched a baby girl (the first woman of the Kayan people) and the second egg hatched a boy (The first man of the Pa-o people, which will be a story for another time). Because the men where monks they had to give the children away. The girl was sent to a small village and the boy was given to a king. When the boy was grown, a wife was sought for him, but he was dissatisfied with all the girls he had been brought. One day the kings solders came to the girl's village, saw her, and told the king about her. The boy visited the village and upon seeing each other they fell in love. The girl followed in her mother's path and emulated a dragon appearance with different hair styles and the boy followed the path of his father, the king. Now the legend does not say if the girl wore neck rings at that time, but with a little imagination one can see how the adornment of neck rings mimic the appearance of a long dragon like neck. This legend is why some believe that the Kayan women wear neck rings, to resemble their ancestor, the first Kayan woman, the dragon mother.

For the Kayan women of today wearing neck rings is very much a choice. At the age of 5, girls have a choice as to if they want to have neck rings placed. While some choose to proceed, others abstain. Many choose to have the rings placed later on in life and many choose to have them permanently removed later on in life. This is because at this age the bones are still soft and moldable. But, how much of a real choice do the girls' have considering they rely on tourism for income? Should a girl choose to proceed, fabric is placed around the neck and a long brass or copper coil is carefully bound by hand around the girls' neck. It is a long and tedious process that can take hours to complete. After the coils are placed, the girls will wear their new companion for the next few years as the coil must be replaced every few years as the girls grow.

You may be wondering as I did how they keep their necks clean. Well it is fairly simple. Because the coil is not a solid mass on their necks, they simply scrub between the coils with a brush type tool. Even though the care process is simple and padding is placed between the neck and the coils, bruising and skin discoloration still occur.

One very well-known misconception about neck binding is that they can never take the rings off on account that their necks will break from having the rings on for too long. While this does to an extent add to the charm of this body modification, it is very much a false representation. While the Kayan women's necks are weaker due to loss of muscle mass on the neck and shoulders, their necks do not snap in half when the coils are removed. Some women must wear a scarf due to the discomfort of atrophy of muscles, but it is not to such an extreme extent of neck breaking.

Another misconception is that the rings actually stretch the neck out. In fact, the neck itself does not change length, but rather the rings (weighing roughly 22lbs) push the collar bone down and compress the rib cage to give the illusion of a stretched neck. There are no actual known health problems associated with neck rings, but one can't help but wonder what kind of impact they could potentially have.

While neck rings at first glance seem to be somewhat of a nuisance when it comes to daily activities, they seem to not be much of a problem. The women seem to be able to bathe, work, eat, and sleep just like anyone without neck rings.

The Ndebele Tribe of South Africa also practice a similar form of neck binding as well. The origin of the Ndebele women wearing neck rings was mainly for marital purposes. After her husband built a home, women would wear copper and brass neck rings symbolizing her bond and faithfulness to her husband. The only time she would remove them was when her husband died. The husband would provide the rings and thus also was a social status symbol. The richer the husband, the more rings the wife would wear. In modern times it is no longer a common practice for women to wear neck rings permanently.

Although this form of body modification has over time lost much of its ritual and spiritual meaning, it remains a fascinating and beautiful form of art.

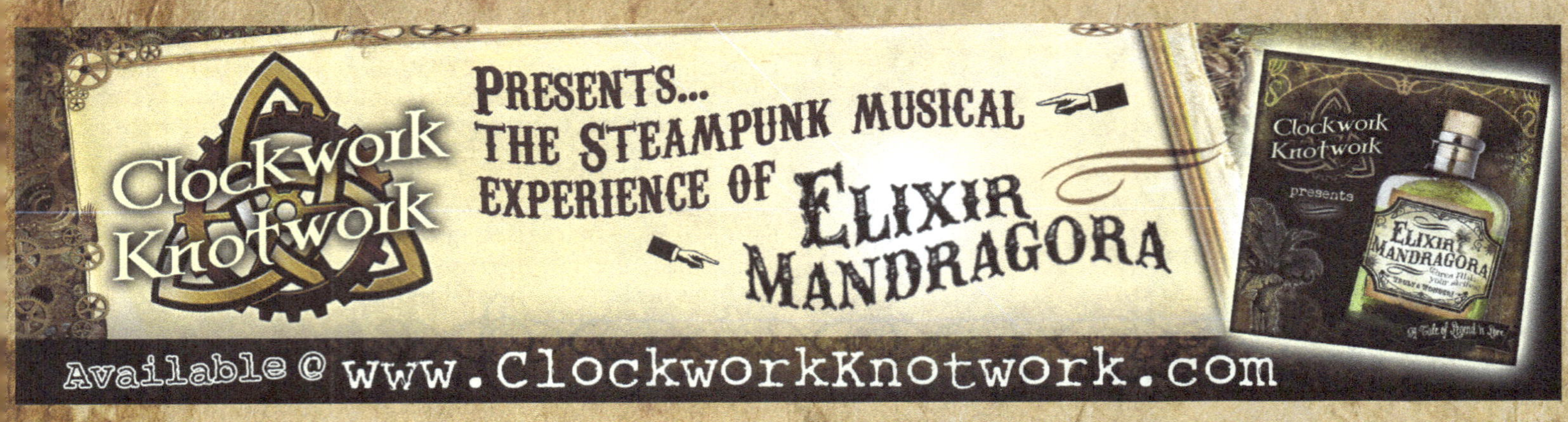

Clockwork Knotwork
PRESENTS...
THE STEAMPUNK MUSICAL
EXPERIENCE OF Elixir Mandragora
Clockwork Knotwork presents
Elixir Mandragora
Available @ www.ClockworkKnotwork.com

Airship Diamter

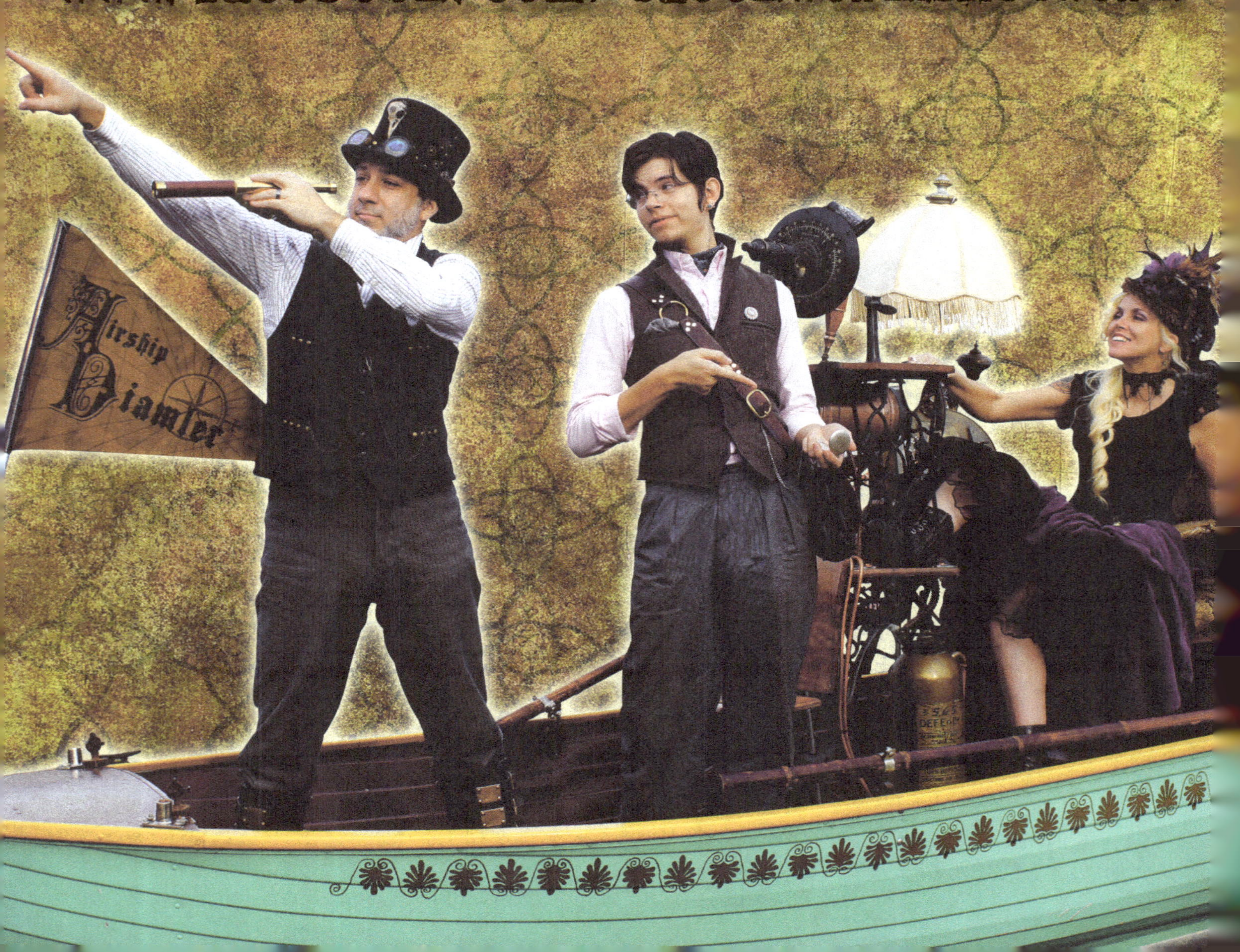